Sociology

JONATHAN H. TURNER
University of California, Riverside

PEARSON
Prentice Hall

Upper Saddle River, New Jersey 07458

Library of Congress Cataloging-in-Publication Data

Turner, Jonathan H.
    Sociology / Jonathan H. Turner.
        p. cm.
    ISBN 0-13-113496-5
    1. Sociology.   I. Title.
    HM586.T87 2006
    301--dc22   2005016533

Editorial Director: Leah Jewell
Executive Editor: Christopher DeJohn
Supplements Editor: Lee Ann Doherty
Editorial Assistant: Kristin Haegele
Senior Marketing Manager: Marissa Feliberty
Marketing Assistant: Anthony DeCosta
Prepress and Manufacturing Buyer: Mary Ann Gloriande
Interior Design and Illustrations: Pine Tree Composition, Inc.
Cover Art Director: Jayne Conte
Cover Designer: Bruce Kenselaar
Cover Image Specialist: Karen Sanatar
Cover Art: Jim Zwaldo
Full-Service Project Management: Patty Donovan, Pine Tree Composition, Inc.

This book was set in 10/11.5 Minister Book by Pine Tree Composition, Inc., and was printed
and bound by Hamilton Printing Company. The cover was printed by Coral Graphics.

Pearson Education LTD.
Pearson Education Singapore, Pte. Ltd
Pearson Education, Canada, Ltd
Pearson Education—Japan
Pearson Education Australia PTY, Limited
Pearson Education North Asia Ltd
Pearson Educación de Mexico, S.A. de C.V.
Pearson Education Malaysia, Pte. Ltd
Pearson Education, Upper Saddle River, New Jersey

10 9 8 7 6 5 4 3 2
ISBN: 0-13-113496-5

Contents

Preface

I have taught introductory sociology for thirty-years, mostly to very large classes. There are many fine texts on the market, but over the years they have become increasingly large and lavish. Indeed, it is often difficult to find the text amongst all of the cartoons, color for color's sake, boxes, diagrams, and other supplementary material. In a sense, introductory books are filled with "pop ups" that mirror the world of the internet. Clearly, there is a large market for these books, and on the whole, they are engaging. Yet, with a sense of disquiet, I have increasingly wondered if they do not contribute to students' sense of a fragmented and frantic world, where the flow of life (including the exposition in a text) is constantly interrupted. My sense is that students are pulled in many directions, all at once, with their cell phones, computer-games, email messaging, and other realities of modern life. One does not have to become a postmodernist to see how these realities have changed sociology textbooks.

It is with these concerns about how to communicate sociology to students that I set about writing this text. I wanted the text, not the supplemental materials, to be the core of the book. Students will not have to look around, behind, and above supplementary materials and four-color graphics to find the text. I have written the book so that students can sustain a line of reading, without being distracted by "pop ups." There are, of course, supplementary materials in this book, but they are not the essence of the book. Rather, it is the introduction of key concepts and ideas from sociology that is at the center of my effort in these pages.

The book is not lavish, nor is its appearance the reason that instructors and students should consider adopting the book. Rather, it is the depth and breadth of the materials covered, as well as the writing style, that will appeal (I hope) to students and their instructors. The book covers a great deal of material, and it is unlikely that any one course can explore every chapter. The chapters are, at one and the same time, modular and yet integrated. You can pick the book up at any point, and the contents will make sense. But, I have also attempted to communicate to students the structure of the social world by allowing them to see the "place" in the sociocultural universe of any particular topic. Thus, I am comfortable with the assertion that the book's materials are integrated in ways that allow students to see the coherence of the social world. Indeed, if I have any unique intellectual qualities, one of them is the capacity to integrate and to see big pictures and how the elements of these pictures fit into place. Students should, I believe, come away from a course using this book with a sense that, for all its diversity, there is coherence and clarity in how sociologists study the social universe.

The text is, I trust, written clearly. I have tried to engage students, without talking down and without simplifying the writing to a remedial level of communication. Thus, the book is more rigorous than most of its competitors. It is long, not so much because of four-color "pop ups" and other distractions but, rather, because there is more substantive material in each chapter.

I have tried the materials out on students for many years, and thus, the book has evolved with constant feedback from students and from the students of my students. I have even written the test bank of questions for instructors; and these too have been vetted through trial and error. Thus, the book and the instructional aids are also integrated, primarily because one person has done them all.

In sum, I hope that you will give this new kind of introductory book a chance. In developing these materials for the introductory course, I have benefited from the reviews of professionals, whom I want to thank. The reviewers were: David Yamane, University of Notre Dame; Markus Kemmelmeier, University of Nevada, Reno; and Jerome R. Koch, Texas Tech University. Thank you for taking the time to offer constructive advice in the final stages of the book's preparation for press.

Jonathan H. Turner

About the Author

Jonathan H. Turner, the Distinguished Professor of Sociology at the University of California at Riverside, has taught numerous courses throughout the years, but always enjoyed introducing students to sociology through teaching the introductory course. Professor Turner received a B.A. with honors from University of California at Santa Barbara, a M.A. and doctorate in sociology from Cornell University.

Dr. Turner has authored, co-authored, edited, or co-edited a number of works, including *The Structure of Sociological Theory, The Emergence of Sociological Theory, Patterns of Social Organization, Inequality: Privilege and Poverty in America* (with Charles Starnes), and many others. His areas of specialization touch many areas within the discipline of sociology such as sociological theory, human and societal evolution, social stratification and inequality, philosophy of science, and historical sociology.

Professor Turner is a member of the American Sociological Association and a former president of the Pacific Sociological Society. He has been the journal editor for *Sociological Perspectives* and is currently the journal editor for *Sociological Theory*.

Prologue:
Gaining Perspective from
a Timeline of Human Society

If the history of life on the planet earth were compressed into one day, it would be less than a tick away from midnight before humans appeared. It would be far less than a millisecond before society as you and I know it emerged. Humans are thus a very recent species on the planet. Somewhere around 150,000 years ago, humans as a distinct species emerged in Africa. The order to which humans belong—termed *primates*—has been around for perhaps as long as 60 million years, but these distant ancestors looked more like a modern tree shrew or rodent than a human. For most of primate evolution, species of monkeys and apes lived in the arboreal habitats of what are now Asia and Africa. Humans are descendants of apes who, as embarrassing as it may seem, lost out in competition to monkeys and were, as a result, relegated to the undersides and outlying branches of the arboreal habitat. Monkeys held the verdant areas, forming larger groups that were well-organized. Around 16 million years ago, the forest in Africa began to recede and apes were forced out onto the African savanna. As marginal tree dwellers who were not particularly well-organized or suited for an open-country environment filled with predators, apes began to die out. Only the handful of present-day apes who now live in or near the trees have survived, and even their survival is threatened by population growth among their close relatives, humans. Only humans' ape-like ancestors found a way to survive the dangers of the African savanna by becoming better organized.

The ancestral lines of present-day primates like chimpanzees, with whom we share 99% of our genes, and the immediate ancestors of humans, whom we call *hominids,* split apart around five million years ago. For five million years, hominids found a way to survive in the open country savanna. During this time, hominids became scavengers, gatherers, and eventually hunters; somehow, they became more organized than any ape before them. They lived a simple life in small bands wandering about a territory, gathering plant life and hunting for meat. For three million years, the brains of hominids were not much larger than those of chimpanzees. And, even as the brain began to grow around two million years ago, it did not reach human proportions until just a few hundred thousand years ago. Indeed, Neanderthals who now appear to have been off the human line had brains that were, on average, larger than modern humans. As the brains of hominids became larger, language and culture emerged, although just when this dramatic evolutionary leap occurred will never be known. Perhaps as far back as two million years, some hominids had a form of language and the beginnings of culture, but we can never know for sure.

Even with their big brains and capacity for language and culture, humans remained hunter-gatherers, wandering a territory in small bands in search of food. In fact, it was not until a few thousand years ago that humans abandoned hunting and gathering as their basic mode of survival and began an entirely new chapter in their evolution. Biological evolution was increasingly replaced by the evolution of culture and social structure leading to the world that you and I now live in. The kinds of societies that sociologists generally study—large, industrial, urban, and complex— are a mere few hundred years old.

Sociology emerged because people were increasingly concerned about what was happening to them as populations congregated into cities and as industrialization transformed the way people lived. Change of this magnitude sparked interest and, in fact, great concern about what was happening. So much change occurring so fast was a new experience in human evolution, forcing people to think about the social world around them. These concerns still fuel the sociological imagination. It is no different today—sociology remains interesting and relevant because the social world around us is once again changing rapidly.

Before we move into how sociology emerged and the topics associated with it, we should pause and take a broad view of how humans have lived over the last 150,000 to 200,000 thousand years. In this way, we can see that modern societies are very different than those in which we evolved as a species. It is a tribute to our flexibility and our capacity to use culture in creative ways that we can live in social constructions that are so divergent from those in which we evolved as a species.

The data from the few hunting and gathering bands that survived into the twentieth century give us a "distant mirror" in which we can see images of how humans lived for most of their time on earth. Hunters and gatherers lived in relatively small bands of perhaps 50 or 60 people. These bands were composed of nuclear families of mother, father, and children—much like today in industrial societies. They would move about a territory in search of food, settling from a few days to a few weeks in one spot until they had exhausted the food supply; and then they would move on. Women did all of the gathering of plant life, which accounted for as much as 80% of the food consumed in the band, while men did the hunting, which was frequently unsuccessful. No one worked for very long, perhaps 10 to 15 hours per week. Children watched and played, learning the skills that they would need as adults. Conflict was probably rather rare, although a band moving into another's territory would, no doubt, be in for a fight. If conflict emerged within the band, its members would typically split apart, with conflicting parties going their respective ways to form a new band or join another. Hunter-gatherers did not have much—their simple tools and personal clothing and artifacts that they could carry—but then they did not have to work very hard. One well-known anthropologist called hunting and gathering the original "affluent society" but it is an affluence born of low stress and little work, compared to our affluent society typified by high stress and much work. As a species we were not programmed to work hard and to live stressful lives, but somehow that is what our lives in the contemporary world have become.

Humans left behind hunting and gathering when they settled down. It must have seemed the obvious thing to do for the first bands that camped near the waters of rivers, lakes, and oceans where fish were plentiful. Still, this big step was not taken until 12,000 years ago and perhaps as recently as 8,000 years ago. When populations settled, they began to grow, with the result that they soon hunted out the wild animals in the area and exhausted the plant life. With a larger population to move, wandering in the old hunting and gathering pattern was no longer viable, at least for many. Some may have moved away to resettle or to adopt the old ways, but at some point, an entirely new mode of survival emerged: horticulture. Horticulture is gardening with human power; and if you have ever had a garden, you know that it is a lot of work. Men would often loosen the soil with sticks that served as makeshift hoes but typically it was the women who tended and harvested the garden. Gardening can produce much more food than gathering, and so, the population would continue to grow and rely upon on gardening. There was no turning back to hunting and gathering once populations became larger and began to fill in a territory. Soon, humans also learned how to herd animals, if such animals existed (as was the case in EuroAsia, but in sub-Saharan Africa, no indigenous animals could be herded). In what is now Europe and Asia, hunting was replaced by domesticated herds of animals as the primary source of meat.

Horticulture changed human society in profound ways. First, community as a distinctive social structure emerged. For most of human history, people lived in groups, such as their immediate family and band. Now, people resided in more permanent settlements that could number several hundred and at times thousands. Second, nuclear families of mother, father, and children were strung together to create the first organizations beyond the group; structures like lineages and clans that organized people into hierarchies of authority. These kinship structures were not a bureaucracy in the modern sense but were the functional equivalent of what bureaucracies do in modern societies because they linked groups and individuals under a command system that perform more complex tasks. Third, with kin authority, inequality entered the human stage. Those with authority had the power to tell others what to do, something that hunter-gatherers would never have dared presumed. Those who can tell others what to do can also garner wealth for themselves and the prestige that wealth brings. Not only did authority create concentrations of wealth and prestige, this authority was increasingly gendered: men now had authority over women, something that was unheard of among hunter-gatherers. And male chiefs could command the resources of their kin groups and village, although they were generally under the obligation to give back what they took (thereby gaining prestige for their "generosity"). Thus, kin authority evolved into political authority that was used to create inequalities of not only power, but also material well-being and prestige. As the population grew, villages became consolidated into larger political units; chronic conflict now appeared among confederations of villages engaged in constant warfare. With war came even more consolidation of power to coordinate men and resources for war. With war, people not only died but were also captured and enslaved; in a few cases, captives were sacrificed and, in even fewer cases, eaten. Within kinship units and communities, bloody feuds often broke out because people resented the authority of kinfolk. Religion became universal with horticulture. Some hunter-gatherers also had religion, but it is with horticulture that pantheons of supernatural forces and beings governing life and fate were conceptualized, leading to the emergence of religious specialists such as shamans and witchdoctors who, in larger populations, would become more permanent priests of increasingly larger temples devoted to organizing rituals toward the supernatural. By the time advanced horticulture was in place some 6,000 years ago, society revealed many features that are familiar to us in the modern age: stable communities; inequality and stratification; slavery and human sacrifice; political and religious elites with the power to tell others what to do; chronic warfare and feuding; and hard work, especially for women. Horticulture is probably not a form of organization that humans would select, if given a choice; rather, it was forced upon them as they desperately tried to get organized because larger populations required new patterns of organization.

Agrarian societies emerged around 5,000 to 8,000 years ago when humans discovered how to use animal power hitched to tools, such as the plow. Now, much more land could be cultivated with less labor; and with more food, populations could grow dramatically. During the agrarian era, the basic profile of complex societies as we know them emerged. Communities became larger, a few numbering into the hundreds of thousands. The state, as a form of political control, was increasingly built around the tax collector, police, courts, laws favoring elites, and jail for dissidents. The state also organized large armies in efforts at conquest, often leading to the formation of large empires that were connected with roads and new forms of travel using animals to draw carriages and wagons. Naval travel and warfare increased, enabling people and supplies to travel long distances. With more people to feed, markets as a mechanism for distributing goods and services emerged; and as markets grew, the use of money and credit also increased, thereby encouraging more market activity. New kinds of economic specialization proliferated to provide an increasing variety of goods. New services such as banking, insuring, and accounting emerged, all made possible by the invention of writing, which dramatically expanded not only economic activity but the codification of religious dogma into canons, political dogma into systems of legal codes, notations for music, and in general, an explosion of culture that could be used to enhance the quality of life. Inequality and stratification reached their peak during agrarianism, however, as elites hoarded virtually all of the material wealth and power, leaving the impoverished peasants to make do on landed estates. However, during the agrarian era, new classes of merchants, traders, wholesalers, artisans, workers, retailers, and bankers were growing; in the industrial era, they would inherit the remnants of the old feudal system that collapsed under industrialism.

In general, the scale and complexity of society changed dramatically with agrarianism. Yet, most people still lived in rural areas; and so communities were relatively small. Literacy was confined to a few elites and service personnel. And so, the complexity of the new social order was not felt by most peasants, at least until this order began to fall apart. Nonetheless, even as most remained oblivious to what was occurring, dramatic changes were in progress. In the economy, the harnessing of nonhuman power to tools set the stage for attaching inanimate sources of power to machines that, in turn, lead to the factory system. In addition, the expansion of markets and the widespread use of money and credit would provide the financial infrastructure to distribute new goods that would soon be produced by an industrial economy. Added to these breakthroughs were new modes of transport that would facilitate movement of goods, people, and services in ways that encouraged expansion of the economy. In the political arena, the bureaucratic state replaced, by and large, kinship systems as the means to organize social control and armies; this breakthrough was essential for the ability to regulate an industrial economy. Law also emerged as a system of codified rules, local and regional courts, and enforcement agents, thereby setting up the primary mechanism for coordination and control in modern societies. Formal education made its appearance with agrarianism, as the sons and daughters of elites were taught culture and as the offspring of the bourgeois learned practical forms of writing and arithmetic. In the religious arena, one large and well-financed system of churches typically controlled worship of the people; as religion became bureaucratized, yet one more template for organizing economic and governmental activity in the future was created. And, an entirely new set of institutional systems that would soon be dominant made its first appearance with agrarianism: science, medicine and, as noted earlier, education.

For most people, life was relatively simple because they lived in rural areas, but in urban areas of the agrarian world, a new complexity was emerging—vast inequalities creating distinctive social classes; large urban communities; differentiated institutional systems (economy, kinship, polity, religion, law, education, science, and medicine); bureaucratic organizations like the state, church, and large-scale economic enterprises; and new cultural forms from books to music made possible by writing. Complex infrastructures of markets, roads, ports, canals, and other public works were created. All of this complexity influenced relatively few people, but as they began to migrate to cities, the scope and scale of society began to engulf individuals as never before in human history. It may have been overwhelming to these migrants, perhaps exciting, or a combination of the two. But life for humans on earth would never be the same.

It was during late agrarianism and early industrialization that the complexity of society and culture began to overtake a species who, we must remember, evolved as simple hunter-gatherers. These changes spawned sociology. People had, of course, always thought about society, but during the eighteenth and nineteenth centuries, thinking about the human condition became more systematic, particularly under the influence of science that for many held out the hope for human betterment through increased knowledge. With industrialization and the revolution that this new mode of economic activity ushered in, sociology was given its subject matter: the study of human society and culture as these influence the lives of individuals.

I need not highlight the industrial era, where a majority of people performed nonagrarian labor in factories, or the era we now live in—the postindustrial—where a majority of workers are engaged in providing services. You live in this world; and I am sure that at times you sense the pace and complexity of postindustrial societies. If life seems overwhelming, it should because at your genetic core you are still a primate who became a hunter-gatherer and, then, was forced to adapt to a complex social world. Of course, many people in postindustrial societies can enjoy the benefits of so many consumer goods and the expanded options made possible by vast markets. Others, however, have been left behind or left out, for inequality along many dimensions—class, region, nation, gender, age, or ethnicity, to name a few—persists, creating new lines of tension in the stratification system. Warfare is chronic, and more deadly than ever. Life is lived in bureaucratic organizations more than groups. Communities are large and, at times, less personal. Adulthood is delayed by needs for more education. Science is capable of providing life-saving as well as life-taking products. Religion continues to be an arena of intense conflict and modern-day terror not imaginable in the agrarian era. The ready availability of food, with fat and sugar that would make a hunter-gatherer sick, now generates diseases like diabetes that people of the past could not imagine. Environmental degradation is now worldwide as the atmosphere grows warmer, as rainforests are chain-sawed into oblivion, and as chemicals permeate the ecosystem and human bodies. The prospect of a pandemic, whether as an intended act of terrorism or unintended consequence of too many people living in too little space, is becoming more and more likely as germs move at the speed of airplane travel. There are, therefore, a lot of things for big-brained primates such as you and I to worry about.

Our big brains have enabled us to create culture that has been used to build complex societies in which we can all take some pleasure. But, these very same societies reveal many problems that give us worry; and with big brains, we are far more likely to worry than our smaller brained hominid ancestors or as our equally smart hunter-gatherer ancestors who lived the simple life. It is this worry and concern that led to the emergence of sociology; and in the end, it is the goal of sociology to understand the social forces that make society work and that systematically generate so many problems. Most of the problems of the world today involve how humans are organized, and so, these problems are sociological in character. Hunter-gatherers did not need sociology; postindustrial humans do. Let us now begin the introduction to how sociologists view the world that you and I live in.

Part I | The Sociological Imagination

Sociology as a discipline with a name emerged in the first third of the nineteenth century. The transformations of society from the agrarian to industrial era prompted scholars to seek an understanding of what these transformations involved and how they would affect individuals and society. From its beginnings, inquiry into the social world has been marked by a debate over the role of science in sociological inquiry. The earliest founders often advocated the application of the scientific method and the search for the general laws of human social organization. But this early optimism was criticized by other founders who saw the nature of society as very different from that of the natural world. These scholars advocated alternatives to a purely scientific viewpoint. Some felt that sociology could seek to be objective, using scientific methods to advantage, even if general laws of human organization were not possible; others argued for an openly ideological sociology, one that criticized patterns of inequality and oppression while suggesting liberating alternatives. These points of debate over science are still with the discipline today. Because of the doubts about the scientific prospects of sociology, theories in sociology range from those that seek to uncover laws of human social organization, through those that provide conceptual frameworks for interpreting the social world, to those that emphasize critique of social conditions. However, all provide a set of lenses or glasses; and depending upon which lenses we put on, different views of the social world become evident.

Chapter 1

Origins and Nature of Sociology

He was the toast of Europe in the early 1830s. Twenty years later, this Frenchman was ridiculed and widely regarded as a fool. What else could be said of a man who now proclaimed himself to be "the Great Priest of Humanity" for a rag-tag following of workers and third-rate intellectuals. As the founder of the new "Universal Religion," he would send messages to his followers, much like the Pope does to Catholics; and indeed, he even sent missives to the Pope himself. The final volume of his famous treatise, which had made him famous in 1830, did not receive a single review in the French press in 1842. He had been arrogant, rude, and unpleasant; and now he was paying the price. Defensive to the end, he even pronounced that he would engage in "cerebral hygiene" and not read the ideas of anyone whom he felt to be his intellectual inferior.

Who was this pathetic figure? He was the titular founder of sociology, Auguste Comte.

Comte preferred the title *social physics* for sociology because in the early 1800s, the term "physics" meant to study "the nature of phenomena." By putting "social" in front of "physics," Comte communicated his meaning: to study the nature of the social universe. Unfortunately, the phrase had already been used by a Belgian statistician; therefore, Comte was forced to construct the Latin and Greek hybrid, **sociology**. He apparently hated the term "sociology" but was forced to adopt it.

What can we say about a madman who was the founder of a discipline whose name was his reluctant second choice? For all of the emotional problems that overcame him in his later years, the young Auguste Comte was a brilliant scholar. As a very young man, he made a huge splash in his advocacy for what he termed *positivism* or the scientific study of society. For Comte, the time had come for the last and, in his mind, the greatest science of all, to emerge: sociology. He outlined what scientific sociology should be like, while at the same time providing a rationale for sociology in a hostile intellectual environment. Let us explore further what the young Comte had to say.

Auguste Comte (1798-1857)

Comte's five-volume treatise, *Course of Positive Philosophy* (1830–1842), was published over a 12-year period. In these volumes, Comte postulated a **law of the three stages.** The first stage is the *theological,* where thought about the world is dominated by considerations of the supernatural, religion, and god; the second stage is the *metaphysical*, where appeals to the supernatural are replaced by philosophical thought about the essence of phenomena and by the development of mathematics, logic, and other neutral thought systems; and the third stage is the *positivistic*, where science, or careful observation of empirical facts and the systematic testing of theories with facts, become the dominant modes for accumulating knowledge.

Comte thus championed the scientific method—the details of which are examined in Chapter 2. He wanted sociology to be like the other sciences, particularly the physics of his time where Sir Isaac Newton's law of gravity served as the model of theorizing. Just like the law of gravity, sociology could develop laws unique to the social universe. These laws were to be tested, and Comte felt that there were several basic methods of inquiry that sociologists could use to gather data to test theories. One was *observation* of the social world, but such observations must be guided by theory because, without a theory to guide the researcher, it is difficult to know what to look for in the flow of social life. Another method was *experimentation*, where pathologies that arise in the "body social" (deviance, crime, violence, etc.) could be used to better understand what is normal or "healthy" in society. Much as a biologist can learn about the normal functioning of the human body by studying ill health, sociologists can come to understand the normal dynamics of societies by examining social pathologies. Another method is *comparison*, in which social processes and structures are compared. Comte had a very broad view of comparison as a method because he advocated not just comparison of one society with another, but also comparisons with animal societies, with societies of the past, and with simpler or more complex societies of the present. A final method is *historical*, which in a sense is a variant of the comparative method because it emphasizes the analysis of past societies to see what they can tell sociologists about societies in the present. These methods are still with sociologists, although they have been refined.

Perhaps Comte's greatest contribution to sociology was his advocacy for the new science of society. Comte was forceful—indeed often rude and arrogant—in making the claim that sociology was a legitimate mode of inquiry. But he had to confront a hostile environment, and so, he developed two lines of argument signaling that the time for sociology was at hand.

One argument revolved around Comte's assertion that ideas move through the three stages—that is, theological, metaphysical, and positivistic (scientific)—at different rates for each major domain of the universe. Astronomy and physics move first, then chemistry and biology, and finally sociology emerges as the last mode of thinking to enter the positivistic stage. Thus, science first penetrates astronomy because this subject matter (at the time) is the simplest to comprehend; then chemistry, which examines the structure of basic elements that make up the physical and biological worlds, enters the positivistic phase. With chemistry and physics, it becomes possible to have a science of life forms, or biology, that moves into the scientific phase. And once biology is in place, it then becomes possible to have the most complex of the sciences: sociology or the study of *relations among* life forms. In Comte's eyes, the analysis of society was ready to take a seat at the table of science—a claim that was challenged in Comte's time, as well as today.

Moreover, Comte forcefully argued that science needed to be used for the betterment of human life. Science is not divorced from the problems of the world; rather, it is the ultimate tool for mitigating these problems. Thus, as the laws of human organization were developed, Comte (1851–1854) believed that they could be used to better the human condition—again, a theme as controversial today as in Comte's time.

A second tactic for legitimating sociology involved Comte's view that there is a hierarchy of sciences. In this **hierarchy of the sciences,** all of the sciences were ranked in terms of their complexity and their movement into the positivistic stage. At the bottom of the hierarchy was mathematics—the language of all sciences higher in the hierarchy—and at the top, emerging out of biology, was sociology. Indeed, in a moment of over-exuberance Comte proclaimed sociology as "the queen science" because it stood above all of the other sciences. For if sociology was the last science to emerge and if it was also the most advanced in terms of its subject matter, it must be a legitimate mode of inquiry—or so Comte hoped.

Comte's view of how sociology could be a science emphasized that the discipline should look for general laws that, much like those in the physics of his time, could explain the operation of the social universe. These laws were to be tested using systematic methods; and if the law withstood these tests, it would become the accepted knowledge about how the social universe operates. Thus, Comte had a vision of sociology as a "hard science" like any other science. As a hard science, sociology could then have engineering applications; that is, the laws of sociology could be used to reconstruct society.

All of these points of advocacy in Comte's thinking have been subject to criticism and intense debate, as we will see in Chapter 2, but without Comte's forceful advocacy, sociology may not have emerged so early in the nineteenth century. Sociology faced a hostile reception from well-established disciplines such as law, philosophy, ethics, and theology that saw pronouncements on social conditions as *their* exclusive mission. For an upstart to come along and proclaim that the "queen science" was here; and moreover, that this new science would impose scientific rigor on the study of the social world was, to say the least, a bit irritating to traditional scholars. It did not help that Comte also saw these scholars as still in the dark ages of "theological thinking."

Someone had to cast the first stone on the establishment, and Comte's arrogance served him well, at least in the beginning. But his personality could be endured for only so long, with the result that Comte managed to lose most of his friends. And, late in his life, when he tried to convert science into a new kind of secular religion, his last supporters in the mainstream scientific community completely abandoned him. Yet, this irritating temperament enabled him to assert what many others had long believed: it was time to study the social world more systematically.

Comte felt that his law of the three stages was much like Newton's law of gravity because it denoted the movement of cultural ideas and the underlying structure of society in a certain direction. No one took this presumption seriously, but there were other, more interesting ideas in Comte's sociology.

Comte saw the basic issue of sociological analysis to be the study of complexity (Turner, Beeghley, and Powers 2002, 26–28). By complexity he meant that as societies evolve they become more **differentiated**; they reveal more types of groups, organizations, communities, social classes, subcultures, and in general, they evidence many new lines of division. Complex and differentiated societies need to be **integrated**, by which he meant there must be forces holding all of the differentiated parts of society together. Much like "Humpty Dumpty" of the children's nursery rhyme, who was cracked into many diverse parts, the social equivalent of "all the king's men" was needed to make sure that all of the different parts of complex societies could be coordinated. If they could not be coordinated, then pathologies would emerge—crime, violence, class conflict, deviance, and other forms that, Comte felt, were abnormal. How, then, was society to be integrated? He argued that there are three basic mechanisms: First, mutual interdependence in which different parts of society depend on each other for resources; and because of this interdependence, coordination of the diverse elements of society could be achieved. Second, the centralization and concentration of power in government could also serve to coordinate the parts of society. By giving government the power to regulate and control, integration would ensue. And finally, the development of a common culture could also hold diverse members and groups in society together because they would believe in the same things and thus see the world in a common light. Comte did not develop these ideas, but they are fundamental to understanding how some degree of social order is possible in modern and complex societies.

Harriet Martineau (1802–1876)

For many years, Harriet Martineau was known in contemporary sociology for translating and condensing Comte's large *Course of Positive Philosophy* into English in 1853—at a time when Comte's star had fallen. Despite the French-sounding name, she was an English woman who did much more than translate Comte; she became an important intellectual in her own right. In fact, she was one of the most-read intellectuals of her time. It is possible that she could have become an academic or a sociologist, but the scientific and academic worlds at the time were dominated by men. If a woman was to make a name and career for herself, she had to move into literature, journalism, and other fields less controlled by men. Thus, we will never know how systematic Martineau's ideas would have become if she had concentrated only on sociology, but she more than Comte and virtually any other sociologist of the last century—save for Herbert Spencer—brought a sociological perspective to the mass of the literate public (Madoo-Lengerman and Niebrugge-Brantly 1998).

If we translate her terminology into more contemporary terms, she viewed the social world as composed of cultural values, beliefs, and norms (what she called *morals*) that proscribed and directed individual behavior and that provided guidance for associations among individuals (what she termed *manners*). Other forces (e.g., geography, material resources, density of settlements organizing a population, history of a society, ethnic composition, and relations with other societies) all influence the culture and structure of relations in a society (Martineau 1838a,

1838b). The culture of a population never wholly accounts for people's behavior because there is always some slippage from what one is supposed to do to what one actually does; as a result, social structures are always changing as people forge new ways of implementing culture. And, as the structure of social relations changes, so does the culture as it is adopted to new structural realities (Madoo-Lengerman and Niebrugge-Brantly 1998, 40–43).

Martineau's sociology appeared in many popular publications, but the ideas above were the underlying core. Like Comte, Martineau also advocated a science of society. Society should be treated as a "thing," just like any other object in the universe; when treated as a thing, it becomes possible to engage in scientific study. The French philosopher, Charles Montesquieu, had made a similar argument 100 years earlier, but Martineau was the first scholar to take this idea to the general lay public. In seeing sociology as a science, Martineau felt that it was important to be impartial. But, like Comte again, she also argued for the role of informed criticism of unfair conditions and for their elimination. Science was, therefore, to be used for the betterment and progress of society.

Sociology and the Enlightenment

Why did ideas like those in Comte's and Martineau's writing appear? Was this a sudden breakthrough in thinking? Like most ideas, Comte's advocacy was the culmination of thinking that had been forming in France and England for over 100 years. As Europe emerged from the "Dark Ages" and the Renaissance was born in the 1500s, the idea of science was slowly resurrected from the middle east as well as from the philosophies of the Greeks and Romans; by the late 1500s and early 1600s, a clear conception of science was emerging. Francis Bacon (1561–1633) codified the essence of the new science: All pronouncements about how the universe operates must be viewed with skepticism and constantly checked against facts that have been systematically collected. Newton's law of gravity served as the exemplar of what science could do: explain with a law the empirical regularities that generations of astronomers had observed.

The application of science to the social universe did not, however, come immediately. A much broader intellectual movement, often termed **The Enlightenment**, was well under way from the beginnings of the Renaissance, although it reached its zenith in the late eighteenth and early nineteenth centuries. The Enlightenment was fueled by the dramatic changes that were occurring in societies of the eighteenth and nineteenth centuries. The old feudal estates were being broken up; market relations were increasing; urbanization was accelerating; skepticism about religious interpretations of the world was challenging the church dogma; medicine was emerging as a skilled profession; exploration was opening up new vistas and sources of wealth and power; and most importantly, by the turn of the nineteenth century, industrialization was accelerating all of these changes.

In France, The Enlightenment was dominated by a century of French thinkers, often called **the philosophes**, who were concerned about the natural rights of humans in the face of oppressive political regimes. Indeed, much of the Declaration of Independence and some portions of the American Constitution come directly from the ideas of the French philosophes—people like Montesquieu, Condorcet, Voltaire, and Rousseau. All believed that humanity was progressing and that with the increasing knowledge accumulated through the methods of science, society would be a better place for humans to live. The French Revolution of 1789 was very much justified by the *philosophes*' idealism, but to their horror, the aftermath of the revolution was hardly liberating for the average person. Ever since the atrocities and chaos of the Revolution, French social thought has focused on the questions that occupied Comte: What is the basis of social order? The French answer always involves an emphasis on common culture—that is, common values, beliefs, and ideologies are essential to maintaining social order.

In England, The Enlightenment is sometimes termed **The Age of Reason.** Like their counterparts among the French *philosophes,* English scholars began, at first, to ponder the natural rights of all humans Yet, because England did not experience the violent revolution of France, scholarly thinking took on a different tone. In the mid-1700s, Adam Smith first posed the question that guided both Comte in France and subsequent generations of thinkers: As society becomes more complex, people live in different worlds and engage in diverse activities; because of this splintering of social life, what force will hold society together? Adam Smith's most famous answer offered in the late 1700s was that markets operating in terms of the "law of supply and demand" would create interdependencies that would bind people together through "an invisible hand of order." He had an earlier answer, however, that resonated with the French: common culture would also maintain a system of "moral sentiments" that would enable people to cooperate because they had a common world view and similar values.

The scholars writing in the generation before Comte all believed in the idea of progress. By rational thought and attention to the inalienable rights of all humans, it would be possible to construct better societies. The transformations ushered in by industrialization—markets, urbanization, and the emerging factory system—would provide one more tool to be used in reconstructing society. Comte's mentor, Henri Saint-Simon, had been a champion of using science to make a better world; and so, it was not a great leap for Comte to pronounce that the science of society was now possible in the new, positivistic age (Turner, Beeghley, and Powers 2002). Virtually all thinkers after Comte also held this vision of The Enlightenment—that society was progressing to a better state. Not all held to the vision that science was the tool by which this new and better world would be built, but the idea of progress dominated thinking well into the twentieth century. Only two world wars and the rise of Stalinism and other dictatorial states eroded the sociologist's faith that sociology could contribute to building a better society.

Herbert Spencer (1820–1903)

Herbert Spencer was one of the most widely read social thinkers of the nineteenth century. His books sold in the hundreds of thousands of copies, but it was only late in his career, in the 1870s, that Spencer turned to sociology. Spencer had a grand vision—too grand, in retrospect—but grand nonetheless. All realms of the universe could be understood with a common set of "first principles" that he roughly took from the physics of his time (Spencer 1862). These realms of the universe included ethics, physics, biology, psychology, and ultimately sociology; and for Spencer, they all could be explained by applications of some general principles. He termed this grand vision *Synthetic Philosophy,* and he spent almost 50 years writing multivolume treatises on psychology, biology, sociology, and ethics. Moreover, he amassed one of the largest collections of historical and ethnographic data ever collected into a 16-volume set of works titled *Descriptive Sociology* that were published from the 1870s and long after his death into the 1930s (he left money in his will to continue the assembling of data).

Like Comte, Spencer (1873) believed that human arrangements could be studied scientifically, and in his monumental three-volume work, *The Principles of Sociology* (1874–1896), he developed a theory of human social organization and presented a wide range of historical and ethnographic data from *Descriptive Sociology* to support this theory. As emphasized earlier, all domains of the universe—physical, biological, and social—evolve in terms of similar principles (Spencer 1862). And the task of sociology is to apply these principles to what he termed the **superorganic** realm, or the study of the patterns of relations among organisms.

Spencer's basic question was the same as the one that guided Comte and before that, Adam Smith: What holds society together as it becomes larger, more heterogeneous, more complex, and more differentiated? In broad contours, Spencer's answer was much the same as Comte's, but he presented the theory in a much more sophisticated form. The theory is very simple: Large, complex societies develop (a) interdependencies among their specialized components and (b) concentrations of power to control and coordinate activities among interdependent units. For Spencer, then, societal evolution embodies growth and complexity that is managed by interdependence and power. If patterns of interdependence and concentrations of power fail to emerge in society, or are inadequate to the task, dissolution occurs. A society simply falls apart.

In developing this answer to Comte's basic question, Spencer analogized to organismic bodies, arguing that societies, like biological organisms, must perform certain key functions if they are to survive: they must reproduce themselves, they must produce sufficient goods and commodities to sustain members, they must distribute these to members of the society, and they must coordinate and regulate the activities of members. As societies grow larger and become more complex, revealing many divisions and patterns of specialization, these key functions become distinguished along three lines: (a) the operative (reproduction and production), (b) the distributive (the movement of materials and information), and (c) the regulatory (the concentration of power to control and coordinate).

Spencer is best remembered for founding an approach in sociology known as **functionalism** (J. Turner 1985b). This approach emphasizes that analyses of specific cultural and social ways in a society should occur with an eye to how they help a society to survive—that is, the *functions* that they serve for the larger society. Functional sociology thus asks a basic and interesting question: What does a cultural or social phenomenon *do for* the maintenance and integration of a society?

Spencer is hardly read today because his name is associated with a school of thought known as *Social Darwinism*. The famous phrase—"survival of the fittest"—was actually coined by Spencer (1850) almost a decade before Charles Darwin published his great work, *On The Origin of Species* (1859). Spencer held to a political philosophy that argued that out of conflict and competition the more fit will survive, thus making society better. He used this idea primarily in his analysis of the history of war. A better organized society usually wins a war against a less organized society; and out of successive wars over the long course of human history, the level of complexity and organization of societies increases. Yet, with the emergence of the industrial world, Spencer felt that war was no longer necessary for societal evolution. He opposed British Colonialism and war making. Rather, in the new era that emerged by the end of the nineteenth century, Spencer advocated a line of thought reminiscent of Adam Smith: markets would become a much superior way to create the competition that would lead to a better society.

Émile Durkheim (1858–1917)

Much of Spencer's mode of analysis was adopted by the first great French sociologist Émile Durkheim, but Spencer's ideas were modified to fit the long French lineage (J. Turner 1984b). Like Comte and Spencer, Durkheim (1895) advocated the search for sociological laws, echoing Montesquieu's, Comte's, Spencer's, and Martineau's view that society can be studied as a "thing." Moreover, like Comte and all French thinkers, Durkheim argued for a sociology that could be used to build a better society.

Durkheim (1893) saw the essential question of sociology as revolving around how to explain the integration of society as it becomes larger and more complex, but unlike Spencer, Durkheim (1891) remained true to his French heritage and emphasized the importance of common ideas as an integrating force. Durkheim (1895) adopted a functional approach, arguing that sociological explanations must seek to discover how an element of the social world fulfills a need of society. But unlike Spencer, he emphasized only one need—the need to integrate members of society into a coherent whole.

What marks Durkheim's contribution to sociology is the recognition that systems of cultural symbols (i.e., values, beliefs, religious dogmas, language, ideologies, etc.) are an important basis for the integration of society (J. Turner 1981). As societies become complex and heterogeneous, the nature of cultural symbols, or what Durkheim (1893) termed the **collective conscience,** changes. In simple societies, all individuals have a common collective conscience that regulates their thoughts and actions, whereas in more complex societies, the collective conscience must also change if the society is to remain integrated. It must become, at one level, more "generalized" and "abstract" to provide some common symbols among people in specialized and partitioned activities, whereas at another level it also becomes more concrete to assure that relations between, and within, specialized positions and organizations in complex societies are regulated and coordinated. Social order, therefore, is possible in large, complex societies when there are some common values and beliefs that all individuals share, coupled with specific sets of rules that guide people in their concrete relations with others (J. Turner 1990). If this balance between the abstract and specific aspects of the collective conscience is not realized, then various pathologies emerge in society (Durkheim 1893, 1897).

Durkheim (1912) later examined society at a more interpersonal level in an effort to understand how the collective conscience is generated. In reading about religion among Australian aborigines (Spencer and Gillian 1899), Durkheim was less interested in religion, per se, than in the interpersonal processes producing a collective conscience. What he discovered was that interaction during periodic gatherings among aboriginals produces a sense that there is a supernatural "force" above and beyond them. In sensing the power of this force arising out of the animation and energy of interaction, the aborigines would construct totems and engage in rituals to honor the supernatural powers symbolized by the totem. From this observation, Durkheim concluded that worship of the gods and the supernatural is, in reality, worship of society and the bonds generated by people's interaction and contact with each other. Thus, the glue that holds society together is sustained by concrete interactions of individuals as they, in essence, worship society. In developing this argument, Durkheim took sociology in a new direction toward the study of more micro, interpersonal activities. For most of the nineteenth century, thinking about society was decidedly macro, emphasizing the big picture—evolution, the state, the economy, the church, the class system, and other structures where the actions of real people were underemphasized. Durkheim was one who began to look beneath the surface at what people actually did in creating and sustaining these "big structures."

Karl Marx (1818–1883)

Karl Marx was German but he managed to offend officials in several countries in continental Europe; and as a result, he moved to London where most of his major work was written, often in collaboration with his patron and friend, Friedrich Engels. Unlike Comte and Spencer, Marx was suspicious of any pretensions that sociology could uncover timeless laws like those in natural sciences. Instead, he felt that each historical epoch was built around a particular type of economic production, organization of labor, and control of property, with the result that historical epochs reveal their own unique dynamics. Hence, feudalism operates by one dynamic, and Marx's (1867) main focus—capitalism—proceeds in terms of yet another set of dynamic processes.

What are these processes? For Marx, the organization of a society at a particular point in time is determined by the **means of production,** or the nature of the economy and the organization of work. Thus, the organization of the economy is the material base, or in his terms, **substructure,** that circumscribes and directs the **superstructure** consisting of culture, politics, and other aspects of society. The operation of human society is thus to be explained by the economic base (Marx and Engels 1846). For Marx (1867), there is always what he termed *contradictions* inherent in the organization of this economic base. For example, in capitalism he saw that the collective organization of production (in factories), where individuals collaborate to produce commodities, stood in contradiction to the private ownership of property and the extraction of profit by capitalists from efforts of collectively organized workers. Whatever the merits of this argument, Marx's approach emphasized a basic source of tension in human societies between those who control resources and those who do not have resources and who are exploited.

In arguing this way, Marx became the inspiration for a sociological approach known as **conflict theory** or **conflict sociology**. In this approach, all patterns of social organization reveal conflict-producing inequalities, where those who own or control resources can consolidate power and develop legitimating ideologies to maintain their privilege and where those without resources eventually become oriented to conflict with the more privileged (Marx and Engels 1848). At the very least, there is always a smoldering tension between super- and subordinates in social systems, and this **conflict of interest**, as Marx phrased the matter, periodically erupts into overt conflict and social change.

Sociological analysis must, therefore, concentrate on the pattern of inequality and the tensions between those with power, privilege, and material well-being, on the one side, and the less powerful, privileged and materially well-off, on the other side. For Marx and subsequent generations of conflict theorists, this is where "the action is" in human social organization.

There is yet another important facet to Marx's work: the activist role of the sociologist. The goal of the analyst is to expose inequality and exploitation in social situations and, in so doing, to play an active role in eliminating these conditions. Sociologists should not just stand on the sidelines; they must work to change the social world in ways that reduce inequalities and domination of one segment of society by another. Marx, of course, wanted to help bring down capitalism, but the general thrust of his program—find inequalities, expose them, and work for their elimination—is still a source of inspiration for many sociologists today—often called **critical theorists**—who wish to intervene in the social world as activists.

Like most early sociologists, Marx was a product of The Enlightenment because he believed that society was marching toward a better state: communism. As each historical epoch reveals its contradictions, the revolutionary conflict ushers in a new era. Marx felt that the time was ripe for the final stage of history. Capitalism had created the new technologies that would, after the revolution, allow humans to eliminate inequality because it was now possible to produce enough for all. Indeed, for all of his brooding about the ills of capitalism, Marx was perhaps the most optimistic thinker of the nineteenth century—an optimism born of The Enlightenment.

Max Weber (1864–1920)

Max Weber is said to have had a "silent dialogue" with his fellow German, Karl Marx. Weber sought to correct for the excesses in Marx's thinking about inequality, power, and social change (Bendix 1968). Like Marx, Weber (1904) was suspicious of any claims that sociology could be like the natural sciences and formulate universal and timeless "laws" of human social organization. Unlike Marx, however, Weber (1904) argued that sociological analysis should be **value-free** or objective and neutral on moral matters. The goal of sociology is to describe and understand how and why social patterns came into existence and how they operate. For Weber, moralizing was less important than objective analyses.

Sociology must, Weber (1922) argued, always seek to understand phenomena "at the level meaning" of the actors. That is, what do the participants see and feel in the course of their involvement in social situations? However, these insights are not enough; it is also necessary to examine the larger cultural and structural picture created when many participants are involved in complex arrays of relationships. Sociological analysis must, therefore, move back and forth between the experiences of individuals and the larger cultural and social patterns in which people live their lives.

As we see frequently in the next chapters, the substance of Weber's sociology still influences sociology. In his silent dialogue with Karl Marx, for example, Weber felt that control of the means of economic production was only one of several bases for inequality; status, honor, and prestige constitute another basis, as do power and politics (Weber 1922). Thus, inequality is not a simple matter of "haves and have nots" with respect to who controls the means of production; it is a more multidimensional process with inequalities and rankings of people along several dimensions—at a minimum class (economic), status groups (prestige, honor), and party (power). For Marx, status and power simply follow from class; for Weber, such was not always the case.

Another silent debate with Marx concerned conflict and change. For Marx, inequality inevitably produces conflict between super- and subordinates and, hence, social change; for Weber, inequality increases the probability of conflict, but the specific conditions of a situation can facilitate or impede the emergence of "charismatic leaders" who can mobilize subordinates to pursue conflict (Weber 1922). Thus, conflict is not inevitable and inexorable; it is more probabilistic. Depending upon chance and other unique convergences of forces, conflict may or may not occur.

A third silent debate that Weber had with Marx was over the impact of "ideas" or systems of symbols in producing social change. For Marx, cultural ideas—values, beliefs, religious dogmas, political doctrines, and the like—are a *superstructure* that follow from a material *substructure* revolving around the means of production. For Marx, it is this *substructure*, or the means of production, that drives social change; for Weber, ideas can also cause social change and alter the means of production. For example, in Weber's (1904–1905) famous *The Protestant Ethic and the Spirit of Capitalism*, he argued that the content of beliefs among early Protestant religious sects—beliefs advocating thrift, frugality, savings, and hard work—were more responsible for the emergence of industrial capitalism in Europe than more material forces in the economy itself, as Marx had argued.

Yet another silent debate with Marx, and indeed all Enlightenment thinkers, was the view that societies are progressing. For Weber, the question of "progress" was a value judgment that had no scientific basis. Moreover, in Weber's analysis of the modern world, the rise of bureaucracy and the large state, coupled with the rationalization of most activities, seemed to create disenchantment and constraint that could not easily be broken. Did "modern" society create a better world? Weber was not so sure, and he increasingly believed that this modern world of bureaucratic authority was an "iron cage" that had the power to dominate people and limit their options.

Weber continues to influence sociology because of his interest in isolating and understanding the basic forces of modern societies—the emergence and operation of capitalism, the domination of social life by bureaucracies, the growing power of the state, the multidimensional bases of stratification, the significance of law in modern social relations, the urbanization of populations into cities, and the effects of cultural ideas. In these and many other specific concerns, Weber sought to sort out the historical causes of a modern situation (or at least modern in his time), to develop objective ways of describing the essence of this modern condition, and to understand what it means to the individuals involved. His insights, as well as the nature of his approach to gathering these insights, still inspire many contemporary sociologists (J. Turner 1993b).

Early American Tradition

Sociology was established in an academic department at a university in the United States before Durkheim in France and Weber in Germany achieved this goal, and yet, early American sociology was highly derivative of European thinking. At first it tended to emphasize Comte and Spencer, but as the twentieth century progressed, Comte and Spencer were forgotten, whereas interest in Durkheim, Weber, and eventually Marx, increased with each decade. To this day, Marx's, Weber's, and Durkheim's ideas exert considerable influence in sociology.

Early American sociology was also very much oriented to amelioration—that is, helping the disadvantaged in society. Few of the first American sociologists were trained as scientists; most came from other professions such as journalism and religion, bringing with them concern for the underdog in social life. Still, American sociology increasingly sought to become more scientific, but unlike Europe, the emphasis in the United States was on the quantification of data collection. Thus, in the first decades of the twentieth century, systematic data collection and statistical analysis were often emphasized, although qualitative and historical work could also be found in leading departments of sociology. Indeed, one of the great patrons of sociology during the first half of the twentieth century was John D. Rockefeller, Sr., who wanted a discipline that could collect data to be used for "practical" purposes (Turner and Turner 1990). Rockefeller soon became disillusioned with sociologists' accomplishments and, in the end, withdrew his support. However, the emphasis on data about life in communities and the analysis of these data with statistics persisted, and with the spread of the computer technologies in the 1960s, sociology could become even more quantitative.

At the turn into the last century, however, the contributions of American sociology to the founding of the discipline as a whole revolved around the concerns of several scholars with the process of face-to-face interaction among individuals—a topic underemphasized in European circles of thinking. The leading figure was George Herbert Mead.

George Herbert Mead (1863–1931)

George Herbert Mead was a philosopher at the University of Chicago, which had also created the first sociology department in the world in 1892. Mead drew ideas from sociologist Charles Horton Cooley (from Michigan where Mead had his first job) and from the Harvard psychologist William James, as well as from philosophers in a tradition known as *pragmatism* emphasizing that the basic force of life is adjustment and adaptation. For Mead, humans are born into a society and must adapt to ongoing patterns of social organization. The young must therefore acquire those capacities that allow them to cooperate with others. As infants, children can survive by cooperating with their caretakers; and, as people mature over the life course, they must cooperate with others in many types of organized groupings. Thus, those behavioral capacities that facilitate adjustment to, and cooperation with, others in organized social contexts will be retained in the behavioral repertoire of the young, whereas those behaviors that do not do so will be extinguished.

Mead saw the process of interaction as the mutual signaling of gestures, such as words and "body language," that carry conventional meanings. Thus, individuals must first learn to communicate with conventional symbols; and as they do so, their ability to cooperate with others is greatly enhanced. From reading the gestures of others, cooperation is facilitated by the ability to take on the role of the other, or **role-take.** By putting oneself in the place of the other, a person can anticipate the other's responses; and because this capacity to role-take facilitates cooperation, it is retained in a person's behavioral repertoire. With role-taking, individuals can also see what others think of them; and as they derive a **self-image** of themselves from the perspective of the other, they evaluate themselves from the vantage point of the other. Eventually, this ability to see oneself from the vantage point of the other evolves, with practice and biological maturation, into the ability to see oneself from a **generalized other** or what Mead called a *community of attitudes.* This more general perspective of the group also becomes a basis for self-evaluation and for behaving in ways that facilitate cooperation. With the notion of the generalized other, Mead now comes full circle and invokes an idea very similar to Émile Durkheim's idea of the *collective conscience.* But unlike Durkheim, who emphasized rituals as activating commitments to the culture of a situation, Mead emphasizes that it is the ability to role-take with more abstract and generalized others that regulates people's conduct.

We explore Mead's ideas many times in subsequent chapters (see, in particular, Chapter 6); and although Mead was a philosopher, his philosophy was not lost on sociologists who were taking his classes. In fact, when he died, it was a sociology graduate student—Herbert Blumer—who took over his class and became an advocate of Mead's sociology for over 50 years (Blumer 1969). Thus, although Mead did not see himself as a sociologist, he was by far the most important American sociologist of the first half of the twentieth century. A theoretical school of thought—labeled by Blumer as **symbolic interactionism**—derives from the core ideas developed by Mead.

Chicago School of Sociology and Its Competitors

From its founding as the first sociology department in the world, the University of Chicago was the center of American sociology for several decades, although by the 1920s strong rival departments had emerged. The first generation of American sociologists at Chicago created what became known as the *Chicago School* of sociology. This "school" was, in fact, not nearly as coherent as retrospective looks back to the first decades of the last century often assume. What distinguished the school was the use of Chicago as a "laboratory" to study the dynamics of immigration, the formation and culture of neighborhoods, deviance activities and careers, and the downtrodden. A variety of methods were used, from taking a census count of people to ethnographies of diverse ways of life. Some Chicago sociologists took a broad view by examining the structure of urban communities in which various groups and interests competed for space, whereas others were more concerned with the practical problems of people.

Thus, compared to the "macro" concerns of European sociologists about the evolution of societies, American sociologists at Chicago were more micro, examining the behaviors and culture of diverse groups. But, Chicago was not the only place that sociology was practiced (Turner and Turner 1990). At Columbia University, other founders of the discipline such as Franklin Giddings were pushing for the quantification of data so that they could be systematically analyzed with statistical procedures— an approach very different than that evident in the Chicago School. Indeed, as the twentieth century unfolded, sociology increasingly became quantitative, emphasizing the use of statistics. Even at the University of Chicago, this reliance on quantification became evident in the 1930s, although the ethnographic collection of qualitative data still remained an important line of inquiry at Chicago and wherever students trained at Chicago migrated. At Yale, William Graham Sumner and Albert Galloway Keller (1927) were pursuing a macro program resembling a European flavor, importing ideas from Herbert Spencer in the study of societal evolution from simple to complex societal forms. Similarly, at Harvard and Brown universities, the influence of Comte and Spencer on the work, respectively, of Pitirim Sorokin (1937) and Lester F. Ward (1883) could be seen.

Early Emphasis on Sociological Practice

From its founding in America, sociology was concerned with what today we call **practice** or the use of sociological concepts and theories to reconstruct social arrangements. Many of the founding generation of sociologists were the children of those who had advocated emancipation of slaves, and so, there has always been a concern in American sociology with helping those who have been victimized by existing social arrangements.

Jane Adams (1860–1935) and Hull House.   One of the unfortunate facts of academic life in the late nineteenth century and first two-thirds of the twentieth century (and sometimes, even today) was the marginalization of women. It was difficult for women to enter academia and pursue careers, and so they often were forced to pursue career paths outside academia—as we saw for Harriet Martineau in England. Indeed, the ameliorative practice of sociology was often left to women, a kind of academic view of "women's work" for the intellectually inclined. Jane Adams's career personifies the pursuit of "applied sociology" at Chicago. Adams became one of the most famous women in America and the world, winning the Nobel Peace Prize; and she did so through her own and many colleagues' efforts to improve the lives of immigrants and others who needed help. Moreover, she became a champion of peace and argued strongly against war; in her deeds and works she became an articulate feminist, pushing for the inclusion of women in politics and other institutional spheres dominated by men (Madoo-Lengerman and Niebrugge-Brantly 1998).

Adams worked outside of the University of Chicago, although she had contact with George Herbert Mead and other professors at the university. Moreover, many of the graduate students at Chicago often participated in the activities of Hull House, which began as a community center and over the years encompassed a whole city block of buildings devoted to the study of the lives of individuals and to the provision of aid and assistance to needy individuals. For Adams, studying the actual experiences of real people—rather than the abstractions of macro approaches—was essential. Like her more academic counterparts in the Chicago School, Adams saw local sites—neighborhoods, schools, unions, factories, political party headquarters, shops, houses, clubs, and the like—as the places where society impinges on the individual (Madoo-Lengerman and Niebrugge-Brantly, 1998:74–81). She argued that the understanding of society and the person come only from knowledge about how these sites are organized, how they related to each other, and how they constrain the individuals who move through them. At the level of practice, where the goal is to help people in need, this practice must be informed by knowledge of the complex interplay of sites as they affect the lives of people. Although the workers at Hull House constructed maps of areas that had a quantitative character, the real thrust of their sociological approach was qualitative. The goal of researchers and practitioners was to learn what the world means to the individuals who carry out their activities at various sites. To help people, it is necessary to know how they think about the world and how they actually adjust and adapt to real life situations.

William E. B. Du Bois (1868–1963).   Over six decades in the twentieth century, William E. B. Du Bois created African-American sociology. Du Bois received his Ph.D. at Harvard and did postdoctoral work with Max Weber at the University of Berlin. He was also one of the founders of the National Association for the Advancement of Colored People (NAACP). His works emphasized, much like Adams', the need to understand the lives of African Americans at the level of meaning—that is, how do African Americans see the world and how is this perception different from that of whites. His works helped whites in America see the "racial divide" and the "double consciousness" of black citizens who must overcome perceptions of their inferiority by whites and, yet, try to participate in the mainstream even as whites discriminate against them. In his early years, Du Bois was optimistic that the racial divide could be overcome, but he later lost hope. At the age of 93 he was so bitter that he left America, moving to Africa where he died two years later. Still, he established a

Box 1.1: Sociology and Other Disciplines

Sociology and Economics

Economics studies the production and distribution of goods and services in a society. It has become a highly technical social science in its emphasis on developing mathematical models of economic processes. In exploring the subject quantitatively, however, economics has not always considered the effects of many noneconomic processes in a society. Sociologists view processes of production and distribution in their larger cultural and social context. The economy is but one set of social relationships within a larger social whole. Sociologists attempt to understand how the events in this larger context influence economic processes. Moreover, even when sociologists focus on a particular economic unit (such as a corporation) or a whole sector of the economy (such as labor or investors), they analyze how the broader social landscape influences events among these economic processes. In particular, they seek to learn how both economic and noneconomic social relationships influence economic events. This may bring about a loss of economists' technical elegance, but it does fit economic events into the larger scheme of things.

Sociology and Political Science

These two fields are beginning to converge on the general question of how power, or the capacity to control, is used and distributed in society. Traditionally, political scientists have studied international relations among nations and the administration of government within nations. In contrast, sociologists have rarely studied international relations; when studying the administration of government, they have been primarily interested in the more general problem of bureaucracy. Also, sociologists have studied many topics that only recently have attracted political scientists: political attitudes, social backgrounds of leaders, social class, and other factors that influence people's political behavior. Sociologists now study intersocietal relations, and political scientists study a wide range of forces that influence political behavior, attitudes, and organization. The concerns of political sociology and political science are likely to be much the same in the future.

Sociology and Psychology

Psychology is the study of behavior. Behavior is defined broadly in psychology and includes thinking, learning, perception, emotions, motives, and increasingly the physiological (organic) and social causes of these processes. Sociology and psychology overlap in an area known as **social psychology,** the study of social factors that influence people's behavior—their cognitions, emotions, attitudes, decisions, and actions. Psychologists usually concentrate on understanding actual behavior, whereas sociologists are more likely to study the social situations that produce certain behaviors. Perhaps the greatest overlap occurs in the study of *personality*, the traits and attributes of people. Psychologists, though, are more likely to study the structure and processes of personality per se, whereas sociologists are usually more interested in how types of social relationships produce certain personality characteristics—and how these characteristics influence social relations and patterns of human organization.

Sociology and Anthropology

Anthropology and sociology have common intellectual roots. Anthropology is divided into several specific areas: cultural and social, linguistics, archaeology, and biological anthropology. Sociology and anthropology overlap primarily in the area of cultural and social organization, although sociologists are becoming more attuned to the biological or physical facets of human behavior. Within cultural (or social) organization, the major difference between the two disciplines lies in the type of societies that each studies. Anthropologists tend to concentrate on simple or traditional systems, and sociologists tend to concentrate on more modern and complex societies. A curious shift is taking place, however. Just as sociologists are becoming more aware of traditional societies, anthropologists are beginning to study modern systems. The following chapters analyze how much the two disciplines have in common.

Sociology and History

History is the study of societal events of the past. Historians seek to chronicle what occurred and to offer some clues regarding how one set of events led to another. Some of the earliest sociologists engaged in historical analysis, but the difference between sociologists and historians persists to this day. Sociologists attempt to generalize from historical events; historians concentrate on the unique features of each event. Historians might, for example, give a detailed account of events leading up to the French Revolution to demonstrate that this revolution was the culmination of a sequence of specific processes in French society. Sociologists, however, would tend to view the French Revolution as an example of revolutions in general. They would try to see how the events leading to this conflict, along with evidence from other revolutions in different times and places, could be considered examples of the general conditions that cause all revolutions. For the most part, historians stay with the particulars, sociologists try to discover the general conditions that such particulars illustrate. There is a trend among historians today, however, to generalize beyond the particulars of events and increasingly to use sociological methods. Thus, although they tend to look upon one another suspiciously, sociologists and historians are converging, to a limited degree, in their interests and methods.

(continued)

Sociology and Social Work

People outside sociology and social work often consider the two areas synonymous. They are not. Social work is a profession for helping people. As such, it draws upon knowledge from all the social sciences and from the individual social worker's intuition and life experiences. Of course, many social workers have received sociological training, for sociology is highly relevant to their work, but sociologists try to understand why certain situations (e.g., crime and poverty) exist. Sociologists do not usually try to intervene in the social world. Rather, they attempt to provide knowledge for those who do intervene. There is, however, considerable disagreement among sociologists over their proper role and responsibility. Should they be detached, or should they be activists and try to change human affairs? The answers tend to vary from sociologist to sociologist.

These comparisons demonstrate that sociology is a very broad discipline, covering almost every facet of human affairs that influences, and is influenced by, patterns of organized social relations. Sociology overlaps and converges with other social sciences and even with some disciplines in the humanities, such as history. To the extent that other fields of inquiry examine human social relationships, their findings are relevant to sociology.

The key to the sociological perspective, which distinguishes it from other disciplines, is the search for common patterns in social relations. The job of the sociologist is to discover the ways that social relationships reveal order, consistency, and predictable change, even when change involves violence and volatility. There is an underlying organization to all human affairs—those of the past and present, those involving economic processes, those revolving around power and politics, and those involving people's personalities. Each social science looks at a piece of social reality, but only sociology and (at times) anthropology seek to put the pieces together. There is, then, a sociological dimension underlying all the social sciences when they address questions of social relationships and human organization. Conversely, all the basic insights of the other social sciences are part of sociology when they deal with the basic ways that human beings form relationships and organize themselves.

brand of sociology that focused on patterns of discrimination and oppression, not just of African-origin Americans but all ethnic groups subject to prejudice and discrimination; to this day, these concerns are at the center of much sociological inquiry.

Study of Sociology Today

Today, sociology is a very broad discipline. It studies just about any aspect of the social world with a wide variety of theories, methods, and agendas. Indeed, some would say that sociology is too broad because there is often little consensus among sociologists about their mission. Should sociological inquiry be guided by theory, as Comte, Spencer, and Durkheim advocated? Should sociology try to make the world better, as Martineau, Marx, Adams, and Du Bois advocated? Should the methods of inquiry be qualitative and interpretive, as many in the Chicago School thought? Or, should data be collected with an eye toward quantification and statistical analysis? Should the focus on sociology be macro and examine the big structures—economy, state, nation—and their evolution, or should inquiry focus on the individual in real-life situations, or perhaps something in between? Thus, the diversity and divisions of present-day sociology were evident at the very beginnings of the discipline.

Yet, as the chapters of this text reveal, there is some consensus over what should be studied. Each chapter and, at times, sections within chapters, represents an important subject matter for sociologists. There are disagreements over *how* topics should be studied, as well as *what kind* of knowledge should be gained and how this knowledge *should be used*. But there is at least a rough consensus over what is the subject matter of sociology. *Sociology* is, therefore, the study of society from (a) the most minute episodes of behavior and face-to-face interaction through (b) all of the structures that humans have created to organize behaviors and interactions into societies to (c) the patterns of relations among societies. Sociology thus overlaps with all of the other social sciences and disciplines in the humanities, such as history. Sociology is not Comte's "queen science," but it is broad. It is a chaotic discipline, but it opens opportunities for people to pursue very diverse kinds of activity.

SUMMARY

1. Sociology is the study of human behavior, interaction, and social organization.

2. Sociology is relevant to each of our daily lives because it provides a vehicle for understanding the sources of constraint in our thoughts, perceptions, and actions.

3. Sociology emerged under conditions of change associated with: (a) the decline of feudalism and the emergence of commerce, industry, and urbanization; (b) the intellectual movement known as The Enlightenment in which science and secular thought about the physical, biological, and social worlds could flourish; and (c) the traumatic shock over the violence and sudden change associated with the French Revolution of 1789.

4. The name, *sociology,* was proposed by the French thinker, Auguste Comte, who believed that a science of society could emulate the natural sciences. Comte also felt that discovery of the laws of human social organization could be used to reconstruct society in a more humane way.

5. Harriet Martineau not only translated Comte's great work, but she took sociology to the larger public and argued that it should address issues and problems of the real world.

6. Herbert Spencer in England argued that laws of human organization could be developed. These laws would focus on the growing size and complexity of

society as these forces created pressures for (a) increased exchange and interdependence among people and organizations of society and (b) increased use of power to regulate, control, and coordinate activities of people and organizational units. Spencer founded a sociological approach known as functionalism, where the effects of a social pattern on the maintenance of society are emphasized.

7. Émile Durkheim borrowed from Spencer, but continued the Comtean and French tradition of emphasizing the importance of cultural ideas for the integration of society. Like Spencer, he was a functionalist and believed that laws of human organization could be discovered, but he added to Spencer's approach the importance of discovering the causes and functions of cultural symbols for integrating society.

8. Karl Marx, a German who was expelled from his homeland and eventually settled in England, emphasized the conflictual nature of society, founding an approach known as conflict theory or conflict sociology. In Marx's view, inequalities in the distribution of resources set the stage for the transformation of society as those without resources to organize and engage in conflict with those who control production, who possess power, and who manipulate cultural symbols to legitimate their privilege. Unlike Comte, Spencer, and Durkheim, Marx did not believe that general laws of human organization, transcending historical epochs, could be developed.

9. Max Weber, the other major German founder of sociology, engaged in a lifelong but silent dialogue with Marx, emphasizing that inequality is multidimensional and not based solely upon the economy, that conflict is contingent on historical conditions and is not the inevitable and inexorable outcome of inequality, and that change could be caused by ideas as well as the material and economic base of a society. He also stressed that sociology must look at both the larger scale structure of society and the meanings that individuals give to these larger scale forces. Like Marx, he doubted if there were general laws of human organization, but unlike Marx, he felt that it is necessary to be value-free and objective in the description and analysis of social phenomena.

10. Early American sociology adopted European ideas to specific problems associated with urbanization and industrialization, but it did initiate two important trends: (a) the widespread use of quantitative, statistical techniques and (b) the theoretical approach that was to become known as interactionism, where concern is with the processes by which society is sustained and changed by the behaviors of individuals in micro face-to-face encounters.

11. Early American sociology also exhibited an agenda for helping people in need, creating a concern for "practice" and "applied sociology" where sociological inquiry seeks to rebuild problematic social structures.

12. Sociology is now a large and diverse field analyzing all facets of human culture, social structure, behavior and interaction, and social change.

KEY TERMS

Age of Reason: eighteenth and nineteenth century thinking on the British Isle, owing its inspiration to The Enlightenment and emphasizing the rights of humans and the nature of social organization.

Collective Conscience: Émile Durkheim's term for systems of cultural symbols that people in a society share and use to regulate their affairs.

Conflict of Interest: Karl Marx's term for the basic tension and incompatibility of goals between those who control resources and those who do not.

Conflict Sociology/Conflict Theory: View that the main dynamic of human social relations and patterns of social organization is tension and conflict over the unequal distribution of resources.

Critical Theorist/Theory: Approach that seeks to expose patterns of inequality and domination, while suggesting ways to eliminate these patterns.

Differentiation/Differentiate: Process whereby individuals and the units organizing their activities become distinctive and differ in their culture, goals, and structure from each other.

Enlightenment, The: Broad intellectual movement, culminating in the eighteenth and nineteenth centuries, in which nonreligious thinking about the universe was encouraged.

Functionalism: Approach to the analysis of phenomena in terms of their consequences for the needs or requisite of the larger social whole in which they are located. This approach was first used in sociology by Herbert Spencer.

Generalized Other: Community of attitudes of social groupings that people use to evaluate themselves and to organize their conduct.

Hierarchy of the Sciences: Auguste Comte's view that the sciences could be arranged in a hierarchy in terms of when they emerged and the complexity of their subject matter. Sociology, not surprisingly, was at the top of the hierarchy, just above biology.

Integration/Integrated: Processes and mechanisms by which differentiated social units are coordinated and controlled.

Interactionism, Symbolic: Approach to the analysis of social phenomena, inspired by early American philosophers and sociologists, that stresses the importance of understanding the dynamics of face-to-face contact and interaction among individuals.

Law of the Three Stages: Auguste Comte's view that ideas, and society as a whole, pass through three stages: (a) the theological, where religious ideas dominate; (b) the metaphysical, where systematic thought is stressed; and (c) the positivistic, where science comes to dominate.

Means of Production: Karl Marx's term for the nature and organization of the economy in a society.

Philosophes, The: Lineage of eighteenth-century social thinkers in France who championed the idea of individual freedom from arbitrary political authority. It was from this lineage that Auguste Comte, the founder of sociology, was to draw many of his ideas.

Practice: Use of sociological data, theories, and interpretations for applied purposes and for changing social relations and structures.

Role-Take: Process of reading the gestures of others to assume their perspective and likely course of action.

Self-Image: View of oneself as seen from the responses of others in a situation.

Social Psychology: Subfield in sociology and psychology that seeks to understand the effects of culture, social structures on behavior, and social interaction.

Sociology: Systematic study of human social behavior, interaction, and organization.

Substructure: Karl Marx's label for the material, economic base that influences other aspects of a society.

Superorganic: Herbert Spencer's view of sociology's subject matter: the organization of living organisms.

Superstructure: Karl Marx's term for those structures and cultural systems determined by the economic base of a society.

Value-Free: Max Weber's term emphasizing that sociology should seek to eliminate bias and moral considerations in an effort to produce objective analyses of social phenomena.

Chapter 2

Scientific Method and Sociology

After spending several months in confinement for reaffirming Copernicus' view that the earth was not the center of the universe and that, indeed, the earth revolved around the sun, a weakened and frail Galileo went before the Inquisition in June of 1616. For years he had drawn the attention of Inquisitors for his views, and now he was to pay the ultimate penalty. He would have to retract publicly all that he believed and beg for absolution by affirming church doctrine that the earth was the center of the universe. At least he would be free of prison, but he was still confined to various residences with his daughter—a nun—in attendance nearby. Yet, he continued to think and tinker with instruments—from the telescope to the idea of a pendulum clock—but he was an outcast in a world dominated by religion. Near the end of his life two decades later, the man who had revolutionized the study of the stars with the telescope lost his sight—perhaps an even greater indignity than having to humiliate himself in front of the Inquisition. Thus, a mere 400 years ago, science was far from dominant.

In the contemporary world, science has become the dominant way to understand the universe. In addition to science, religion, ideologies, philosophies, and personal intuition are also used to make sense of the world. Thus, science has competitors; this competition is more intense in some arenas than others. Unlike the Inquisition, few nonscientists today question the claims of physicists about how the physical universe works; the same is true of chemists, biochemists, and biologists, although deeply held religious beliefs about "creationism" often conflict with biologists' commitment to Darwinian evolution. Religion and science can come into conflict, even at the beginning of the twenty-first century.

In the social arena, science hardly reigns supreme. Religion is less the culprit than intellectual doubts about the prospects for a science of society. For many, humans and their creations—society and culture—are not seen as amenable to scientific study. And so, 175 years after Auguste Comte's (1830–1842) confident presumption that sociology could be a natural science, sociologists themselves are still divided on the question of how scientific sociology can, or should, be. Just as Karl Marx and Max Weber questioned the possibilities of scientific sociology, so do many contemporary sociologists (Denzin 1970; Halfpenny 1982). Still, for the moment, let us assume that this controversy over the scientific status of sociology did not exist and examine how scientific sociology proceeds.

The Nature of Science

The goal of **science** is to understand how the universe, in all its dimensions, operates. The vehicle for such understandings is **theory.** Scientific theories seek to explain why phenomena exist and how they operate (J. Turner 1991). To "theorize" in the lay public's mind is often seen as the equivalent of "speculation" and offering of unproven and perhaps unproveable ideas. This connotation of the word "theory" is unfortunate because it implies the very opposite of what scientific theory attempts. The goal of scientific theory is to state ideas about how the universe operates with sufficient precision that they can be rigorously tested. Scientific theories have some special characteristics that set them apart from other types of explanations like those in religion, political dogma, and personal opinions (J. Turner 1985a).

One distinctive characteristic of scientific theories is *abstractness*. Theories are stated abstractly in an effort to explain phenomena in all times and places. Scientific theories are not about the unique and particular but, rather, about processes that operate universally. For example, Albert Einstein's famous formula, $E = mc^2$, says nothing about a particular emission of energy (E), or body of matter (m), or the speed of light (c) in a specific context; what it says is that energy, matter, and the speed of light are fundamentally related in all times and in all places. Sociological theories can also display this quality of abstractness. For example, as noted in Chapter 1, Herbert Spencer (1874–1896) proposed that as a population grows, its members become differentiated into ever more specialties and partitions that are then integrated by interdependencies and concentrations of power. This theory is also abstract because it does not address a particular population at a specific point in time, but *all* populations in *all* times and places.

A second unique characteristic of scientific theories is that, as emphasized earlier, they are subject to **tests.** Some have even proclaimed that scientific theories are designed to be proven wrong (Popper 1959, 1969) because the goal is to subject theories to tests and retests until we have some confidence that the theory is highly plausible. If a theory stands intact after repeated assaults from empirical data, it is considered for the time being to be the best explanation of the way things are (Popper 1969). Thus, in contrast to the population's perception of theories as idle speculation, the goal of scientific theory is to conduct tests that eliminate any speculation or doubt about their plausibility.

This is the way all science works. It is not an efficient process, but it keeps theories tied to real events. We hold theories skeptically and constantly check them against the facts. Compare this approach to alternative ways of trying to understand the world. In religious interpretations, the powers of gods and supernatural forces are seen to control the flow of events, and if this view does not correspond to the way actual events unfold, beliefs in the power of the gods or the correctness of one's presumptions are not rejected, as they would be for a scientific theory. Rather, a new interpretation is offered that sustains beliefs. Similarly, personal biases are often retained when the facts contradict them; indeed, we cling to our prejudices and perceptions because they give us comfort and because we are used to them. Political ideologies have this same quality;

Box 2.1: What Makes Science Unique?

1. Science does not seek to evaluate what *should,* or should not, exist or occur.

2. Science seeks only to understand why phenomena exist and how they operate.

3. Science generates such understanding by developing abstract and nonevaluative theories explaining the how and why of phenomena.

4. Science then subjects these theories to empirical assessment, rejecting or modifying theories if the facts do not support them.

5. Science uses methods of data collection that can be replicated by others to make sure that the data used to test theories are not biased.

6. Science accumulates knowledge when theories find consistent support in empirical tests and when those that do not receive such support are rejected or modified.

people hold on to their political beliefs even when programs enacted in the name of these beliefs fail. In contrast, scientific theories are ultimately rejected or changed when they do not correspond to the empirical facts.

Theories are not casually tested, although scientists often begin with only an intuitive sense that the data correspond to the theory. Eventually, the theory must be assessed in a systematic way in terms of some general procedures, often termed the **scientific method.** The general idea behind the methods of science is to develop unbiased procedures for collecting data and then to specify clearly the steps that were taken in data collection. In this way, others can come along and check up and verify that we were honest and did not make any dumb mistakes or impose biases. Without data that have been carefully and systematically collected, we do not know if we have accurate records of events nor do we know if the data really do bear on the theory that we are testing.

Science seeks to be "objective" in the sense of collecting data without prejudice and bias, and then, letting the facts speak for themselves in assessing whether or not a theory is plausible. In the long run, science is self-correcting, but in the short run, biases often creep into inquiry along several fronts. First, scientists typically have a favored theory that they want to see confirmed and, as a result, they may stay with an explanation long after it should have been discarded or changed. Second, science is expensive, and so, whoever is paying the bills has an interest in some kinds of knowledge over other lines of inquiry. If the military is funding research, for instance, they have a clear interest in weapons, and this will bias scientific inquiry; if a drug company is paying for research, they have an interest in disease-curing that biases research; and so it goes. Third, political agendas and ideologies often determine what kinds of research are considered desirable, especially when particular avenues of research are funded by the government. If the agricultural department wants pesticides, research will be tilted toward these rather than other forms of pest control; or if government wants to eliminate welfare, it will fund projects that seek ways to do so. And most recently, if government for political (and religious) reasons wants to ban most stem-cell research, it has the power to do so, as it has over the last few years. Thus, science exists in an institutional environment that exerts considerable influence on how it goes about developing and testing theories.

Despite these influences from the institutional environment, the goal of science is to be, as Max Weber argued, "value-free," but this ideal is always hard to sustain. In the long run, relatively accurate knowledge about how the universe operates will accumulate. And compared to alternative belief systems, science is the most objective. One way to compare science with alternatives is outlined in Table 2.1. In the table, two questions are asked: (a) Is the belief system evaluative, stating what should and ought to occur? (b) Is the belief system empirical, oriented to data about the actual world? If the answer is "yes" to both questions, then the belief system is an ideology that states what should occur in the empirical world. If the answer is "no" to both questions, then the belief system is a logic of some sort, such as mathematics or a computer language. If the answer is "yes" to the first question (i.e., evaluative) but "no" to the second (referring to the nonempirical), then an example of this kind of belief system would be religious conceptions of a supernatural realm inhabited by gods. And finally, if the belief system is nonevaluative (or seeks to be) and is oriented to the empirical world, then science is the preeminent belief system falling into this box.

Recall Auguste Comte's *hierarchy of the sciences* with mathematics at the bottom (as the ultimate language of all science). Science uses logics for communication and formulation of ideas, but ultimately, science must seek to test out ideas in the empirical world. So, the boundary between science and logics is porous, as logics are formulated to deal with problems confronted by scientists. The boundary between ideology and

Table 2.1   Types of Belief Systems

		Is It Empirical?	
		Yes	No
Is It Evaluative?	Yes	Ideology	Religion
	No	Science	Logics

science is also somewhat porous because ideological agendas, especially when backed up by funding, often dictate the kinds of research problems pursued by scientists. Within the social sciences, ideology is particularly difficult to keep out of inquiry because we all have views about what should and ought to occur and be in society. And the boundary between science and religion has always been problematic. Indeed, science replaced religion as the dominant belief system in industrial societies, but religion has not fully accepted this fate, nor have most people abandoned a religious interpretation of events.

Within sociology proper, there are many who simply do not believe that sociology can or should be a science. For others, the goal of sociology is ideological advocacy, usually for the poor and oppressed. Thus, there is no consensus within the discipline about how scientific, if at all, sociology should be. My bias is for a scientific sociology that seeks to be, as Comte advocated, a science of society, but this bias is hardly shared by all.

Methods in Sociology

In science, **data** on the actual world need to be systematically and carefully collected so that procedures can be replicated by someone else. If we simply describe some data without telling others *how* and *why* these data were collected, no one can check up on us to see if our "facts" are really true. Thus, in science a general procedural approach—*the scientific method*—guides research, or the collection and analysis of information about the world.

This scientific method is often viewed as having stages or steps, but we should not get too carried away here and view science as a kind of lock-step march to truth and knowledge. Rather, the practice of science, or carefully crafted research, simply depends upon attention to several questions (Babbie 1992).

One is a statement of a **research problem,** or what one is trying to discover. This may sound obvious, but it is fundamental because one needs to narrow the focus of inquiry. Otherwise, we will run around like data-collecting magpies. In science, research problems are often dictated by a theory and a desire to see if the theory is plausible. However, in sociology as well as in the more advanced sciences, research is often conducted for reasons other than explicit theory-testing. One reason for conducting research is that we are just curious about some aspect of the world. Another is that a client (e.g., a governmental agency, a business, a charity) desires information on a topic. Yet another is that previous research reveals gaps in our knowledge, or stimulates new questions. Thus, although the idealized view of science would see all research as guided by theory, the reality is quite different. There are many other reasons for conducting research, and the scientific method can be easily accommodated to them.

Another important matter in the conduct of research is the question of what a researcher expects to find. It is often useful to formulate a **hypothesis,** which may be taken from a theory but not necessarily, about the expected results. In this way, researchers have a criterion or yardstick against which to measure their findings. Without a hypothesis to guide the collection and analysis of data, or at least a loose expectation about what is likely to be found, it is once again difficult to focus one's efforts;

indeed, we might gather unneeded, or even irrelevant, information that does not bear on the research problem or hypotheses.

Eventually, after stating a problem and what your expectations are, a **research design** is constructed. This design is a game plan and set of procedures for gathering information as it relates to one's research problem and hypotheses. There are many basic types of designs, but they all try to state clearly *how* information is to be collected. The choice of a design depends upon many factors—the nature of the problem, the amount of money one has to spend, and the preferences of the researcher. In sociology, there are four basic types of designs employed in research: (a) experiments, (b) surveys, (c) observations, and (d) histories. Each of these is briefly summarized here.

Experiments. The idea behind an **experiment** is to test the effect of a particular phenomenon on some aspect of the social world, typically people's responses to a particular stimulus or situation. The key ingredient of an experiment is the control of extraneous influences that might contaminate the researchers' ability to assess the effects of focal stimulus in a situation. In the classical **experimental design,** this is achieved with two matched groups of subjects: (a) the **experimental group,** which receives the stimulus or is exposed to the situation of interest; and (b) the **control group,** which does not receive the stimulus or is not exposed to the situation. The differences between the two groups allow the investigator to determine how much, if any, the stimulus or situation affected individuals. An example of a controlled experiment can be found in drug research where an experimental group receives a new drug, while a control group takes a harmless placebo. These kinds of experiments often involve "blinds" where neither the doctors giving the drugs nor the patients know who gets the experimental drug and who receives the placebo. In this way, researchers can be sure that they can isolate the effect, if any, of the drug when compared to the control group.

Surveys. The most common research design in sociology is the **survey,** where people are asked questions about a topic of interest to the investigator (Rossi, Wright, and Anderson 1985). These questions can be asked by an interviewer who sits down with the respondent, or more typically, by a questionnaire that the respondent fills out. The most ideal survey is one that has the following characteristics. First, the respondents are the entire population of interest, or more typically, a representative sample from this population. Second, all respondents agree to answer the questions. Third, the respondents answer precisely the same questions. These three features are often hard to achieve in practice, however. It may be impossible to ask all of the population; there may be too many, or they may be hard to reach. It may be difficult to get them to respond, because they are busy, unconcerned, forgetful, or even hostile to intrusions in their lives. It may be that items on a questionnaire are interpreted differently by varying respondents, or if actual interviews are conducted, the interviewers ask the questions in a different tone or the synergy of the interaction between the interviewer and respondent produces different responses. If samples are large enough, many of these problems are obviated, or cancel each other out. However, the extensive use of surveys reveals other problems (Cicourel 1964): they only reveal what people *say,* not what they may actually think and do; they structure respondents' answers, rather than letting respondents communicate in their own way; they are easily subject to lies and misrepresentations; and they do not easily examine phenomena that cannot be collapsed into questions. Nonetheless, sociologists use them because they are quickly administered and amenable to the application of statistics (Collins 1984; Lieberson 1985, 1992). Moreover, sociologists are often interested in what people think, perceive, and believe; a survey is a relatively easy way to get at surface cognitions, perceptions, feelings, and emotions.

Observations. Sometimes it is best to leave the confines of the experimental lab, throw away the questionnaire, and go out among people in real life situations and observe what they are actually doing. **Observational research designs** do just this (Whyte 1989; Whyte & Whyte 1984): they place investigators in a more naturalistic setting, and they have investigators observe and write down what they see. In this way, nuances, context, interactions, histories, and flows of events can be discovered. One type of observational study is **participant-observation**, where the investigator actually becomes a member of the group, organization, or community being studied. As such, the observer cannot only be intimately involved, but he or she can actually experience the world in a manner similar to those being observed. Another type of observational study is the **unobtrusive-observation**, where the investigator does not actually participate as a member, but stands aside out of the way and records what is occurring. This type of study loses some of the intimacy and insight possible with participant-observation, but it does mitigate against the pitfall of having the researcher's actions influence the flow of events and, hence, the research findings. Often, observational studies are a preliminary step in survey research because they enable those designing questions to select and phrase them in ways that will make sense to the respondents. The great advantage of observational studies is that one is examining the real world, not the artificial constructions of experimental designs and lists of survey questions (Whyte 1989). The great disadvantage, however, is that different investigators may see different things in terms of their personal biases. Moreover, observational studies are hard to replicate—to see if indeed what the investigator says occurs actually does—because the group may no longer exist or because various investigators simply observe different things or elicit different responses from subjects.

Histories. At times, we want to know what happened in the past. One can, of course, ask people in interviews about their past, but often we want to look further back at the longer reaches of history. It is at this point that history and sociology converge. Most of the early founders of sociology—Comte, Spencer, Marx, and Weber, in particular—used history to develop or illustrate their ideas; in recent decades there has been a dramatic revival of historical research to test or illustrate theories, or to describe the ebb and flow of events in past societies. At times, **historical research** draws upon the previous research of historians who have gone to the archives and dusty records or upon the data of archeologists who have dug up the past; at other times, sociological researchers go themselves to the records or to the archeological dig. The major difference between history and historical sociology is that the sociologist is often interested in using history to test or illustrate a more general theory, whereas the historian seeks only to describe the events of a particular time in the past. This is a blurred distinction, but it does capture a sense of the differences between history and sociology. The great problem with using historical records is that they are always incomplete and subject to different interpretations (which, of course, keeps historians in business); as a result, history can rarely provide a definitive and conclusive "test" of a theoretical idea.

Once the data are collected by one of these research designs, they are subjected to **analysis.** The type of analysis depends on the research design and the nature of the data, but the goal is to be careful, systematic, and unbiased. From the analysis will come our conclusions about what we found; and so, we had better be careful because others will check up on us.

A final step in the scientific method is to assess the plausibility of the hypothesis or, if hypotheses were not offered, to indicate what the data tell us about the phenomena studied.

The steps in the scientific method are outlined in Figure 2.1. These steps may seem like common sense, but they are more than this: they force us to be systematic, to remain unbiased (or at least to reduce our biases), and to let others know *what* we discovered and *how* we discovered it. Without the guidelines of the scientific method, we could not trust each other's findings, and we would not know how to check them and reassess them. The result would be that knowledge would be haphazard and often inaccurate; and we would not accumulate trustworthy knowledge about the world.

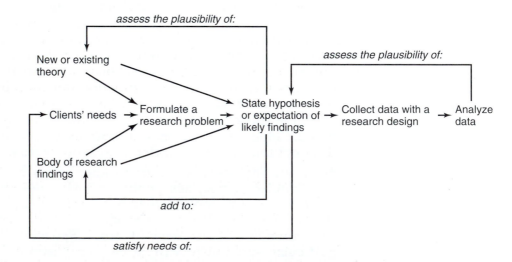

Figure 2.1   Elements of the Scientific Method

Does Science Take Away Humanism?

My fellow sociologists often proclaim that sociology is "an art form." The general idea behind such proclamations is that sociologists should stop handing out impersonal questionnaires and, instead, get in touch with the actual behaviors and thoughts of real people in their daily lives. Moreover, we should use our intuition as much as our intellect to extract information about the world. Sociology should still involve the use of general conceptual ideas, it is held, but only as these are influenced by our active participation with people in real-life settings. By knowing first-hand about the concerns, dilemmas, problems, and frustrations of individuals in society, we can use our conceptual knowledge to help them and make their lives better and more satisfying. Sociologists of this persuasion see their mission as diagnosing those sources of strain among individuals that stem from patterns of social organization and then suggesting possible solutions.

Many professional sociologists first went into sociology for humanitarian reasons. They felt that certain social conditions were wrong—ethnic and sexual discrimination, privilege in the face of abject poverty, unhappiness and alienation, and other social ills—and they wanted to do something about them. Indeed, this desire to help people was certainly the motivation of such early sociologists as Karl Marx, Harriet Martineau, and Jane Adams; and humanism has attracted many contemporary sociologists to the discipline. They want to help people and make a better world. Scratch the surface of even the most hard-nosed methodologist or climb into the armchair of a good theorist, and one can find humanistic motivations in the most professional of our professionals. Of course, this fact means that there is always an implicit ideology lurking in the thinking of a sociologist. Sometimes this ideology is explicitly advocated, but whether implicit or explicit, most sociologists do hold views about "what's wrong with society" and a general plan for "what should be done to solve these problems." True, at the same time we are realists and recognize that it is impossible to mold society to our will and fervor. Moreover, we recognize the bias in our thinking, and we try to suspend it when "doing science." Indeed, something often happens to sociologists as they move through school, especially on the road to a Ph.D. Somehow, the humanistic motivations and ideological fervor recede and get buried under a veneer of technical skills and academic professionalism. One consequence of this is that those scholars who remain openly humanistic and ideological tend to view experiments, statistics, impersonal scientific methods, and abstract theory as the "enemy" to their more practical concerns. They tend to see theory and methods as negating both their intuitions of sociological situations and their desire to help people.

This apparently unbridgeable gap between intuition and research is unnecessary. Our reasoned hunches, feelings, and intuitions are marvelous sources of sociological data. Although the methodological problems of personal bias are often emphasized when people study people, we should also recognize the great advantage they give us over natural scientists. Because we are humans who study humans and their patterns of social organization, we can use our intuition to gather information. We often have intimate familiarity with our subject matter in a way that a geologist or a physicist can never have. In short, our intuition and feelings can give us an advantage over what is occurring. However, we should not go overboard on this issue, as many sociologists do.

Our intuition can be wrong, biased, or only partly right. And if we try to base a corrective program on faulty information or on ideological grounds (i.e., on what we think *should* occur), we can potentially do more harm than good. Indeed, we can hurt people and create even more difficult social settings for those we are trying to help (J. Turner 2001). Thus, we need to qualify our enthusiasm for intuition and for data gathered and interpreted in light of our actual experiences in a social setting. We should not throw this intuitive advantage away or suppress it, any more than we should repress our humanistic concerns and desires to help people and make a better world. But we need to supplement these motivations with scientific inquiry.

If we want to realize our humanism—and this motive is what gets most of us started in sociology—we need to be skilled at gathering and interpreting information about situations we want to change and people we want to help. We also need theory to understand *why* and *how* the situations operate. We need to be able to anticipate the consequences of any changes we initiate and to collect accurate information about these changes. We cannot rely only on intuition and our personal ideologies. We need theory that has withstood efforts to disprove it to tell us how and why things operate, and we need to use this theory in ascertaining what needs to be done to improve a situation. We also need to collect accurate information and analyze it carefully to know just what exists in a situation and just what the consequences of our theoretically informed actions are.

If we have no theory, we have no framework for understanding and interpreting the social world. Hence, we do not know what we have done or what to expect. If we do not have methods, we cannot have confidence in our theories because they have not been tested, and we cannot know exactly what in a situation needs to be changed. We can use our familiarity with a situation and our creative intuition to bring to bear relevant theories and to develop systematic ways of gathering information. But our intuition cannot substitute for theory, carefully constructed methods, and detailed analysis. This is why science is an important tool for approaching social issues and problems of interest to humanists.

Scientific Sociology and Social Practice

As mentioned in Chapter 1, the titular founder of sociology, Auguste Comte, believed that a science of society could be used to make a better society. He realized that if sociology could develop and test theoretical laws like those in the physical and biological sciences, it would be possible to achieve a level of understanding about human organization that would facilitate the construction of new social forms. Thus Comte saw science and humanism as complementary: once there is an understanding of how and why the social world operates, this knowledge could be used to construct a better world. In entirely different guises, Karl Marx and Émile Durkheim felt the same way. They desired to *use* their conceptual understandings of how the world works to *construct* a better society.

Words like "construct" smack of social engineering, of social control, of an Orwellian world of Big Brother, and of a dull and lifeless society of technocrats. Engineering is fine, many would argue, as long as it is used to build bridges and roads. But unfettered engineering of theoretical knowledge creates things like nuclear bombs and other potentially harmful devices. These fears about engineering are, of course, well founded. But it could be argued that harmful uses of engineering are the result of organization into societal forms that encourage and sustain the misuse of engineering. If we knew more about the social universe, we might be better able to limit the misapplication of knowledge. On the other side of the issue, however, we might misuse knowledge of social organization to create even more monstrous things (J. Turner 2001).

This issue is moot in some ways. The development of theory and the use of research methods are going to produce more knowledge about how the social world operates. This knowledge—even in its current crude state—is going to be used for social engineering (Hunt 1985), although social engineering is typically called by another name in sociology—such as sociological **practice**, at other times **clinical sociology** and **applied sociology.** But we should know what these more benign labels mean: efforts to construct certain types of social relations using theoretical ideas and research findings. As with all engineering, this knowledge can be used for both good and bad purposes—what is "good" and "bad," of course, being a matter of people's values. Thus, we should not view scientific sociology as an arcane activity, for in point of fact, it is being used to change our daily lives; and it is likely to be used even more in the future.

SUMMARY

1. Science is the systematic effort to understand the universe in terms of theoretical ideas that have received consistent support in carefully conducted research.

2. Theory is, ultimately, the vehicle for understanding the universe, and it reveals two distinct characteristics: (a) abstractness and generality and (b) testability. Knowledge accumulates when abstract theories are tested and retested.

3. Data on the empirical world are collected systematically in accordance with the tenets of the scientific method. These tenets include (a) stating a research problem; (b) formulating a hypothesis; (c) collecting data, which in sociology is done with experiments, surveys, observations, or history; (d) analyzing the data; and (e) drawing conclusions with respect to the plausibility of theory, previous research, or needs of a client.

5. Although there are biases when humans study humans, the fact that social scientists can have an intuitive familiarity and actual experience with their subject matter can also be an advantage. Social scientists are not studying an alien world apart from their own experiences; they are, in a sense, studying the world they make in their daily lives.

6. Sociological knowledge will, as it accumulates, be used to construct and reconstruct social relations. Such efforts do not need to be antihumanistic; indeed, they can be done in the name of humanism. Hence, science and humanism need not stand in contradiction.

KEY TERMS

Analysis: Stage in the scientific method in which the data collected are systematically assessed to determine what has been discovered.

Applied Sociology: Effort to use sociological knowledge in dealing with problems and events.

Clinical Sociology: Term used to describe the activities of sociologists who use sociological knowledge to assess a situation for a client and develop solutions for this client.

Control Group: Those subjects in an experimental design who are not exposed to a stimulus of interest and who are used as a basis of comparison with those exposed to the stimulus.

Data: Information about the empirical world.

Experimental Group: Those subjects in an experimental research design who are exposed to a stimulus of interest to the investigator.

Experiments/Experimental Designs: Research design in which extraneous influences are controlled in an effort to isolate the effect of some specific stimulus.

Histories/Historical Research: Type of research design in which information about the past is gathered systematically.

Hypothesis: Statement of what one expects to be found in a research project. Hypotheses are often derived from theories and represent the predictions that a general theory makes for a specific empirical case(s).

Observations-Observational Research Design: Activities of individuals in their natural setting are recorded.

Participant-Observation: Type of observational research design in which the researcher becomes actively involved with those being studied.

Practice: Term often used to describe sociological work that is used for practical purposes and for changing a situation.

Research Design: Explicit procedures that are used in collecting empirical data.

Research Problem: First step in the scientific method devoted to establishing what kind of information is to be gathered in a research project.

Science: Process in which theoretical explanations about the operation of phenomena in the universe are systematically tested with empirical data.

Scientific Method: Procedures employed in the collection of data. These procedures are designed to test theories or, at the very least, to collect data in ways that are objective and replicable by other researchers.

Survey: Type of research design in which a sample of respondents is asked an established set or schedule of questions.

Tests: Careful gathering of empirical data to assess the plausibility of a theory or hypothesis derived from a theory.

Theories: Abstract statements that explain how and why phenomena in the universe operate. Theory is the vehicle in science for understanding.

Unobtrusive-Observation: Type of observational research design in which the investigator seeks to remain uninvolved with those being studied.

Chapter 3

Theoretical Perspectives in Sociology

Problems in Developing Scientific Theories

Theories are stories about how the world works. The most elegant theories are stated in very precise terms so that they can be tested. In sociology, there are many such theories, but they do not dominate sociology the way they do in more mature sciences. Part of the reason for this failure to develop a body of accepted theories is that many sociologists do not believe that the **scientific method,** as described in Chapter 2, is appropriate for the social sciences. Unlike the physical and biological universe, there are no timeless laws that govern how people behave, interact, and organize. People are creative, unpredictable, and able to refashion the fundamental nature of their social world; hence, it would be impossible to have timeless laws about the dynamics of the social universe (Giddens 1993). In addition to these critics of scientific sociology, there are others who, whatever their feelings about the prospects for scientific theory, believe that sociology should be explicitly ideological. It should take the side of the "ordinary person," especially those subject to abuse by elites with money and power.

Another factor working against science in sociology is the unfortunate tendency of some theorists to state their ideas in such imprecise terms that researchers have little interest in testing them. Moreover, many researchers, who carefully follow most of the steps in the scientific method listed in the last chapter, simply do not have an interest in testing theories. They are more interested in gathering data on some topic of interest (Turner and Turner 1990). Thus, it is sad but true that theorists and researchers tend to go their own separate ways. And, if we add to these problems the fact that some sociologists do not believe that scientific theory is possible or desirable or that sociology should be more ideological than scientific, it is easy to see why theories in sociology are less developed than those in the "hard" sciences.

There are many rather sophisticated theories in sociology, but they are often not known by sociologists outside narrow professional circles, and equally often, they are not accepted by many sociologists who have a nonscientific agenda. Nonetheless, most sociologists work within one or several general theoretical perspectives. These are not precise theories, but are conceptual eyeglasses for looking at the social world. Some have rather precise theoretical formulations, others retain rather loose conceptual frameworks, and still others revolve around ideological agendas.

However, as a way of getting a minimal appreciation for theories in sociology, let me summarize some of the most prominent theoretical perspectives. We have already encountered some of these perspectives in
our review of the emergence of sociology in Chapter 1. Here, I am more
explicit on the underlying elements of these broad approaches (J. Turner,
2003). As we move into the substance of sociology, we can explore these
perspectives, where relevant, in more detail.

Theoretical Orientations in Sociology

Functional Theorizing

Functional theory was created by Herbert Spencer and carried forward
by Émile Durkheim into the twentieth century. At one time in the 1950s,
this kind of theory dominated sociology; now, it represents just one of
many approaches. All functional theories examine the social universe as
a system of interconnected parts (Turner and Maryanski 1979). The
parts are then analyzed in terms of their consequences, or *functions,* for
the larger system. For example, the family might be seen as a basic social
institution that helps sustain the larger society by regulating sex and
mating among adults and by socializing the young so that they can become competent members of a society. Moreover, one can examine any
structure (e.g., your current college or university) in functional terms. All
that is necessary is for you to ask one question: How does some aspect
of your school—the student body, fraternities and sororities, student
government, faculty, staff, administrators, and so forth—contribute to
the operation of the overall system?

Most functional theories posit "needs" or "requisites" of the system.
When this is done, a part is examined with respect to how it meets a
need or requisite. For example, many social systems have needs for making decisions, coordinating people, and allocating resources; and so, if
these constitute a basic set of requisites, one would ask: What parts of
the system meet these related needs? And then, we would explain how a
particular part (e.g., government if our focal system is a society) operates
to meet this basic need.

There are many problems with functional theories. One of the most
important is that they often see society as too well integrated and organized (Dahrendorf 1958, 1959). If every system part has a function or
meets a need, societies would seem to be smooth-running and well-oiled
machines. We all know, of course, that such is not the case; conflict and
other dysfunctional processes also exist. However, functional approaches
still have an appeal because they force us to look at the social universe,
or any part of it, as a systemic whole whose constituent elements operate
in ways that have consequences for this whole.

Evolutionary Theories

There are two types of **evolutionary theories** in sociology—one focuses on the development of human societies from simple to complex
forms and the other focuses on the effects of natural selection on
human genes as these influence behavior. **Stage-model evolutionary
theories** all examine societies as having moved through certain discrete phases or stages. Among early sociologists, Auguste Comte, Herbert

Spencer, Karl Marx, and Émile Durkheim all saw society as moving from simple to more complex forms, with discrete stages along the way. Most functional theories of societies also posit evolution as a process of increasing *differentiation* of society into ever more distinctive structures and systems of cultural symbols. Evolution for functionalists is thus a process of increasing complexity of human society (Durkheim 1893; Luhmann 1982; Parsons 1966; Spencer 1873–1894), with each stage of societal development revealing a certain level of complexity (e.g., consult the Prologue where the most prominent stages of evolution are summarized).

More recent stage-model theories document the movement from hunting and gathering through horticulture (gardening with human power) and agriculture (farming with animal, wind, and water power) to industrial and postindustrial societies of today (Nolan and Lenski 2004; J. Turner 2003). Typically, these theories emphasize the effects of technology (knowledge about how to manipulate the environment) and economy in transforming societies, although some also stress the effects of war and the rise of the state on the evolution of societies from simpler to ever more complex forms.

Evolutionary theories emphasizing the effects of natural selection shift the focus from the evolution of societies to the genes of the human genome. Many behaviors are viewed by theorists in this tradition as directed by genes; hence, the crucial structures of society are the product of genes as they push humans to behave in certain ways. **Sociobiology** is an approach that views organisms as "survival machines" for genes that are driven to sustain themselves in the gene pool (Lopreato 1989; van den Berghe 1981, 1991). Human behavior and social structures are viewed as "strategies" of genes to sustain themselves in the gene pool by pushing for behaviors and social structures that enable the organisms housing these genes to survive and reproduce. For example, the evolution of the family is a strategy that evolved to assure that individuals who share genes would protect each other and, thereby, enable their genes to stay in the gene pool; the more genes that individuals share, the more intense are their protective behaviors (hence, mothers and fathers who share 50% of their genes with their children are highly protective, being driven by their genes to assure that this genetic material stays in the gene pool). A more recent variant of sociobiology is **evolutionary psychology**, which argues that natural selection, as it worked on the genes regulating human's neuroanatomy, creates "modules" in the brain that guide behavior (Tooby and Cosmides 1989). Genes survive, therefore, because natural selection wired the brain so that humans are driven to behave in ways that assure that genes will stay in the gene pool.

These kinds of biologically oriented evolutionary theories have not gained wide acceptance in sociology. It has been very difficult for sociologists to see humans and their creations—culture and social structures of enormous complexity—as being guided by genes. Still, the theories do draw attention to an important fact: Humans are animals and evolved like all other animals through a process of natural selection. The majesty and complexity of human culture and society can blind us to this simple fact; we are an animal, and therefore, it is likely that some aspects of human behavior have a biological basis. The problem, of course, is sorting out what behaviors have a biological basis because of the conflating influences of socialization in society. For now, these biological theories remain on the fringes of sociology, but they are being actively pursued in biology and, to a lesser extent, in psychology.

Ecological Theories

Another kind of biologically inspired theory emphasizes the ecological aspects of evolutionary theory. All social structures exist in an environment containing the resources necessary for survival. When social structures must secure resources of a given kind from the environment, this is the "niche" of these structures; if there is high niche "density" (i.e., many organizations in the niche), competition will be intense and selection will favor those structures that can more effectively secure the resources in a niche, with the result that the less fit structures in a niche either die off or restructure themselves and move to a new resource niche. **Ecological theories** thus take the notion of natural selection from Darwin and apply it to populations of social structures trying to survive in a resource niche. For example, particular kinds of organizations such as retail stores (e.g., say, Sears or Wal-Mart) compete with each other for resources in a particular niche (customers seeking discounts across a wide array of products), with the more fit surviving (Wal-Mart and Sears) and the less fit going out of business (Montgomery Wards) or changing niches (JCPenney's, which once looked like Sears). Or, different families can be seen as competing for housing in a desirable area of a town where the supply of houses is limited (the niche), with the real estate market assuring that the more fit (those able to pay for rising prices) will be able to out-compete the less fit and settle in the neighborhood, with the result that families with less money will have to move to a new, lower priced housing niche.

These ideas are now part of a school of theorizing termed *human ecology* that first appeared in the functional theories of Herbert Spencer and Emile Durkheim, but these theories have long been separated from functional approaches to explanation. The Chicago School of sociology was the first to downsize Spencer and Durkheim to study patterns of neighborhood development and succession as different individuals, groups, and organizations competed for urban space. Today, the basic thrust of all ecological theories is to view social structures competing with each other for resources in their environment; although the first distinctive ecological theories emphasized competition over land use in urban areas, more recent theories stress the ecology of organizations as they compete for resources.

Conflict Theories

Karl Marx and Max Weber were the intellectual fountainheads of **conflict theories**, although other early sociologists also saw the social world in conflictual terms. Unlike functional theories, which emphasize the contribution of parts to a larger whole, conflict theories see any social structure as rife with tension and potential conflict. Although there are many diverse conflict theories, they all share this point of emphasis in common: Inequality is the driving force behind conflict, and conflict is the central dynamic of human relations. Indeed, it would be hard not to notice the tensions and conflicts that emanate from inequality. For example, in your sociology class there is an inherent tension between you and your instructor over a basic resource: your grade. The instructor controls the grade, and this means that he or she has power over you. Therefore, you are in a situation of great inequality, and the tension is just beneath the surface. If you do not get the grade that you wanted, you may get angry; and if you could, you would do something about it. The same basic force operates in all social relations between such diverse actors as individuals, ethnic groups, personnel in an office, society-wide strata, or relations among nations in a world system.

If we look around our own society, we see the tension-producing effects of inequality everywhere. Workers and managers in companies often exist in an uneasy standoff; poor people have aggression for affluent people; women have resentments for the extra income and power that men can command in the society; ethnic minorities intensely resent their second-class status; and so it goes. All of these sources of tension that erupt into many diverse forms of conflict—violence, crime, riots, protests, demonstrations, strikes, and social movements—stem from the unequal distribution of valued resources like money, power, prestige, jobs, housing, health care, and opportunities. Conflict is, therefore, a basic contingency of social life; we feel its potential everywhere, from interpersonal relations between men and women, through the often strained interaction with different ethnics, to the resentments against the power of parents, teachers, and employers.

Critical Theories

Critical theories are sympathetic to the general points of conflict theory, but they go a step further and adopt Karl Marx's view that theory should be used to emancipate people from bonds of oppression. As the name implies, the goal of critical theory is to call attention to inequalities, to analyze the processes generating inequalities, to critique these processes, and to propose ways to eliminate inequalities and the patterns of domination associated with inequality. Generally, the world is seen as controlled by those with power—whether political, economic, or religious. The goal is to expose this disproportionate power and how it is used to oppress others by denying them resources or by controlling their options in life. Critical theory is self-consciously ideological, advocating a social world where there is little or no inequality; where people have true freedom to do as their desires and abilities dictate; and where people are free from domination by centers of economic, political, or religious power. Indeed, in many critical theories, science is seen as a form of domination because it is used by economic and military elites to build a world that oppresses others (Habermas 1968). For example, science is used to make machines that oppress workers, or science is used to create a disenchanted world of technocrats and bureaucrats who destroy the richness of culture.

Many critical theories focus on a particular social category, such as gender, social class, and ethnicity, and then seek to document the mechanisms by which the powerful exploit and/or dominate members of these categories. Feminist critical theories seek to expose patriarchy and, thereby, provide guidelines for how to eliminate male domination. Class theories seek to expose the subordinate position of workers and to lead the way for them to secure resources while working under more desirable conditions. Ethnic and race theories attempt to show how discrimination has operated to oppress a particular minority (e.g., African Americans) and how the culture and structure of society needs to be changed to achieve equality with the dominant ethnic group—white Americans of European ancestry.

Most sociologists are drawn to the discipline by the issues raised by critical theorists. As undergraduates reading a book like this one, many students over the years have found sociology to be the most relevant discipline for their concerns about inequality and injustice; and they pursued sociology because they wanted to acquire knowledge that would help eliminate the causes of inequality and injustice. As these undergraduates entered graduate school, they often adopted the views of science—that the problems raised by critical theorists needed to be studied objectively—but most sociologists retain the critical edge that they had as undergraduates without becoming full-fledged critical theorists.

Postmodern Theories

Postmodern theories all argue that a fundamentally new stage of human evolution has been reached, and in this sense, they are like stage-model evolutionary theories. But in the end, these theories fall toward the critical theory end of the spectrum because they imply a critique of the new postmodern stage of human evolution. For postmodernists, the explosion of media technologies and the globalization of capitalism are changing the very nature of human beings and the societies in which they live. There are two somewhat separate lines of postmodern theory (Allan and Turner 2000). One emphasizes the effects of media and communication technologies on increasing the salience of culture, while at the same time destroying the connection among local cultures, local social structures, and individuals' attachments to both. The media plugs individuals into a vast world of cultural symbols; and in so doing, the power of local and traditional symbols to regulate people's conduct has been broken, freeing the individual but at a very high cost. With no guidance, the individual has no anchor; the world is a buzz and blur of symbols without any real meaning. The individual wanders in a symbolic world detached from real social structures that have a history and that embody traditions. Video games, advertising that promises a new person and lifestyle, sanitized media images of war and other horrors, and many other media representations have lost their connection to a substance that can give individuals sustenance. Culture has thus become more powerful in postmodern societies, but unlike culture of the past, it cannot regulate and control the way it once did because it is not attached to local structures. It is disembodied and floats in virtual worlds and the media. And without attachment to local groups and communities, culture cannot regulate, with the result that individuals have trouble developing stable identities that can guide their conduct and give them a sense of psychological well-being.

The other branch of postmodernism is economic (Harvey 1989; Jameson 1984; Lash and Urry 1994). Here, emphasis is on how transportation and communication technologies have the capacity to compress time and space. We have instant communication all over the world, and travel time is short. Time and space are thus compressed, making the world speed up and increase the pace of social life in potentially unhealthy ways. Along with this recognition about time-space compression comes the realization that the flows of capital that fuel production and consumption can also move, literally, at the speed of light through fiber-optic technologies connected to computers. Vast sums of money are exchanged every day, creating industries in virtually any part of the world. As a result, corporations are truly global, moving to where labor is cheap or markets are robust, without consideration of the nations in which they are chartered or workers in their homeland. This form of economic postmodernism often blends into a new kind of Marxism: as the world becomes capitalist, the contradictions of capitalism will become ever more evident and will lead workers to see their interests in opposing global capitalists, leading to a revolution and the collapse of global capitalism. Whether pursuing a Marxist agenda or not, economic postmodernists examine the effects of globalization of the economy on people and the communities and societies in which they live.

Interactionist Theories

Not all theories are as "macro" as those discussed earlier. The social universe is ultimately composed of individual people interacting with each other; and so, some theories try to understand this micro universe of face-to-face contact. **Interactionist theories** are all inspired by the work of George Herbert Mead, whom we encountered in Chapter 1 and will encounter again in chapters to come. This interactionist framework has been expanded, and for now, let me outline the interactionist approach in broad strokes.

Humans interact by emitting symbols—words, facial expressions, body position, or any sign that "means" something to others and ourselves. By signaling with symbolic gestures, we mark our mood, intentions, and course of action; and conversely, by reading the gestures of others, we get a sense for what they think and how they will behave. We can even do this when the other is not physically present—for example, when you think about asking for more money from your parents, protesting a grade, or dazzling someone of the relevant sex. Here there is an exchange of gestures in your head as you mentally interact with this person. Thus, the world as we experience it is mediated by symbols and gestures; we use these gestures to adjust to each other; build up images of ourselves as certain kinds of persons; and construct a definition of what will, or should, occur in situations.

For interactionists, the explanation of social reality is to come by carefully examining the micro world of individual people who mutually interpret gestures, build up images of themselves, and define situations in certain terms (Blumer 1969). The macro or "big structures" of society—the state, economy, stratification, and the like—are constructed and sustained by micro interactions (Collins 1981, 1986). For interactionists it would be impossible to understand the social world without examining these micro-level encounters. Imagine yourself, for example, in a classroom: All that occurs in this setting is a constant flow of gestures, you move to your seat past others who may have to accept your apologies as you squeeze by them, as you and others talk before (and often during) lectures, or as your instructor's words seek to penetrate your mind. So, a "structured" classroom is teeming with gesturing, interpreting and reinterpreting, and defining situations. From an interactionist perspective, you are not a "worker bee" who dutifully follows the script of classroom demeanor (though this is certainly relevant); you are constantly signaling and interpreting to adjust and, at times, create new scripts for interaction. Interactionism thus provides a correction to any tendency to view "structure" and "culture" as somehow outside of us or as imposing itself on passive interpersonal robots.

Utilitarian Theories

A final group of theories borrows a simple set of assumptions about humans from modern economics that, in turn, adopted the core ideas of Scottish philosophers such as Adam Smith (1776) during the Age of Reason (Camic 1979). In the eyes of **utilitarian theorists**, humans are rational at least to the extent that they set goals and purposes, calculate the costs of various alternatives to realizing these goals, and choose the alternative which maximizes their benefits (or what economists call *utilities*) and minimizes their costs. We are thus beings who try to derive some benefit in a situation while reducing our costs (Coleman 1991; Hechter 1987). For example, you may calculate how much work you are willing to put out (your "cost") to receive a particular grade (your benefit) in this course, or, if I can be idealistic for a moment, a body of knowledge that you can use over a lifetime (in the long run, a much more rewarding benefit). Thus, all situations involve an "exchange" of resources: You give up some resources (your cost) to receive something that you perceive to be more valuable (your utility or reward).

For utilitarian theorists, all social relations are ultimately exchanges among actors who incur costs to get benefits from each other and who calculate the cost-benefit ratio. Your instructor incurs a cost (energy and time in preparing lectures, talking to students, reading exams, etc.) to receive a salary (from the university) and, perhaps, your undying loyalty and admiration. Similarly, you come to class, read, think, and humble yourself on exam days (your costs) to receive grades, knowledge, and perhaps a monthly stipend from someone like your parents (your benefits or utilities). We do not have to be consciously aware of these calculations; more often than not, we make them implicitly. It is only when we are not sure of what to do in a situation that we become aware of hardnosed cost-benefit calculations. But ultimately, utilitarian theorists argue, you exchange time, energy, and money in school settings for grades, credentials, and knowledge that you calculate to be even more valuable than alternative avenues for spending your time, energy, and money.

For rational choice and exchange theorists, interaction, society, and culture are ultimately created and sustained because they offer payoffs to rational individuals. These payoffs are rarely monetary, although they certainly can be, but more typically they are less tangible "goods"—self-feelings, affection, pride, esteem, power, control, and other "soft" currencies that cement society together. You can see this by simply looking at a situation where you got mad or perhaps had your feelings hurt; in such a situation, an anticipated reward (usually nonmonetary) was not received proportionate to your costs and investments, a fact that indicates that beneath the surface of your feelings are implicit calculations about costs and rewards.

State of Theory in Sociology

There are many specific variants of these broad theoretical perspectives. We will encounter many of these variants as we move into the subject matter of sociology. From the point of view of **science**, it would be nice to have more focused and precise theories that have been systematically tested and that would now organize this introduction to sociology. But such is not the case. Moreover, as I have emphasized, many sociologists do not believe that scientific theories can, or should be, developed (Seidman and Wagner 1992). Instead, current sociological theories can only help us interpret particular facets of the social world, and so, for now our theories are not like those in the "hard" sciences (Giddens 1971, 1976, 1984, 1993).

Sociology has many pieces of theory, typically inspired by the early founders, but most have not been systematically tested or accepted as the best explanation of the social world. For some, the goals of science in sociology are illusionary, and Comte's dream for a science of society is just that, a dream. For others, scientific sociology would be a nightmare. And for many others, sociology has not yet become a mature science, but the potential is there in the theoretical ideas that have developed within some of these approaches: functional, evolutionary, ecological, conflict, critical, postmodern, interactionist, and utilitarian theories. Moreover, there are many less "grand" theories, only loosely connected to these and other general approaches, that help us understand many social processes, as we will come to see.

SUMMARY

1. Science is the systematic effort to understand the universe in terms of theoretical ideas that have received consistent support in carefully conducted research.
2. Theory is the vehicle for understanding the universe, and knowledge accumulates when abstract theories are tested and retested.
3. Theory in sociology is not as well-developed as in the natural sciences. Among the general theoretical approaches guiding sociological analysis are: (a) functional theorizing where concern is with understanding how social phenomena operate to meet the needs of the larger social whole in which they are implicated; (b) stage-model evolutionary theory that tries to document the phases of societal development from simple to ever more complex forms, typically seeing technology, economy, and politics as the driving forces of evolution; (c) biologically inspired evolutionary theories emphasizing that human behavior and, hence, social structure and culture, are to some degree directed by hard-wired genetic propensities that have evolved by virtue of natural selection on humans and their ancestors; (d) ecological theories that view the social world as partitioned into resource niches in which social structures seek to adapt and survive, with those structures most fit outcompeting less fit structures, and thereby, pushing the less fit

to new niches or, at times, killing them off; (e) conflict theorizing where emphasis is on the conflict-producing effects of inequalities; (f) critical theory emphasizing that inequalities always involve the domination of some categories of people by those with power and that the goal of theory is to expose this domination and suggest ways it can be eliminated; (g) postmodern theories—whether cultural or economic—stressing the effects of communication and transportation technologies as well as the spread of capitalism to truly global proportions on the fate of individuals, communities, and societies; (h) interactionist theorizing where attention is drawn to the use of gestures in face-to-face communication and adjustments of individuals to one another; and (i) utilitarian theorizing where emphasis is on the calculation of costs and benefits in the pursuit of goals.

KEY TERMS

Conflict Theory: Theorizing that emphasizes the tension-producing inequalities that pervade all aspects of social life and that systematically generate conflict between those who have resources and those who do not.

Critical Theory: Theorizing that emphasizes the role of the sociologist as a critic of inequalities that allow one group to dominate another and as an advocate for alternative patterns of social organization that reveal less inequality and oppression of one group by another.

Ecological Theory: Theorizing that views the social universe as composed of resource niches in which various social actors compete, with selection of the more fit actors leading to their survival and with selection of the less fit causing them to die off or to move to a new resource niche.

Evolutionary Psychology: Theorizing that emphasizes the process of natural selection as it builds modules in the human brain that direct human behaviors in ways that enhance fitness, or the capacity of the genes of individuals to stay in the gene pool.

Evolutionary Theory: Theorizing that examines either the stages of development during the course of societal evolution or that explores the effects of natural selection on humans as a species.

Functional Theory: Theorizing that examines the effects of particular sociocultural processes or structures in meeting the requisites or survival needs of social systems.

Interactionist Theory: Theorizing that explores the face-to-face process of individuals mutually communicating with symbols as they attempt to cooperate and confirm their conceptions of themselves.

Postmodern Theory: Theorizing that emphasizes the effects of transformations in communication and transportation technologies on the organization of people in contemporary societies. Cultural postmodernists emphasize the transforming effects of media and marketing on disconnecting symbols from the groups and social structures in which they originally evolved, whereas economic postmodernists stress the effects of new technologies in compressing space and time and in moving people, capital, and goods rapidly around the world system.

Science: Process in which theoretical explanations about the operation of phenomena in the universe are systematically tested with empirical data.

Scientific Method: Procedures employed in the collection of data. These procedures are designed to test theories or, at the very least, to collect data in ways that are objective and replicable by other researchers.

Sociobiology: Theorizing that sees humans and society as survival machines for genes and emphasizes the process of natural selection as it generates behavioral and organizational propensities that enhance fitness of organisms, or the capacity of their genes to remain in the gene pool.

Stage-Model Evolutionary Theory: Theories that attempt to explain the movement of human societies from simple to ever more complex forms in terms of changing levels of technology, economic production, and mobilization of political power.

Utilitarian Theory: Theorizing that emphasizes the rational calculation of the costs and benefits to be gained from pursuing various courses of action and that sees social life as a constant exchange of resources among actors who seek to make a profit (rewards or utilities minus the costs in getting them) in relations with others.

Part II Basic Elements of Social Organization

Human behaviors, interactions, and patterns of social organization are built from certain key elements. These elements are what make possible the social world as we know it, and as it has existed in the past. One element, often underemphasized by sociologists, is biological. Humans are animals who evolved, and from this evolution, the biological capacities that enable humans to act, interact, and organize were forged. The biological element is, however, greatly overshadowed by the power of culture to provide the information and codes necessary for social life. With their large brains and capacity for language, humans can generate systems of symbols or culture that they can then use to manipulate the environment, direct behavior, structure interactions, and regulate complex patterns of social organization. Human behavior and interaction are constrained not only by cultural codes but also by social structures that place people in positions where they play roles. These structures can be relatively simple but they can also become quite large and complex. Much of the subject matter of sociology revolves around the analysis of different types of social structures. Ultimately, culture and society are produced and reproduced by people engaged in face-to-face interaction. Thus, like biology, culture, and social structure, interaction is a basic element of human social organization. A special type of interaction is denoted by the notion of socialization in which individuals learn how to interact, pay attention to culture, and play roles in the positions of social structures. And finally, all social life is a process of social control in which pressures for deviance, dissent, and disorder confront forces of order and control.

Chapter 4

Biology

At the time that most dinosaurs went extinct, a small rodent-like mammal clawed its way up into the dense forest canopy and began to adapt to this arboreal habitat. You and I are descendants of this rather unimposing animal. Over millions of years of evolution by natural selection, prosimians (pre-monkeys) first emerged, followed by full-blown monkeys and apes. Humans are basically evolved apes; and indeed, we share 99% of our genes with the two species of chimpanzees that can currently be found in Africa. We are more distant relatives of gorillas and orangutans, and even more distant kin to gibbons and siamangs. The most noteworthy feature of apes is that there are only nine species left; indeed, apes are one of the great evolutionary failures of the last few million years, especially compared to monkeys, who number over 130 species.

I emphasize our primate lineage because it is often easy to forget that humans are animals who evolved like any other animal. Classification systems put humans alone in our own genus on the primate family tree, but increasingly, it is argued that humans and chimpanzees belong in the same genus, *Homo,* because genetically chimpanzees are much closer to humans than they are to mountain and lowland gorillas. This closeness to chimpanzees gives us a "distant mirror" in which we can gaze into the past and see what our ancestors might have been like. Some five million years ago, our ancestral line—called **hominids**—diverged from the ancestors of present-day chimpanzees; even though chimpanzees of today are the outcome of evolution, their biological characteristics, behaviors, and patterns of social organization can still give us a sense for our biological heritage.

Virtually all social thinkers have thought about "human nature" or the behavioral propensities that are common to humankind. Much of this speculation about human nature is just that—speculation. Even more scientifically oriented efforts to ponder behavioral propensities involve considerable speculation because it is so difficult to separate what is learned from what is in the genes as they build life forms. Indeed, natural selection enlarged the brain of our hominid ancestors over the last two million years so that culture could be used to organize activities among hominids; once culture directs so much social behavior, it is difficult to disentangle nature from nurture. Yet, chimpanzees offer at least some clues about what might be—and I emphasize, *might* be—the biological basis for human behavior and, by extension, patterns of social organization. We do not want to get carried away with this idea, but it is at least worth thinking about before we move into the analysis of the social structures that culture and big brains have made possible.

Natural Selection As a Driving Force

If we are to address the question of the biological basis of human behavior and organization, we need to understand how evolution operates. All life forms are given structure by genetic codes, or the **genotype** of a life form. The expression of this genotype is termed the **phenotype,** or actual structure of a life form as it emerges. There is a common misunderstanding that the phenotype is rigidly determined by the genotype, but in fact, there is considerable influence of environmental factors on how a genotype gets expressed in a phenotype. Genes contain potentialities, and these can encompass considerable latitude in the life form that will be produced. Because of this latitude, the actual expression of genes will be influenced by environmental factors. Even the structure of very complex systems like the human brain, for example, will be altered by environmental influences such as socialization, diet and nutrition, and varying experiences. This process of gene-environment interaction as it leads to the formation of a biological structure is sometimes called **epigenesis.**

Thus, in considering the biology of humans, as expressed in our genotypes and emergent phenotypes, we must immediately abandon any view of rigid genetic determinism. There are always environmental influences in how the potential in genes gets expressed in the actual structures of a human being. There is another important point that follows from this one: human behavior is influenced by *systems* in the body, not by discrete genes. There is unlikely to be a gene for a specific behavior because how people behave is related to complicated systems, such as the hormonal systems, the emotion system, the neurotransmitter system, the neuroactive peptide system, the musculoskeletal system, the immune system, and so on. These systems, like the genotype that generates them, are also subject to environmental influences, especially socialization and experience. And because they are systems, environmental influence on one element of the system, say the emotion system, has influence on the others, such as the immune system. My point here is that when analyzing the biology of human behavior, we should not get carried away with images from the newspaper that there is a discrete gene for this or that behavior, or even the idea that behavior is rigidly determined by our genetic makeup.

The human genome, whose genetic codes have only recently been mapped, is the outcome of millions of years of evolution by natural selection. **Natural selection** is the process whereby the conditions of the environment select those variants of phenotypes (and the underlying genotypes) that facilitate survival and reproduction of a life form. If one variant of an organism can adapt to its environment, it is likely to reproduce itself and thus pass on its genes to the next generation; if another variant of this species cannot adapt and dies before it reproduces, then its genotype is taken out of the gene pool. Because environmental factors, such as culture and social structures, dominate our lives, it is sometimes easy to forget that we are the result of natural selection as it worked on variants of our ancestors. We are just another animal that evolved like all other animals, but we are special in the sense that natural selection produced an animal capable of structuring most behaviors with cultural rather than genetic codes. Yet, even though culture and experience influence each of our behaviors, the question remains: Are some human behaviors influenced by the biological systems that make up our body? The obvious answer is "yes" because talking, walking, gesturing, shouting, crying, breathing, sweating, and many other behaviors are directed by biological systems. But, the question that we are most interested in is deeper: Are there propensities to behave *in particular ways* that are guided by our biological systems? To answer this question, we need to review briefly our history of evolution, as natural selection worked to make humans a very special kind of primate.

Evolution Of Primates

By 34 million years ago, species that would eventually split into monkeys and apes could be distinguished from prosimians, but they could not be clearly differentiated from each other (Maryanski & Turner 1991). Monkeys and apes looked and acted much the same. But, sometime around 30 million years ago, monkeys began to split away from apes. Monkeys, as it turns out, were the more adapted or fit species because they developed dietary specializations that allowed them to out-compete apes for food and thus take control of the verdant portions of the trees. Apes were relegated to the tops of the trees (the ends and undersides of branches) and forced to adapt to the more hazardous and less verdant niches of the arboreal habitat. Monkeys controlled the central portions of the trees where the best food was and where larger groups of individuals could be supported.

It may seem unsettling to realize that we evolved from an ancestral line that lost out in competition with monkeys, but such is the case. Pushed to the extremities of the forest canopy, apes underwent evolution that increasingly distinguished them from monkeys in several ways. First, apes became smarter than monkeys because to live in the dangerous parts of the forest required intelligence so that a false step would not lead to death by gravity. Second, apes developed physiological features that enabled them to move from branch to branch efficiently. One of these features is the capacity to brachiate or rotate the arm in a circle over the head; only apes and humans can do this, and this ability allowed apes to swing from branch to branch much like children today do on a jungle gym. Another feature was a heightened haptic sense on the fingers that enables apes to feel the texture, strength, and other features of branches. Still another was stronger wrists and hands, along with more dexterous fingers, thus allowing apes to move rapidly across the branches of trees. Along with these more specialized features, like all primates apes retained their generalized skeleton consisting of a large trunk with four appendages, as well as a generalized teeth structure that allowed them to eat a variety of plant and animal life.

Because apes were forced to live in the terminal feeding areas of the trees, they could not sustain large groupings as could monkeys who controlled the central portions of the trees. Monkeys are organized along two main axes that give order to monkey groupings. One is the male dominance hierarchy. Males compete for dominance of a troop, with the most dominant male seeking to control exclusive access to females, although females and other males often have secret meetings when the dominant male is not looking or is not around. The other axis of social order is lines of related females, or **matrilines.** Female offspring stay with their mothers for their entire life, and so the real backbone of monkey groupings is the related females who stick together, groom each other, and otherwise sustain the continuity of the group, especially as dominant males come and go. Male offspring leave the group and transfer to another group at puberty; males from the outside transfer into the group and compete for dominance, although some males do not bother in this competition and find other ways to have sexual relations with females. Thus, because females stay in the group, generations of females can be found in most monkey troops.

Ape groupings stand is stark contrast to monkeys. There is relatively mild competition for dominance; compared to what is evident in monkeys, dominance hierarchies are rather muted or, for some species, simply do not exist. Even more dramatic is the lack of female matrilines among apes. Unlike monkeys, females *always* transfer from the ape community at puberty and migrate to another community; except for chimpanzees, males also leave their natal group, although they stay within a larger community that can be as big as 10 square miles.

This lack of strong social ties and group structures represents an adaptation to living in those portions of the arboreal habitat that could not sustain large numbers of individuals. Natural selection thus made apes much more individualistic than monkeys and more mobile from group to group. Some apes like the orangutan are virtually solitary and live alone, coming together occasionally for mating. Chimpanzees are more social because, although the females leave, a son may stay around his mother and male siblings.

Thus, the current data on apes, especially chimpanzees, can give us a sense for what natural selection had to work on as it altered our distant hominid ancestors of some five million years ago. Like all primates, our ancestors were visually dominant, a fact that has enormous significance for making us humans, as I explore shortly. Our ancestors were big-brained compared to most other mammals. They had a generalized skeleton and four limbs with five sensitive digits on hands and feet. They had strong wrists and hands. They could brachiate or rotate their arms in a circle over their heads. And, they revealed some interesting behaviors and patterns of social structure: Most ties among adults were rather weak; females almost always left their natal group in which they were born as well as the larger community, migrating to another community. Males may have also left, but if chimpanzees are a guide to what our distant ancestor was like, males may have stayed in their natal group; they always stayed in their larger home range or community and defended its boundaries against males from other communities.

By 16 million years ago, the forests were receding in Africa, forcing many species of primates onto the open country savanna where predators were abundant. For monkeys who had to begin living out in the grasslands of the savanna, this necessary transformation was less problematic because they were better organized. Contemporary monkeys, such as several species of baboons, march across the savanna in military-like formation, with the larger males in the front, rear, and flanks, whereas smaller females and offspring stay in the middle of this imposing legion. Most predators are reluctant to attack such a well-oiled military machine. In contrast, apes do not have the strong tendencies for hierarchy that would allow them to march in military-like formations; indeed, they are rather individualistic and often scatter when threatened, thereby making them easy targets for predators. How, then, were the apes to get organized? The answer is that they had great difficulty becoming more organized, and as a result, most species of apes went extinct over the last 16 million years. The only apes that survived, save for our ancestors, are those who lived in the forest or on the edge of the forest. All other apes who were forced onto the savanna except humans eventually perished.

How did the ancestors of humans, or hominids, beat the odds and survive in the open country? We can never know for sure, but somehow our ape ancestors became better organized. Aside from their lack of tight-knit social structures, apes like other primates had some additional disadvantages on the savanna. One is that they have a reduced sense of smell that was lost during adaptation to arboreal habitats. Smell is the best way to detect predators, and without this sense, apes were at an extreme disadvantage because they had to see or hear danger before responding (and then it might be too late). Another disadvantage is that apes are slow compared to most savanna-dwelling mammals. Apes are built for rapid movement in the trees, not on the ground, with the result that it would be easy for a predator to run down a fleeing ape. Thus, it is even more remarkable that the ancestors of humans survived, but how? An answer to this question must incorporate what natural selection did to ape anatomy and behavioral patterns to forge species that somehow managed to survive on the African savanna. This answer can give us some interesting leads about what is biological about human behavior and organization.

Biological Parameters of Human Organization

Consequences of Visual Dominance

As I noted earlier, one of the most unique characteristics of primates is that they are visually dominant—that is, vision is the sense modality that dominates the other senses for hearing (auditory), touch (haptic), and smell (olfactory). This fact may seem so obvious that it is not worth mentioning, but it is very important. Most mammals are olfactory- or smell-dominant; they sniff their way around the world with vision and touch being subordinated to their sense of smell. Some animals are auditory-dominant, such as bats. What do we mean by dominant? The brain must be wired so that the senses can coordinate inputs from the environment. Imagine if your brain received information from smell, touch, hearing, and vision that was discordant; you would soon be confused. For example, when people are overwhelmed by vertigo, they become highly disoriented because their haptic sense (for balance) overwhelms their visual sense. Thus, the brains of all mammals are wired so that all other senses are integrated, with one being dominant. Thus, when you hear something, you immediately turn to see it; if you smell something, you look; if you feel something, you direct you eyes to what you are sensing with touch.

The primate ancestors of humans became visually dominant because adaptation to an arboreal habitat is facilitated by being able to see where you reach and jump. If you have to feel your way around a tree (haptic dominance), you will move slowly and tentatively. If you have to smell your way around a tree, you are very likely to fall out of the tree. And, it is hard to imagine hearing your way around a tree. Thus, natural selection required that the brain and the visual cortex, the optic nerves, and the positioning of the eyes be such that monkeys and apes would see the world in color and stereoscopically (i.e., three-dimensionally).

Humans are the product of this selection; and although we do not live in the trees anymore, vision remains humans' dominant sense modality. Thus, although it may seem obvious, it is nonetheless a fundamental part of human nature for us to see very well. And with vision, we can do amazing things like read, write, drive cars, use tools, see small numbers on cell phones, perform complex and intricate tasks, and do many other things that most animals could not possibly do. Moreover, we interact with vision. True, we talk to each other through the auditory channel with speech, but we rely to a very great extent on seeing the "body language" of others—their face, lips, and the flow of blood in the face (as in blushing). Thus, the fine-tuned and fine-grained interactions that make life meaningful are not possible without a heightened sense of vision.

The rewiring of the brain for vision did something else: it also rewired the brain for the capacity to use language (Geschwind 1965a, 1965b; Geschwind & Damasio 1984). This capacity was a by-product of creating the association cortices that integrated the other senses under visual dominance, but it gave natural selection something to work on when selection began to expand the brain in ways that allowed hominids to have language and culture. Thus, without the shift in the brain's wiring to visual dominance, language and culture—the very things that makes human society possible—could not ever have evolved.

We can see what this potential for language was like among our earliest hominid ancestors by studying the use of language among the Great Apes: chimpanzees, gorillas, and orangutans. In their natural habitats, these animals do not use language as you and I know it, but they do communicate in subtle ways through eye contact and touch as well as by calls. But, when exposed to human language, they can also learn the rudiments of our language at about the level of a three-year-old child. The first studies on language acquisition were conducted on chimpanzees using the sign language of the deaf; later, pictograms on a board wired to a computer were used so that when a sequence of symbols is punched by an ape, the computer translates the ape's actions into verbalization. Apes cannot talk because they simply do not have the physical equipment to make fine-grained vocalizations, but they can "talk" to us using hand signs or pictograms wired to a computer.

The most amazing case of how apes learn language comes from Kanzi, a bonobo chimpanzee (sometimes called "pygmy" chimpanzees). His handlers were actually trying to teach his mother, an adult, how to use the pictograms to make sentences, but because she was an adult, she was not doing so well (just as you might have trouble learning a new language as an adult). Kanzi was simply climbing around and over the lab area as his mother was being coached; no one was really paying any attention to him because the focus was on his mother. Then one day, Kanzi spontaneously began to use the board to communicate with the handlers; he had obviously learned language just as human children do, by simply being immersed in an environment where language is spoken. Soon, Kanzi could construct sentences and communicate rather complicated requests. Moreover, unlike earlier studies with sign language, Kanzi could understand naturally spoken English. You can talk to Kanzi, and he responds by punching the pictograms in a particular sequence (Savage-Rumbaugh et al. 1985, 1986a, 1986b). Thus, humans are not wholly unique in their ability to use language, but we use it in much more complex ways than a chimpanzee whose brain is less than half the size of a human brain. The wiring is there, which means that it was there among our hominid ancestors, waiting for natural selection to work on the brain to expand the capacity for language.

Consequences of Having a Large Brain

Humans have very big brains relative to their body size (brain size and body size are roughly correlated among mammals). Apes also have large brains for a mammal, and this too is the result of adaptation to an arboreal habitat. As I noted earlier, animals that must move around in a three-dimensional world need to be more intelligent so that they can remember routes, sense strength of branches, assess risks, and otherwise be aware of the environment as they fling themselves about the trees. And so, humans' large brains are, once again, the outcome of our ape ancestors' adaptation to the arboreal habitat. Still, compared to humans, the hominids trying to survive on the African savanna had small brains that were about the size of a present-day chimpanzee (around 400 cubic centimeters compared to the human range of around 1000 to 1200 cubic centimeters); and the brain did not grow significantly for several million years. By two million years ago, natural selection was working on the brain, making it larger and more complex relative to body size than any other animal that had ever lived. Why was this so?

The obvious outcome is that a larger brain makes an animal smarter, thus able to think and reason in ways to outsmart predators and prey. Another outcome was the ability to symbolically represent the world and self, or in other words, to produce and use culture to regulate behavior and organize activity. But, the brain of *Homo erectus*, who emerged around two million years ago, was only 750 cubic centimeters; and so, we can ask: Is a 750-cubic centimeter brain big enough to enable an animal to have language and culture approaching the human measure? There is no clear answer to this question, but perhaps this is large enough to engage in more complex communication and to develop rules regulating conduct; once this push toward the rudiments of language and culture was made and facilitated survival and reproduction, this rudimentary capacity for culture was selected again and again to enhance the cultural abilities of hominids.

There is another less obvious consequence of the larger brain. The cerebral cortex gets most of the press in discussions of the human brain. And indeed, it is dramatically larger relative to body size than any other animal on earth. But there are older areas of the brain below the cerebral cortex, termed *subcortical areas*. In these areas are lodged the many basic systems that guide and direct behavior. Neurotransmitters, neuroactive peptides, autonomic responses, hormones, short-term memory, and most important, emotions all come from systems that are subcortical and out of consciousness. When measurements are taken comparing ape and human brains, the neocortex is, as might be expected, dramatically larger in humans than apes (controlling for body size which, as noted earlier, correlates with brain size), but the centers responsible for the production of emotions are also larger than those for apes. Thus, as the brain grew, the centers for emotion also expanded (Stephen 1983; Stephen and Andy 1969; J. Turner 2000). Why would the emotion centers be enhanced?

One answer is that with emotions, animals can be more rational. There is a common misconception that emotionality and rationality are at the opposite ends of a continuum, but in fact, rationality is not possible without emotions. To decide rationally upon a course of action, you need to be able to assess what will bring the most reward; and the only way you can assess payoffs is by attaching positive or negative emotions to various lines of potential conduct. Damasio (1994, 1997) reports data on subjects in whom the neuro-nets connecting the cerebral or neocortex to the subcortical emotion centers have been severed; what he finds is that these individuals have trouble making decisions and when they finally are able to make decisions, they make poor choices that are hardly rational. Without the neurological capacity to attach emotional valences from subcortical areas of the brain to conscious thinking about alternatives in the neocortex, people cannot be rational. Thus, expanding emotion centers is critical to rationality that, in turn, would increase the chances of survival for an animal.

Another answer as to why emotion centers grew is that with emotions, animals could form more intense bonds. Recall that, compared to monkeys, apes do not reveal very many strong ties (Maryanski 1997; Maryanski & Turner 1992), and so, enhanced emotionality would allow an evolving ape to generate more intense emotional bonds that could overcome the low sociality of being an ape. Enlarging areas of the brain for emotions not only allows for increased emotionality, it enables animals to generate a more complex array of emotions above and beyond the primary emotions that all intelligent mammals reveal for aggression, fear, satisfaction, and sadness. At some point, emotions like pride, guilt, and shame—all critical to maintaining social order—could emerge and give social order a moral compass (J. Turner 2000). Moreover, as the emotional repertoire of emotions grew among hominids, more nuanced and fine-grained emotional responses of individuals to each other could occur. These more complex and subtle emotions—love, disappointment, hopefulness, awe, nostalgia, reverence, yearning, hope, wonder, and the like—could be used to forge bonds of solidarity on weak-tie animals, enabling them to overcome the tendency for individualism and mobility of their ape cousins and form stronger, more permanent bonds that would enhance their chances of survival (see Table 8.1 on page 122 for a list of human emotions).

Thus, a larger brain does more than increase intelligence, it expands an animal's emotional horizons; and with emotions, not only is rationality enhanced but new kinds of solidarity-producing relationships can be built from the signaling of emotions back and forth among individuals. Because emotions are mostly read visually—in the movements of face and body—primates' keen vision can be used to see how others respond emotionally and adjust to their emotional moods. You can see this today when someone is emotional; you look at the face and body for cues, although auditory sounds like crying or laughing are also used to assess another's emotions. But, the face tells most of the story, and there are good evolutionary reasons why we rely so much on visual cues to tell us about how others are feeling and how we should respond to them. Without the larger brain, especially in the emotion centers, and without a keen sense of sight, this kind of nuanced and fine-tuned emotional interaction could not occur. It is, therefore, in our nature as humans to use our primate vision to assess the emotions as activated by subcortical areas of the large human brain.

Consequences of Being Bi-Pedal

Apes have little difficulty standing up on their back feet and walking around on two legs, or in a *bi-pedal* manner. It is now clear from the archeological data that hominids were bi-pedal before they were smarter (as measured by brain size). One of the first adaptations of apes trying to survive on the savanna was to become bi-pedal, walking and running upright. This is not a dramatic alteration, because apes can do this now but not with the same efficiency as hominids five million years ago. Why was this one of the first adaptations? One answer is that bi-pedalism was one of the easiest anatomical changes for natural selection. And, for an animal that cannot smell predators hiding behind tall grasses, it is wise to get up on hind feet and use the visual sense to see what lurks in the grasses and behind bushes. Bi-pedalism does something else: it frees the hands and arms. A bi-pedal ape can pick up things (with its fine sense of touch and flexible fingers and wrists), and it can throw things with its capacity to brachiate (rotate the arm), even putting a little "heat" on what it throws as it uses its fingers and wrists to generate whip action. With the ability to pick up and carry, an ape can scavenge for leftovers from predators or it can carry its own prey to safer quarters; and with the ability to throw objects like rocks and sticks, it can defend itself. Moreover, with dexterity in the fingers and the ability to throw objects at a fast pace, the making of tools was inevitable in hominid evolution. Because chimpanzees can make tools, natural selection certainly enhanced this ability; and with full bi-pedalism, these tools could be carried and used as needed—thereby increasing the chances for survival of hominids.

Standing upright does even more; it exposes individuals' full bodies face-to-face. We see not only the face, but the rest of the body as well. And, this mutual exposure greatly enhances visually based interaction. Hominids gestured with their hands, much as you and I do when we talk; they could read body countenance for signs of emotions; and of course, they could read the face and eyes for further signs of emotions. If we had to interact with each other on all fours, it would be difficult to read gestures and cues. If we were a dog and had a great sense of smell, interaction would not be so difficult; we would simply put our noses in glandular areas to read emotions. But we are visually dominant; and so, standing upright gives humans a much bigger canvas on which to see emotions painted. Bi-pedalism thus enhanced hominids' capacity to use emotions to forge strong social bonds.

Human Nature

If we know the biological stock from which we evolved and, in general terms, the selection pressures that worked on this stock, perhaps we can make some guesses as to what is biologically in us. In other words, what is human nature? But again, we must emphasize that genes do not dictate behaviors; rather, their influence is only indirect because within wide parameters they direct the formation of biological systems that, in turn, have effects on behavior. And, recall epigenesis whereby the environment shapes just how the genotype is expressed in the phenotype of an organism; the more complex the organism and the more complex the systems of the organism-guiding behavior, the more epigenesis is at work.

Sociology is the study of behaviors that allow people to interact and build up patterns of social organization. What biological features of humans, then, facilitate these processes? An answer to this question can be of two kinds: one is the biological capacities of humans that *enable* people to interact and form social relationships from which all social structures and cultural patterns are built; another is the biological drives that *push* humans to behave in certain ways. The first influence of biology is less controversial, and so, let us begin here.

Human Biological Capacities

Large Brains and Culture.   The most distinguishing characteristic of humans is a large brain that allows for the use of symbols to represent aspects of the world and to communicate through language. Together, the capacities that are lodged in the neurology of the human brain allow humans to create **culture,** or systems of symbols, that can be used to guide and regulate human conduct (see Chapter 5). For most sociologists, this capacity to create and use culture obviates biology. Humans' large brains have created an alternative set of codes in culture that regulate behavior, making concern with how biology may influence behavior unnecessary. Once humans could create culture, they acquired the ability to construct vastly different systems of information for controlling behaviors, interactions, and patterns of social organization that far outweighed any direct bioprogrammers for behavior. Indeed, the wide variability in the cultures of the world and in the structures organizing social life attests to the power of culture to overwhelm the effects of biology. Is this line of argument correct? The *sociobiology* perspective reviewed in Chapter 3 would dispute this claim by most sociologists, but it may go too far in the other direction, seeing too much of human behavior as directed by biological systems devoted to preserving genes in the gene pool. Let us for the moment, then, simply conclude that humans are probably unique in the extent to which they use culture to regulate behavior and social organization.

The Brain and Emotions.   Culture is stored primarily in the neocortex, but as I noted earlier, the subcortical portions of the brain also grew disproportionately during hominid evolution. Thus, humans have the capacity to experience, signal, and interpret a wide array of emotions that would not be possible without an expanded set of emotion systems, sometimes called **limbic systems,** connected to the large neocortex. This capacity to use emotions is perhaps as important as culture in regulating how people interact with each other. Moreover, the moral codes of culture telling people how they should behave would have no "teeth" if emotions were not attached to them. If we did not feel guilt and shame when we behaved improperly, or if people did not get angry when others violated norms, culture would be ineffective. Culture would be like the instructions in a manual for how to put something together, but it would not reach deep, literally, into the subcortical core of our brains and compel us to act in certain ways.

The Brain and Vision.   What you see when gazing at the world is the result of brain systems. Sensory inputs come to your optic nerve, and then move to subcortical areas of the brain that send the signals to emotional centers of the brain and onto the occipital lobe where you have the experience of sight. Your entire brain has been reorganized, by virtue of your primate heritage, to be visually dominant, with all other senses subordinate to vision. This rewiring of the brain allows people to read each other's gestures, particularly emotions, in a fine-tuned and fine-grained way; and because we can become so visually attuned to each other, we are able to coordinate our actions. Also, because emotions are read primarily through seeing others, especially their facial gestures, vision is the key to enhancing social bonds and attachments to people. We do not sniff each other, and although touch and talk can certainly enhance the emotional experience, much interaction is built from face-to-face visual contact.

The Brain and Language.   The brain makes language possible by virtue of systems of neurons that download thinking into words (Broca's area) and that upload what you hear into the brain's way of processing information (Weinerke's area). Talking obviously facilitates interaction because people can be very specific about topics; moreover, language allows for culture because it is through the symbols of language—spoken and written words, mathematics, computer codes, and other "languages"—that culture is built up and used by people to organize social life. I should also note that spoken language comes from the effects of natural selection on reworking the vocal cords, larynx, tongue, lips, and the muscles serving all of these. Still, even though these organs are not in the brain, they are activated by brain systems. And, as I emphasized earlier, language is only possible as a result of the rewiring of the ape brain for visual dominance.

The Body and Culture.   Bi-pedalism that frees the hands represents an enormously important capacity, especially when coupled with a brain that can generate language and culture. Not only this, the dexterity of our wrists, hands, and arms coupled with a very fine sense of touch enables humans to make tools that, in turn, allow for the construction of physical facilities. A snake, for example, cannot make very much because it has no hands or feet, to say nothing of having a very small brain. Not only does freeing the hands allow for tool-making and all that this means for human societies, it gives humans the capacity to interact in more complex and subtle ways because we see the whole body, which, as we all know, reveals a "body language" of gestures that carry meaning and that allow people to become even more attuned to each other's responses.

Human Biologly and Behavioral Propensities

Now we come to the more controversial issue revolving around behavioral propensities that may be programmed by the human genotype into the phenotypical systems—neurological, hormonal, muscular, skeletal, circulatory, autonomic, and the like—that activate human behavioral responses. Most sociologists would, once again, discount some of the arguments enumerated here, but they are at last worth considering.

Sex and Behavior.   Humans are either male or female biologically, with a few exceptions where people possess the organs of both sexes or the organs not appropriate to their genotype. The controversial question is not that the sexes are different in some obvious biological ways, but whether or not these biological differences lead men and women to have somewhat different behavioral propensities. On the women's side, most sociobiological arguments revolve around the female's need (as implanted by natural selection) to assure that the relatively few eggs that she will produce in her lifetime will be fertilized by the sperm of fit males who can help assure that her children are raised and reproduce themselves as adults (thereby keeping her half of the offspring's genotype in the gene pool). On the male side, sociobiological arguments emphasize that men need to assure that their plentiful sperm find eggs that will live to adulthood and reproduce. Most sociologists are highly critical of these kinds of arguments, which are used to explain everything from the family to male promiscuity. Instead, sociologists stress that sex is culturally elaborated in gender roles and that social structures are the products of culturally induced codes rather than genetic codes.

Human Sociality.   It has often been said that humans are "naturally social." Yet, our ape cousins are not so social, especially compared to monkeys. Females leave their group and community, and males often do so as well, and there are relatively few strong ties, save for those of mothers to their offspring (a trait characteristic of all mammals). Indeed, the big roadblock to ape survival on the savanna was the lack of strong group ties and comparatively weak dominance hierarchies. Natural selection could have altered the human genome to make our hominid ancestors more social because there are areas of the brain that could be selected to enhance sociality. Also, in expanding emotions, natural selection may have worked indirectly on forming stronger social bonds and solidarity by making people more emotionally responsive to each other (J. Turner 2000). Still, humans may not be quite as *social* as much social philosophy and most sociologists would argue. More controversial is the debate as to whether humans are "collectivistic" or "individualistic." Those who see humans as highly social imply biological drives for collectivism in which people seek solidarity with others and enjoy being in groups that coordinate their behaviors. Those who see humans as more like their ape cousins would argue that collectivism is more culturally directed than genetically programmed into humans and that humans have behavioral propensities for freedom, choice, individualism, and mobility.

Reciprocity.   There is some indirect evidence that there are brain systems devoted to monitoring reciprocity (Cosmides 1989; Cosmides & Tooby 1989) in which people note if others give back favors for those received. Sociologists have long argued that the "norm of reciprocity" is universal (Mauss 1925;) but they have left open the question of whether this norm is a cultural manifestation of a deeper biological programmer. Studies of exchange, where people give and take resources from each other, show that when people do not receive expected resources, they become angry at the injustice; and so, it is clear that people do indeed "keep score." Moreover, studies show that humans understand delayed reciprocity, where a favor given at one time may not be reciprocated until much later; and because humans have large brains, they can remember who has and has not reciprocated. Sociobiologists and evolutionary psychologists would argue that the brain was wired to assess and monitor reciprocity because if reciprocity was the core of social organization and long-term social relations, natural selection would work on the brain to generate a "module" or brain system devoted to pushing people to reciprocate when given favors and to monitoring whether or not others reciprocate favors given.

Attention to Face.   The phrase "I never forget a face" may have a biological basis. The heart of interaction, particularly emotionally laden interactions that create social bonds, is visually based. As a result, some would argue that people are born with propensities to pay attention to each other's faces where emotions are most readily revealed. Newborn infants can, for example, focus on their caretaker's face more readily than on any other object in their environment (Ekman 1982), and within a very short period of time, they can read and emit smiles that promote bonds with caregivers. Other studies of both children and adults find that people can remember faces more than other objects. Thus, we are led to the intriguing notion that humans are biologically disposed to search out, focus on, and remember faces because it is through face-to-face interactions that emotions are aroused in ways promoting bonds of solidarity.

Attention to Emotions.   Newborn infants can read their caregiver's emotions within days (Ekman 1982, 1992a, 1992b), and as noted earlier, they can respond with emotions such as a smile very early in life. Long before children can speak, they can communicate with others through emotional displays, as any mother with an infant can testify. Because emotions are responsible for social bonds, it is possible that natural selection not only expanded humans' emotional capacities (by enlarging and rewiring subcortical areas of the brain), but it may also have made people disposed to seek out emotions to get a "read" on others so as to bond with them or at least coordinate actions with them.

Rationality.   In Chapter 3, I noted that all **utilitarian theories** emphasize that humans are rational in the sense of always trying to get more resources than they must give up. Some versions of this approach emphasize that humans engage in rational choices where they try to maximize their payoffs, getting as much as they can for as little cost (Coleman 1990; Hechter 1987). As I noted earlier, rationality is only possible with emotions (Damasio 1994) that give "value" to resources and that define what constitutes a "cost." It is perhaps possible that in rewiring the human brain for enhanced emotionality, increased rationality was a by-product. Expanded emotional capacities would give people heightened rationality because they could fine-tune with a greater array of emotions their payoffs relative to costs. It is clear that humans make implicit and explicit calculations about their costs and investments to get rewards of a given kind. Certainly, the big brain of humans makes rationality possible, but the key question is whether or not rationality always drives human behavior.

Nature versus Nurture

The debate over what is biologically based and what is the result of socialization into culture will, no doubt, continue. Most sociologists do not even enter the debate, simply rejecting nature-based arguments in favor of nurture. But, as a great deal of data now document for other animals, a genotype can indirectly affect learning through what is sometimes called **biased learning** (Machalek and Martin 2004), whereby an organism has genetically directed bias (via neurological systems) to learn some types of information. The substance of what is actually learned is not genetically programmed in any direct or precise sense, but the bias for learning certain kinds of information is. For example, perhaps human propensities to focus on the face and to learn about the face and emotions are biases that stem from the effects of genes as they wired particular neurological systems. Or, maybe humans are biased by programmers in the brain to learn about the rules of reciprocity in a culture.

Whatever the merits of any of the above arguments, sociology may need to reconsider its prejudices against biology. Most scholars working in the area of biology recognize that learning and experience change how genotypes become manifested in phenotypes and that experience and environment dramatically shape how phenotypes develop and mature. Moreover, most biologists understand that most human behavior is to be understood by the power of culture and social structure to circumscribe what people learn, perceive, and believe as well as how they behave. At the same time, it is still important to recognize that humans are animals who have evolved over the last 60 million years and who may have biologically based biases in learning and biological propensities to behave in certain ways. It is an issue that will not go away because biologists are interested in pursuing the topic, and so, like it or not, sociologists are going to have to engage biologists and biology.

SUMMARY

1. Humans are animals with a 60-million-year history. Humans are a member of the primate order and are closely related to apes, particularly chimpanzees.
2. By examining the features of primates, especially those of chimpanzees, it is possible to gain some insight into what the humans' distant ancestor who initiated the hominid line was like.
3. As a primate, humans carry the legacy of the initial adaptation of animals who evolved in an arboreal habitat, and more particularly, the legacy of apes who were pushed to the terminal feeding areas of the trees. This legacy includes: visual dominance, high intelligence, strong and sensitive arms, wrists and hands, brachiation, generalized skeleton and teeth structures, and

loose- and weak-tie patterns of social organization (in which females leave the group and community at puberty and males typically move about from group to group).

4. Most apes went extinct when forced to live on the African savanna, but the ancestors of humans found a way to become better organized.

5. The biological capacities of humans are the joint outcome of initial adaptation to the arboreal habitat and the subsequent adaptation to the open-country grasslands of the African savanna.

6. Because of the adaptation of hominids to these two habitats, humans have large brains that enable them to use language to build culture, to fine-tune interactions through the visual reading of emotions in the face and body, and to impose moral imperatives through the mobilization of emotions like anger, guilt, shame, and pride.

7. More controversial speculations on biological propensities for behavior include differences in behavioral propensities of the sexes, sociality, reciprocity, and attention to face and emotions.

8. Although most sociologists are highly suspicious of any explanation that invokes biology, sociologists will have to engage biologists because they are trying to explain sociological processes in terms of biological ideas.

KEY TERMS

Biased Learning: Propensity driven by the genotype of an organism as it structures the phenotype of this organism to learn certain kinds of information.

Culture: Systems of symbols that humans create and use to guide behavior, interaction, and patterns of social organization.

Epigenesis: Processes whereby the environment and genotype interact as they generate a phenotype.

Genotype: Information contained in the genes of a life form.

Hominids: Ancestors on or near the human line of evolution.

Limbic Systems: Subcortical areas of the brain that generate human emotions.

Matrilines: Generations of related females who stay in proximity to each other within a group or troop of primates.

Natural Selection: Process whereby the environment selects those traits of a life form's phenotype that facilitate survival and reproduction.

Phenotype: Actual expression of the genotype in the structures of a life form.

Sociobiology: Theorizing that sees humans and societies as survivor machines for genes and emphasizes the process of natural selection as it generates behavioral and organizational propensities that enhance fitness of organisms, or the capacity of their genes to remain in the gene pool.

Utilitarian Theory: Theorizing that emphasizes the rational calculation of the costs and benefits to be gained from pursuing various courses of action and that sees social life as a constant exchange of resources among actors who seek to make a profit in relations with others.

Chapter 5

Culture

A World of Symbols

Humans, and to a limited degree a number of nonhuman animals as well, can do an amazing thing: they can represent facets of the world, their experiences, and virtually anything with arbitrary signs. We call these signs *symbols* when people come to agree on what a sign stands for and what it represents. The words that you are now reading are signs (black marks on a page) whose meaning we agree on; and hence, each word is a symbol. These words are organized into sentences, paragraphs, and chapters. They are part of an organized *system* of symbols.

What is true of language is true of almost anything we can think up. Flags, crosses, clenched fists, a raised middle finger, facial frowns, books, bibles, and computer programs are all signs that carry agreed upon meanings. And typically, they belong to systems of symbols, for they invoke other related symbols and meanings. It is through such systems of symbols that we remember the past, take cognizance of the present, and anticipate the future. Without this amazing capacity, our world would consist of mere sense impressions. We would be enslaved in the here and now. We would have no music, art, mathematics, joking, swearing, reading, worshipping, or any of the other things we as humans take for granted. Our life would be dull and routine, but we would not "know" this because we would be incapable of representing it with symbols.

We can get a sense for the significance of symbol systems by observing ants and other "social" insects, like termites and bees. We call them "social" because they are organized, but they are organized by information much different than our systems of symbols. The information guiding these insects and their conduct is built into the biology of insects so that their place and role in insect society are largely predetermined, although environmental influences will also affect how behavioral propensities become coded into the biology of even insects.

Human systems of symbols are not biologically programmed, except in the sense that large brains make the development and use of symbol systems possible. Symbol systems among humans are imaginatively created, used, and changed as individuals confront each other and the conditions of their environment. But they are the functional equivalent of the more biologically based codes of social insects in that they shape actions and, most importantly, patterns of social organization. The sum total of these systems of symbols among a population of humans is what sociologists generally call **culture** (Kroeber and Kluckhohn 1973;

Parsons 1951). In everyday talk, we often use the term "culture" differently to refer to fine wine, good scotch, tasteful dress, or premium beer. But these are not culture, per se, but the material products of activities guided by culture. They are physical things created by using symbols to organize people to produce things. Yet, they can also be cultural symbols in themselves if they "say something" about us to others. Thus, serving a premium beer as opposed to an "el cheapo" discount brand is a statement and it affects the nature, in however slight a way, of your relation to others, as does driving a Mercedes Benz, Lexus, or BMW. Thus, cultural products (which result from cultural symbols as they organize manufacturing) can become symbols themselves and influence the behavior, interaction, and organization among people.

I should add a note of caution and qualification here: This emphasis on culture as systems of symbols is not universally accepted. There are many diverse definitions of culture (Kroeber and Kluckhohn 1973) and some want to see culture as the sum total of all human creations (Singer 1968)—symbols, material artifacts, and ways of organization. When this more global definition is used, a distinction between **material culture** (physical artifacts) and *nonmaterial culture* (systems of symbols and social ways) is sometimes drawn. I will, however, employ a more restricted usage, but it is important to be aware that there is no agreed upon definition of culture in the social sciences (Gilmore 1992).

Thus, our world is constructed from and mediated by symbols. Virtually everything we experience, do, desire, and see is tied to symbols. Understanding ourselves and the broader social world thus requires a greater knowledge of culture. We need to recognize that symbols structure our world for us, although not to the extent they do for genetically preprogrammed ants, bees, or termites.

Symbols and Society

At one level, culture and the products of culture are simple resources that enable people to get things done. Without language, our communication is limited. Without technology (information about how to manipulate the environment), we could not eat and house ourselves. Symbols, then, are the medium of our adjustment to the environment, of our interaction with others, of our interpretation of experiences, and of our organizing ourselves into groups.

Symbols are more than a convenient medium, however. They also tell us what to do, think, and perceive. Culture does not shackle us in the same way as the genetic information on the genes of ants, bees, and termites ultimately does, but it does limit our options. Even a seemingly neutral symbolic resource like language carries a hidden message (Hall 1959). For example, the language of the Hopi is different from English in the way it treats the notion of time (Carroll 1956). In English, "time" is a noun, which means that it can be modified—cut, saved, spent, lost, wasted. (For example, you may be having a "bad time" reading my words, or you may consider this all to be "a waste of time.") But for the Hopi, time is a verb and cannot be modified or manipulated like a noun; time simply flows and humans bend to its way. (A Hopi will probably complain less about this book.) Thus, the respective perceptions of the person using Hopi or English will vary, as will their behaviors and patterns of social organization. Culture, then, is rarely just a neutral resource. Culture is a constraint and it is this constraining aspect of culture that most interests sociologists.

Sociologists study culture by examining how symbolic systems constrain human interaction and organization, and in turn, how patterns of social organization operate to create, sustain, or change culture (Kroeber and Parsons 1958). We are not interested in every symbolic system, only in those symbols that influence how people see things, act in the world, interact with others, and coordinate actions and behaviors.

Systems of Symbols

Symbols are organized into systems that enable them to get quite complex. Although there is enormous diversity in systems of symbols among human populations, these systems are of several basic types.

Language

One type is the *system of language codes* that can range from spoken words and the words on this page to complex mathematical representations and computer algorithms. The basic kinds of language codes that a population possesses will greatly influence how it will become organized. For example, if a population only has a spoken language, its patterns of social organization will be limited, whereas if this population can develop a written language, it can store information more effectively and, as a result, elaborate its patterns of social organization. And if new languages—mathematics, logic, computer algorithms, and other symbolic codes—can be developed, the range of responses of this population to its environment can increase; and the nature of its members' social relations and their patterns of social organization will be dramatically altered. Think, for example, of what computer language has done to the speed, scale, and scope of relations in the modern world, and you can see the power of language to transform society.

Technology

Another basic cultural system is **technology**, or the organization of information and knowledge about how to control and manipulate the environment. If gathering plants and hunting animals is the basic store of information among a population—as it was for 150,000 to 200,000 years of humans' existence as a species—social organization and adaptation to the environment will be limited. As technology expands, so does the scale of society: more can be produced to support larger and more complexly organized populations. Thus, technology is one of the driving forces of human organization, and once it reaches certain levels and becomes intertwined with science and engineering, it becomes a cultural juggernaut, transforming how we live, relate to each other, and organize ourselves (Lenski 1966; Lenski, Lenski and Nolan 1991). Indeed, just about every aspect of your daily life—your dress, transportation, living arrangements, perceptions, aspirations, and modes of communication—is circumscribed by the products that come from new kinds of knowledge or technology. Indeed, we cannot even imagine life without a telephone, television, car, apartment, DVDs, computer games, and so the list goes. If personal relations get lost in this technological shuffle, it should not surprise us.

Values

Humans always hold ideas about what is good or bad, appropriate or inappropriate, and essential or unessential. These are **values;** when these are organized into a system of standards or criteria for assessing the moral worth and appropriateness of conduct, they constitute a *value system* (Rokeach 1973, 1979; Williams 1970).

Values possess a special feature: they are abstract in that they are so general as to be applicable to many diverse situations (Kluckhohn 1951). Without this abstract quality, which allows us to tailor values to specific situations, people would have a hard time communicating and getting along, because they would have no common moral yardstick to assess others', as well as their own, actions. Imagine a conversation between two individuals holding very different sets of values. They would not agree on what should occur, what would be fair, and what would be appropriate behavior. What is remarkable about most human populations is how they reveal at least some consensus over values. This consensus is rarely perfect, I must caution, for one of the most interesting and volatile dynamics of a society is conflict over values. But a society without some degree of value consensus would be characterized by considerable conflict and tension. It is striking that in a society as large as the United States, spread across such a huge geographical area and revealing such diversity, there is some agreement on what is good, bad, appropriate, and inappropriate. In large part, this general consensus over values is what makes us uniquely "American," and it is what enables individuals to move into and out of new situations without great stress. When we share basic values, we can interact, even though we may disagree on many things.

What are some general values (Williams 1970)? Table 5.1 lists some of the most powerful values in the United States. In America, we agree on such values as *achievement* (doing well, trying to do well), *activism* (trying to master and control situations), *freedom* (being unrestrained for pursuit of our fancy), *progress* (improving ourselves and the world around us), *materialism* (acquiring material objects, tastefully, of course), and *efficiency* (doing things in a rational and practical manner). We tend to share these and other ideas and they serve as a moral yardstick for evaluating ourselves and others in most concrete situations.

We do not agree on all of these values; indeed, some people reject them all. But there is an amazing degree of consensus over them among most people. Although you and I might, for example, assign these values different priorities, we probably agree about them in general terms. And as a result, our interaction proceeds with less effort.

Equally important, every encounter, group, organization, community, institutional complex, and society as a whole is guided, to some degree, by values. For example, think of education as an institutional system. The values of achievement (doing well and getting good grades), individualism (doing well on your own), progress (moving up the educational hierarchy), and materialism (getting a degree to make more money) structure the organization of schools and the entire system of schools, from kindergarten to the university. Values not only influence

Table 5.1 A List of American Values

Values are abstract and general standards of what is right and wrong in all situations. The following lists prominent American values (Williams 1970).

1. **Achievement and success:** It is appropriate and, indeed, mandatory for individuals to strive to do well in all situations. The more one achieves, the more worthy he or she is.

2. **Activity:** It is desirable to master and control their environment through hard work and effort. We should always be active, trying to master each situation.

3. **Individualism:** It is the individual who should be active and try to achieve. The burden is always on the person, not the group, to be successful.

4. **Progress:** It is necessary to improve one's standing and place over time. We should all seek to be better than we were in the past.

5. **Materialism:** It is appropriate for those who are active, who achieve, and who progress to enjoy more material well being than those who are less active and less accomplished.

6. **Equality of opportunity:** It is desirable that all should have an equal chance to be active, achieve, progress, and have material well being. Equality of opportunity does not, however, mean equality of result—only that there should be a level playing field for all individuals.

7. **Efficiency and rationality:** It is appropriate to use the best means to an end and to be practical about one's activities.

8. **Conformity:** It is appropriate that people conform to norms and try to get along, even as they also seek to assert their individuality. One must go along to get along.

9. **Morality:** It is necessary to evaluate all situations in terms of their worth and value.

10. **Humanitarianism:** It is desirable to help out those who are less fortunate than ourselves, as long as their misfortune is not their own fault and that they are, thereby, deserving of assistance.

Note: These values are very general; they do not say exactly how to achieve, be active, be an individual, progress, and the like. These values apply to all situations, with the details about *how* you are to realize these values defined by ideologies and norms.

social structures, but the ways that people in them think and act. For example, a student reading this book is guided by these core American values: activism (I'll master this book), achievement (I've got to take a test on it), progress and materialism (I've got to get a degree that certifies me as eligible for a good job), and efficiency (I'm not going to waste time rereading). These values guide your conduct in an educational system *organized around* these moral premises. Furthermore, entrance into school marked an implicit acceptance of these values by students and willingness to perpetuate the educational system organized around activism, achievement, individualism, and materialism. And what is true for school is also the case for almost all situations: some profile of values from a value system is guiding the perceptions and conduct of individuals.

A functional perspective stresses these consequences of values for guiding people's actions and motivating them to participate in society. If we think back to Émile Durkheim's analysis of the "collective conscience" and its integrative functions for society, we can see that consensus over values is crucial to a society. There is a great deal of merit in analyzing these functions of values, as Durkheim did long ago and as I have done here, but we must not forget that values can be a source of disintegration in a society. When segments of a population hold differing values, or as I will discuss shortly, different beliefs, the stage is set for conflict. People will clash over their moral standards, and because they hold these dearly, they cannot back down. A conflict perspective would emphasize this aspect of social life, but it would do more: it would stress that values are often tools for the more privileged who have the power to define *which values* people should hold. I return to this point later, but it is important to bear it in mind.

Beliefs

Yet another type of symbol system revolves around **beliefs**, which are people's cognitions and ideas in *particular types* of situations—education, work, family, friendships, politics, religion, neighborhood, sports, recreation, and all basic kinds of social situations in a society (Turner and Starnes 1976). For virtually every type of situation that we encounter, we all hold ideas about what *should* occur in this situation and what actually *does* occur. Some beliefs represent the application of basic values to particular situations, and we might term these evaluative beliefs or ideologies. **Ideologies** indicate what should transpire and they represent the application of core values to specific contexts. In a college or university, for example, there is an ideology emphasizing that one should get good grades (achievement), try hard (activism, efficiency), and move through the system and know more (progress). Almost all situations—work, play, parties, friendships, sports, and the like—involve beliefs that stem from the application of these and other general values. Even in a personal relationship in America, we wonder how "well we are doing" (achievement), if we are "going somewhere" in the relationship (progress), and what we need "to do to improve it" (activism). Depending on the type of relationship—lovers, parents, casual friends, close friends—somewhat different beliefs apply, but they all invoke the same value premises. In so doing, they give us guidance and make us confident that we are doing the right thing.

Other beliefs are on the surface more factual. They are ideas we hold about "what is" and "what exists" in a situation and we might term these **empirical beliefs.** By "knowing what exists," we feel confident about approaching and acting in a situation. We also hold beliefs about situations that we have not experienced, have yet to experience, or will never experience—work, marriage, old age, poverty, and other distant situations. Members of a population can be seen as "plugged into" each other's social worlds in this way. By holding beliefs about other social arenas and contexts, we vicariously "know about" and can potentially "act in" these arenas. For this reason, new situations are not so totally unfamiliar. We have learned the general values, ideologies, and empirical beliefs necessary to guide us as we initially fumble about.

Our factual or empirical beliefs are not always accurate, however. They are greatly influenced by values and ideologies about what *should* occur or exist in a particular situation. But because we are convinced that we do indeed know about other worlds, we feel a vicarious comradeship with others and a sense that we could function in these other worlds. For example, most Americans believe that there are job opportunities for anyone who really wants to work and that many welfare recipients are lazy and misrepresent their need (Kluegel and Smith 1986; Smith 1985). This belief represents an invocation of such values as activism, achievement, progress, and efficiency to the world of work and welfare. It also contains some supposedly neutral facts: there are lots of jobs out there and lots of people who are too lazy to take them. And it carries a presumption: If I were poor and out of work, I would take any job and preserve my dignity. Thus, we feel knowledgeable about a world that, realistically, we are not likely to experience. But the "facts" in these beliefs may be wrong: Most people on welfare cannot work; they are too old, too disabled, and too sick; and about half of them work full time or were laid off (J. Turner 1993b). Thus, the more accurate "facts" are that the economy does not have enough jobs to employ all of its citizenry and that wages for many jobs are not high enough to keep people out of poverty (Beeghley 1983; Ropers 1991). So our beliefs about what actually exists and occurs can be biased by values and evaluative beliefs. This is not bad; rather, it is inevitable in human affairs.

Indeed, in modern society an entire industry has emerged to poll the public on its attitudes and opinions—which are, in essence, expressions of beliefs. The public opinion industry extends far beyond election polls and general surveys, such as the Gallup and Harris polls; polling is also the basic methodology behind market research and public relations inquiries. The recognition that people's behavior—from voting for president to buying a product—is influenced by their attitudes that, in turn, are shaped by their general values and beliefs, has greatly changed the way politicians run for election and the way that corporations do business.

Norms

Values and beliefs are too general to regulate and guide behavior precisely; they give us a common view and perspective; and they also get us mobilized to behave in certain general ways (Blake and Davis 1964). But they do not tell us precisely *what* to do. **Norms** make up for this deficiency in other symbol systems by telling us what is expected and appropriate behavior in a particular situation. Imagine yourself coming to class not knowing the "rules" of, and expectations for, student behavior. You are mobilized to achieve, be active, and progress mentally, but you do not know what to do—where to sit, how to act, and what to do with your hands, legs, mouth, and mind. This may be hard to imagine because you do know the general rules of school behavior so well. Yet, if you have never been in a big lecture hall, if you have never owned your own books, and if you have never attended a college lecture, then you may have some early feelings of discomfort. Indeed, you may find yourself watching how to sit in lectures and how to take notes. Thus, one may know the general norms pertaining to basic types of situations—what some sociologists call **institutional norms**—but each person must learn additional norms to fine-tune behavior in a special setting.

From an interactionist viewpoint, this process of discovery is very complex and subtle. If we do not know the relevant aspects of culture that apply to a situation, we become intensely attuned to the actions and gestures of others. We read their gestures, seeking to plug ourselves into their mental states in an effort to learn how to behave. We often carry the relevant values, beliefs, and norms already, but lack complete knowledge of *which* ones are most salient, and of course, we may even be ignorant of relevant norms and beliefs. Our mistakes give us away, and we experience the sanctions and disapproval of others, with the result that we become attuned to others' gestures. Or, we may know of our ignorance before we make a mistake, and as a consequence we act tentatively as we pay attention to the movements, words, and gestures of others. Once we acquire a sense for the relevant cultural symbols, interaction processes sustain these symbols in a mutually reinforcing way. Each of us behaves in the appropriate way; such behaviors reinforce values, beliefs, and norms; and as these are reinforced, they gain power to constrain behavior. Acts of deviance do occur and break this cycle of reinforcement, but we usually try to bring the deviant back into line and sustain the cycle. Such is how culture is maintained by the micro interpersonal actions of individuals.

Norms vary in their generality—from broad institutional ones, which are general instructions about how to behave in basic social spheres (work, school, friendships, home, etc.) to more specific ones, which tell us precisely how to function in a concrete setting. We all carry with us the knowledge of crucial institutional norms, and as a result we can enter new situations with at least some guidance. Once there, we can learn the additional norms by reading the gestures of others. We must also learn how to create new norms in some situations as we interact with others, and this process can become very difficult, especially if people hold somewhat different beliefs and invoke variations of norms that are at odds. When people marry, for example, they often need to negotiate new agreements about how they are going to behave because beliefs about the role of men and women are in rapid flux and because norms about wife and husband activities can differ greatly. In light of this fact, it is not surprising that most marriages begin to degenerate in the first year because the husband and wife carry very different beliefs and normative understandings about their respective behaviors. Most couples have only some highly romanticized beliefs, knowledge of general institutional norms about marriage, and perceptions of their parents' and friends' marriages to guide their relations. There is often just too much to work out, normatively; as a result, the marriage fails.

Some situations in modern societies, then, require us to improvise and develop normative agreements on the go. Others, such as an assembly line job, are highly constrained, but even here people develop normative agreements about how they are to work on the job. Much of our social life consists of our learning, fine-tuning, creating, and renegotiating norms. This is particularly so in modern societies, where constant social change forces us to move about into ever new situations.

Stocks of Knowledge

Aside from language, technology, values, beliefs, and normative systems, people carry with them more loosely and implicitly held stores of information. The German sociologist Alfred Schutz (1932) coined the phrase "stocks of knowledge at hand" to describe the catalogues of relevant information that individuals can draw upon in adjusting to situations. Schutz was a key figure in a theoretical and philosophical tradition known as *phenomenology*, a perspective that seeks to understand how people know and develop knowledge about the world. For example, a student entering college possesses stocks of useful knowledge about schools, classrooms, rank differences, occasions for formality versus informality, lectures and speeches, and appropriate sitting and talking demeanor. These are used to guide a student's orientation to those first classes and encounters while the more fine-tuned norms of each new situation are learned.

Thus, each of us has many **stocks of knowledge**, forged out of experiences. We use these stocks to orient ourselves to situations and when people share similar stocks of information, they can construct a common view of a situation. Even when we do not speak the same language, this is possible, as anyone who has traveled in a foreign country can testify. By using nonverbal gestures like pointing, we can usually get foreigners to draw from their stocks of knowledge information close to our own, especially with respect to the common situations. This ability to use these implicit systems of symbols gives humans enormous flexibility in their adjustment to new situations.

Part of culture, then, is a quiet "knowledgeability" that is drawn upon constantly, as we adapt to each other, norms, and other features of situations. If we only could catalogue values, beliefs, and norms, we would be stiff and robot-like; and if something new came along outside our "programming," we would not know what to do. But we can adjust to nuances because we all carry vast storehouses or stocks of knowledge that can be drawn upon. Indeed, one of the problems in creating machines with "artificial intelligence" is that it is difficult to program the stocks of knowledge and the capacity to assemble these on the spot; as a result, the machine often seems "dumb" or at least "out of it."

To sum up thus far, the organization of human society is greatly facilitated by cultural symbols. Conversely, cultural symbols are created, sustained, or changed by interaction among people. Indeed, as functional theorists argue (Alexander 1985; Parsons 1951), the integration of society cannot occur without common systems of symbols. Culture thus meets a basic need of society. And as interactionists emphasize, these systems of symbols are sustained by the fine-grained reading of each other's gestures. The most crucial symbols for understanding our actions and patterns of organization are systems of language, technology, values, beliefs, norms, and stocks of knowledge. These are the functional equivalents of genetic codes in social insects, but with a big difference: they can be changed and used to create new social forms. If we all did not participate in a common culture, we would be bumping into each other, insulting our friends, and otherwise doing the wrong thing. However, we are not insects, and because our guidance system is not genetically coded, there is lots of room for misinformation, inadequate information, conflicting information, and ever changing information. Thus, society is not like the well-ordered beehive or ant hill because we organize ourselves with cultural, as opposed to genetic, codes. And in cultural symbols there is a great potential for ambiguity, dissension, conflict, and most important, innovation and change.

One way to visualize culture is as a loose hierarchical system that successively penetrates the structures of society. At the top of this system is language that is used in every social context. Also at the top is technology, or the general knowledge base of a society about how to manipulate the environment. Both languages and technologies become more specialized as they are adopted to various social contexts. High in the hierarchy are values that are society-wide systems of ideas about what is right and wrong. Values are, in turn, made more concrete to specific situations by evaluative beliefs or ideologies and empirical beliefs. Below values and ideologies are broad institutional norms about how people should behave in basic institutions like family, economy, government, law, religion, medicine, sports, and education. And below these are the more specific norms that emerge for structures operating within an institutional sphere, like your particular family, school, study group, and other unique contexts. Figure 5.1 represents this hierarchical structure of culture, but we should not view it as a rigid system. The important point is that culture comes to us as an individual in any particular situation well organized: we know the language, we generally understand the technology, we take cognizance of the relevant values, we possess an ideology about what should occur, we have some sense of what does occur, we know the institutional norms, we possess tacit understandings in our stocks of knowledge, and we know or soon learn the more specific norms guiding our conduct.

Culture has power, as the illustration tries to document. Unlike Atlas who had to hold the world on his shoulders, we hold the culture of the society on our shoulders, as is illustrated in Figure 5.2, but it is not heavy *unless* we violate the values, ideologies, and norms. When you feel embarrassed, ashamed, guilty, outraged, or any number of very negative emotions, you can be sure that you or someone else has violated a cultural

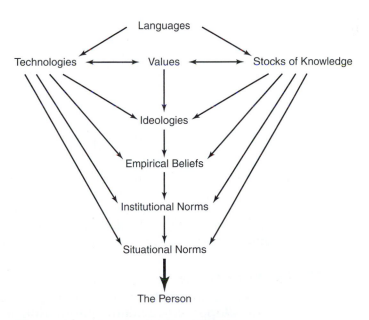

Figure 5.1   Constraints of Culture

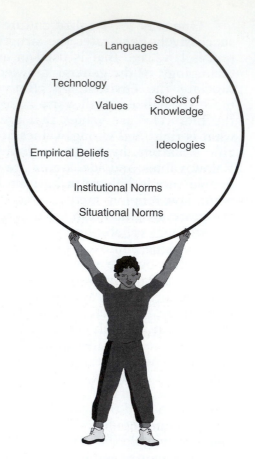

Figure 5.2   The Weight of Culture on the Person   When all is going well in a situation, culture is like a beach ball: light and hardly noticeable. But if there is a problem or if a person is unsure about what aspects of culture apply, the beach ball becomes like the weight of the earth.

code. Thus, the world of culture travels rather lightly on our shoulders, most of the time, but we suddenly feel its weight when we fail to follow dictates of culture. Most of the time, then, we need not shrug as Atlas had to; we can stand tall, but as soon as we violate a value, institutional norm, ideology, or more specific norms that have emerged in a situation, we are virtually flattened by the weight of culture, as others look at us strangely or as we sanction ourselves for our stupid conduct.

Cultural Variations

Humans create systems of cultural symbols because we need them. They are developed to facilitate interaction and organization, as functional theorists argue. And because people live and operate in diverse environments, culture will vary. As a conflict theorist would emphasize, cultural variations are a source of constant conflict and tension in a society. Just as languages differ, so do other cultural systems, such as technology, values, ideologies and beliefs, norms, and stocks of knowledge. This fact has enormous implications. Let me review some of them.

Cultural Conflict

Cultural systems like values and beliefs are a set of eyeglasses or a colored prism through which we see the world. Our perceptions are biased by culture so that we see some things and are unaware of others. This is why science has been created as a conscious effort to reduce the biases inherent in the fact that we must have culture to organize our daily lives. Science is also a type of belief system and like other aspects of culture, it emerged to deal with human problems. In the case of science, the desire to gather accurate information and to check ideas against the facts led to the development of beliefs that knowledge is generated by theories that are constantly checked against carefully and systematically collected data. Initially, beliefs about science, and later the development of norms about how to conduct inquiry, were viewed with hostility by others holding different beliefs. And some people still view science with great antipathy. Such antipathy can create conflicts for individuals who simultaneously hold a number of different beliefs, as well as larger conflicts between groups of individuals adhering to different beliefs. Religious fundamentalists question science when its conclusions violate the tenets of religious dogma. And ideologues, whether Marxists, right-wing politicians, or something in between, often refuse to accept scientifically based knowledge. Even in the United States, where science is a dominant cultural belief, this conflict surfaces over such emotionally charged issues as the teaching of Darwinian evolution instead of creationism.

When differences in cultural beliefs become the basis for political organization and action, **cultural conflicts** become more intense. For example, the current conflict over abortion involves not just disagreement over beliefs about motherhood, life, and conception but actual combat among organized groupings (Luker 1984). Such conflicts are difficult to resolve because the combatants' beliefs are so different and so strongly held. Similar conflicts have occurred again and again in the United States and in all complex societies where complete consensus over symbols is simply impossible.

Subcultures

Different subpopulations within a larger society like the United States often hold somewhat different beliefs and at times even different values. These diverse cultural worlds are built up and sustained by face-to-face interaction, as interactionist theorists would stress. Subcultures emerge because those in frequent interaction develop common symbol systems to give meaning to their affairs. And so, through interaction, people in different subcultures develop somewhat different beliefs, normative expectations, speech patterns, and ways of expressing themselves in bodily movements. For example, blue-collar workers exist in a somewhat different cultural world than white-collar workers, as do blacks and whites, Hispanics and Anglos, rich and poor, executives and clerks, professors and students. These subpopulations can be termed **subcultures** because their members see the world through somewhat different symbolic glasses and behave differently; often, these differences cause conflict, especially when they are accompanied by differences in power, income, wealth, and other valued resources in a society. But we all get along, to a degree, because we share some of the same culture. Our relations are often strained because we recognize our differences and try to tiptoe around them with stylized and ritualized interactions. Of course, at times these differences in beliefs and norms erupt into overt conflict—and then no amount of effort can save us from confronting our differences.

As Karl Marx and most conflict approaches stress, some subcultures possess more power and material resources than others. The wealthy, the holders of political power, and the owners of large corporations, for example, are better able to impose their beliefs and to define the norms on those subcultures without wealth, political power, or economic power (Mills 1959). Just *how far* they can go is a subject of great debate (Alford and Friedland 1985), but there can be little doubt that basic values and key beliefs in a society are those of the wealthy and powerful (Bourdieu 1984). At times, this disproportionate influence is resented by the less influential, and conflict emerges. For example, women, African Americans, gays and lesbians, and other subcultures in America have pushed for redefinition of beliefs and norms about, respectively, gender roles, white Anglo-Saxon culture, and sexuality.

Cultural Contradictions

Not only can subpopulations hold different cultural beliefs and other symbols, but the components of cultural components can themselves be somewhat inconsistent and contradictory. We often hold inconsistent values, beliefs, and norms. Fortunately, humans have large brains that allow them to partition or reconcile much of this inconsistency in an uneasy armistice. Thus, biologists who can adhere to Darwinian evolution when they do biology can believe in biblical accounts of creation in their personal and everyday lives; whites can believe in equality and freedom while holding discriminatory stereotypes about blacks; students can believe in learning and still cheat on exams; and professors can believe in a dispassionate search for truth and hate those whose research conflicts with their own. But there are limits to these mental gymnastics. Too much inconsistency can create a problem for the individual; and if too many people in a society are confronted with **cultural contradictions**, widespread personal pathologies can result. Or, cultural contradictions can lead people to change society, as was the case in pre-Civil War days when abolitionists reacted against the beliefs of people who asserted both that "all men are created equal" (women too, let us hope) and, yet, who still believed that slavery was acceptable. Thus, major contradictions in values, beliefs, and norms usually create both personal and social turmoil. They are the stuff of change and reorganization in a society.

Ethnocentrism

Finally, all cultural systems make people in a society ethnocentric—that is, individuals tend to view their system of values, beliefs, and norms as better than those of others. Ethnocentrism leads to intolerance, and intolerance in turn leads to conflict and tensions. Thus America's belief in its moral superiority can lead it to interfere in the affairs of other nations whose ways are, from an ethnocentric view, inferior. Many other societies have done this, and so we should not be too hard on ourselves. Ethnocentrism also operates within a society: Members of certain subcultures can view those in other subcultures as inferior, and this, too, can lead to conflict.

By looking around virtually any college campus in America, ethnocentrism is immediately evident. The effort to increase the cultural, class, and ethnic mix of students has brought individuals with somewhat different beliefs and normative expectations about demeanor and behavior. Various subcultures—African Americans, Hispanic Americans, Anglo and Angloized white Americans, Asian Americans, students from middle class backgrounds, students of the working class, and so on—can view each other suspiciously and apply the standards of their subculture in evaluating the others. This ethnocentrism is, of course, aggravated by the dominance of white, middle class, and Anglo-Saxon values, beliefs, and norms in most American colleges. Members of other subcultures must constantly confront the domination of many cultural symbols different from their own.

Culture and Media

Two trends have changed the dynamics of culture. One is the expansion of the media so that virtually every human on earth can potentially be exposed to the culture of others. The second is globalization in which the economies of the world are increasingly interconnected. As **postmodernists** argue, the confluence of these two trends changes the nature of culture. Symbols of a population can be lifted from their local context and presented to others, far away; and globalization of capitalism as an economic form creates incentives for profit in marketing the cultural symbols of local populations.

One line of argument by postmodernists is that the symbols of any local group can be commodified, or converted into a commodity that can be marketed. At one time, for example, the symbols of the motorcycle gang, The Hell's Angels, were tied to a local group that originated in San Bernardino, CA. Now, one can buy imitations of these symbols, such as the jean-style coat with cutoff arms and insignia on the back, at any motorcycle dealer, if not the local department store. Indeed, these symbols have been presented to the world via the media (advertising and movies) so that they can be found in Japan and Europe, much less the parking lot of any city in America. The reason that these symbols have been lifted from their local culture is that they present the prospects for profits by corporations that now market globally. And through advertising in all forms of media—from television through newsprint to computer games—demand is created for the selling of these symbols.

Postmodernists probably overstate their case, but the argument is that all symbols can be lifted from their local context, where they carry meaning, and mass marketed. When this kind of mass marketing occurs, the symbols of the culture become free floating because they are no longer attached to the local context where they emerged and gave meaning to the daily lives of individuals. In marketing the symbols of one group or subpopulation to another, the symbols are trivialized because they are converted from something that carried important meanings into a commodity to be bought and sold like toothpaste or cars. Thus, department stores carry "gang banger" clothing for middle class suburban youth; sports logos of teams are marketed world wide in areas where people have only a vague idea of who Kobe, Shaq, or the Lakers are; and so it goes.

There is no firm evidence as to whether or not cultural symbols that are commodified lose their meaning to local populations. Just last week I watched a line of Hell's Angels roar by and they looked as menacing as ever and would not be mistaken for the doctors and attorneys who dress up on weekends and take their Harley-Davidson motorcycles to the country club. Thus, even as symbols are marketed, they may still retain their original meaning to the groups who invented them and who still use them. But, even if the postmodernist case is overdrawn, the general argument has merit: Media and globalization dramatically increase the circulation of cultural symbols; and as a result, in the modern world people are exposed to far more culture than was ever possible before the mass media and before profits could be extracted through the marketing of people's culture. Whether this proliferation of culture diminishes its power is perhaps doubtful, but we are nonetheless in the middle of a true cultural revolution.

SUMMARY

1. The information guiding much human activity is symbolic rather than genetic. Unlike social insects, humans create the codes guiding their behaviors, interactions, and patterns of social organization.

2. Culture is the system of symbols that a population creates and uses to organize activities, facilitate interaction, and regulate behavior.

3. There are many systems of symbols among a population, but among the most important are (a) language systems that people use in communication; (b) technology systems that embody knowledge about how to manipulate the environment; (c) value systems that carry the principles of good and bad, right and wrong; (d) belief systems that organize people's cognitions about what should and does exist in particular situations and domains; (e) normative systems that provide the general and specific expectations about how people are to behave in situations; and (f) stocks of knowledge that provide the stores of implicit information that people unconsciously use to make sense out of situations.

4. Culture varies within and between societies, and this situation often leads to conflict between those holding different values, beliefs, norms, or stocks of knowledge. Some conflict remains at the symbolic level, but conflict often erupts into open combat between parties with different ideologies.

5. Subcultures emerge and persist in complex societies, each revealing some distinctive symbols. At times conflict is evident among subcultures, especially when some subcultures have been able to impose their symbols on others.

6. Systems of symbols often reveal contradictions and inconsistencies, a situation that can put individuals in personal turmoil and, at times, groups into conflict.

7. Ethnocentrism is an inevitable by-product of cultural variations, with individuals viewing as inferior those cultural symbols unlike the ones that they hold. Such ethnocentrism produces prejudices that often erupt into conflict.

8. The rise of the mass media and globalization of the economy have created the conditions whereby the circulation of cultural symbols is increased. Symbols of one subpopulation can be lifted, marketed via the media, and sold as commodities to other subpopulations. Just what these dramatic changes in the capacity to move symbols about markets mean is still an open question.

KEY TERMS

Beliefs: Systems of symbols organized into cognitions about what should and does occur in specific types of social situations.

Cultural Conflict: Differences in cultural values and beliefs that place people at odds with one another, and hence, in potential conflict.

Cultural Contradiction: Inconsistencies in the various systems of symbols making up the culture of a society.

Culture: Those systems of symbols that humans create and use to guide behavior, interaction, and patterns of social organization.

Culture, Material: Term used by some analysts to denote the artifacts and objects created by humans.

Empirical Beliefs: Cognitions that people hold about what actually occurs in situations.

Ethnocentricism: Tendency to view one's own culture or subculture as superior to the culture of other people or societies.

Ideology: Evaluative beliefs that say what should occur in situations.

Institutional Norms: Systems of symbols organized into very general expectations about behavior in basic types of situations in a society.

Language: Systems of symbols used in communication.

Norms: Systems of symbols informing individuals about how they are expected to behave and interact in a situation.

Postmodernists: General school of thinking, some of whose practitioners emphasize the effects of media and global capitalism in commodifying symbol systems.

Stocks of Knowledge: Implicit stores of information that individuals use to guide their behavior and interactions.

Subculture: Subpopulation of individuals in a society that possesses at least some symbols that are unique to this subpopulation and, at times, at odds with the broader culture of a society.

Technology: Systems of symbols organized into knowledge about how to manipulate the environment.

Values: Systems of symbols organized into abstract moral ideas about good-bad, appropriate-inappropriate, and right-wrong. Values cut across diverse situations because they are general and abstract.

Chapter 6

Social Structure

If you stand on the sidelines and watch the world pass you by, what you see is people moving about and somehow avoiding each other, people talking, people going in and out of buildings, people sitting on benches, people driving cars, people congregating, and in general you see just a maze of activity as individuals move about in physical space. There is a fluidity to social life when examined this way, but there is also order, at least most of the time. People are not randomly moving about, talking, driving, entering and exiting buildings, or sitting around; they have purposes and goals as they move in space and talk to each other. But there is more than just purpose; there is a structure to what you see as you look at the ebb and flow of human activity. Part of this structure inheres in the organization of symbols into culture, as it directs and guides individuals to act in certain ways. But for culture to really be effective in regulating conduct, it must be attached to something that orders social life. This extra "something" is social structure. Social structures constrain who is present, where they stand, what they can do, and how they are to relate to each other. This structure is as real as the buildings that people occupy.

Indeed, we can view social structures like the physical layout of a house. There are entrances and exits that determine where you can come and go from the house, unless you try a window. There are partitions and walls that divide the internal space, there are hallways that direct your movement, there are doors in and out of rooms, and there are different kinds of rooms where varying functions are performed. You, as an individual, have choices about when to enter or leave the house, when to walk down the hallway, when to use one room as opposed to another, and in general, you are the master of this home. But you cannot walk through walls, go to a room without using the doors and hallways, and do other things that only Superman could do. Thus, for all of the seeming freedom, the structure of the house constrains your actions in very fundamental ways. Social structures are no different; they give you freedom of choice in your actions—to a point. But if you try to be Superman and go through the hidden walls of a social structure, you will soon discover that you are not as free as you may have thought. You will bump into a reality as solid as a house, only less visible. You implicitly recognize the power of social structure because you will generally play by the cultural rules and do what is expected. But sometimes it is easy to underestimate the power of social structure to determine what you think, what you can do, and how you behave.

Most activities in our daily lives are carried out within social structures. In fact, try and think of situations where you are away from other people and outside of expectations and constraints. Even when alone, we are often part of a larger structure whose presence is felt. For example, you may be reading these words in your private room or at a table in the library or cafeteria, but you are not alone; you are part of a structure—home, dorm, apartment, or library—in which others and their expectations are not far away. Moreover, the very act of reading this page is done because you are part of a college or university that imposes expectations and constraints. And even if you think about doing something more interesting, your thoughts probably revolve around choices among alternative social structures.

Social life is thus organized within structures, and because of this obvious fact, we need a vocabulary for talking about structure. Let us begin with the basic elements of all structures; then we can see how they are combined to produce ever larger and more encompassing structures that constrain all of our lives.

Basic Building Blocks of Social Structure

Positions

Social structures are ultimately composed of **status positions**, which are the place we occupy in a system of interconnected positions (Nadel 1957; Parsons 1951). For example, you currently occupy the status position of "student" and this fact locates you within a larger system of positions—fellow students, teaching assistants, professors, staff, administrators or counselors, and all those other positions in a college or university.

By knowing our position, we know where we stand and what is expected of us. Thus, positions make sense only in relation to other status positions, a topic that we discuss shortly, but for the present, I want to emphasize a simple point: Positions carry with them cultural content. For each position, there are usually expectations or norms about how we should behave (Linton 1936), and these normative expectations are impregnated with values, beliefs, stocks of knowledge, language, and even technology. The position of student carries certain clear norms—come to class, study, take exams, be respectful to teachers, be quiet in class, ask questions, and other expectations that can be listed on a piece of paper. But these norms embody aspects of other cultural systems: a profile of values is being invoked, particular beliefs are being applied, stocks of knowledge are being used, and certain technologies are being employed. Thus, there is an enormous amount of cultural coding for a particular position. In one sense, this can seem like a burden, but in another sense the existence of so much information gives a person options about exactly which codes will be used and how they will be used. There is, then, a dynamic quality to a status position and the cultural systems impinging upon this position. This is so because an active, thinking, and potentially creative human being ultimately occupies a position and must decide how and in what way cultural forces are to guide behavior in a particular position. We are not worker bees or ants; rather, humans have the capacity for agency in their behaviors (Giddens 1984).

Roles

When we behave in a position, we take account of norms and other systems of symbols; then we fashion this behavior in ways that fit our needs and personality as well as the particulars of a situation. This behavioral activity associated with incumbency in a status position is termed **role.** It is the dynamic aspect of a status position and it reveals how cultural systems are being invoked (Biddle 1992; Heiss 1981; Linton 1936). To occupy the status of student, for instance, involves paying attention to prescribed behaviors dictated by a cultural script while at the same time reconciling expected behaviors with (a) personal needs and (b) the expectations of others occupying the same or different positions in a situation (R. Turner 1978). Roles are thus complex activities because they involve interplay among many forces—culture, personality, other people, and other positions. Let me explore this complexity by introducing some additional concepts.

Status-Sets

All of us occupy many different status positions, lodged in various structures. For example, we have positions in families (child, father, or mother), in churches (worshiper), in organizations (student, worker, fraternity or sorority member), in groups (friendship, study, lunch time), in communities (resident), in political parties (voter), in society (citizen), and so on. The complex of positions that each of us occupies is often termed **status-set** (Merton 1957).

A status-set marks the structures in which we belong and the systems of culture that we are plugged into. Figure 6.1 presents a hypothetical status-set. By knowing people's status-sets, we can learn a great deal about them because we can get a sense for the cultural systems and attendant expectations that orient and guide their behavior. For example, it is easy to spot different types of students—let us say, "party animal," "married with children," "part-time," "full-time with job," "commuter," "dormy," "greek," "geek," and so on: The differences in these students reflect varying webs of affiliation with social structures. For each position in a particular configuration, somewhat different cultural systems are invoked and used to orient perceptions and guide behavior. By listing all the positions that each of us occupies, and then assessing the structures and culture in which these positions are lodged, it becomes possible to get a rough picture of "who we are" sociologically.

Role-Sets

For any particular status position, there is always a cluster of behaviors to be emitted. The total of these behaviors constitutes a **role-set** (Merton 1957). For example, as is illustrated in Figure 6.2, the role-set of a student (the status position) might include going to class, being with friends, using the library or computer room, studying, taking exams, participating in fraternity or sorority activities, holding a part-time job, and playing a sport. By virtue of occupying one master status—student—a variety of role behaviors can become relevant. Some of these place individuals into new status positions—say, "jock" on a particular team or "worker" in a part-time job—but our focus here is on the configuration of behaviors associated with a particular position. Some status positions are

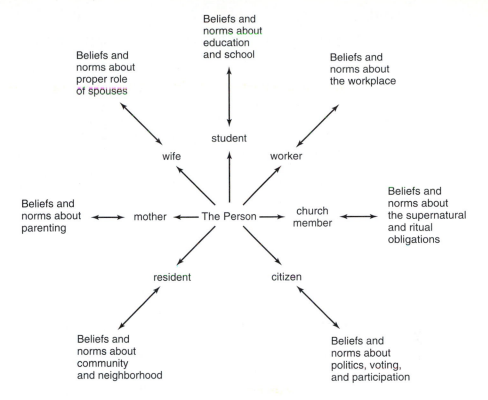

Figure 6.1   A Hypothetical Status Set   Each position in this person's status set plugs her into somewhat different cultural scripts composed of beliefs and norms that, in turn, reflect values and other cultural systems such as technology. By constructing a similar diagram for each of us, we can learn a great deal about ourselves and about the symbolic codes that guide our perceptions, orientations, and actions.

robust and require many different behaviors, whereas others are simple and do not demand too many different behaviors. Compare the difference between "mother" or "student" positions, on the one hand, and "shopper" or "customer" in a store on the other; there are great differences in the amount and variety of behaviors associated with these roles, and so the role-sets are very different.

Role-Conflict and Role-Strain

Participation in social structures is rife with conflict and strain. **Role-conflict** comes when we occupy different status positions that come into conflict or are incompatible. A mother of three children (one status position) who goes to school as a student (another status) is likely to experience considerable role-conflict, trying to juggle and balance very different demands. For example, the hypothetical woman, whose status set is delineated in Figure 6.1, is a very likely candidate for role-conflict, and certainly role-strain. Similarly, a student who has a part-time or, worse, a full-time job will also experience role-conflict. Role-conflict is inevitable in complex societies where we all occupy different positions in

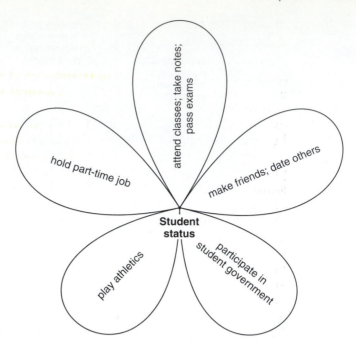

Figure 6.2   Role Sets   Here the role set of the student status is illustrated. We all have many such role sets, some of which come into conflict. Few of us could do all of this and still find time to sleep and eat. Just doing academic work and socializing can pose potential role conflicts. Such conflicts are inevitable, because most status positions involve multiple behaviors.

varying structures with their own demands. Usually, role-conflict can be mitigated by separating occupancy in different positions in time and space. If a student-mother could do all of her work at school, and then go home to assume her mother status, the conflict would be reduced. But in this instance, the student-mother must also study at home, and here is where the conflict becomes more intense.

One source of strain is that the behaviors associated with a position are too robust and demanding, requiring too many different or even incompatible behaviors. If such is the case, **role-strain** is likely (Goode 1960). A full-time student who is active socially will often suffer role-strain by trying to engage in too many activities. First year college students are the most likely to suffer role-strain as they jump into far too many social activities, leading them to suffer fatigue, physical illness, or even emotional distress. Thus, depending on the number, variety, and intensity of behaviors associated with a position, the level of role-strain will vary.

Thus, built into status-sets and role-sets are sources of tension, strain, and conflict. These problems are the price we pay for living in complex societies. Each of us must learn to manage these sources of strain and conflict or suffer the consequences.

Networks of Positions

So far, I have not really said anything about structure, only some of the elements of structure. Let us now take this matter head on: *social structures* are composed of (a) **networks of status positions**, (b) the roles for each status position, and (c) the cultural systems associated with the positions in this network. Structure is thus evident when positions are *connected* to each other, such that our roles in one position are affected by, and conversely have an effect on, roles in other positions and when culture directs how positions are connected and how roles are to be played. For example, a family is a structure composed of three basic positions—father, mother, children. But, it is the relationships or network connections among these positions, the cultural scripts that apply to these positions, and the reciprocal roles played by incumbents in each position that make the family a social structure.

This may seem so obvious that it is a waste of time to talk about it, but when social structures get big and complex, we need some way to look at them and talk about them. By visualizing social structures as networks of status positions in which individuals play roles regulated by culture, we have the elementary tools to analyze large-scale structures (Wellman and Berkowitz 1988; Burt 1980; Marsden and Lin 1980). But we need to introduce some simple ideas if we are to use the notion of networks to examine social structures (Maryanski and Turner 1991, 540–557).

Dimensions of Structure

What are some of these simple ideas? One is very obvious: the number of different types of positions in a network. Structures with two or three positions are very different than those with many positions, as a simple comparison of your family and your college will immediately reveal. Another dimension is also straightforward: the number of people in positions of a given type. A network with 1,000 incumbents in a particular position (e.g., the student position) and comparatively few in other types of positions (e.g., faculty) will be very different than one where the distribution of people in various positions is more equal (e.g., a friendship network like a lunch group or, more formally, a sorority).

Yet another useful consideration is the nature of the connection among positions. Is the connection loose, as is the case among casual friends? Is it temporary as will be the case with students in a class? As utilitarian exchange theorists (Coleman 1991) would emphasize, are there important resources—for example, money, love, honor, grades—flowing among the positions, and if so, which ones? As conflict theorists (Collins 1975) might stress, are there differences in the power of positions, and if so, how much? And, to what degree is every position in a network connected to every other position (this is often termed "density" of the network)?

By considering these various dimensions of networks among positions, we can describe very different kinds of structures. An American family is a simple structure; it is composed of a few positions and relatively clear cultural guidelines for role behaviors of incumbents in these positions; these positions are densely connected to each other (i.e., its members are all directly connected to each other); there are only a few people in each position; the connections are usually close; they are rarely temporary; the resources flowing among the positions are highly valued (love, affection, support, and, of course, money); and the power differences (parent-child and perhaps mother-father) have a great influence on how roles are played. Compare this kind of structure with a classroom, sorority or fraternity, athletic team, or work place: The nature and types of positions, the number of people in positions, the density of connections, the permanence of connections, the resources being used, and the power relations are different from the family and, as a result, the underlying structures are different.

Types of Social Structures

Stripped to their basic forms, there are relatively few types of social structures. Of course, once cultural content is added, the range of substantive diversity for each type increases, but the underlying structure of the type remains. For example, a group is a small, face-to-face cluster of positions and, as such, constitutes a basic structural form; but the substance of a group—family, work, play, recreation, and so forth—can vary enormously in terms of the cultural symbols guiding its operation.

What, then, are some of the basic forms of social structure? An answer to this question frames much of the subject matter of sociology, as will be evident in later chapters. For the present, let me briefly discuss basic forms of structure, leaving a more detailed explanation for later chapters.

Box 6.1: Comparing Social Structures

1. Social structures are composed of networks connecting status positions, cultural symbols associated with these positions, and roles dictated by cultural scripts, personal needs, and expectations of others.

2. These networks of positions can be described by some basic dimensions:
   a. the number of different types of positions
   b. the number of people in each type of position
   c. the nature of connections among positions, including:
      1. looseness of ties
      2. duration of ties
      3. resources exchanged in ties
      4. variations in power among positions
      5. density of ties

3. By examining any structure—from our family through our workplace to the entire economy—in terms of these dimensions, it is possible to compare and contrast social structures. Use number 2 as a checklist in describing the social structures in which you participate.

Corporate Units

Corporate units are social structures that reveal a division of labor, with individuals playing distinctive roles by virtue of where they stand in this division of labor. Sometimes the division of labor is only implicit, as when two friends exchange greetings, but it is there nonetheless. In the case of two friends who, say, pass each other and pause to say hello very briefly, each occupies the position of friend and plays out the role of friend in a brief episode of interaction. Corporate units can also reveal a formal division of labor, as when a student plays a particular role in relation to professors and teaching assistants within a university or college. Corporate units are thus created, sometimes very briefly as is the case with a passing encounter with friends, to get something done. A university seeks to educate; a community tries to organize schools, housing, jobs, and transportation; small groups often assemble to get something done, even if only to have a good time; and even an encounter seeks to organize the exchange of pleasantries so that a sense of solidarity is produced. Let me now outline several basic types of corporate units.

Encounters.   An encounter is the most elementary social structure. It involves two or more people taking cognizance of each other and adjusting their behaviors to facilitate communication or, alternatively, to avoid each other. There are two basic types of encounters. A **focused encounter** is a situation where two or several individuals form an ecological huddle, face each other, and engage in direct communication. Each person in the encounter recognizes the status of the other, the appropriate roles, and the relevant norms as they mutually communicate (Goffman 1961). Focused encounters rarely last very long—a few seconds, as when individual pauses to say hello and then moves on their way, to perhaps a few hours when people get carried away with their talk, or when they are required to achieve some task. **Unfocused encounters** are just the opposite of focused encounters because people take cognizance of each other but at the same time try to avoid direct communication (Goffman 1963). When individuals move about in public space, for example, they implicitly monitor the movements of others without actually focusing on them, as would be the case with a stare, and on the basis of an assessment of these movements adjusts role behaviors. It is because of unfocused encounters that people are able to avoid bumping into each other or threatening others. The goal is to avoid face-to-face contact. Unfocused encounters are thus very brief, lasting only so long as people become mutual of the other's presence in space, assign positions to each other, invoke the relevant norms, and play roles so as to avoid focusing on each other. We examine encounters in Chapter 10 as the most elementary social structure, from which all other structures are ultimately constructed.

Groups.   Groups are comparatively small social structures composed of one or a few types of status positions, small numbers of incumbents in these positions, dense ties among some of the positions, and clear cultural expectations about what people are supposed to do. Groups vary in their permanence—from a temporary gathering of friends over lunch to permanent ties among members of a close-knit family. The line between an encounter and group can often be difficult to distinguish when individuals only interact for a short time. Thus, a lunch with a friend is an encounter, but if it is also part of a larger network of friends who see each other often, it shades into a group that periodically assembles. Thus, the more permanent the network of positions connecting individuals, the more likely that this set of relationships will constitute a group. When the group assembles, this face-to-face contact is also an encounter, but it is more because the encounter is repeated over time and part of a more inclusive group structure. Thus, groups are ultimately made up of encounters, but encounters become groups when they are iterated and involve the same individuals occupying particular status positions, playing roles, and attending to a common culture.

Another important consideration is that groups vary in size which, in turn, influences important dimensions of their structure. Sometimes this difference is described in terms of a distinction between *primary* and *secondary* groups. Primary groups are small, close-knit, and intimate, whereas secondary groups are larger and more impersonal (Cooley 1909). The difference between a small seminar class (where personal ties develop among members) and a large lecture class (where personal ties among all its members are impossible) captures the essential differences between primary and secondary groups.

Much of our participation in social structure begins with a position in a group which, in turn, is lodged in a larger structure like an organization. For instance, your classes, friendships on campus, and other group activities at school are embedded in the more inclusive organizational structure of the college or university; and hence, it is your membership in a series of groups that ties you to the larger college structure. Encounters in groups plug us into larger structures, and as a result, they are critical for understanding not only ourselves but the larger society as well. Each time a group assembles, this encounter of individuals locates each person in a position, invokes particular aspects of culture, and structures the enactment of roles. We explore the properties and dynamics of groups in Chapter 11.

Organizations.   Organizations are larger and more formal structures composed of a diversity of status positions, revealing differences in authority and, at the lower levels, evidencing larger numbers of incumbents in each position (Weber 1922). Organizations are assembled to get something done—making money, educating students, winning a war, producing a good or service, and so on—and they tend to develop distinctive cultural systems revolving around their goals and structure. We usually think of organizations as "bureaucratic" structures, although it is best to conceptualize them more generally as *complex organizations* because of the unsavory connotations of the term "bureaucrat" and because organizations evidence considerable diversity in their structure. Complex organizations are, as we will come to see in Chapter 12, the principle integrative structure of modern complex societies because they connect people in groups to the broader forces in society.

Communities.   People reside and move about in physical place; when there is organization to this place—roads, schools, churches, government, work place, and other structures—it can be termed a **community**. Communities are thus social structures organizing people's residence as well as their activities in physical or geographical space (Hawley 1981). As is perhaps obvious, but nonetheless fundamental, communities can vary in size, from the small rural town to a giant megalopolis. And hence, our goal in Chapter 13 is to understand how the size of communities has changed how we all live.

Categoric Structures

Humans classify each other in terms of distinguishable characteristics and, then, respond to each other differently. When placed into a social category, a person is assigned a position that carries a cultural evaluation and set of normative expectations for how individuals in a category are to play roles. The only universal categories are sex and age, which means that all human populations that have ever existed have categorized people on the basis of their sex and age and, as a result of these distinctions, respond to them differently and expect certain kinds of role behaviors. For example, we evaluate and expect different role behaviors from males and females as well as babies, young people, old people, and middle-age persons; on the basis of these varying expectations, people placed in a category behave in similar ways, thereby reinforcing assumptions about the characteristics of people in a category. **Categoric units**, therefore, are created and sustained by virtue of differential treatment of those who reveal identifiable characteristics (Hawley 1986).

As populations grow and as societies become more complex, many additional kinds of categoric units are created: ethnic categories, social class distinctions, religious categories, occupational categories, regional distinctions, and educational differences. Among the most important of these additional categories are ethnicity and social class because members of such categories usually receive varying shares of valued resources (e. g., money, power, prestige, health, opportunities) as a result of differential treatment; as conflict theories would emphasize, categories often become a source of intense conflict in society. Because these categoric structures are so important to understanding society, especially its tensions and conflicts, they are sometimes viewed as a distinctive kind of structure, a **stratification system**.

Stratification Systems

When the valued resources of a society are distributed unequally and when, as a result, people can be categorized by virtue of their shares of resources and come to define themselves as distinctive, a stratification system exists in a society (J. Turner 1984a). There are many bases for stratifying categories of people: sex, age, income, ethnicity, and religion. All that is essential for stratification is that members of a category get a distinctive share of some valued resource. For example, if dark skin color is used as a basis for economic, political, and educational discrimination, then the low shares of money, power, and prestige among those who have dark skin will become codified into a system of ethnic stratification. Or, if sex is used for differential treatment of men and women with the result that men have better jobs, more income, more prestige, and more power than women, then a system of sexual stratification exists. Or, to illustrate further, if there is a correlation among people's incomes, education, and jobs and if individuals become distinctive by virtue of this fact, then class stratification exists (say, among poor, blue-collar workers, low-income white-collar, high-income-educated white-collar, and rich individuals). In Chapters 14, 15, and 16, the stratification structures emerging from categoric distinctions will be examined; as we will discover, these kinds of categoric units are among the most volatile in any society because they are created and sustained to give some people more of what is valued in a society. Rarely do those on the short end of the stick take their plight lying down.

Institutional Systems

Groups and, at times, organizations are organized to meet basic contingencies of biological and social life. For example, to survive biologically, humans must eat and reproduce, and so there will be social structures—the economy and kinship systems, respectively—designed to assure that this is so. Or, to remain effectively organized, especially as the size of a population grows, it will be necessary to develop political structures to regulate and control the larger population. Those structures that are created to solve basic human and organizational problems are termed **institutions** (J. Turner 1972, 1997, 2003); as the problems of organization for a population increase, so do basic institutional structures. For example, in very simple societies, only a few basic institutions are evident—family, economy, and religion—but as the scale of society increases, additional institutions— government, law, education, science, sports, and medicine—become elaborated to deal with new human needs and organizational problems.

Social institutions are ultimately built from the ground up by encounters, groups, organizations, communities, and categoric units. For example, an industrial economy is built from complex organizations engaged in the production and distribution of goods and services, as well as the categoric distinctions (worker, manager, entrepreneur) that are often made for people engaged in economic activity. Organizations are composed of groups that, in turn, are built from encounters. Thus, from the micro to the more macro institutional level of social organization, we can say: Groups are composed of encounters iterated over time; organizations and categoric units are built from encounters and groups as they sustain the division of labor in the organization and as they reinforce categoric distinctions among individuals; and institutions are constructed from organizational and categoric units, while being located within communities.

Societies

When a population with distinctive systems of cultural symbols is organized within a clear territory by political institutions, we can call it a **society**. Societal structures can be very simple and small, consisting of only a handful of people. However, as larger societies have gobbled up, destroyed, or displaced smaller ones, societal structures increasingly embrace larger populations, although larger societies can disintegrate into a series of smaller ones (as was the case over the last decades with the breakup of the Soviet Union, Czechoslovakia, and Yugoslavia).

In the course of human history there have been just a few basic types of societies (Lenski 1966; Lenski, Lenski and Nolan 1991; J. Turner 1972, 2003; Maryanski and Turner 1992). *Hunting and gathering societies* organized virtually all of human activity until just a few thousand years ago. These societies were composed of small, wandering bands of 30 to 80 people, organized by their families and making only basic distinctions between sex and age categories. There was little inequality; men hunted but in reality sat around a great deal; women gathered indigenous plants and prepared food; and no one worked very hard, perhaps 15 hours a week. Conflict was rare, and if a dispute could not be resolved, the band split up and moved on. As a species, our natural tendency is *not* to work very hard, or to be locked into highly constraining structures (Maryanski and Turner 1992). Therefore, we can see how far our current lives are from the societal form in which our biological propensities were forged. Then, about 18,000 to 15,000 years ago, people began to settle down and a new form of existence for humans emerged. *Horticulturalists* were the second type of society to emerge. Here, people lived in small villages composed of groups that included numerous kin related by blood and marriage and linked together by political ties and authority. These kin groups, under the direction of a headman, cultivated gardens with women performing much of the dull work. Men helped at times, but they became involved in a new pastime: war. Horticulturalists were often in conflict with their neighbors, and a new chapter in human history was born. *Agrarian societies* were the third basic type, and they were built by the use of nonhuman power—animals, wind, and water—to cultivate much larger tracts of land that, in turn, created enough surplus to build roads and cities, while sustaining great inequalities between the nobility and peasants. With agrarianism the scale of society shifted; societies became bigger, more complex, more oriented to distant conquest, more unequal, more urban, and more politically centralized. Then, a few hundred years ago, the *industrial society* emerged based upon the use of fossil fuels for energy. New social constructions developed—factories, huge bureaucracies, large urban centers, open markets, political democracy, complex infrastructures for transportation and communication, mass education, and all the basic structures with which you are familiar. You and I now live in yet another societal type—the *post-industrial*—where most people work in nonmanual jobs for the first time in history and where new modes of transportation and communication reduce physical distances among people in even the largest society, and for that matter, in all the world. (For a more detailed review of societal types, see the timeline at the beginning of this book.)

Yet, no matter how grand societies become, they are ultimately composed of all those positions ordered into all those types of social structures discussed earlier and all those types of cultural systems examined in Chapter 5. Most sociological analysis examines culture and structure within a particular society, but increasingly there is concern with intersocietal structures for the simple reason that contact and communication among societies have increased dramatically.

Inter-Societal Systems

Trade, migration, political and economic coalitions, and warfare have typified relations of societies in the past and today (Chase-Dunn and Hall 1997). As politically organized populations have bumped into each other, it has become necessary to form some kind of relation, or **inter-societal** system. War has been a most typical response; trade and exchange have been another; political and economic alliances in the face of a threat have been yet another kind of response; and migration from one society to another has frequently forced societies to form some kind of relation.

If we ponder some of today's big issues for Americans—the aftermath of the collapse of the Soviet empire, the increasing formation of a common European community, the patterns of trade with the Japanese and other societies, the prospects of war, the immigration of foreigners (legally and illegally), the effects of globalization, and a world filled with terrorism—the importance of unraveling the complex web of intersocietal connections becomes clear. For what goes on *within* a society is greatly influenced by what transpires between them. For example, who would deny that events in Israel, Iraq, Iran, Afghanistan, and elsewhere in the world do not affect the internal structure and dynamics of American society. Indeed, we now operate in a world system, composed of trade and political networks as well as intense conflicts that influence most aspects of our daily lives (Wallerstein 1974).

Levels of Social Structure

One way to visualize social structure is in terms of whether the structure is micro, meso, or macro, as is illustrated in Figure 6.3. This three-part distinction is only approximate, but it gives us a sense for how large and encompassing a structure is. At the macro or "big" level of social reality, we have intersocietal systems, societies, institutional systems, and stratification systems. These are macro because they cut across a whole society and often beyond its borders. For example, when a society is part of an intersocietal system, it reaches outside its borders to other societies. Moreover, macro structures within a society often reach out beyond a society's borders. For example, a multinational corporation is part of the institution of the economy within a society, but it is also part of a world economy. Similarly, Christianity or Islam is part of the institution of religion in many societies, but they are also world religions that cut across societies. The military of one society such as the United States extends far beyond its borders into various alliances such as NATO and patterns of conquest like the recent war in Iraq. Even stratification systems reach beyond their borders, as is the case when the poor of one country migrate (legally or illegally) to another society, thereby changing the demographic composition of the new society, its system of stratification, and perhaps several of its institutional systems such as economy, education, and religion.

At the meso or "middle" level are corporate units and categoric units. These units are meso because they stand between micro- and macro-level units. They are built from micro units, and in turn, they are the units from which institutional and stratification systems are ultimately constructed. Corporate units reveal a division of labor that directs the activities of individuals, whereas categoric units mark important distinctions that make a difference in how people treat each other. Corporate units at the meso level include communities and organizations. Meso-level categoric units revolve around sex and gender, age, ethnicity, race, and various categoric distinctions that emerge from the division of labor in corporate units (as is the case when the position of

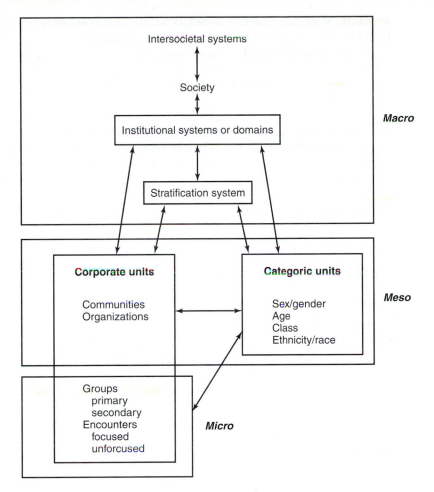

Figure 6.3 Levels and Types of Social Structures   The bold boxes give a rough outline of what is considered macro, meso, or micro levels of social reality. Within these boxes are various kinds of social structures that sociologists study. Corporate units reveal a division of labor and internal organization, if only fleeting as is the case with many encounters. Some corporate structures are micro because they are dominated by person-to-person interaction, whereas others are more meso because they are built from groups and encounters into larger social structures. Categoric units are social categories that make a difference in how people respond to each other. Any basis of difference can become a categoric unit, with the most common being age, sex and gender, social class, ethnicity, and race, although other categoric distinctions come from people's membership in corporate units (student, worker, mother, father, and other points in the division of labor that become transformed into categoric distinctions). Categoric units are often the basis for a stratification system in which valued resources are unequally distributed to various social categories. Stratification systems tend to be macro phenomena because they cut across an entire society. Corporate units are often part of the system of stratification because they are the arena in which people discriminate against members of categoric units and deny them access to valued resources. In addition to stratification systems at the macro level of social organization are the institutional systems—economy, family, religion, law, polity, medicine, sports, education—that are built from corporate and categoric units and that have effects on stratifying members of categoric units. A society is composed of its institutional and stratification systems at the macro level as well as its corporate units at both the meso and macro levels and and its meso-level categoric units.

student, worker, mayor, politician, mother, father, and other status positions within communities and organizations).

At the micro level, where people come face-to-face and respond to each other in episodes of interaction, there are two basic types of corporate units: encounters and groups. These are where people directly respond to each other; and ultimately, all other corporate units—organizations and communities—and all categoric distinctions—age, gender, class, ethnic—are built from episodes of interaction in encounters and groups. Thus, the meso-level structures are constructed from encounters and group dynamics, whereas the macro-level structures of the social universe are built from corporate and categoric units.

The Power of Social Structure

Each of us is but a cog in a vast web of structural forms. True, we have big brains and can be creative, but our daily lives are highly circumscribed by structure, as well as by the cultural symbols associated with structures. One way to visualize the power of social structure, and the culture that attends social structure, is as a process of successive embedding of smaller structures inside of larger structures. Figure 6.4 seeks to give you an image of how social structures impose restrictions on each individual person. Let us start at the top of the figure, with systems of intersocietal relations. Societies are embedded in such systems, and by virtue of this embedding, the structure and culture of an entire society are, to some degree, influenced by what transpires in this system of intersocietal relations. Culture is also influenced by this system because the values, beliefs, technologies, and other elements of culture will be shaped by what occurs in the world system.

Next, let us move to society as a whole. A society is composed of institutions—economy, kinship, polity or government, religion, medicine, sports, law, education, and the like. Each institutional domain translates societal values, beliefs, ideologies, and technologies into sets of institu-

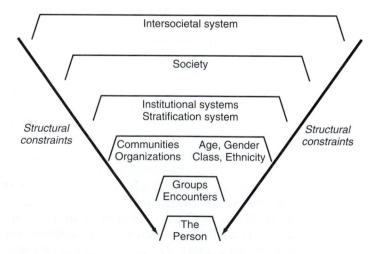

Figure 6.4   The Embeddedness of Social Structures

tional norms that regulate conduct in an institutional sphere. Thus, the beliefs, values, and norms of the kinship system are different than those of the economy or education. Each institution is built from organizations and communities. Organizations tend to specialize in a particular institutional domain—a company for the economy, a school for education, a clinic for medicine, a court for law, an agency for government, a team for sports, and so on—for all the organizations from which an institution is ultimately constructed. Organizations have to be located in physical space, and so institutions are also built from the communities in which their constituent organizations are located. Institutions are also built from categoric units. Sometimes these categoric units follow from distinctions in the division of labor of complex organizations, as is the case when student (schools), doctor (medicine), worker (economy), mother (family), jock (sports), and the like are at one and the same time a position and role in an organization as well as a categoric unit that defines a person and imposes broader expectations on them, above and beyond the norms of an organization. Thus, students are not only expected to behave in certain ways in schools, but there are more general evaluations and expectations for one categorized as a student in the broader society. Organizations and categoric units are constructed, respectively, from the groups that organize activity within a complex organization and that reinforce categoric distinctions. And finally, groups are constructed from encounters of face-to-face conduct.

This embedding of social structures (i.e., structures inside of ever larger structures culminating in the world system) can be looked at another way. Encounters are often embedded in a group, and almost always in a categoric unit. When two females meet in an encounter, for example, its dynamics will be different than when a male and female meet, which tells us that when an encounter is embedded inside different categoric distinctions, its dynamics will vary. At first, it may be hard to visualize an encounter as being embedded in gender, age, class, ethnic, and other social categories, but a moment's reflection tells you that all encounters are so embedded. What happens in the encounter will change depending upon which categories of individuals are present. Like encounters, groups are also always embedded in categoric units; depending upon age, ethnicity, gender, social class, and other categoric distinctions, what happens in the group will vary. Most groups are, in turn, embedded in complex organizations with a division of labor and distinctive culture. Complex organizations are, in turn, embedded in communities; organizations, communities, and categoric units are embedded inside of institutional spheres with their own culture and norms; and institutions are embedded inside a society that is often part of an intersocietal system.

This layering of social structure gives it power. Imagine yourself in an encounter. Most encounters are lodged, successively, inside a group that is inside of a complex organization and set of categoric units that are inside of a community that is inside of an institutional system that is part of a whole society that is often a link to a system of societies. The culture and structure of each of these more inclusive structures impose constraints upon the encounter. Take an encounter at the university or college that you attend. This encounter occurs within a world system that influences the level of resources that are available to your school as well as the composition of the student body if you have international students. The school is part of the institution of education that has its own distinctive culture as it translates societal values and uses other culture elements, such as knowledge and technology, to organize the division of labor. The college is located in a particular community with its own structure, which may impinge on the encounter. The encounter may be embedded inside of several categoric units (e.g., foreign students, gender, class, and age). And the encounter may be part of a more stable group, such as a network of friends who meet for lunch. Each of these layers of structure and culture imposes itself on the encounter. The most immediate structure has the most effect, say the group that encourages encounters among certain individuals. Next in influence is the organization in which the group is embedded—in this case the university or college—and various categoric units (class, student, ethnicity, gender). Next in influence is the institutional system—education—in which the categoric units and organization are embedded. Then, the broader society structure and its culture, and finally the world system. You as an individual are at the bottom of this hierarchy of structures. You are part of the encounter that, as we see in Chapter 10, has its own dynamics that constrain what you can do, and this encounter is part of a whole complex of layered structures and their cultures.

Of course, we rarely feel oppressed by the weight of so much structure and culture, but even if we cannot see the complex webs of connections among these embedded structures, they are like the walls of a house. As long as you move down the hallway and through doors, you hardly notice the existence of the structure, but when you bump into a wall, the power of the social structures is all too evident. For example, let us say that you are from the working class (your parents are blue collar) and that you are an ethnic minority. Almost every encounter you have will be embedded in your class position and ethnicity. Let us say that you are a male, making an encounter embedded in at least three categoric distinctions (gender, class, ethnicity), to say nothing of the social categories that distinguish other participants in an encounter. You are trying to do well in school, which means that your motivations are probably the result of general cultural values of American society about achievement and about the importance of trying to move up the organizational and stratification ladders. You have chosen to go to college, and so, the culture of this system and its structure has you working and studying hard as you try to meet expectations of professors in classes and get good grades. And you have various friendship groups—say, you are also an athlete and have close friends on a team. All these structures and the culture associated with each exert power over you.

Social structure and culture thus have power over us; they force us to do what they want. For example, right now, you are reading these words because you are part of a class in a college or university system that, to be blunt, has you doing what it wants. I am sure that most of you would prefer to be elsewhere, but you persist, because there is a power beyond your control, a system of relations dictating your actions. So it is in social life, from the day each of us was born until the moment of our death. Our life is a constant and incessant movement in social structures—family, friends, schools, work organizations, communities, and other social aggregations. What we are as individuals is the product of these structural affiliations. Indeed, all of social life is a web of interconnected social structures in which we are at times merely cogs or pawns.

True, we can choose to move in or out of many structures. We can often choose which ones are to be our oppressors or our taskmasters. But unless we can find a vacant mountaintop for social contemplation and tolerate the loneliness of it all, we must be involved in social structures. Each type of structure has its own dynamics and the goal of sociology is to understand these dynamics.

To some extent, the field of sociology is organized around basic types of social structures. Individual sociologists tend to concentrate on a particular type of structure. We can view the social world as organized around encounters, groups, organizations, communities, social categories (social classes as well as sexual, age, ethnic, and racial categories), various social institutions (economic, political, kinship, educational, and religious), and societal and intersocietal systems. Because the world is organized in this way, so is the discipline of sociology that studies this world. For all of us, most of our waking hours are spent embedded within these basic social structures; because of this fact, social structure has great power to influence our thoughts, perceptions, emotions, actions, and interactions. And, it is this power of social structure on our lives that makes sociology an important discipline.

Box 6.2: What is the Difference Between Sociology and Psychology?

We often prefer to think about our world in psychological terms—feelings, moods, motivations, and the like. From a sociological perspective these psychological states reflect our experiences in social structures. This point of emphasis is what distinguishes sociology from psychology. Psychology is primarily concerned with personality, cognition, behavior, and other dimensions of the person, per se, whereas sociology is devoted to the study of culture and social structures as these influence interaction, behavior, and personality. The two fields meet, and indeed often clash, in the area of *social psychology*, but even here where the subject matter overlaps, large differences are evident. A psychologist will emphasize the effects of social situations on the operation of basic psychological processes—perceptions, cognitions, emotions, and the like—whereas a sociologist will stress how culture and social structure constrain behavior and the interaction of individuals in social contexts and, then, how these constrained behaviors and interactions sustain or change culture and social structure. Thus, psychology will tend to focus on the properties and dynamics of the person; sociology will concentrate on the properties and dynamics of the person, behavior, interaction, social structure, and culture as these mutually influence each other.

SUMMARY

1. Virtually every aspect of our being—thoughts, perceptions, feelings, and behavior—is influenced by participation in social structures.

2. Social structures are constructed of status positions, roles, and networks of positions. Each person reveals a status-set, perhaps a master status, and for each status position occupied, a role-set. Role-strain and role-conflict often ensue because of too many role obligations in a single position or conflict between obligations in different positions.

3. The networks of positions that comprise social structures vary in terms of basic dimensions: number of positions, number of people in each position, and nature of connections among positions. These connections can be loose or dense, involve power or hierarchy, transmit varying resources, and exist for varying lengths of time.

4. Basic social structures organizing human populations include: (a) encounters or episodes of personal contact; (b) groups composed of relatively small networks of people in face-to-face contact; (c) organizations pulling together larger numbers of individuals and groups in hierarchies of authority; (d) communities ordering individuals, groups, and organizations in geographical space; (e) institutional structures composed of complexes of groups and organizations devoted to resolving basic contingencies of human existence and social organization; (f) categoric structures in which identifiable characteristics of people become the basis for differential treatment; (g) stratification structures in which categories of people receive different shares of valued resources; (h) societal systems organizing (a) through (g) in space and territory; and (i) intersocietal structures connecting societal systems together.

5. Social structures can be visualized as operating at different levels of reality, with intersocietal systems, societies as a whole, institutional systems, and stratification systems constituting a macro level of reality, with corporate units (organizations and community) and categoric units (class, age, gender, ethnicity) a meso level of reality, and with groups and encounters a micro realm.

6. Because each person is embedded in a matrix of social structures—from groups to intersocietal systems—human thoughts, perceptions, feelings, actions, and interactions are highly constrained.

KEY TERMS

Community: Social structures organizing residence and activities of people in physical space.

Encounters, Focused: Episodes of face-to-face interaction revolving around an ecological huddle, eye-to-eye contact, focused talk, and solidarity.

Encounters, Unfocused: Episodes of mutual monitoring of people's movements without focusing attention on each other.

Group: Small social structures composed of only a few different status positions, small numbers of incumbents, relatively dense ties among positions, and clear cultural expectations about role behaviors.

Institutions: Society-wide structures that organize groups, organizations, social categories, and communities to resolve problems.

Inter-societal Systems: Processes that create relations among societies, including trade, war, migrations, and political or economic coalitions.

Networks (of Status Positions): Ties and connections that link status positions together, thereby forming a social structure.

Organizations: Goal-directed social structures revealing a division of labor and hierarchies of positions linked together by authority and clear norms.

Role: The behavior of individuals in status positions, as they take account of each other, norms, and other cultural symbols.

Role-Conflict: A situation where the roles associated with different status positions are incompatible, placing the individual trying to play the roles of these different positions in a situation of conflict.

Role-Set: The expected array of behaviors for a given status position.

Role-Strain: A situation where there are either too many or contradictory expectations in the role-set of a status position, thereby creating tension and strain for individuals trying to meet all expectations.

Social Categories, Categoric Units: Structures that are created when cohorts and types of individuals are defined and treated differently on the basis of their perceived attributes and characteristics.

Society: Structures encompassing all other structures (groups, organizations, institutions, categories, and stratification) that organize a population and provide political regulation for these structures in geographical space and in relation to other societies.

Status Position: The location of an individual within a network of positions; the basic element of all social structures.

Status-Set: The complex or array of positions that an individual person occupies.

Stratification System: Structures revolving around (a) the unequal distribution of valued resources to the members of a society and (b) the distinctive categories thereby created by virtue of the shares of resources held by different subpopulations in a society.

Chapter 7

Social Interaction

Shakespeare once wrote "all the world's a stage, and all men and women merely players: they have their exits and their entrances; and one man in his time plays many parts." Much of human life is indeed performed on a stage, but in contrast to theatrical life, our stage is set by cultural symbols and social structure. We play roles on a stage in front of an audience of those who are immediately present and those whom we can imagine. And, just as actors try to impress their audience and receive applause in return for their performance, so individuals in society seek to cultivate an audience and receive its approval. Ultimately, human societies are created and sustained by individuals engaged in mutual dramatic performances; for without interaction, social structures and culture have no life. Interaction is thus a fundamental element of human social organization.

Symbolic Interaction

At the beginning of this century social scientists did not understand the key dynamics of human interaction. All could agree that interaction among people is the fundamental process underlying the social world, but how did it operate? What were the specific mechanisms and processes involved? A University of Chicago philosopher, George Herbert Mead (1934), unlocked the mystery of this process, as noted in Chapter 1. Mead did not have a blazing insight, but rather, he took bits and pieces from the works of others and combined them in ways that made sense.

The essence of **interaction**, Mead argued, is the emission of signs and gestures. Any organism must act within its environment, and as it does so, it emits signs or gestures that mark its course of action. *Inter*action occurs, Mead felt, when (a) one organism emits signs as it moves through its environment; (b) another organism sees these signs and alters its course of action in response to them, thereby emitting signs of its own; and (c) the original organism becomes aware of the signs of this responding organism and alters its course of action in light of these signs. Let us imagine a cat and dog. The dog is looking for a post to relieve itself (emitting the appropriate signs); a lounging cat observes the dog moving toward it and panics, running away (its gestures); the dog sees the cat and readjusts its course of action, forgetting about its bladder and instead giving chase.

When these three stages have passed, interaction has occurred. Note that signs or gestures are the critical vehicle of interaction and note also that these signs do not need to be symbolic in the cultural sense. That is, the cat may not be able to read or interpret the dog's gestures, nor does the dog necessarily understand the panic of the cat. But "their conversation of gestures," as Mead put it, is nonetheless interaction.

Mead also thought that humans interact in a unique and special way, however. The signs that humans send, read, receive, and respond to are symbolic in that they mean the same thing to the sending and to the receiving organisms. In a word, they are cultural. The words on this page mean more or less the same thing to both of us; as a result, interaction is special because it is mediated by signs that are given cultural definition. Indeed, with our large brains, we can attach common, agreed upon meanings to virtually all our movements—talk, facial gestures, bodily stance, spacing relative to others, clothing, hair style, or almost any sign or gesture that we make. This is why we feel "on stage" when in front of others, for we implicitly know that others are reading *all* of our gestures and interpreting our performance. And although some animals can also interact symbolically, they cannot do so to the degree of humans (Aitchison 1978; Maryanski and Turner 1992; Seboek 1968).

Mead observed that the ability to read symbolic gestures allows humans to **role-take** or *take the role of the other.* What he meant is that by reading the gestures of others, we can imagine ourselves in their place; we can take their perspective and sense what they are likely to do. Thus, if someone comes up to you glaring, fists clenched, and calling you obscene names, you can imagine yourself in his or her position and adjust your responses accordingly. All of us role-take in every situation, but we are usually not that conscious of this process, until we find ourselves in an awkward situation where we literally hang on every word and gesture emitted by others. Imagine a first date with someone, or going to a party where you do not know anyone, or entering a school or dorm for the first time, or any number of new situations where you only have broad institutional norms to guide you. You cope—that is to say, you learn the more situationally specific norms—by role-taking or seeing others' perspectives and using what you see to guide your responses. This is *symbolic interaction* and it is the means by which we plug ourselves into culture and its values, beliefs, and norms. Conversely, by being aware of cultural symbols, we can role-take and thus get along with others in various positions of a specific social structure. As a functional theorist might argue, the function of role-taking is to connect people to each other and the broader culture, thereby facilitating their cooperation and, ultimately, the integration of society. And so, if we were unable to use cultural symbols and role-take, interaction would be very awkward indeed, and society would collapse.

Mead also emphasized other processes involved in human interaction. One is the process that he termed **mind.** For Mead, mind is not a thing or entity, but a series of processes. For Mead, mind is the covert and behind-the-scenes process of first anticipating the consequences of various possible courses of action and then, on the basis of this assessment, choosing or selecting a particular action. Mead characterized mind as the process of "imaginative rehearsal" in that, like any good actor who must go on stage, we rehearse our act in different ways and assess our audience's reaction to these alternatives. Such mind processes are an intimate part of human interaction, for as we role-take with others, we assume their perspective, and as we become aware of relevant beliefs and norms, these become a part of our mental deliberations. We then imagine how others will respond to us, and we deliberate on whether or not we are doing the proper thing in terms of cultural codes. A utilitarian theorist would add something to Mead's portrayal: We calculate our costs and benefits as we imaginatively rehearse alternatives, trying to choose that option that would give us the greatest payoff.

Because we are so facile at this process, we are often unaware of its operation. But think again about a situation where you felt awkward or unsure. Remember how you rehearsed your lines and anticipated what the reaction of others would be. Naturally, one cannot be this attuned all of the time; that would be too exhausting. But all of us are always involved in reading gestures, role-taking, and covertly (in our minds, as it were) imagining outcomes of alternative responses. For if people could not engage in these processes, interaction would not be flexible, and it could not involve more than just a couple of people.

Yet another crucial process involved in interaction is what Mead labeled self. Each of us sees *ourself* as an object in each situation, just as we see other objects like other people, cars, chairs, or houses. When we communicate with someone, we read gestures and, by doing so, get an image of ourselves from the perspective of others. Thus, the gestures of others become what Charles Horton Cooley (1909), a contemporary of George Herbert Mead, termed a *looking glass* or mirror in which we see ourselves reflected. We are all, in a sense, implicitly saying "mirror, mirror on the wall," except our mirror is not on the wall but in the gestures of others. In each situation we get an image of ourselves, but we also bring to a situation a more stable and enduring conception of ourselves or self-conception as a certain type of object or person. Each of us has a self-conception, seeking to interpret the gestures of others so that they are consistent with this conception and adjusting our behaviors so as not to violate this conception. Thus, our actions in most situations reveal a consistency as we seek to sustain our conception of ourselves as a certain kind of person. We come to behave in predictable ways, and because of our consistency, others are able to coordinate their responses to us. In the same manner, we adjust our responses to others who display a typical interpersonal style.

When you say things like "Sorry, I'm not acting myself today," you are acknowledging that others will not see you in the usual way because you acted contrary to your self-conception. Or, when you say "I can't figure out where he's coming from," you are really saying two things: your role-taking has been ineffective, and you cannot see consistency, as dictated by his self-conception, in his responses. Hence, you are uncertain as to how to respond.

Thus, George Herbert Mead viewed interaction as a process of sending and receiving gestures, and in the case of humans, sending culturally defined symbols that carry common meanings. These gestures are used to role-take and to become aware of others' expectations and their possible lines of conduct. With the cognitive abilities provided by "mind," we can rehearse alternatives, imagine their impact, inhibit inappropriate responses, and select a mode of conduct that will facilitate interaction (or, from a utilitarian perspective, maximize utilities or rewards). Furthermore, we can see ourselves as objects in situations and bring to all interactions a stable self-conception that gives us a compass for guiding our responses in typical and consistent ways. Such is the nature of "symbolic interaction" as viewed by Mead, and his views on this most fundamental process represent the starting point for further inquiry.

Dramatic Presentation of Self

Because we are all actors on a stage, we are performers who orchestrate our emissions of gestures to present ourselves in a certain light—as a certain kind of person, and as an individual who deserves certain responses from others. Some of us are, of course, better actors than others. But all of us are performers who manipulate the emission of gestures. This view of interaction is known as *dramaturgy,* a term made popular by the late sociologist Erving Goffman (1959, 1967).

Goffman utilized our analogy of the theater and the stage by distinguishing between frontstage and backstage regions of interaction (Goffman 1959). On the formal **frontstage,** people consciously manipulate and orchestrate gestures in ways to elicit desired responses from others—responses that uphold their self-conception and that conform to the normative demands of the situation. In the **backstage** area, people relax a bit and lower their respective fronts. Backstage allows some privacy with companions who share their knowledge of the rigors of going onstage. For Goffman, much interaction involves moving back and forth between backstage and frontstage areas. If you doubt that such is the case, examine your own daily routines. You are backstage when you are getting ready to go to school, with showers, toothbrushes, hair dryers, curlers, make-up, deodorants, and hair sprays. You are frontstage when you are sitting in class, lounging in the student union, or flirting at a dance. We are more relaxed and less self aware in the backstage and more aware and conscious of what we say and do on the frontstage.

Without the backstage, life would be unduly stressful. And yet, without the frontstage, social order would be problematic. As a functionalist would argue, society requires that things get done and actions be coordinated; this fact, in turn, demands that humans perform and conform. We go by the rules, we say the right thing, and we carry ourselves in the appropriate way. If people refused to do so, social reality would be cluttered and chaotic.

Another aspect of dramaturgy is what Goffman (1959) termed **impression-management,** where we orchestrate gestures to present a front. We do so to present a particular self to our audience and receive certain kinds of responses. And so, as we move to the frontstage, we begin to manage our gestures. Such management gives each person's behavior a consistency and facilitates the alignment of behaviors, while contributing to the general order of society. Of course, as Goffman emphasized, fronts can be both deceptive and manipulative, as when a "con-man" presents a front that masks his true intentions to steal. All of us do so at times, hopefully to a lesser degree, but we still find ourselves presenting a front that is not quite genuine.

Implicit Use of Folk Methods

Dividing the world into stages and following cultural scripts are not enough to sustain a sense of order during interaction. We have all met someone who seemingly does everything in just the right way, and yet, we feel uneasy. Something is missing—we are not quite sure what it is—but something is wrong in how this person talks, gestures, and acts. One possible reason for this sense of uneasiness is the failure or inability of this individual to utilize certain tacit and yet crucial techniques of interaction. When these techniques are not used, our sense of continuity and orderliness in interaction is disrupted (Handel 1982; Mehan & Wood 1975). Thus, interaction depends on some additional processes that the sociologist Harold Garfinkel (1967) labeled **ethnomethods**, or simply "**folk methods**." As we interact with others, we use a variety of interpersonal methods or techniques to create and sustain a *sense* of orderliness and to provide continuity to interaction. These folk methods are so unconsciously employed that we only become aware of them when someone does not use them or uses them incorrectly.

Using one of Garfinkel's (1967) examples, try to imagine your response if you were the subject of this interaction:

> *Subject:* "I had a flat tire."
> *Experimenter:* "What do you mean, you had a flat tire?"
> *Subject:* "What do you mean 'what do you mean'? A flat tire is a flat tire. That is what I meant. Nothing special. What a crazy question!"

Obviously, this interaction is losing its continuity and sense of order, but why? The reason is that the experimenter has violated an implicit and agreed upon technique in all interactions: the tacit rule that "we don't question the obvious and the presumption (not to be challenged) that we share certain life experiences." Ethnomethodologists (those who study such folk methods) have termed this particular method the *et cetera principle* because we communicate with our gestures the implicit command not to question certain things. Let me now reconstruct for you a conversation I had with a student (again, imagine yourself in this interaction).

> *Student:* "I'm having trouble with this material, you know."
> *Me:* "No, I don't know."
> *Student:* "The material is so, so abstract, you know?"
> *Me:* "No, I don't know."
> *Student:* "Well, I . . . I'll come back some other time."

People frequently use the phrase "you know" in conversations. When that little phrase is used, the *et cetera principle* is being invoked. The speaker is, in essence, asserting that we are to accept his or her pronouncement, even if we "don't know" what is meant. By nodding or by saying "yeah, I know," we create a sense that the two people share the same world and that the world is orderly.

Another kind of implicit method revolves around "turn-taking" in conversations. Ethnomethodologists have studied this process in detail, but let me give you a sense for some of their findings. When one person talks, there are gestures—clearance cues—telling others that they can now talk. People can lower their voice, nod their head, look at you directly, and employ other gestures to allow others to jump in. Similarly, there are vocalizations, such as the "ah" "ah" filler, when a person appears lost for words, that tell others that the speaker has not yielded the conversational floor. These methods of turn-taking are critical to keeping a conversation in rhythm; when they are not used or responded to, a conversation becomes out-of-sync and the implicit sense of order necessary for people to interact comfortably becomes problematic.

Thus, there are some implicit folk methods that people use to create a *sense* of order. When not used or when others fail to respond in the proper manner, reality itself seems more ephemeral.

Interaction in Roles

A role is simply a configuration of behaviors (gestures) that people emit and that others accept as signifying a particular kind and course of action. As we saw in Chapter 6, many roles are dictated by norms and by our position in a social structure (Parsons 1951). For example, as you play the role of student (dressing a certain way, talking in a particular manner, taking notes, attending lectures, etc.), your configuration of behaviors reveals a consistency and style that almost everyone can recognize as "just a student." This distinctive role is, in large part, dictated by cultural norms and location in a college or university structure.

Cultural codes and one's position in a social structure are at best only general frameworks (R. Turner 1962). There is always a lot of room in which to maneuver; it is always possible to present oneself in a particular way (as student-jock, student-beauty queen, student-sorority member, student-fraternity member, student-intellectual, student-crazy, student-party animal). This is what Goffman termed impression-management.

Box 7.1: Conducting a Breaching Experiment

One way to discover the subtle universe of folk methods is to conduct your own breaching experiment. These are very easy to execute because each and every face-to-face interaction involves the use of "folk methods." Here are a few suggestions: The next time someone uses the phrase "you know," tell them that you don't know, or take the most obvious statement a person makes ("I'm late for class") and ask them what they mean ("what do you mean, late?"), or best of all stand impassively as someone talks to you and do not utter a sound and try not to gesture with your face or body. If you follow any of these suggestions, an interaction will probably crumble before your eyes.

Act like a guest in your parents' house. Ask if you can use the bathroom, seek permission to grab something to eat, ask if it is okay for you to go to bed, and so on as if you were a guest. Your parents will wonder "what's wrong" and attempt to reconstruct a common sense of order.

Part of this impression-management involves orchestrating gestures to assert *what* role we are going to play. Indeed, others are waiting to read our gestures to discover this role. As part of our stocks of knowledge (Schutz 1932), all of us carry within ourselves generalized conceptions of various roles—that of student, mother, father, lover, worker, beauty queen, stud, jock, grind, comic, flirt, teacher, jerk, nerd, friend, acquaintance, and so on. For each role we probably have many conceptions about the behaviors appropriate to the role. Interaction is greatly facilitated by the ability to store inventories of roles in our memory and then draw upon this inventory to establish the exact role that another is playing. For, once we have established someone's role, we can anticipate, at least to a degree, how that person will respond to us. Life is much less stressful when we are able to place someone into a role, for we can then take up the reciprocal role and, in a sense, go on "automatic pilot." It is when we do not know the role of an individual that we have to work at the interaction. We have to read gestures more actively, role-take more cautiously, gaze into the "looking-glass self" more carefully, remain more mentally alert, and do a host of rather tiring mental exercises. Life is so much easier when others orchestrate their gestures to tell you *what* role they are playing.

Interaction with Reference Groups

Henry David Thoreau implicitly captured an important dynamic of human interaction when he wrote "if a man does not keep pace with his companions perhaps it is because he hears a different drummer. Let him step to the music he hears, however measured or far away." In all interactions, we deal not only with those immediately present, but with many "distant drummers." We can simultaneously interact with immediate others and with others not present. This process is sometimes obvious with young children who, as they play together, invoke their parents ("well, my dad says . . ."; "what's your mother gonna think about that?"). All of us also interact with important others who are not present—a spouse, lover, parent, philosopher, or anyone we deem significant to us. Often, the perceived or imputed reaction of these remote others is far more important than the reactions of those right in front of us. We all like to think of ourselves, especially in America, as rugged individualists; so we disguise or refuse to be conscious of the extent to which vicarious role-taking with remote others guides our conduct.

Often these remote others personify cultural values and beliefs and role-taking with them plugs us into the general culture or a particular subculture (Kelley 1958). And equally often, we assume the perspective of a large group of individuals, without singling out, or even knowing, a particular individual who personifies this perspective (Shibutani 1955). Rather, we have a general sense for what these **reference groups** expect, and we thereby adjust our conduct. George Herbert Mead referred to this process as role-taking with the *generalized other*.

The fact that interaction often involves role-taking with remote others and reference groups can potentially create tensions with those who do not know about these distant drummers. What they may see is someone who misses cues or who violates the norms of the present situation. Normally, we are quite good at reconciling our behaviors with those both close and afar. But at times, we have difficulty; as a result, we say and do stupid things, at least from the perspective of those in front of us. At other times, we recognize that we march to different drummers and ritualize our interactions. For example, jocks and intellectuals, blacks and whites, Hispanics and Anglos, old and young, rich and poor, educated and uneducated all ritualize their initial encounters to avoid the tensions and awkwardness created by role-taking with unfamiliar remote others and reference groups (Merton & Rossi 1968).

Interaction and the Social Order

As we see in Chapter 10, episodes of face-to-face interaction reveal a microstructure—what Erving Goffman called the **encounter**. The processes examined in this chapter are the core of an encounter, but as we will see, encounters add to these basic processes of interaction.

Society is ultimately held together by people in face-to-face contact, typically organized by the most micro social unit: the encounter. Of course, individuals create a universe of cultural symbols and large-scale structures that constrain what they can do when facing each other and when mutually signaling and interpreting gestures. Indeed, systems of symbols and social structures have a life of their own, being driven by dynamics that can overwhelm individuals; and yet, it is people who occupy positions in social structures, play roles, hold symbols in their heads, and sustain the culture and structure of a society. Thus, the process of interaction undergirds the majestic structural edifices and cultural constructions of societies.

It is often difficult to make the connection between micro-level interaction and macro-level structures and cultural systems. We know that there is a connection—but the mutual influence of the two levels is often hard to discern and dissect. This issue is often termed the problem of micro-macro *linkage* or the micro-macro *gap* (Alexander et al. 1986; J. Turner 1983). Yet, for our purposes, we need only recognize that the processes outlined in this chapter are what sustain the structures and symbols of the social world, and conversely, as I emphasized in Chapters 5 and 6, interactions are embedded in corporate and categoric units, and their respective cultures, and by extension, in large-scale institutional spheres. Thus, any given interaction is constrained by the structures in which it is embedded, but culture and structures operating at the meso and macro levels are not viable without real people actively interacting with each other in face-to-face encounters. People in interaction are the energy that drives the formation of culture and society. Without the ability to use gestures, role-take, role-make, present self, manage impressions, present fronts, mutually typify, use rituals, and employ remote others and reference groups as a frame of reference, the structures of society and the symbol systems of culture could not exist. But again, we should never forget that these structures and symbol systems constrain and guide the course of interaction.

SUMMARY

1. Interaction involves the mutual signaling and reading of gestures and the adjustment of responses to the emission of gestures. For George Herbert Mead, human interaction is symbolic in the sense that the gestures emitted by individuals mean the same thing to the sending and receiving parties. Mead also emphasized that human interaction involves the capacities for mind (thought, deliberation, and covert rehearsal of alternatives) and self (seeing oneself as an object).

2. In Erving Goffman's analysis, interaction occurs on a stage, both a frontstage and backstage, and each individual orchestrates a personal front as part of a more general process of impression-management.

3. Ethnomethodologists stress that much of humans' sense for order is sustained by implicit "folk methods" that are implicitly used by individuals to preserve the presumption that they experience the social world in similar ways.

4. Interaction occurs in social structures, where considerations of roles become important. People manage their emission of gestures to make roles for themselves, and they actively read the gestures of others to discover the roles that others are trying to establish. This process is possible because individuals carry in their stocks of knowledge inventories of roles that they draw upon in making a role for themselves and in interpreting the gestures of others.

5. Interaction involves awareness of, and adjustment to, the expectations of others and group perspectives not physically present in a situation. Such reference groups and remote others often guide and direct the behaviors and responses of individuals.

6. Interaction, social structure, and culture are interrelated. Each could not exist without the other.

7. Most interaction occurs in encounters, which are the most micro social unit of society.

KEY TERMS

Backstage: Places where the self-conscious manipulation of gestures can be relaxed.

Ethnomethods: Concept introduced by Harold Garfinkel to denote the implicit interpersonal signals emitted to create the presumption that people in interaction share a common view of reality.

Encounter: Episodes of face-to-face interaction in which individuals present fronts and play roles.

Front: Erving Goffman's term to denote the use of gestures to present oneself in a particular way and in an identifiable mode of action.

Frontstage: Erving Goffman's term denoting situations where individuals consciously manipulate gestures in ways designed to elicit desired responses from others, especially with respect to one's sense of self.

Impression-Management: Erving Goffman's term to denote the deliberate manipulation of gestures and physical props to project a particular image of oneself to others.

Interaction: Process of individuals mutually emitting gestures, interpreting these gestures, and adjusting their respective courses of action.

Mind: George Herbert Mead's term to designate the process by which individuals covertly rehearse alternative lines of conduct, anticipate or imagine the consequences of each of these potential lines of behavior, and select that line of behavior most likely to facilitate cooperation.

Reference Group: Perspectives of groups, both those in which one is participating and those that are remote, which are used as a frame of reference for self-evaluation and for guiding conduct.

Role-Take: Concept introduced by George Herbert Mead to denote the capacity to read the gestures of others and, thereby, to sense what they are likely to do in terms of their dispositions to act and the cultural symbols relevant to a situation.

Self/Self-Conception: Capacity to see oneself as an object in a situation and to carry cognitions, feelings, and evaluations of oneself as a certain type of person who is deserving of particular responses.

Chapter 8

Socialization

In 1920, the Reverend A. L. Singh was told of a man-ghost haunting a village in India (Brown 1972). The ghost had been seen in the company of wolves who apparently lived inside an abandoned anthill near the village. Intrigued, Singh set up a shooting platform from which he and some of the villagers could observe any activity. What he saw was surprising. A mother wolf and her children would go in and out of the anthill, but two of them looked to be human. They crawled on all fours, had matted hair, and for all intents and purposes looked and acted like wolves. The villagers and Singh decided to dig into the den concealed in the anthill, an act that brought the mother out to defend her cubs. She was killed, and what they found inside was four little creatures clinging together—two cubs and two little girls. Kamala was about eight and Amala only one and a half years old. They were thoroughly wolfish in appearance and behavior: they had hard calluses on their knees and palms from crawling and they would eat and drink by lowering their face into their food. When brought to "civilization," they would prowl at night, sometimes howling. They preferred the company of dogs and cats to children and they slept together rolled up on the floor.

Cases of feral children like Kamala and Amala document the plasticity of humans when born. So much of what makes us human is learned in interaction with others in social structures regulated by culture. As Kamala and Amala document, if you are raised by a wolf, you become a wolf; if you are raised as a human, you hopefully become a human. The philosopher John Locke once noted that, when born, humans are like a blank sheet of paper on which experience will write a story leading to a person and personality. Locke overstated the case because it is clear that we bring with us from the womb some biological propensities and potentials that are hard-wired.

Still, many of these biological programmers must be activated by experiences. Studies of other feral children shed some light on what happens when the human potential in our biological systems is not activated. Anna was an illegitimate child, a fact that displeased her grandmother greatly. As a result, Anna was locked into a small area of an attic for the first years of her life (Davis 1940, 1947). She received enough care to keep her alive, but little more. When finally discovered by social workers, it was clear that Anna had been isolated from all human contact. She could not walk or talk, and she appeared retarded, deaf, and blind. She was a human in body only, but when placed into a school, she was found not to be deaf, blind, or dumb; indeed, she showed marked improvement in her ability to communicate to others. She died before reaching adulthood, and so, it can never be known if she would have become fully human and able to function as a normal person in society. In cases like Anna's, where the child has been in isolation for longer periods and has lived into early adulthood, studies have documented that such children always have trouble in communicating, learning, and acting like a normal human being.

What these tragic cases document is that there is a window of opportunity for learning many of the basic skills and behaviors that make us all human and that allow us to play roles in society; if this window of opportunity—from birth to perhaps 10 or 11 years of age—passes, it is closed forever. Thus, human potentials that are hard-wired into our neuroanatomy must be activated within a certain timeframe; if they are not activated, it will be difficult to acquire in full human measure those capacities that make us human and allow us to participate in society. Another case of an isolated child, Isabelle, demonstrates that when isolation is not so complete, early deficiencies can be overcome through intense training. Like Anna, Isabelle was illegitimate, and had been isolated by her mother, who was a deaf-mute. She had not learned how to use conventional language, but unlike Anna, she had learned how to communicate; and so, because the centers of her brain responsible for communication had been activated, Isabelle was able to become almost normal when given special training.

The conclusion to be drawn here is that our most basic human capacities, such as discriminating sounds, seeing and using nonverbal gestures, walking, talking, and responding to others are, to a great extent, learned. Our genetic endowment provides the capacity to learn these behaviors and may even direct us to learn them, but it does not guarantee their emergence and development. We become human through interaction with others in a variety of cultural and social structural contexts. The interactions influencing the development of those capacities that allow us to participate in society are termed **socialization**. We carry into this world a genetic heritage—a human physiology, cognitive capacities, emotional propensities, and perhaps some basic drives for food, companionship, and later, sex—but just *how* this heritage is manifested is in large part the result of our interaction with others in social and cultural contexts. Our goal in this chapter is to understand the dynamics of this key form of social interaction.

Socialization and Society

Each of us is made unique by socialization—that is, by our biography of specific interactions with others in a cultural and social context. This may be what interests us most about socialization. We all want to know what made us into the person we are. Far more important sociologically, however, is the socialization experience of whole populations. What is it that people have *in common* by virtue of socialization? A society can only be sustained if its new members acquire capacities that enable them to participate fully in the society. As functional theories would stress, our unique qualities are far less important than what we share: the capacity to function in the same society (Parsons 1951).

What are these capacities (J. Turner 1985c, 100–104)? One essential capacity is the acquisition of the **motives** that direct us to occupy positions and to play essential roles. We all must be energized to play such roles—as worker, father, friend, mother, or citizen—if a society is to be sustained. Alienation, disaffection, and dissatisfaction are, of course, prevalent in large and complex societies. And if significant numbers reveal these attributes and fail to perform basic roles, society begins to crumble or at least change.

Another capacity is cultural (Parsons 1951). All of us must, to some degree, share commitments to common values, beliefs, and institutional norms, or we must agree to disagree and separate ourselves into different subcultures. But a society composed of too many highly diverse subcultures is likely to reveal conflict and tension, as people clash over their respective views of what is right and wrong, of what should and should not be done, and of what actions are proper and improper. Thus, to some degree, each of us must be guided from within by common cultural symbols—what we can call **cultural directives.** Only in this way can our interactions proceed on the basis of similar moral assumptions, commonly accepted beliefs, and agreed upon norms.

Yet another key human capacity is to see ourselves as an object, or to have a conception of ourselves as a certain kind of person, as interactionist theories stress (James 1894; Mead 1934). If we lack this **self-conception,** our behaviors will not reveal consistency, and we will have no stable object or point of reference to assess and evaluate with cultural symbols (Bandura 1977; Epstein 1980; Gecas 1982, 1985; Rosenberg 1979). People without a stable sense of self-esteem, even when they abide by the norms, are "flighty" and "flaky." There is a lack of an inner compass guiding their actions (Gecas and Schwalbe 1983). In addition to a more stable self-conception, we also carry a more *situationally based sense of self* (Goffman 1959) or **identities** (Burke 1991; McCall and Simons 1978; Stryker 1980). We see ourselves somewhat differently in varying situations, but we are not chameleons. Our more stable sense of self places limits on how we think about ourselves in life's diverse contexts. Moreover, sustaining this general self-conception as well as situational identities becomes a powerful motivational force in human interaction, giving our behaviors a direction and pattern that facilitates interaction with others (Gecas 1986, 1989, 1991; Miyamoto 1970; J. Turner 1987).

Still another crucial capacity stressed by interactionist theories is a collage of **role-playing skills** and abilities. All of us must have the ability to read the gestures of others and role-take with them. In this way, we can take on the point of view of others and even the broader cultural guidelines or directives guiding a situation. If people are bad at role-taking, they will have trouble coordinating their actions with others. We must also be able to role-make for ourselves, to assert through the orchestration of gestures the role that we are playing so that others can see how we are likely to behave (R. Turner 1962). There is always a certain skill in making a role for oneself in a situation; if we do not orchestrate our gestures well, others will see us as brutish and avoid us. Thus, in seeing the role that others are trying to make for themselves through role-taking, while at the same time emitting gestures to communicate to others the role that we are making in a situation, we become able to cooperate with others.

Yet another personal capacity revolves around **emotions.** Much research has been done on the basic or primary emotions possessed by humans at birth (Ekman 1982; Kemper 1987; Plutchik 1962; Plutchik & Kellerman 1980). Although some disagreement exists, the emotions of assertion-anger, satisfaction-happiness, disappointment-sadness, and aversion-fear, appear to be inborn (J. Turner 2003). What is remarkable, however, is the elaboration of these basic emotions into many additional ones. In essence, the human brain seems to combine or mix primary emotions to elaborate more complex and subtle emotions, as suggested in Table 8.1 (J. Turner 1999, 2000). These emotional states are learned, but it is the neurology of the brain that makes such a diversity of emotions possible. Thus, by using the capacities of the brain to generate an array of emotions, humans are able to acquire a complex array of emotional states through socialization. The reason for so many emotions is that they facilitate fine-tuned interaction (J. Turner 2000, 2002; Turner and Molnar 1993). If we can display and read many diverse emotions, we can signal our moods and intentions, and others can respond to us in appropriate ways. Imagine a social world where the only emotions that we could read were the primary ones—fear, anger, happiness, and sadness. Such a world would lack the emotional richness of our daily lives, but more importantly, it would be very difficult to construct and sustain the complex, fluid, and robust interactions, social structures, and cultural symbols that order human society.

From a sociological viewpoint, it is the acquisition of these capacities through interaction with others that allows us to participate in ongoing patterns of social organization. Each of us reveals a unique profile in terms of our motives, cultural directives, self-conceptions, role-playing skills, and ability to display emotions. But to a minimal degree, we all must have these basic capacities if society is to exist. This is what is sociologically important, because the job of the sociologist is to understand what makes social relations and social organization possible. The dynamics of socialization as it leads to the acquisition of these basic capacities are thus critical to understanding not just ourselves as individuals but also the operation of society.

The Process of Socialization

When we were born, we were narcissistic. We wanted this and that, and we wanted it now. If we did not get it, we would cry and scream. However, immediately after each baby is born, socialization begins to tame this narcissism because the infant finds itself in a social structure—hospital, home, family—where it *must* interact and get along with others, such as nurse, mother, father, siblings, and others. Thus begins a lifelong process of interaction in an ever increasing variety of contexts; it is out of these interactions that a profile of motives, a system of cultural symbols (language, values, beliefs, norms), a self-conception, a distinct role-playing style, and an array of emotional capacities are developed.

Several rather obvious, but nonetheless critical, principles operate during socialization. First, infants possess a series of biological tendencies and capacities that are "hard wired" into their biology. At a minimum, infants have some biological needs and drives, complex neuro-nets, numer-

Table 8.1   The Mixing of Primary Emotions

Primary Emotion	Variations in Intensity			First-Order Emotions	Second-Order Emotions
	Low Intensity	**Moderate Intensity**	**High Intensity**		
Satisfaction-Happiness	Content, Sanguine, Serenity, Gratified	Cheerful, Buoyant, Friendly, Amiable, Enjoyment	Joy, Bliss, Rapture, Jubilant, Gaiety,	+ fear: wonder, hopeful, gratitude, pride + anger: vengeance, appeased, calmed, soothed, relish, triumphant, bemused + sadness: nostalgia, yearning, hopefulness	
Aversion-Fear	Concern, Hesitant, Reluctance	Misgivings, Trepidation, Anxiety	Terror, Horror, High anxiety	+ happiness: awe, reverence, veneration + anger: revulsed, repulsed, dislike, envy, antagonism + sadness: dread, wariness	
Assertion-Anger	Annoyed, Agitated, Irritated, Vexed, Perturbed, Nettled, Rankled	Displeased, Frustrated, Belligerent, Contentious, Hostility, Ire, Animosity	Dislike, Loathing, Disgust, Hate, Despite, Detest, Hatred, Seething, Wrath	+ happiness: snubbing, mollified, rudeness, placated, righteousness + fear: abhorrence, jealousy, suspicion + sadness: bitterness, depression, betrayed	
Disappoint-ment-Sadness	Discouraged, Downcast, Dispirited	Dismayed, Disheartened, Glum, Resigned Gloomy, Woeful, Pained	Sorrow, Heartsick, Despondent, Anguished	+ happiness: acceptance, moroseness, solace, melancholy + fear: forlornness, remorseful, misery + anger: aggrieved, discontent, dissatisfied, unfulfilled, boredom, grief, envy, sullenness	+ anger, fear: shame + fear, anger: guilt

Source: Turner (1999).
At the far left are the four primary emotions that all researchers agree are lodged in human biology. The next three columns list various levels of intensity for these primary emotions. The First-Order Emotions are the emotion labeled on the far left plus a less amount of another primary emotion (e.g., *satisfaction-happiness,* plus a lesser amount of *fear* produces emotions like *wonder, hopeful, gratitude,* and *pride*). The last column emphasizes that guilt and shame are the outcome of linking *fear* and *anger* to *disappointment-sadness.* Thus, *shame* is mostly *disappointment,* combined with a lesser amount of *anger* (at self), and an even lesser amount of *fear* about the consequences to self, whereas *guilt* is mostly *disap-pointment-sadness* coupled with a lesser amount of *fear* and an even lesser amount of *anger* (at self). Just how this "mixing" occurs neurologically is not clear, but at an early age, children begin to learn how to feel and express the aforementioned emotions listed above.

ous glands for hormonal secretions, repertoires of primary emotions, minimal needs for affiliation, and many latent biological capacities that will eventually become manifest in later life (see Figure 8.1). Second, early socialization has more influence on the activation of these biological potentials than later socialization. Moreover, early socialization also has more impact on the formation of a person's personality than does later socialization. As infants learn to interact, they read the gestures of others and

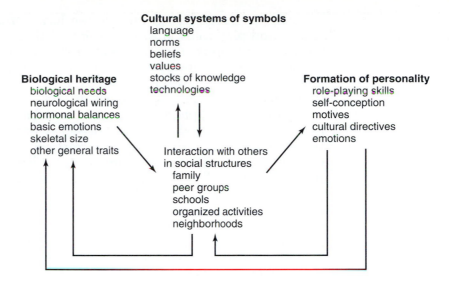

Figure 8.1   The Interplay of Biology, Culture, Interaction, and Social Structure

derive their first self-images in the looking glass (Cooley 1909). Infants and young children begin to feel the expectations of others and experience their first contact with cultural codes; they begin to develop their own ways of gesturing and role-playing so as to get along with others; they start to channel and direct energies toward others in ways that will eventually become stable motivations; and they expand their emotional horizons. Because infants have had no previous social interactions, they do not have a legacy of role-playing style, sense of self, motives, culture, or emotions; and so early interactions have a disproportionate influence on the kinds of basic capacities that a person will develop.

A third principle of socialization is that interaction with significant others—people who are emotionally important to us—is more influential than interaction with ordinary individuals (Sullivan 1953). At first, of course, parents and relatives are significant others. As children learn to role-take and role-make, they assess themselves in the mirror provided by the gestures of others and begin to assume their perspective and, hence, the cultural codes that they personify. Furthermore, children acquire a style of role-playing; in presenting themselves so as to get along with significant others, they direct our motivational energies in ways that enable them to meet the expectations of others, social structures, and cultural codes. And slowly, children learn to manage their emotional displays. Later in life, we all acquire many significant others—peers, teachers, lovers, spouses, our own children, employers, and even media personalities—but they never have quite the same influence as the significant others with whom we first interacted.

A fourth principle is that interaction in primary groups, where relations are more personal and emotional, exerts more influence on the formation of personality than contact with others in secondary groups where the interaction is less immediate and more formal (Cooley 1909).

It is not that secondary groups do not have influence on how individuals behave and play roles, how they think of themselves, how they interpret cultural codes, how they channel motivational energies, and how they display emotions. However, the influence of secondary groups is never as great as that of family, close friends, and other groupings where people have "face-to-face" contact and are intimate with each other.

Another principle is that long-term relations with others have more influence on personality than short-term interactions. True, individuals can come into our lives briefly and exert an enormous influence, but feelings about ourselves, commitments to cultural codes, style of playing roles, and channeling of emotions and motivational energy are most typically shaped by long-term relationships that have endured for many years.

Thus, early primary group interactions among significant others with whom relationships endure are the most influential in the development of personality. These ideas may seem obvious, but they are not trivial. These principles have been in place for all of us and help account for who and what we are.

The development of our basic capacities to participate in society does not occur in a short time, nor does it ever truly end. But by the time a person is an adolescent or teenager, many basic capacities have begun to crystallize. The individual reveals a stable self-conception, and a series of identities, a particular role-playing style, a profile of values, a set of commitments to certain beliefs, a knowledge of crucial norms, a profile of motivational energies, and a tendency to react emotionally in predictable ways.

We must be careful not to view these capacities as too fixed or crystallized because after adolescence, all of us encounter new significant others in a variety of social structures. There are new friendships yet to be made. There are new groups to join. There are new organizations to enter. There are new communities to live in. Still, to some degree, later significant others and new social structures with distinctive cultures must take us as we already are. One is no longer the "blob" to be molded at will; and hence, motives, cultural codes, self-conceptions, emotional tendencies, and role-playing styles are unlikely to change dramatically. Change will probably be gradual, at times imperceptible. This is why someone whom we had not seen for many years seems very much the same as before.

A great deal about humans as social beings can be learned by examining efforts to change them and by looking at cases where people do seem to undergo dramatic transformations. Indeed, there is a vast industry—clinical psychology, psychotherapy, psychoanalysis, group therapy, and hundreds of applications of ideas in these fields—devoted primarily to changing people. Some change is possible in these efforts—more so for some capacities of individuals than others. Much change can occur in cultural values and beliefs; and people can become more aware of crucial norms. It is also possible to alter emotional propensities and role-playing style by dramaturgical coaching. Thus, individuals can become somewhat different with conscious effort. They can become better role-takers and role-makers; they can change their beliefs and their capacity to abide by norms; and they can become better at regulating some emotions. If these kinds of changes are sought, various programs do help. If, however, people want to change their self-conception and motives, then a long and difficult journey lies ahead. One does not so easily eliminate deeply held self-feelings with short-term coaching, nor does someone suddenly change motives from, for example, a strong need for affiliation to one for power or achievement. Change here will be slow and in most cases not so dramatic.

Yet, in real-life situations, fundamental changes sometimes occur. For example, an ex-alcoholic is often a very different person after treatment because he or she had previously sunk to such depths of maladjustment—loss of job, family, friends, and self-esteem. Starting from this devastated personal landscape, rehabilitation does indeed create a new self-concept and new motivations. But few humans would willingly strip themselves bare in this way; and thus, our old self-conception and motives resist transformation. They place constraints on what we can do to ourselves.

These situations tell us something about adult socialization. As we move into various new phases of life—and into new jobs, families, work-places, communities, clubs, and organizations—it is our role-playing style and cultural directives that are the most likely to be altered. Our self-conception will, of course, change somewhat, depending on our successes and failures as well as on our satisfaction with others, but not to the same degree as cultural codes and role-playing styles will. Our motives and emotional propensities may shift around somewhat as our lives run their course, but again not dramatically. Only with real physical decline do motives begin to change, and even then, old desires and passions often persist.

From the standpoint of maintaining social order, it is probably best that personality is not wholly fluid. And it is significant that role-playing abilities and cognizance of cultural codes are the most readily changed. If people could readily change their self-conceptions and motives, it would be difficult for others to respond to them. There would be no consistency in their actions, making it hard for others to adjust. But if people can change and even improve their role-playing abilities, interaction is facilitated, and easy cooperation becomes more likely. If they can also acquire new cultural directives, this too can facilitate interaction with others and integration into the existing social order. If they can better signal and control their emotions, then this will further cooperation and adaptation.

Changes in role-playing abilities and cultural directives do not always promote social order. Just the opposite is often the case, as people who once accepted the social order rebel against it or become increasingly deviant. Our more flexible capacities are also the most crucial to making adjustments and readjustments to social situations, and this fact is very important. It means that people are capable of flexibility in their relations with other individuals and in their involvements in collective enterprises, whereas those components that are least flexible—self and motives—provide a sense of stability and continuity for both the individual and those in his or her environment, even in the face of readjustments to changing circumstances. Thus we can, in a sense, maintain our core compass and at the same time alter our more peripheral course. Without this dual capacity, social change in human affairs would be even more awkward and traumatic than it already is.

Box 8.1: Resocialization Through Brainwashing

During wartime, prisoners of war have often been subjected to "brainwashing." As this term connotes, the object of brainwashing is to "wash" the "brain" clean of its content. The fact that brainwashing is not very successful in inducing permanent change in the vast majority of prisoners attests to the stability of personality. But even when successful, the severity of techniques that must be employed reveals the resistance of personality to change. A review of these techniques demonstrates the kind of assault that must be mounted.

First, to be successful, brainwashing efforts must place the prisoner in a state of extreme physical discomfort. Food and water deprivation, torture, and, most important, sleep deprivation are essential. For example, a prisoner might be denied food and water for several days and denied sleep for weeks.

Second, a prisoner must be socially isolated from other prisoners. As long as prisoners can receive support from fellow prisoners, it will be very difficult to break them down.

Third, interrogators must instill a sense of paranoia in the prisoner, indicating that the prisoner's country and fellow prisoners have abandoned him or her. Such efforts are only successful when a prisoner is in a weakened physical state and in emotional turmoil as a result of sleep loss and social isolation.

Fourth, at that point when a prisoner seems to "weaken," losing his or her grasp on reality, interrogators take on a more sympathetic role. They pretend to be the prisoner's friend, offering help, food, water, and of course a new political ideology. During this process, new images of oneself are generated, new values and beliefs are acquired, motivation is restructured, and role-playing styles are altered. In essence, a new personality has emerged.

Yet, rarely is such a drastic alteration of personality effective. More typically, attitudes, values, and beliefs are changed, at least temporarily until the prisoner is reintegrated into his former society. Changes in self and motives are rarely long term and permanent. The lack of success of brainwashing is thus ample testimony to the strength and stability of human personality.

Stages of Socialization

Socialization into Early Adulthood

Socialization occurs over time. We all must first learn to communicate with others; once the young can communicate, they can interact with others in ways that plug them into the broader culture. Increasingly, these others are characters in the media or in the virtual world of games. With practice and exposure to different types of status positions and roles in varying social structures, children begin to develop a role-playing style; learn more about cultural norms, beliefs, and values; and see themselves as a certain kind of person. By the time individuals are adolescents, much of their personality is shaped. Their biological heritage is now almost fully developed, ready for the long decline that imperceptibly begins around 20 years of age; their motive states—or those arenas where one is willing to mobilize energy—are becoming clear; their conception of themselves as a certain kind of person deserving of particular responses from others is crystallizing; their internalization of culture is sufficient for a basic morality to have emerged; their role-playing skills and style of role performance are beginning to reveal a typical pattern of response to others; and their way of responding to situations emotionally becomes increasingly predictable. Table 8.2 outlines some of the most noticeable stages in socialization from birth to early adulthood.

From birth to around the age of three, a tremendous amount of neurological growth and muscular development must occur. Because humans have such large brains, infants must be very immature if they are to leave the female womb. This immaturity makes infants helpless and fully dependent upon caretakers who communicate and coach infants to respond back. It is clear that humans are programmed to learn language rather effortlessly; by the time a child is three years old, he or she can role-take with others, talk with a vocabulary of around 1,000 words, read the emotions of others, and present self in a particular way. Moreover, by three years of age, children have confronted morality and the power of culture to specify right and wrong, appropriate and inappropriate; as a result, three-year-olds have learned to pay attention to norms, values, and beliefs in most situations. Children have also learned that emotions must be regulated and that some emotional displays will bring punishment, whereas others will bring praise. They will understand many of the emotions listed in Table 8.1, and particularly important, they will experience shame for incompetent behavior and guilt for behaviors that violate moral codes. Children are also beginning to see themselves reflected in what Charles Horton Cooley called "the looking glass" provided by others' responses to them; as a result, their conception of themselves as a certain kind of person is beginning to form.

From four to seven years of age, neurological and muscular growth continues, giving children ever greater cognitive skills and muscular coordination. Moreover, hormones are beginning to influence behavior, although the full hormonal assault does not begin until adolescence. Children's role-playing style and skills are being honed, and depending upon the nature and number of contexts in which a child is able to interact, he or she will evidence either considerable skill or seem immature or unable to interact with others easily. Children are also learning how to control emotional outbursts and, more importantly, to manage how they reveal emotions to others. A child's self-conception is also becoming more clearly formed as experiences with others tell them what kind of person they are. And finally, motive states are taking on greater focus and intensity, clearly guiding the interests and role-playing style of children by the age of seven.

Full neurological and biological development, with hormones clearly differentiating the sexes, will be evident between 8 and 16 years of age.

Table 8.2 Stages of Socialization

Ages	Biological Heritage	Role-Playing Ability	Components of Personality				
			Self	Motive-States	Cultural Directives	Emotional Responses
1–3	Neological growth; development of muscular coordination	Use of language; capacity to read gestures and role-take with others	Initial images of one-self as an object in the environment; beginnings of self-evaluation	Biological needs for food, affiliation, and exploration dominate	Vague sense of moral codes, becoming more explicit by three years; more precise understanding of situational norms	Capacity to read and experience primary emotions; beginnings of the ability to experience shame and guilt; only partial control of emotional outbursts
4–7	Neurological growth; greatly expanded cognitive skills; dramatic increase in muscular coordination; hormones begin to influence sexual differentiation	Expanded capacity with language, with use of verbal and nonverbal gestures; greatly increased capacity to role-take with individuals and group perspectives; ability to role-make and present self; beginnings of a distinctive role-playing style	Beginnings of a self-conception and sense of self-esteem; early identities for gender and other roles emerging	Socially acquired motives for achievement, affiliation, recognition, and power begin to surface and guide conduct; no clear hierarchy or pattern to diverse motive states	Knowledge and rigid interpretation of values and general beliefs and ideologies; growing awareness of basic institutional norms; knowledge of norms for many specific situations; dramatically expanded stocks of knowledge	Capacity to interpret many diverse and complex emotional responses; increased ability to control emotional outbursts; ability to experience shame and guilt (if this ability is not evident at this stage, child becomes a sociopath)

(continued)

Ages	Biological Heritage	Role-Playing Ability	Self	Motive-States	Cultural Directives	Emotional Responses
8–14	Full neurological and cognitive development is reached; increased muscular coordination; rapid growth of skeleton; hormones cause clear sexual differentiation	Fluency in language; high competence in reading and using nonverbal gestures; capacity to role-take and role-make in diverse contexts; clear role-playing style evident	Self-conception and self-esteem established; behavior becoming predictable in light of global self-conception; increased repertoire of identities for situations and roles	Motives are now ingrained and reveal a hierarchy of drives that push individuals to behave in certain ways, thereby giving behavior predictability	More flexible interpretation of values and ideologies; clear understanding of basic institutional norms; expanded knowledge of a wider variety of situational norms; stocks of knowledge are rapidly expanding	Capacity to experience, interpret, and consciously manage emotional displays; control of emotions is only partial because of rapid hormonal changes
14–20	Full biological maturity; long period of biological decline begins	Basic ability to role-take and role-make established; distinct role-playing style now evident	Self-conception and level of self-esteem is now established and not easily changed; new situational identities are being acquired	Motives guiding actions are now clear and hierarchically arrayed in terms of most likely behavioral tendencies; motive-states are now relatively fixed and not easily changed	Basic values firmly set; beliefs and ideologies are codified, but may change with new experiences; knowledge of basic institutional norms is extensive, as is knowledge of situational norms; stocks of knowledge are extensive and continue to expand	Capacity to experience, interpret, and manage emotional displays is more developed and will continue to develop, although a basic pattern of emotional responses is established; emotionality declines as hormonal changes stabilize

Language fluency is well developed; speech styles and other behavioral patterns in playing roles are now evident and, in all likelihood, these patterns will stay with an adolescent into young adulthood. By early adolescence, the ability to role-take with others is well developed. Indeed, the often seemingly compulsive chatter of adolescents and their high levels of sociality may well mark an effort to hone and fine-tune role-taking and role-playing skills. The ability to read emotions in others, control one's own emotional responses, and orchestrate emotional behavior has dramatically increased, although hormones exploding through adolescent bodies often make expressive control difficult. Motives are now formed, dictating the kinds of interests and activities toward which an adolescent will focus their energy. By this time, a considerable amount of knowledgeability and other elements of culture will have been acquired; moreover, the internalization of basic moral codes and increased understandings of many key norms in a wide variety of contexts will have occurred. Perhaps the biggest obstacle for adolescents is the formation of a stable self-conception. Identity crises are quite common during early adolescence, as individuals play roles, read the reactions of others in the looking glass, evaluate themselves, and begin to develop more stable feelings about who they are.

In traditional societies of the past, by the time a person reached 16 years of age, the individual was close to being a full adult. In modern societies, however, adulthood is pushed back because of the need to acquire occupational skills in the education system. Thus, as the young grow into mature adolescents of 18 or 19, they are fully formed biologically. Their basic cognitive abilities are established, their muscular-skeletal system is fully formed, and their hormonal balances are in place. Indeed, they are now ready in their early 20s to begin the long decline into old age and death, although this decline will be hardly noticeable for at least a decade. By 18 an individual's core self-conception is formed; although many situational identities are yet to be acquired during the life course, the individual's sense of worth and adequacy will be fully developed by 20 years of age. The uncertainty over identity should be resolved by the end of adolescence, although the many new roles to be played in later years set the stage for refinements to a young person's self-conception. By 20, a person's role-playing style will be evident, although it will become refined with age and practice in new social contexts. The cultural directives, particularly basic morality and willingness to abide by norms, will be in place, although each individual expands his or her knowledge of cultural directives throughout the life course, at least to old age. The habitual ways that a person reacts emotionally and uses emotions in playing roles will be established by 20, although emotional dispositions undergo refinement during adulthood and, in many cases, change with old age.

Adult Socialization

People never stop learning, even those who seem pig-headed and bigoted. Although early stages of socialization are more critical to the formation of personality than later stages, individuals change with age. The decline in their bodies becomes more noticeable and, in many cases, limits the kinds of roles that can be played. And, people's experiences in new and varied social settings—work, family, education, community and neighborhood, religion, recreation, and the many differentiated spheres of activity in modern societies—can subtly alter each basic component of personality. Individuals will change their role-playing styles, emotional responses to situations will often be modified, motives may be readjusted in light of successes and failures, new knowledge and understandings about cultural directives will be acquired, and even self-conceptions will undergo change with biological decline and experiences in different structures and roles.

Table 8.3 arranges data and ideas from a variety of theories to understand the life course of adults. From Table 8.3, you can get a sense of what lies ahead if you are just leaving the stages presented in Table 8.2. Of course, if you are older than the typical college student, you already have experienced some of the effects of later socialization. I have made the table simple, highlighting three basic stages in adulthood in modern societies. The first stage is young adulthood, from the age of around 20 to the late 30s. During this phase, individuals create new families; have children; buy homes in communities; take jobs and pursue professions; establish the level of income they are likely to have; and in general, participate in the full array of institutional systems, groups, organizations, and communities available in a society. They will also be marked by basic social categories—age, gender and sex, social class, and ethnicity—as these shape how others respond to them. During the initial phase of full adulthood, individuals' conceptions of themselves may undergo some change as they evaluate their success and failure in key roles, such as father, mother, and worker. Role-playing skills will be honed, and role-playing style will be adjusted to changes in self-conceptions and identities as well as to success or failures in varying groups and organizations. Cultural directives will be fine-tuned and knowledge will increase, although basic morality will not likely change in significant ways. Motives will be adjusted to experiences, although the arenas in which people are willing to mobilize their energies will not change dramatically unless they have been unsuccessful in efforts to occupy positions and play roles in particular types of social structures. Emotions will generally be more easily regulated, although the basic way in which individuals read, use, and display emotions will generally not change dramatically, unless life has been emotionally difficult.

The late 30s to the late 60s is a period of mature adulthood. During this period, individuals experience significant transitions in the positions they occupy and the roles they play. Within the family, children grow up and leave, and perhaps a spouse leaves as well. New family roles such as grandparent are assumed. At work, an individual may have changed jobs several times or had even more devastating occupational experiences, such as losing a job and being out of work for significant periods of time. One's ultimate social class positions will be established. Health problems may begin to emerge with increasing frequency. And, by the time one is 65, the reality of old age can no longer be avoided. In a sense, individuals have reached whatever summit they sought to scale and begin to recognize that they are now on their way down from this peak. These kinds of changes often change personality, sometimes in significant ways.

The reality of biological decline is, for most individuals, clearly evident by the end of mature adulthood. The inability to engage in certain

Table 8.3 Stages of Adult Socialization

			Components of Personality			
Ages	**Biological Heritage**	**Role-Playing Ability**	**Self**	**Motive-States**	**Cultural Directives**	**Emotional Responses**
21–38	Biological decline begins, but adults typically feel and appear robust	Role-playing skills are expanded with experience in new roles in varying social structures	Experiences in adult roles may add new identities and lead to some re-valuation of self	Willingness to deposit energy in roles will be adjusted in response to experiences	Values and beliefs are generally stable, although new experiences may alter these, especially ideologies. Expanded knowledge of norms and dramatically expanded stocks of knowledge	Capacity to experience, interpret, and manage emotions is expanded, especially as individuals learn how to control their emotional reactions and displays. Basic pattern of emotional response to situations is now set
39–65	Biological decline is now increasingly evident and may affect emotional reactions, roles played, and some identities	Role-playing skills and style adjusted to positions that have been lost and gained during this period	Identities may be lost (e.g., father, worker, spouse); re-calibration of self in light of age; basic self-conception remains intact despite changes in certain identities associated with roles	Willingness to deposit energy in roles may be adjusted as key roles—worker, father, spouse—may be lost. New interests emerge, although motive-states from old roles will be likely carried into new ones	Values unlikely to have changed; beliefs may change with changes in roles played and in light of experiences in key adult roles of work and family	Basic emotional responses to situations remain the same, although success or failure in key adult roles may lead to global emotional reactions that are energizing or depressive
66–80	Biological decline accelerates; chronic health problems may emerge; and identities and emotional reactions changed in light of health issues	Role-playing skills and style adjusted to new realities of age; some skill may be lost, especially if adult experiences have not been positive	Identities may be lost as adult roles are lost and new roles of retired or chronically ill are assumed; basic self-conception is unlikely to have changed	Overall level of physical energy declines dramatically with aging; willingness to deposit energy in new roles may remain high if physical health is good and if depression and other emotional reactions to the life course can be avoided	Values and beliefs are unlikely to change from this age on	Basic emotional responses remain intact but the degree of biological decline and health problems, coupled with assessments of how successful life has been, can effect overall emotional reactions that can range from positive to highly negative
81–death	Biological decline accelerates dramatically; health problems are almost universal	Role-playing skill and style adjusted to realities of very old age; because limited roles are played, skills may decline with very old age	Most role identities outside those of gender and old age are lost or kept only as memories; basic self-conception will be unlikely to change	Overall level of physical energy declines significantly; willingness to mobilize energy for activities declines, except perhaps in a few roles	Values and beliefs are unlikely to change	Basic emotional responses remain, but are altered by physical decline and the ability to mobilize energy; depending on life's experiences, people feel despair or a sense of integrity about a life well lived

activities or health problems forces individuals to adjust at least some elements of their self-conception, role-playing style, and emotional reactions. Although stable for most of this period, self-conceptions and identities may be readjusted as individuals lose family and work roles; correspondingly, their-role-playing style may change as new roles are assumed and as old age begins to become increasingly evident to a person. New cultural directives may take on greater salience and importance, although basic morality is unlikely to change. And, by the end of this period, motives that were stable for most of adulthood may be adjusted as work and family roles are altered. During this phase of adulthood, the psychoanalyst Eric Erikson (1950) sees the biggest challenge to be one of **generativity**—or giving of self to others and the sharing of accomplishments—versus **self-absorption and stagnation** in not being able to give to others.

The next stage of adult socialization comes with the categorization of a person as elderly. From around 66 to 80, it is no longer easy to avoid such categorization; as a result, others respond to a person as elderly, forcing this individual to take a new look at who they are and make adjustments to their self-conception. Moreover, during the latter phases of this period, biological decline is rapid, once again requiring most people to adjust to a new reality. Except in a few cases, individuals are now out of work and active family roles, thereby forcing them to make further adjustments in their role-playing style, their emotional responses, their motives, and perhaps even their self-conception. These necessary transitions can become more difficult when an individual must adjust to the loss of a spouse or when a person suffers from chronic illness. By the time individuals are 80 years old, they have passed the average of longevity in modern societies and, thus, must face the prospects of death.

The very old enter this last phase with varying orientations. Those who have been successful, who have a strong and positive self-conception, and who have been able to occupy positions and play roles that have brought income and prestige will generally approach death in a positive frame of mind. They will see the inevitability of death and appreciate a life well lived. In contrast, those who have not been successful, who have never had a strong and positive view of themselves, and who have been unable to occupy prestigeful positions and play gratifying roles will often end life bitter and resentful, seeing death as yet one more cruelty that they must endure. Eric Erikson termed very old age the challenge of *integrity* versus *despair*, as individuals look back on their lives and see the positive things that have been done or accomplished or, alternatively, look back at what has not been achieved and continue to be self-absorbed.

Agents of Socialization

Individuals

Parents are the first agents of socialization in a child's life, particularly the mother. Parents are more than caregivers; they are also representatives of culture; and through their responses to a child, they pass on the cultural traditions of a society—from its language to its core values and beliefs. Moreover, they are also the primary sources of emotional support for the young, and so, the flow of positive and negative emotions between parent and children will influence just about every aspect of the child's personality. If the child experiences positive emotions from parents, he or she is more likely to develop a sense of trust in others, experience positive self-evaluations that will lead to a strong self-conception, accept the values and beliefs of the culture, be willing to play roles in the manner dictated by norms, and be able to give off positive emotions to others. When parents are inconsistent in their emotional responses, especially if they become excessively angry and out of control, it is likely that the formation of each element of personality will be problematic as the child gets older.

Parents are not the only individual agents who exert an influence on a child's personality. Other members of the family—from siblings to grandparents through cousins, aunts, and uncles—also exert an influence if a child has high rates of interaction with them. Over time, when a child becomes an adult, marries, and has his or her own children, the individual's spouse and children can become new agents of socialization. Indeed, very few parents could argue against the conclusion that they are socialized by their spouse and children.

At any time in life, particular individuals in groups, organizations, and communities can exert a significant influence on a person. A teacher, fellow worker, friend, or even character presented in the media can influence each aspect of an individual's personality, although rarely to the extent that early, face-to-face interaction does in the family and early peer groups.

Groups

Groups have power, especially primary groups where rates of face-to-face interaction are high and where emotional bonds are strong. When we find ourselves in a group, we role-take with others and try to get along. Because we generally want to fit in, the norms of groups and the reactions of others in groups have the power to shape role-playing, self-evaluations, motivational energies, and expressions of emotions. The family is probably the most important group because it comes early in a child's life, contains others whose opinion is valued, and persists during the formative years of socialization. Other groups that come early in life, or that are highly salient and valued in later life, also exert considerable influence on the formation of personality. Early peer groups, where nonfamilial roles are played for the first time; where nonfamilial self images are received and evaluated; where new norms, beliefs, values, speech styles, and other new cultural directives are present; and where new and varied emotions are expressed and experienced for the first time will also exert considerable influence on personality as a child grows up. Later in life, groups formed in work, recreation, community activity, and in other spheres will, to some extent, influence at least the role-playing style, emotional displays, and adherence to cultural directives. Such groups are less likely to alter motivations and self-conceptions significantly, unless the person becomes highly dependent upon the group.

Organizations

The first formal organization for most children is the school, or in many cases, the preschool. Here the child encounters the world of formal rules, monitoring and sanctioning of conformity to the rules, and the impersonality of much social life in the modern world. In a sense, socialization in schools teaches an individual how to play roles, express and control emotions, define self, channel motivations, and even present the body in ways demanded by bureaucratic organizations. The hidden curriculum of schools, then, is to socialize children through adolescence and, indeed, often well into adulthood into the ways of organizations. The more salient an organization is to an individual and the more the person relies upon an organization for resources that are valued (such as money, prestige, power, or knowledge), then the greater will be the power of this organization to influence the formation or, in the case of adults, reformation of personality. Much of this power comes through the groups that are lodged in organizations, but these groups generally channel the culture of the organization as they regulate conduct. Thus, individuals will learn to direct their energies (motives) into avenues available in the structure of the organization, to define and evaluate self by the cultural standards of the organization and those who have power, to play roles in ways demanded by the culture and structure of the organization, to accept the cultural directives imposed by the organization, and to display the emotional demeanor demanded by the organization.

Humans are not robots, and so, rarely is the power of organizations over personality complete. And indeed, groups in organizations often rebel in both quiet and raucous ways against the demands of the organization. Still, most people in modern societies will spend at least 40 hours per week in an organization; it is unlikely that such long-term and intense exposure to the culture and structure of an organization will not exert considerable influence on personality.

Categories

At first glance, it would seem improbable that membership in a social category would socialize a person. Being young or old, being a member of an ethnic group, being located at a particular class position, or being gendered are not the same as being in a group or organization. However, when a person is defined as belonging to a certain category, this individual is treated according to the expectations and images associated with this category. For example, no matter where a man or woman may go, he or she will be treated as a member of a distinctive gender category. People acquire knowledge via all socializing agents about the relative value and worth as well as expectations for members of a particular category. Once this knowledge is acquired, any time one's categoric unit membership becomes salient, just how one presents self, how one plays roles, how one channels motivational energy, how one expresses emotions, how one plugs into culture, and even how one presents body will be guided by categoric membership. Those social categories that last a lifetime—such as ethnicity and gender—will exert even more influence on the formation of personality because an individual will constantly be called upon to bring to bear the expectations associated with membership in this category.

Community

Communities organize activities in physical space. Where one lives influences personality indirectly by circumscribing the groups and organizations in which a person is likely to participate. Communities also organize categories of people by social class and by ethnicity, increasing (or decreasing) rates of interaction among members of these categories and thereby increasing (or decreasing) the salience and influence of expectations associated with categories on people's personality. Thus, people in an ethnic ghetto or in an area inhabited by members of a particular social class will interact with each other in terms of the culture, interpersonal styles, emotional demeanor, motives, and identities appropriate to this ghetto or class.

Communities can also influence personality directly when they reveal a particular culture and structure that limits the roles people can play, the identities they can present, the emotions they can display, and the motives they can mobilize. Compare, for example, the vast differences in the culture and structure of a poor rural community, a plush suburb, or a large city. These community structures and the culture associated with them will socialize each element of personality so that the individuals who grow up and live in these very diverse communities will reveal personalities that are often quite different.

Media

There is considerable debate on how the media influences the socialization process, but there is no doubt that most people in modern societies are exposed to the media for several hours each day. And, if video games and virtual tours on the Internet are added to television, radio, newspapers, magazines, and movies, the exposure to the media could be greater for many individuals than actual interaction with real people. It is clear that media exposure can reinforce existing behavioral propensities, but what is not so clear is whether or not the media can actually generate these propensities. Thus, aggressive images in the media can reinforce aggressive role-playing styles of individuals, but can aggression in the media, by itself, socialize aggressive role-playing styles? There is some evidence that the media can do just this, if the images are sufficiently graphic, but again, the data are not without ambiguity. In either case, the media is an important socializing agent because it presents images of how people should play roles, deal with and express emotions, present and see self, and channel their motivational energies, while at the same time communicating particular values, beliefs, and norms. Media can even influence biological processes, as a recent study on gaming demonstrated that hand-eye muscular control increased with the amount of video gaming a person engaged in.

Institutional Spheres

For the most part, institutions socialize via the groups, organizations, and social categories from which they are built. We are raised in a family that is part of the institution of kinship; we work in a company that is part of the institution of economy; we worship at a church that is an element of the institution of religion; or we go to specific schools that are part of the institution of education. The culture of institutions is thus filtered through the groups and organizations, as well as categoric units, that make up an institutional sphere. Yet, institutions can directly socialize individuals, independently of the groups, categories, and organizations from which they are constructed. For example, much of your definition of success, your conception of yourself, your motives, your role-playing styles, and your emotions is currently tied up in the institution of education. Specific individuals in groups within schools may have exerted considerable influence on these components of your personality, but there is also a more generalized influence of education as an institutional system on your personality. Your self-definitions, your motives, your playing of the student role, your emotional involvement in school, and your reactions to tests and grades are all influenced by the broader institution of education, independently of any particular classroom, college, or university. In fact, when you study, define yourself by the standards of performance in the classroom, adjust to schedules and roles to be successful in school, mobilize your energies to study, assess what is right and wrong, and experience emotions, you do so in reference to *generalized images of education* that you have acquired. In some ways, you are socializing yourself as you take cognizance of education as a whole and use the general values, beliefs, norms, and other features of the entire system of education to structure your personality. What is true of education can also be the case with the economy, family, religion, politics, science, law, and any other institutional sphere that you use as a frame of reference to order your behavior and perceptions of yourself as a certain kind of person motivated to pursue particular goals.

Stability and Change in the Social Order

One reason for the relative stability of personality components, once formed, is that these elements of personality are integrated. Our self-conception is the result of evaluating ourselves in terms of cultural codes; our role-playing style and role-taking with others are greatly influenced by our self-conception and cultural codes; our emotions are tied to our interpersonal experiences, motivations, self-evaluations, and cognizance of cultural codes; our motives are guided by cultural codes and emotions, and in turn, our interpretation of these codes and emotional states is influenced by our motives; finally, our role-playing style is also greatly influenced by our motives and emotions, as we selectively role-take and role-make in efforts to consummate our needs. The elements of personality thus constitute *a system* whose interrelations resist dramatic change.

We all need this integration because, without it, our emotional lives would be tumultuous. Many people do reveal inconsistency in these traits, and they lead a miserable existence. For example, their ability to play roles and evaluate themselves positively may fall short of their cultural directives. Or, their role-making may be inconsistent with their sense of self. Or, their motivational energies may be inadequate to the cultural expectations that they place on themselves, and as a result, they feel and must deal with negative emotions like frustration, anger, hurt, and shame. We have all known individuals in such situations, and to a degree, we all reveal such incompatibilities.

Some inconsistency in our basic human capacities can be endured, but if the inconsistency is great, change in personality is likely or emotional problems can ensue. The converse is also true: relative consistency among these capacities is a force that resists change. If self, cultural directives, motives, emotions, and role-playing are in reasonable harmony, we are unlikely to change, unless we find ourselves in dramatically new social situations requiring changes. Typically, we seek out and interact in situations where we feel comfortable and experience positive emotions. We attempt what we can achieve. We selectively filter our inconsistent inputs from others. And we avoid situations where our cultural codes are inappropriate. As a consequence, we find comfortable social niches for ourselves, and our lives become predictable, perhaps even a bit boring. This is the appeal of vacation spots like Las Vegas and Atlantic City; they allow you, if only briefly, to get "out of your rut." But society as a whole depends on such ruts, because as people find niches that are compatible with their personality, social life becomes predictable. Predictability, routine, and perhaps boredom are the binding stuff of social order (J. Turner 1988).

Once in place, this compatibility between our social niches and personality becomes yet another force working to maintain the stability of personality so essential for continuity of social order. In societies where people feel out of their niches, their personality is under great strain to change or, as is also the case, people feel pressure to change the "system" to fit their needs, aspirations, self-feelings, and abilities. For example, revolutions in a society often come when a period of "rising expectations" (cultural beliefs that life is getting better and should continue to get better) is followed by a downturn or leveling off in people's social and economic conditions (Davies 1969; Phillips 2001). Here, the inconsistency between cultural codes and people's sense of self-worth, their motivational needs, and role-taking skills, on the other, is sufficient to move them against the social order. When such dislocations between personality and social conditions hit large numbers of people, change in social structures is as likely as alterations in personality. Social movements, revolt, and protest require a large number of people who cannot find social niches compatible with their human capacities (Smelser 1963; Turner & Killian 1978). Just as consistency among our traits and harmony between these traits and the social conditions are the stuff of social order, inconsistency and lack of harmony are the impetus behind social change.

SUMMARY

1. Socialization is a particular type of interaction—one that shapes the nature of human personality and, in turn, human behavior, interaction, and participation in society. Without socialization, neither humans nor society would be possible.

2. In general terms, the basic components or capacities of personality relevant for understanding human behavior in society can be labeled (a) motives, (b) role-playing skills and style, (c) cultural directives, (d) self-conceptions and identities, and (e) emotions.

3. As a rule, interactions that are initiated early, are long-term, are in primary groups, and are with significant others will have the most influence on how these components of personality are forged and developed.

4. Socialization occurs over time and, to a degree, reveals "stages" that mark the acquisition or change in components of personality. In early socialization, the ages of 1–3, 4–7, 8–14, and 15–20 mark significant changes in personality; the stages of adult socialization in postindustrial societies are more elusive but roughly correspond to 21–37, 38–65, 66–80, and 81–death. At each stage of socialization, personality changes somewhat as its components are altered.

5. Personality tends to stabilize, to some degree. This fact gives each person some equanimity in their life, while facilitating the maintenance of social order.

KEY TERMS

Cultural Directives: Profile of values, beliefs, norms, and other symbol systems that individuals use in guiding their behaviors and interactions.

Emotions: Moods or states of individuals revolving around, and involving elaborations of, such primary states as anger, fear, sadness, happiness, and surprise.

Generativity versus Self-Absorption or Stagnation: Seventh stage in Erik Erikson's developmental scheme, lasting through mature adulthood, and during which success in family, work, and community lead to a feeling of being able to give to others, or if not, to self-absorption and stagnation in life.

Identity: Conception that people have of themselves in a particular social context and role.

Motives/Motivation: An individual's level of energy, and nature of energy, devoted to occupying positions and playing roles in society.

Role-Playing Skills: An individual's ability and capacity for role-taking and role-making in interactions with others.

Self-Conception: An individual's view of himself or herself as a certain type of person with particular attributes and, hence, deserving of certain kinds of responses from others.

Socialization: Those interactions instilling in individuals the basic components of personality that are necessary for their participation in society.

Chapter 9

Social Control

The Problem of Order

Social life involves a perpetual standoff between those forces that operate to maintain the social order and those forces that produce deviance, dissent, disorder, and change. In a real sense, we live in the midst of a constant struggle between mechanisms of social control and social tendencies for deviance, conflict, and dissent. This societal battlefield often has no right or wrong side; the forces of control are not always benign nor are those of deviance and dissent always malevolent. Thus, the imputed rightness or wrongness of these dynamics is less relevant than their inevitability. The battle never ends, for it addresses the most fundamental sociological question: How is some degree of order to be maintained in a society? Indeed, the very founding sociologists examined in Chapter 1—Comte, Spencer, Marx, Durkheim, and Weber—wanted to know the answer to this question. For them, as for us today, the social world is rife with tension and conflict and with change and transformation. One does not need to advocate the status quo to realize that societies that cannot provide some provisional answers to this question are marked by constant turmoil and change. Although conflict and change can often improve unpleasant conditions, there must also be some way to create cooperation and consensus among people in society. Without these, society collapses or, as is often the case in human affairs, it becomes an arena of constant upheaval.

Thus the problem of order revolves around questions of social control. As a functional theorist might ask: How are people to play roles in ways that allow them to interact and cooperate? How are people to come to agree about what is right and wrong, proper and improper? How are disputes and disagreements to be resolved and mitigated? In some societies, answers to these questions come effortlessly, without great thought or reflection. In other societies, control is a constant headache. People are alienated; they deviate from accepted norms; they disagree over core values and beliefs; they fight as they pursue their interests; and in general, they refuse to get along. Here is the stuff of conflict theory. These problems of social control are most likely to occur in societies that are large, complex, and stratified. Let me elaborate on this point.

Forces of Disorder

Population Size.   One force that escalates the problem of order in society is the size of a population. Large populations are always more difficult to organize than are smaller ones, because as the number of people increases, face-to-face contact among everyone becomes more problematic. There is not enough time to see, talk to, and know others. Moreover, the quality—the intensity of emotion, affection, and mutual trust—of the interaction decreases. And so, when people cannot interact directly and cannot feel a sense of solidarity with one another, a very powerful force of social control is weakened. In addition, those who do interact frequently come to form subpopulations, and they often develop their own subculture and lifestyle that deviates from the culture and behavioral patterns of the majority. These interactions provide a sense of solidarity, but they also do something else: Members of subcultures become distinctive and different. When subpopulations in a society are strangers to each other, the conflicts and disagreements increase. What results are problems of control among diverging subpopulations.

Larger populations also present real difficulties for distributing resources and coordinating activities. When people cannot talk things over and agree informally, how do virtual strangers come to decide on who does what and who gets what? The market economy, where people buy and sell goods and services, is one answer but an incomplete one. Another answer is the consolidation of power so that there is a "political force" that can coordinate actions, distribute resources, and regulate potential conflicts in markets.

Differentiation.   A second force that escalates problems of order is social differentiation. *Differentiation* is simply the process of creating differences—in culture; occupational roles; income; family structure; types of economic arrangements; and in all the things that people, groups, and organizations do. The greater the number of differences, the more differentiated a population will be. Differentiation results from increases in population size, because people get isolated from each other and develop their own distinctive subcultures and ways of doing things. In addition, supporting a large population requires new, more complex economic arrangements, with people playing specialized roles and working in organizations that produce the volume and varieties of goods and services necessary to support a larger number of people. The degree of differentiation can vary depending on particular circumstances, but in the end, differentiation will increase with population growth. Such differences always create problems of social control: How are people in different subcultures, economic roles, neighborhoods and communities, regions, and work organizations to be coordinated? Who is to keep them from fighting? Who is to regularize market exchanges among them? The answer to these kinds of questions is that government's regulatory activities expand, creating yet another source of social differentiation.

Inequality.   Population growth and social differentiation are linked, in turn, to a third force escalating the problem of order in societies: inequality. As populations grow and people do different things, it is inevitable that some people get more money, power, and prestige than others. Complete social equality is really possible only in very small populations where the differences in people's activities and lifestyles are not great. But as populations grow and differentiate, inequality increases and

represents a truly volatile force behind conflict and tension in human societies. Inequalities sometimes create society-wide revolutions. More
often they generate limited skirmishes between those who have and
those who do not have particular resources. As conflict theories emphasize, many of the most interesting events around us are over inequalities—labor strikes, demands for equal rights for women, and ethnic
tensions—among members of different categoric units. Change-producing
social movements—the labor movement, the abolitionist movement, the
women's suffrage movement, the current women's movement, and the
civil rights movement—all emerged and spread in response to inequalities (see Chapter 23). Confrontation and violence are often a part of
these movements as forces for change and forces for social control clash.
The reconciliation of these forces eventually comes from governmental
responses—for example, new laws, new enforcement agencies, and new
procedures for redressing grievances. Without government, inequality
would be a perpetual conflict-producing machine. With it, someone is at
the controls for at least some of the time.

Macro Forces of Social Control: Markets and Government

Thus, social life in large, differentiated societies characterized by inequality is filled with potential for disagreement, dissent, and disorder. In his
Leviathan, the seventeenth-century British social philosopher Thomas
Hobbes (1651) proposed that the only solution to such problems is for
everyone to agree to subordinate themselves to political authority—to government and to rule by Big Brother. In contrast to Hobbes, the eighteenth-
century economic philosopher Adam Smith (1776) took a utilitarian view,
seeing an "Invisible Hand of Order" as emerging out of unregulated, free
competition in markets where the laws of supply and demand would create exchanges that led to interconnections and interdependencies among
people and the social structures organizing their activities.

Although the debate of these old social philosophers may not seem
relevant today, American society reflects a kind of compromise between
their conflicting ideas. We live in a society where cultural values extol
freedom and individualism; our dominant system of economic beliefs
stresses laissez-faire and economic competition among individuals; our
social beliefs emphasize "doing your own thing," "being your own person," "sticking to your convictions," and "not knuckling under." Many of
our political beliefs involve a distrust of "big government" and a convic-
tion by many that all government is inefficient. Our heroes are rugged individualists who do what they want rather than what they are told. Thus,
our cultural beliefs clearly favor Adam Smith's position over Thomas
Hobbes'. But as I have already mentioned, big government is inevitable
as size, differentiation, and inequality increase. And so, many of our
most cherished cultural beliefs or ideologies do not correspond to the realities of social life in large, complex societies. Imagine a society like
ours governed solely by the laws of supply and demand. How would
greed be controlled? What would keep people from cheating? And, how
would basic services—from roadways to schools and police—be delivered? Inevitably, whether we like it or not, political authority as it generates laws, police, courts, and jails must emerge to maintain control;
ultimately, it is the government that must fund expensive services like

fire protection, education, health care, welfare, social security, and other social programs. Adam Smith's "Invisible Hand of Order" becomes very visible as government expands its functions.

A society without extensive government control could not answer the following questions: Who would build roads? Who would control pollution? Who would check consumer fraud? Who would keep banks from collapsing with your and my money? Who would take care of the poor, the indigent, the crippled, and the helpless old? Who would keep corporations from getting so large that they could wipe out their competition and charge us at will for basic services? Who would deal with criminals? Who would stop conflicts? Who would run the schools? Who would build universities and colleges? Who would finance disease control? Who would preserve natural resources for recreational use? These and thousands of other tasks cannot be performed by private corporations operating under the profit motive in a free market. If this were actually attempted, society would collapse. The problems of social control would simply overwhelm us and leave us isolated in a rather cold world. True, we have much to grumble about, but without government we would not even have the luxury of grumbling.

But Hobbes probably went too far in his advocacy of governmental power, as power alone cannot maintain order. The use of power generates resentments on the part of those subject to power. Indeed, power is not only used to control others; it is also used to hoard wealth and other desirable resources. As a result, power becomes a source of inequality and hence potential conflict, as conflict theories always emphasize. A society that must be perpetually conquered cannot be ruled, as the Soviet Union discovered in 1990 and as conflicts in the middle east so clearly document.

Thus, the social order cannot be sustained for long either by Smith's "Invisible Hand" or by Hobbes' *Leviathan.* True, markets and government are essential to social control in complex societies, but either alone produces social disorder. Moreover, macro-level forces of control never work effectively unless reinforced by people's daily interactions and routines at the micro interpersonal level.

Micro-Level Forces of Social Control

Much social order comes, as interactionist theory would emphasize, from informal interpersonal processes. While the macro dilemma of power versus markets plays itself out, people manage to get along, conform, and remain satisfied in their daily encounters in groups, organizations, and communities. Such is not always the case, but the problem of order is greatly mitigated by processes of interaction.

Socialization.   One crucial interaction process is socialization. By learning a common culture or repertoire of symbols through interaction with others, we go a long way to resolving the problem of order. If you and I did not have some level of consensus over values, beliefs, and norms, we would enter situations with no clear expectations, no standards by which to evaluate each other's and our own conduct, and no instructions about how to behave. We would have to create these, and as a result, our interaction would be awkward, stressful, and perhaps conflictual until we negotiated a common understanding. Thus, one of the essential processes of social control is our socialization into a shared repertoire of symbols and symbol systems, a force of social control that is also emphasized by functionalists (Parsons 1951). And once we implicitly recognize the importance of such shared symbols, we socialize ourselves. We actively look for and learn about the operative norms, beliefs, and values in situations. When you enter into a new situation where you are a bit uncertain of the relevant cultural beliefs and norms, you become highly sensitized and aware. You want to know the cultural codes. And the desire and willingness to be guided by such codes are a powerful mechanism of social control.

This need to know the cultural codes, like the acquisition of the codes themselves, is largely the result of socialization. In addition to the need to know the culture of a situation, we also acquire motives that energize us to occupy social positions and to play roles. If we were apathetic and alienated, we would not want to play roles, and we could not depend on others. Society could not control us because we would not care. Without socialized motivations, therefore, the commitment to the social order and the willingness to subject oneself to cultural guidance would not exist. And no matter how motivated we are to abide by cultural codes, we must have the interpersonal skills, such as role-taking, role-making, and management of emotions, to function in society. Socialization gives us these; without them, we could not adjust, readjust, and fine-tune our responses to each other. Finally, our acquisition of a self-conception gives us a steady compass by which to assess our conduct and the reactions of others to us. If we did not have a self to sustain in interaction and if we did not constantly evaluate ourselves, it would be hard for others to respond to us or to control us. The confirmation of self gives us a stake in interaction; this fact is what gives others the power to control us—within limits, of course.

Sanctioning.   The process of mutual sanctioning is also an intrinsic part of all interactions, and it is crucial to social control. As you and I role-take with others, reading gestures and thinking of appropriate responses, we are also being sanctioned. Those gestures are telling us how well we are doing in the situation; if we are doing something wrong, the gestures of others—their frown, hurt look, or their words—tell us, and we change our behaviors. If we could not assign gestures symbolic meaning, and if we could not role-take and imagine ourselves in each other's place, social control would lose its subtlety and grace. We would have to club people into submission. We still do this occasionally, but far more important and effective are the subtle and sometimes unconscious orchestration of gestures that tells people when they are doing things right or wrong.

Rituals.   Most situations require the use of stereotyped behaviors or rituals. They are yet another way of controlling our responses to each other and of maintaining the social order because they help us typify each other; frame the situation; and take cognizance of relevant cultural norms, beliefs, and values. They assure that certain predictable responses will occur. When we buy goods at a store, we engage in rituals— "hello, how are you," "just fine," "nice day," "yes it is," "have a good day," "thanks," and so forth—and the interaction moves smoothly. In other words, it is controlled and regulated. And we are grateful because it keeps us from having to do too much interpersonal work with a stranger. All rituals thus control interaction. We are being told what to do and we know how to respond to one another.

Segregation of Activities.   The separation in time and space of potentially incompatible activities—activities where different cultural symbols, interpersonal styles, and rituals apply—is yet another process of social control. Much of this separation is done for us by the larger social structure, and so this process of control comes from the outside from meso and macro structural arrangements. But we implicitly recognize its importance as we shift from one stage to another. For example, family activities are segregated from work activities in complex societies because the expectations placed on family members are different from those placed on workers. People thus leave the home for work, thereby separating in time and place conflicting norms and role enactments. If family members "bring their work home with them," there are usually tensions in the household; or, if people work in their home or have a "family business," then there are extraordinary burdens on everyone. In complex societies, it is essential to segregate incompatible activities, thereby avoiding the tensions of having to reconcile different cultural expectations and dramaturgical requirements. Or, if individuals wish to pay for sexual contact or use drugs, there is almost always a "red light district" or a place where drugs can be purchased that is separate from other kinds of activities.

Meso-Level Forces of Social Control

Organizations.   Between the micro-level interactions in encounters and groups, on the one hand, and the macro-level structures of government and law, on the other, there is a variety of middle- or meso-level structures of control. These structures are typically organizations of various types. One kind of organization for controlling deviance is what is often termed a *total institution* in which people are confined until they can cease behaving in a deviant manner. Prisons, mental hospitals, camps for juvenile delinquents, jails, isolated camps for suspected terrorists, and other complex organizations that confine and segregate deviants and others perceived to be dangerous are typical examples.

Another type of organization is a *reintegration structure* that seeks to rehabilitate the deviant so that the individual can eventually become part of normal social life. Many total institutions are also reintegration structures, but the amount of rehabilitation is generally very limited. Other organizations such as those for drug and alcohol problems are more likely to engage in active efforts to change the deviant.

Another kind of meso-level structure of control is what we might term *safety-value* organizations. These structures are generally separate from the mainstream of normal life and are geared toward providing outlets for deviant behavior that will be practiced no matter how reprehensible to the general public. Houses of prostitution, opium dens, gay bars, and other structures provide outlets for deviant behaviors while segregating these behaviors from the normal flow of social life. Some safety-valve structures such as gambling casinos have become mainstream with the spread of "Indian gaming" or with building of Disneyland-like destination resorts such as Las Vegas. Thus, what was once deviant is now mainstream. Similar transformations may be occurring for other types of deviance, such as gay bars, that are now more accepted by the general public.

Aside from these organizations for managing deviance, we should not forget that the regular organizations of a society operate as a mechanism of social control. Work, school, recreation, church, stores, and the many other organizations that we move in and out of regulate behavior. They have "entrance rules," as once we enter, we know how to behave (Luhmann 1982); when we leave, these norms stay in the organization, and as soon as we enter another organization, we adjust behavior to the new rules. Because so much of our lives is spent moving from one organization to another, these norms operate as effective mechanisms of control.

Communities.   We should also remember that organizations are part of communities that also operate as social control mechanisms. Much of the very visible hand of order is wielded by community-level government—police, traffic control, municipal courts—and the organization of space through roads, neighborhoods, shopping districts, business centers, schools, and other structures all order social life. Just looking at the movement of people and cars in space in a community is orderly; because most people are using the structure of community infrastructures to go to and from organizations, community and organizations control much of our daily routines.

In sum, then, social control is a complex set of processes and structures that emerges to manage deviance from cultural norms and to control dissent that can lead to social disorder. Social control is never complete or wholly successful. Still, without mechanisms of social control operating at the micro, macro, and meso levels of social organization, the social order would be overwhelmed. And, as societies become large and complex, micro-level social control operating at the micro level must increasingly be supplemented by the macro-level organization of power in the institutions of the polity and law as well as the meso-level structures that confine and reintegrate those who are seen, whether rightly or wrongly, to pose a threat to society.

Deviance and dissent are thus systematically generated by the organization of human populations into societies. They are inexorable and inevitable, especially as societies become larger. For now, I will only focus on deviance and save the topic of dissent and collective behavior that can transform the structure and culture of societies for the last part of this book (Chapter 23), after we have examined the structures of human societies. Various theoretical traditions have developed explanations for deviance; by reviewing them, we can get a sense for how and why deviance is systematically generated by the very nature of human society.

Deviance

Deviance is behavior that violates widely held norms; as societies get larger, more complex, and more diverse, the rates of deviance increase because both formal and informal forces of social control become inadequate. Émile Durkheim (1893, 1897), one of the founders of sociology, was perhaps the first to fully recognize that the price for large-scale complex societies was an increase in all forms of deviance. Thus rates of deviance will inevitably increase, despite moralizing from public figures. New mechanisms of social control are necessary in large societies, but they are never as effective as those face-to-face mechanisms that were typical of smaller, traditional societies. And, as the study of deviance now reveals, these new mechanisms of social control, especially those operating at the macro and meso level, can actually work to produce deviance.

The Functional Theory of Structural Strain

The functional theorist Robert K. Merton (1968) proposed a theory of **structural strain**—often termed *anomie theory*—to explain deviance. In any society, Merton argued, there are culturally defined success goals and various legitimate means to achieve these goals. High rates of deviance emerge when the legitimate avenues to these success goals are limited, creating a structural strain between means and goals for those who do not have access to legitimate means. A society like ours, for example, stresses monetary and occupational success, but limits the available means to achieve this success, thereby generating structural strain. You are pursuing a legitimate means to the success goals of the United States; in Merton's terms, you are a "conformist" because you accept goals as legitimate (indeed, you may lust after material success) and you use legitimate means to achieve them (unless, of course, you cheat on your exams).

Other people, however, experience strain, leading them to deviate in several ways. One form of deviance is what Merton called "innovation" where success goals are accepted, but the legitimate means are rejected in favor of illegal and illegitimate means—that is, crime. Criminals want what you want—material success—but they use illegitimate means to pursue this goal. Another kind of adaptation to structural strain is "ritualism," where the success goals are rejected or forgotten in favor of slavish conformity to legitimate means. The slavishly conformist bureaucrat who "goes by the book" is such a ritualist. Yet another adaptation to means-ends stress is "retreatism," where both the success goals *and* means are rejected. Dropouts, drug addicts, members of deviant sects, and the like fall into this category. A final adaptation is "rebellion"—a topic to be examined in more detail in Chapter 23—where the culture and structure of a society as a whole are attacked, with the rebels proposing new goals and new means.

In Merton's theory, then, a wide range of behaviors is to be understood in terms of the disjuncture between the availability of legitimate means and the intensity of success goals. A society like the United States, revealing considerable inequality (see Chapter 14) and extolling the virtues of material success, should have high rates of deviance. And not surprisingly, we do. Crime is high, and retreatist subgroups exist; although a society-wide rebellion is not likely, there are some rebellious subgroups.

The Conflict Perspective on Deviance

Merton's structural strain theory emphasizes that legitimate means are not equally available to all, and conflict theory focuses on this point. Lower class persons, women, and many ethnic minorities simply do not have the same degree of access to the means for success as more affluent, white males. Access to legitimate means is, therefore, a valued resource over which there is conflict. Conflict theory also stresses that those who hold power are also able to define success goals as well as legitimate and illegitimate means in ways that favor them.

Although the conflict theories are often stated in the extreme (Quinney 1970, 1979, 1980), the general argument is worth reviewing. The norms that define deviance are, conflict theorists argue, those of the powerful. Laws and their enforcement emphasize the illegality of activities that are offensive to the morality of the privileged classes and that threaten their property and affluence (Turk 1969). Stated less stridently, the laws and their enforcement are greatly influenced by the distribution of power and privilege. Poor people who are more likely to steal, use drugs, and carry weapons must confront strict laws against them and harsh enforcement of these laws compared to affluent people who commit white-collar and corporate crimes like embezzlement, industrial pollution, health and safety violations, consumer fraud, election fraud, political dirty tricks, stock manipulation, and the like. In addition, the more powerful can usually enlist the support of the broad middle classes to support them. Indeed, by focusing law enforcement energies on the crimes of the poor, there is less enforcement of those crimes committed by the nonpoor (Chambliss 1978), thereby enabling many of the rich to "get away" with their forms of crime.

Interactionist Approaches to Deviance

For interactionists, the behaviors of individuals are shaped by the responses of others. And when others *label* a person's acts as deviant, the individual can often be forced into the role of deviant. How is this possible?

Labeling theory emphasizes that the labels attached to people's behaviors are crucial in the genesis and maintenance of deviance (Lemert 1951, 1967; Scheff 1966). When people are labeled deviant—as criminals, delinquents, crazy persons, drug users, alcoholics—they can often respond to these labels by fulfilling the expectations contained in the label. We all know, to some extent, the roles of deviants; if we were consistently labeled, how would we respond? We might well be driven to act as we were labeled.

But the process of labeling is more complex (Liska 1981). When a person is labeled deviant—say, as alcoholic, criminal, delinquent, prostitute, or mental patient—this individual will typically accumulate written transcripts of this label, such as a police file, a blank period of biography, or a hospital record. The label thus becomes formalized and institutionalized with the result that employers, landlords, potential friends, welfare agencies, and others respond *as if* the person were deviant. Such labels deny people the chance to escape from deviance and force them back into deviant roles. These pressures are compounded by the inability to acquire new, nondeviant interpersonal ties, for who wants to interact with a prostitute, homeless person, delinquent, mental patient, or alcoholic? Over time, as the label is applied and enforced, people acquire a self-conception of themselves as deviant in terms of the label, and they come to act in ways that reflect this deviant self-conception, thereby assuring that the label sticks.

These labeling processes are, no doubt, part of the biography of any deviant. Sometimes the labels have been informal; at other times an "official" record is accumulated. But for each, the label often has generated interpersonal and institutional responses that kept people from escaping their label and that have communicated the evaluation, assessment, and expectation of others about their deviance. Thus, whatever the initial causes of deviance, there are powerful forces operating to sustain deviance once labeling occurs.

Another type of interactionist theory about deviance emphasizes the transmission of deviance through interaction and socialization. Perhaps the most famous of these is the **differential association theory** (Sutherland, 1939; Sutherland and Cressey 1986). In this theory, individuals who interact in situations where deviance is approved will acquire a high ratio of deviant to nondeviant images and definitions. The result is that these individuals will be disposed to commit deviant acts, especially when they encounter deviant orientations early in life and in long-term interactions with those they admire and care about. Thus, if people must live in environments where there are many images, definitions, and role-models of deviance, they are more likely to have early, close, and long-term interactions with others who impart these deviant orientations. As a result, their patterns of differential association will distort their definitions of proper behavior, their self-definitions, and their perceptions of opportunity in ways that encourage deviance. Once labeled as a deviant, it will become difficult for these individuals to alter this preponderance of deviant definitions about how to view themselves, assess opportunities, and act in the world.

Utilitarian Theories of Deviance

Control theory blends many aspects of these other theories into a "rational choice perspective" (Hirschi 1969). The basic question is: What keeps people from being deviant in light of the fact that there are many rewards or utilities for being deviant? Ultimately, the answer to this question is that it would cost too much to deviate because of social attachments to nondeviant others and groups, because of investments in nondeviant activities, because of the time spent in nondeviant activities, and because of acquired beliefs in conformity to norms. Conversely, for those who are deviant, these costs are not so great.

For deviants, there are no strong *attachments* and bonds to others who would disapprove of deviants. Indeed, from a control theory perspective, the career of any deviant is punctuated by a lack of attachments, or very weak attachments (Hirschi 1969; Kornhauser 1978; Liska 1981) to others, even those engaged in deviance. Without attachments, there is less to lose from being deviant; and because much deviance is highly rewarding, it will increase among those whose attachments are weak. There is also the question of "investments" in nondeviant careers. The more we have invested in education, years on the job, house, family ties, car, and other relationships and possessions, the more we risk by being deviant. We could lose these investments, and so, we perceive deviance as very costly. But for those who do not have these investments, the costs of deviance are much less. There is also the matter of "involvements," or time and energy spent in conformity to norms. Time and energy are limited, and if our attachments and investments have created pressures to conform, there is less time and energy available for deviance. The extra energy is costly to mobilize, and the time is difficult to find; and so, when people are involved in nondeviance and are spending much time and energy on conformity, they have less to expend on deviance. Finally, there are "beliefs" and other cultural symbols about how people should behave; and if we have internalized those stressing conformity, it becomes psychologically and emotionally costly to violate them. Having a conscience is another way of saying that it is too costly to violate norms and values about what should be, and what should occur.

Thus, from a control theoretical viewpoint, those who deviate have weak attachments to others, few investments in nondeviance, less time and energy committed to conformity, and fewer beliefs about conformity to mainstream norms. As a consequence, the costs of deviance are less to these individuals; and because deviance can be rewarding, they become more likely to perceive "rationally" the rewards of deviants as exceeding the costs of deviance. For you and me, the reverse is true: attachments, investments, involvements, and beliefs make it too costly to deviate.

In sum, these various theoretical approaches can provide much insight into deviance today in America. There is enormous structural strain stemming from inequality; we are all bombarded in the media with the notion of material success in a society that limits the opportunities for many to achieve this success. There is also considerable inequality in how deviant acts are defined by laws and enforced by agencies; and this inequality favors the rich over the poor in how deviance is treated. When deviant acts are committed, labels are easily applied by police, courts, hospitals, and other agencies that stigmatize deviants and help sustain deviant careers, especially for the poor who have no other resources to fight against labels. There are clear areas and regions in America where definitions supporting deviance exceed those against it, forcing people who must live in these regions to differentially associate with definitions, techniques, beliefs, and norms favoring a deviant career. And there are rewards for deviance—instant money for selling drugs, local fame for acts of violence, "easy" income from robbery, quick gratifications for murder and assault, and so forth—that are not counterbalanced by high costs from attachments, investments, involvements, and beliefs.

We should expect, therefore, high rates of deviance in the United States; and perhaps it is wise to be less shocked and morally outraged. Instead, we should be more attuned to what needs to be done in light of these theories. More punishment and enforcement will not work to stop crime and other acts of deviance; rather, policies must be directed at reducing the disjuncture between success goals and available means, at redressing the imbalance in how poor and rich criminals are treated, at mitigating the effects of labels, and at increasing the human costs of deviance by increasing attachments, investments, and involvements in the mainstream culture and structures of society.

SUMMARY

1. Society is always an uneasy standoff between the forces promoting order and those causing deviance, dissent, conflict, and disorder.

2. A number of interrelated forces inevitably generates pressures for disorder: (a) increases in population size, (b) escalated differentiation, and (c) increased inequality.

3. At the macro level of society, social control is promoted by (a) governmental regulation and (b) market exchanges.

4. At the micro level of social organization, social control is promoted by (a) socialization of personality, (b) mutual sanctioning, (c) rituals, and (d) role segregation.

5. At the meso level of social organization, social control is promoted by the rules governing behavior in organizations and the structures of communities ordering the location and movement of people in space. Organizations can also be created as (a) safety-valve organizations, (b) reintegration structures, and (c) total institutions.

6. Each of the major theoretical perspectives offers a theory on the causes of deviance. Functional theories stress the structural strain between cultural goals and the distribution of means. Conflict theories argue that laws and enforcement procedures help the affluent and work against the poor. Interactionist theories stress the labels given to people and the socialization process. Utilitarian theories emphasize the calculations of costs, investments, involvements, and beliefs in the genesis of deviance or conformity.

KEY TERMS

Control Theory: Utilitarian theory of deviance, stressing that calculations of cost and investments determine whether or not people will deviate.

Deviance: Behavior that violates accepted norms.

Differential Association Theory: Theory arguing that deviance is created when there is an excess of criminal to noncriminal definitions of appropriate behavior in a person's biography.

Labeling Theory: The view that the labels bestowed on individuals become self-fulfilling prophecies that create expectations for deviance which, in turn, lead to deviance and deviant careers.

Structural Strain: Robert Merton's "anomie theory" between goals and means to achieve these goals.

Part III Types of Social Structures: Corporate Units

Human behavior and interaction are organized by culture and social structures. Corporate units, as outlined in Chapter 6, reveal a division and labor and generally have goals or purposes, however transitory. These stand in contrast to categoric units that are created when people categorize others and, on the basis of this categorization, evaluate and respond to these others differently—as is explored in Part IV. In this section, our focus is on the basic types of corporate units that organize people's behaviors and interactions. At the most micro level of social structure is the encounter of focused and unfocused interaction that organizes people's responses to each other when they are co-present. All social structures are ultimately constructed from encounters. Groups are often coextensive with encounters; the groups organize chains of encounters over time. Organizations are formal structures that structure encounters and groups into hierarchies of authority to achieve specific goals. Encounters, groups, and organizations all exist within communities that organize institutional activities—economic, political, religious, educational, medical, family, and the like—in physical space. All social structures, except perhaps a few that now appear to exist in virtual reality, are located in a place; this place is organized into a community as a basic form of social structure.

Chapter 10

Encounters

You are walking across the campus at night, alone in your thoughts. You see another person approaching you from a distance. It is dark and you cannot see precisely who this person is, but you become alert as you monitor the other's movements. As the individual approaches, you implicitly know to avert your gaze and avoid looking at them directly while at the same time monitoring this person's movements, body countenance, and other gestures. You begin to assess this person's gender, ethnicity, and perhaps even dress and body countenance for signs of social class. Suddenly, you are relieved to see that this person is someone you know from class, and when this recognition is reciprocated, you both realign your movements, stop, offer mutual greetings, share some pleasantries, say goodbye, and move onto your respective destinations.

This unfolding series of events was labeled by Erving Goffman (1961, 1963, 1967, 1971) as an *encounter*. The encounter is the most elementary and fleeting structure of society because it involves individuals becoming mutually aware of each other in a place, monitoring each other's conduct, and making behavioral adjustments to others. Goffman saw two basic types of encounters: (a) focused and (b) unfocused. When you saw your classmate at a distance, the encounter was unfocused; you were prepared to keep your distance, perhaps offer a passing hello, and go about your way. When, however, you recognized the other, you engaged in a short but focused interaction, exchanging pleasantries, asking after the other, and only then going on your respective paths. In some ultimate sense, society is constructed from these two types of encounters; therefore, an understanding of these two forms of encounters represents a good starting point for analyzing the structure and culture of human societies.

Focused Encounters

A **focused encounter** involves individuals who, as the name implies, are focused on each other. They are open to verbal communication. They have aligned their bodies in a kind of ecological huddle to facilitate face-to-face contact. They are on heightened alert to the meaning of each other's words, facial expressions, and body. And, as the interaction proceeds, a "we" feeling develops that distinguishes the encounter from the buzz and noise occurring outside the temporary ecological huddle.

Even an encounter like the two acquaintances passing in the night is fundamental to the social order. Indeed, the social order is ultimately composed of these encounters as they are repeated and strung together over time. Because focused encounters are so fundamental to the social order, they reveal complex and powerful dynamics. They often seem casual, perhaps even trivial, but when something goes wrong in an encounter, the arousal of people's emotions indicates that something much more important is at stake. Imagine what happens if one person misspeaks and says something that throws the interaction out of line. People fall silent, the speaker turns red-faced, others pause to give the speaker a chance to engage in corrective action, and when the proper response is forthcoming, everyone feels relieved that the breach to the interaction will not require more emotion work.

What is at stake in virtually every encounter is the moral order of society. If social structure and culture are ultimately built from focused encounters, it is not surprising that everyone senses what is at stake. When an encounter goes badly, it is emotionally upsetting because each individual's sense of what should occur and must occur has been violated. Of course, when an encounter turns ugly, civilization does not collapse around us, but we all implicitly recognize that social order depends upon the smooth flow of interaction. If you question this generalization, imagine situations that seem unimportant but that had the ability to arouse emotions: the clerk at the store who is unfriendly, the fellow student who passes you but does not say hello to your greeting, the person who leaves the encounter without saying goodbye, and many other small gestures that would seem trivial but that can arouse emotions when not performed. Why would one get mad at a clerk who was not friendly, why would you care if someone did not say hello or goodbye? The answer is that much is on the line with each and every encounter.

Not only is a lot on the line, but the dynamics of encounters are surprisingly complicated. A great deal is going on and, we should try to isolate some of the key dynamics.

Rituals

All encounters begin and close with **rituals** or stereotyped sequences of behavior. Handshakes, smiles, greetings, and goodbyes open and close the encounter. But why, we can ask, should this be necessary? Why do people need to say hello, goodbye, and engage in other stereotyped sequences of behavior? If you doubt the necessity of these interpersonal rituals, think of a situation where the proper ritual has not been performed. Someone walks away from you without saying goodbye (in some ritualized way, such as "see you around" or "nice talking to you"). You will find yourself upset at the end of the encounter, as you watch the person walk away, but more fundamentally, how will you feel at the next meeting? There will be a tension in the air because the previous encounter was not ritually closed.

Rituals not only open and close an encounter, they also structure the flow of interaction. When a person wants to change topics, this is often done with a short ritual like "can I ask you a question?," "what do you think of?," "can we move onto something else?," and the like. Without the use of these ritualized phrases, sudden shifts in talk seem awkward and, indeed, often breach the flow of interaction, leaving everybody to scramble for a way to get the interaction back on track.

Rituals also repair breaches to an interaction. When a person utters something wrong, individuals often sanction this individual with rituals: "what do you mean by that?," "are you sure about that?," "how can you say that?," and the like. The use of rituals takes some of the sting out of the negative sanction, but it does more; it gives the other the chance to offer the appropriate apology, which is often given in highly ritualized form: "sorry, I wasn't thinking," "you're right, that was a stupid thing to say," and other highly stylized sequences. In turn, people accept the apology in a ritualized way: "no problem," "that's okay," "we all make mistakes," and the like. Without the use of rituals, the negative emotions of anger by those engaged in sanctioning and the sense of fear and anxiety from those who have been sanctioned can send the encounter out of control. Rituals regulate the process of pointing out breaches, giving people opportunities to make repairs, and allowing others to accept the repair. We all sense this emotional dynamic, and we have all been party to encounters that have suddenly gone out of control as people's emotions are aroused to the point where they cannot control them; given the problems in putting these encounters back together again, we all implicitly understand the need for rituals to keep them going.

Erving Goffman (1967) was the first sociologist to recognize that the rituals of everyday life are probably more fundamental to the social order than the "big ticket" rituals, such as religious, graduation, and marriage ceremonies in institutional spheres like religion, education, and family. Each and every interaction is opened, closed, and structured by rituals; when these are not emitted properly, the encounter soon degenerates into an awkward and tension-filled scene.

Forms of Talk

Goffman also emphasized that **forms of talk** vary from encounter to encounter. There are, in essence, implicit rules about how you are supposed to talk in an encounter. Indeed, if these rules are violated, the interaction is breached or, at the very least, stressful. Individuals will be forced to use rituals to sanction and bring those who have violated the rules back into line. How each of us talks in an encounter depends upon who is present, their prestige, their power, and their place in the larger social structure within which the encounter transpires. You do not talk to your professors, for example, as you do to your friends; a low-ranking employee does not talk to the boss like fellow employees; you do not ask a question in class as you do at the dinner table or in the dorm. If you doubt the power of these rules, adopt a manner of talking that is inappropriate to the cultural rules of the encounter: talk to your professor as you would with a fellow student, talk to your parents at home as if you were a guest in their house, or otherwise break the proper form of talk.

There are also rules about other aspects of talk in encounters. One set of rules governs what Goffman called *response cues,* such as "wow," "oops," "yikes," "yo," and other verbal utterances that are not words but that demonstrate responsiveness and keep the interaction in flow. There are also rules about *verbal fillers,* such as "ah," "um," "uh," and the like. These are used to maintain the conversational floor, indicating to others that a person is not done and, therefore, is not be interrupted. Yet, people who use these fillers to distraction also violate cultural rules by holding the floor too long. There are also norms about *clearance cues,* which indicate that a person is done speaking, leaving the floor open to others. These cues can be done with the body, such as a nodding of head, but they are often done with voice, as when a person's words trail off or with an explicit ritual ("that's all I can think of," "what do you think?"). People are supposed to signal to others that the coast is clear for others to talk; when they do not, the interaction becomes strained because others may interrupt or be unsure about when they can respond.

Finally, successful interactions always involve a rhythmic synchronization of talk and other gestures (Collins 2004). One person says something, another responds, and the person picks up on what is said and responds appropriately. There is thus a rhythm to talk—a give and take that when in sync will resemble a rhythmic flow of body gestures and facial expressions back and forth. We are immediately aware when rhythmic synchronization is off. You say something, for example, and the other person just stands there looking at you; you say something again and the same thing happens; eventually, the interaction becomes so awkward that you want to leave. We all know people who always seem out of sync. Perhaps they are shy, maybe they are too self-conscious, or maybe they are just weird, but we all know that interaction with such individuals will be stressful. Thus, any encounter seeks to establish a rhythm of talk, of give and take, that heightens the pleasure of the interpersonal flow of verbalizations and other gestures.

Frames

Erving Goffman (1974) also introduced the notion of **frame** and framing to the study of encounters. The basic idea, which I extend here, is that individuals in an encounter establish implicit boundaries of what is to be included and what is to be excluded from an interaction. These boundaries are like a picture frame because they establish what is to be inside the frame and, hence, an appropriate topic of conversation and what is to be outside the rim of the frame and not a topic of conversation in an encounter. Rituals are often used to **key the frame**—that is, establish what the frame is. For example, if an encounter opens with a reserved "hello" and movement of the head in acknowledgement of your presence, it is safe to say that personal matters such as your sex life are outside the rim of the frame. In contrast, a big hug and kiss on the lips may open up such topics. Often the structure of the more inclusive situation sets the frame, as is the case when you enter a classroom, work setting, dorm, or your parent's house. These structures carry a culture or set of understandings pulled from stocks of knowledge about what are appropriate and inappropriate topics. The process of framing is an amazingly complex process, and yet, unless frames are established, individuals do not know how to behave. If you can imagine a situation where you simply do not know the frame, you will probably find yourself very actively searching the ritual responses of others to determine just what the frame of the situation is.

Rituals are also used to **re-key** or shift the frame. For example, when a person says "would you mind if I asked a personal question?," this ritual phrase shifts the frame to a more personal and potentially intimate conversation. Or, if an individual says "I don't want to talk about that," this moves the frame and excludes certain topics. Thus, anytime a person wishes to re-key the frame they will typically do so in a highly stylized or ritualized way. To shift the frame without the groundwork laid down by the ritual risks breaching the interaction. Indeed, rude people are often those who do not pay attention to frames, or break them without the necessary ritual work.

Categorization

Each encounter involves a process of **categorization** along several dimensions. One is the situation itself. Erving Goffman (1967) thought that situations are one of three basic types: (1) *work-practical,* or where the encounter is devoted to getting some explicit task done; (2) *ceremonial,* in which the encounter is intended to mark with rituals some event or transition (such as encounters devoted to marriage, graduation, promotion, retirement, and initiations); and (3) *social,* where people are gathered primarily to enjoy each other's company. Rarely is a situation wholly work-practical, ceremonial, or social, but one orientation typically dominates the other two. Thus, at work, people are often social and even at times ceremonial, but work-practical orientations still dominate. Even at a social gathering, people can "talk work" or "talk about classes" and other work-practical matters. And, ceremonies can also be social and work-practical.

Another dimension of categorization is the level of intimacy appropriate among participants of the encounter. Frames help establish the intimacy, but we typically know the level of intimacy that should be evident. One level is where individuals are simply *social categories.* When you check out your groceries at the store, the check-out person is treated as a category (clerk) and you can go on automatic pilot when interacting with them. Professors teaching large classes will generally treat students as members of a category, and vice versa, unless out-of-class encounters ensue. A second level of intimacy is to treat individuals as *persons* in that you know something about them but at the same time are not intimate. A casual friend, a check-out clerk you have come to "know" casually, a professor whose office you have visited, and many others whom we have encountered before are treated as persons about whom we know something unique but with whom we are not intimate. A third level is actual *intimacy,* whereby we know highly personal things about the other, and vice versa. Thus, when encounters form, we do a quick and generally implicit assessment of the appropriate level of intimacy; from this categorization, we adjust our responses accordingly.

A third dimension of categorization revolves around what were termed categoric units in Chapter 6. People are always members of social categories, such as gender, ethnicity, and social class. On the basis of our perceptions of the categories of those in an encounter, individuals adjust their behaviors. For example, an encounter of all men or all women will be very different than one composed of both men and women, or an encounter of whites and African Americans will flow differently than one composed of only members of one ethnic group. Interactions between upper class and lower class individuals will be very different than among those in the same class. In a very real sense, every encounter is embedded in categoric units. We have distinctive expectations for members of categoric units and we behave in accordance with these expectations. Over time, as people get to know each other, these expectations can change, and a person's membership in a categoric unit can decrease in salience, but such changes only occur as individuals become persons and perhaps intimates. Even here, when the transition to greater intimacy has occurred, categoric membership can remain highly relevant. For example, a husband never forgets that his wife is a female, or if he does, he does so at his own peril.

Thus, in each and every encounter we do some quick calculations about the nature of the situation, the level of intimacy that is appropriate, and the expectations associated with our own and others' categoric unit memberships. It is remarkable that people can generally do this categorization with ease, without great agonizing or reflection. Only when we are unsure about how to categorize the situation do we realize how much we rely upon this process. If a person does not know how much work-practical, ceremonial, or social content is appropriate; if they do not know the right level of intimacy; or if they have no experience in interacting with members of a particular category, this individual will feel ill at ease until they sense that they have successfully categorized the situation and others in the proper manner.

Body Language

Much communication in encounters is conducted nonverbally, through the language of the body. Facial expressions, body countenance, hand and arm movements, and many other gestures of the body that carry common meanings are critical to the smooth flow of interaction. We can immediately recognize this fact when the spoken words emitted by a person do not correspond to his or her body language. For example, if a person says that she is not angry but her face and body tell us otherwise, we immediately rely more on the body language than on the spoken word. In fact, we almost always feel uncomfortable around individuals who are not very demonstrative with their face and bodies. We do not know what they are feeling or how they are likely to respond to our gestures. A simple kind of breaching experiment can also demonstrate the importance of body language: When talking with a friend, try to avoid making any expressions with your face and body; become like a robot and simply rely only upon the spoken word with few voice inflections. You will find that others will immediately want to know "what is wrong" with you.

Thus, for an encounter to proceed smoothly and for individuals to feel like they are "in sync" with each other, nonverbal gestures are critical—the smile, a nod of the head, a touch of the hand, an animated movement of hands, a rhythmic sway of bodies vis-à-vis one another, and many other gestures of the body that carry common meanings. In fact, these nonverbal gestures are probably more important than spoken words in generating a sense of rhythmic flow and solidarity among participants in an encounter

Body language is essential in communicating emotions and affect. Words simply cannot communicate the full range of emotions without nonverbal gestures. To say "I love you" with a stone face and no appropriate gestures with the body would immediately indicate the opposite: "I *don't* really love you." For almost all emotional responses, then, people rely primarily on body language to get a sense for what others feel; and we use the gestures of the body to communicate our feelings to others. In fact, when nonverbal gesturing is in sync, words can become unnecessary, if not an intrusion to the smooth flow of an interaction.

Emotions

All encounters have rules about the appropriate kinds and levels of emotions to be displayed. A funeral and a fraternity bear bust reveal very different expectations for the kinds of emotions that are to be emitted in the varied encounters that make up these events. Framing and categorizing dramatically reduce the effort needed to understand what emotions are relevant, and once a person has categorized and framed the broader situation and the specific encounters that ensue, this individual generally understands the feeling rules and display rules that are guiding the interactions (Hochschild 1979). **Feeling rules** dictate what one is supposed to feel in a situation—say, sadness at a funeral or hyper-joviality at a keg party. **Display rules** indicate how one is supposed to behave in revealing to others their emotions. When individuals do not feel the right emotion, they often must engage in considerable **emotion work** to get into the proper emotional mood or to act out in their behaviors emotions that they do not feel. If you are happy that someone is dead, you may engage in "method acting" to see if you can evoke the feeling of being sad, or if you cannot do this, you will act sad by giving a performance to others about your grief.

In complex societies, we are often required to engage in considerable emotion work. People are often put into encounters where they are required to display particular emotions that they do not feel. For example, Arlie Hochschild (1979) studied airline stewards who are supposed to remain friendly, even when passengers are rude; this kind of emotion work was psychologically costly for the stewards. Similarly, when in class, on the job, in public, and in many contexts, feeling and display rules often work against a person's emotional states. Indeed, students will often work to stifle their yawns in lectures, especially in small classes where their behavior can be seen by their professor, because display rules indicate that they are supposed to be attentive and motivated rather than bored.

Emotions are also very important in sustaining the flow of an interaction. We all need to emit the appropriate type and level of emotions to others for them to feel "connected" to us. For example, individuals who do not give off much affect are often difficult to be with because others rely upon a certain level and type of affect to signal that the interaction is on track. Emotions are thus important markers of internal dispositions, and when people do not or cannot reveal expressiveness, the interaction is strained. Indeed, norms regulate how expressive people are supposed to be in an encounter. If the proper emotions are not emitted, or even worse, if the wrong emotions are given off, the interaction will be breached, leading to ritualized sanctions, hoped-for ritual apologies, and ritualized acceptances of corrective behaviors.

Roles

Individuals seek to "make" a **role** for themselves in all situations. Each individual emits a sequence of behaviors that marks them as a certain kind of person engaged in a recognizable line of conduct. Often roles are associated with each individual's position in a larger social structure, as when a student and professor enact their respective roles in an encounter. When social structure does not dictate the roles that individuals are to play, they must work at the process of making a role for themselves. Sometimes they do so unconsciously, and at other times they strategically manipulate their gestures and behaviors to communicate to others the role they are playing. For example, if a male is trying to "impress" a female with his qualities as a potential love partner, he will orchestrate his behaviors into an identifying role. The roles can vary, as would be the case for trying to present oneself as an intellectual, a stud, or a sensitive type. Thus, people generally have some leeway in the style of role that they play, even in situations that are highly structured. For instance, although the general expectations for the role of a professor are well understood, this role can be played in very different ways such as "friend of students," "mean and demanding," or something in between.

People carry in their brains conceptions of various types of roles. When they read the gestures of another, they interpret these gestures and scan their minds to see what kind of role a person is trying to make for himself or herself in an encounter. Indeed, we all implicitly assume that others are making a role, and as a consequence, we look for syndromes or configurations of signs marking a role. And, when we recognize the role that someone is making, we can then more readily interact with this person. Conversely, when the signals being emitted do not conform to any configurations that we recognize, we will immediately become uneasy. We have trouble understanding a person, and as a result, we feel uncomfortable until we understand how the behaviors of another person mark a role.

Thus, individuals operate with the folk assumptions that the behaviors of others do indeed mark a role, and we read their gestures and behaviors in an effort to understand the underlying role. People also work to assert or make a role for themselves in a situation, and some of the most interesting dynamics of an encounter revolve around people's efforts to make a role and others' recognition of this role. At times, others will not allow a person to make a role for themselves, sanctioning their behaviors as inappropriate. "Don't be a jerk," "who are you trying to kid," "get real," "not in this world," and other ritualized phrases often signal to a person that they have not successively made an appropriate or acceptable role. People typically understand the limits of what they can do in a situation, however, because they are aware of the relevant norms, frames, rituals, forms of talk, and categories. Of course, some people are just boorish and unaware, and they go through encounter after encounter trying to make roles that few are willing to accept. But, most people cannot stand the negative sanctions that ensue and are quickly brought back into line.

Self and Identity

In making a role for oneself, individuals are also engaged in a very serious effort to present themselves as a certain kind of person, or **self**, who is deserving of respect and other responses from others (J. Turner 2002). People carry a self-conception that operates at two levels. One level is a *role identity,* whereby a person sees himself or herself as a certain kind of person in the particular role that they are playing. Thus, a student, professor, mother, father, or worker all attempt to assert to others in encounters their role identity as a *certain type* of student, professor, mother, or father; if others will confirm this identity, they will be satisfied and indeed may experience pleasure. Another level of self is more trans-situational and involves people's general *self-conception* of themselves as a person. Each of us seeks to present to others this more stable and global conception of who we are, and when others confirm that this presentation of self is acceptable, we will experience satisfaction if not pleasure.

Most interesting is when the presentation of self is not successful because others will not confirm either the role identity being asserted or the more general self-conception. When a role identity is not accepted by others, a person will seek to convince others that this identity is appropriate, but if the individual is unsuccessful in this effort, another role identity will be presented. When the more general conception of oneself is not accepted by others, the negative emotions aroused can be intense. People feel angry, shamed, humiliated, and fearful that their view of themselves is not viable. Most of the time, people will avoid rejecting an identity because the negative emotional arousal is highly disruptive to the smooth flow of the encounter. But, at times, people cannot or will not accept a person's presentations of self; as a consequence, the encounter will be filled with emotional tension.

Props

In an encounter, there are physical props to be utilized. The way each person dresses and grooms represents a stage prop, as something that is used to signal a role and self to others. If one person dyes their hair purple and wears dark clothing, these acts signal something to others; or if another wears button-down clothing and cuts his hair into a "flat top," something else is communicated. We are all aware of these differences in how body and its adornment can be used as a staging prop, but we also use other physical features available in an encounter. How one sits in a chair, uses a desk, or aligns body vis-à-vis other bodies represent's a kind of stagecraft. For example, a professor who stays behind the podium versus one who wanders down the aisle is using props in different ways to communicate a role and identity to others. Thus, individuals always use props that are available in encounters. Just what props they adopt and how they deploy them can dramatically influence the flow of the interaction.

Demography and Ecology

All encounters reveal a **demography:** how many people are co-present, what characteristics (age, gender, ethnicity, status, power) do they have, and how do they move in and out of the encounter. There is also an

ecology to an encounter: how people are spaced and how props and other fixed equipment circumscribe not only people's location but their opportunities to make face-to-face contact. An encounter in a large lecture hall will reveal a different demography and ecology than a small seminar class. Or, as any professor knows, when students come and go during a lecture, this movement changes the nature of lectures (and how the professor feels about the students in class). And, depending on the demography and ecology, different expectations for how people are to behave will exist. In the large class, you may get away with talk whereas you would be mortified to try this in a small seminar; or if an encounter has very old and very young people in it, the interpersonal flow will be very different than if people are of the same age. Thus, we are always highly attuned to the demography of who is present in what numbers and of how people are distributed in space by props and other physical features of the situation.

The Person, Culture, and Social Structure

The encounter is where you as a person meet culture and social structure. As we respond to others and read their gestures, each of us feels the pressure of others' expectations on how we should behave. We are also cognizant of the broader culture and of our position in social structures. It is the meeting of the macro, meso, and micro realms of reality that makes the encounter so significant sociologically. Each of us as a person seeks to play a role and confirm self, but we must do so in ways that are acceptable to others, that are in accordance with cultural scripts, and that are appropriate to our position and the positions of others. Thus, much more than our personal well-being is on the line; the culture and structure of the social world is also being supported, challenged, or changed by the actions of individuals when they meet face-to-face in focused encounters. Rarely can any one person in any one encounter change much of anything; indeed, most encounters reinforce the cultural rules and respective positions of individuals. But when people find most of their encounters less than gratifying and unfulfilling, negative emotions are aroused and people seek change; if enough individuals in enough encounters feel this way, social change is sure to ensue, eventually. However, culture and social structures are not easily changed because, as we will see, they carry a power and weight that constrains our options in almost every focused encounter we have. Indeed, sociology is about the properties and dynamics of meso-level and macro-level structures that constrain encounters. Each encounter is embedded in the culture and structure of corporate and categoric units that in turn are embedded in the culture and structure of larger institutional systems. The combined power of these meso and macro structures makes large-scale change by actions of individuals in micro encounters difficult, but obviously not impossible because the social world is constantly changing. There is a majesty and power to culture and social structure, but it must confront efforts by individuals to maintain their dignity, to confirm self, to play viable roles, and to experience positive emotions. There is always a potential for tension in this intersection of powerful social forces.

Unfocused Encounters

For most of humans' evolutionary history, the vast majority of encounters were focused. But, as the scale and complexity of society increased, **unfocused encounters** increased. Just like the person discussed at the opening of this chapter, we often walk in public places, adjust our bodies so as not to bump into each other and, most importantly, remain aware of each other's presence but remain unfocused on the person as an individual. Large, urban populations always reveal the movement and positioning of people in public places. We move down sidewalks; cut across streets; sit on benches, chairs, and other equipment in public places; and through it all, people manage to navigate a complex social grid. We rarely bump into each other; we usually understand where we can move, stand, and sit; and we know how much contact we can make with strangers. All of these accomplishments involve unfocused encounters where we take account of those around us but do not focus on each other.

Like focused encounters, unfocused encounters are governed by cultural rules. If you doubt this, walk down the street and try to make eye contact with a stranger coming toward you. Just stare at this person, trying to engage them in face-to-face eye contact. You will find the other person becoming very uncomfortable, averting their eyes, and moving away; and this individual might become angry and engage you aggressively for your violation of the rules of public behavior. Or, sit close to someone on a park bench when there is still plenty of room to keep some distance; the other will soon move, or at least give you a dirty look. Or, enter an elevator with only one person and stand near them rather than going to the furthest neutral corner. Or, take someone's backpack off a chair in the student union and sit in it, waiting for them to return with their tray of food. In all of these behaviors, you will have violated powerful but hardly acknowledged cultural norms about appropriate behavior.

As with focused encounters, Erving Goffman (1963, 1971) offered many key insights to the dynamics of unfocused encounters. Unfocused encounters begin with scanning the environment, noting who is present and where they are going. We note the social categories to which others belong, the speed and direction of their movements, the resoluteness that they reveal, and other features of their behavior. We do this without zooming in on them and without making direct eye contact, which would immediately focus the encounter. As individuals move in space, they send out signals to others indicating that they are engaged in a recognizable and acceptable line of conduct and that they are not going to invade another's personal space. Of particular importance is respect for others' **territories of self.** Each culture has rules about just what constitutes a territory of self. One territory is the appropriate distance between you and others, relative to the overall space available. Other territories include *fixed equipment* that can be appropriated for a time (benches, stalls), *objects* that can be arrayed around an individual (animals, strollers), and *conversational preserves* that limit others from making verbal contact.

When another violates these territories of self, negative sanctions are often given—a hostile look or actual words. And, when a person must violate a territory of space, this incursion is usually predicated with rituals.

For example, if you need to ask someone the time or need directions, this request is typically highly stylized in an elaborate ritual sequence of words. The use of ritual—"excuse me, but can I trouble you for the time" or "I am really sorry to disturb you but I am lost. . . ."—tells others that you are a normal person and that you are only temporarily intruding on their territory. When violations of the territories of self are accidental, as when you bump into someone, this violation is immediately followed by high ritualized apologies and accounts—for example, "oh, I am so sorry; I was not looking where I was going!"

The fact that violations of territories of self lead to use of rituals underscores how important they are for sustaining social organization. Much social organization in modern complex societies involves moving larger numbers of people across public space; the social order depends upon these movements occurring with the least amount of disruption. As a result, norms emerge to regulate contact and keep people moving without focusing their actions directly on each other. People keep their distance, overplay their intentions to assure others that they are normal and behaving appropriately, offer rather elaborate and ritualized apologies for violations of public space, and otherwise keep their place by body positioning and allow others to sustain their territory of self. Indeed, it is a remarkable achievement that humans who evolved in small bands of hunter-gatherers can assemble in such large numbers and still manage to move about smoothly. Only when we go to a very different culture where the rules of public behavior are different do we encounter problems.

SUMMARY

1. The most elemental social structure is the encounter. Encounters can be focused, whereby individuals form an ecological huddle and engage in face-to-face communication, or unfocused, whereby individuals monitor each other's movements in space without making eye-to-eye contact or focusing the interaction.

2. Focused encounters revolve around all of the key processes of interaction: rituals, the forms of talk, keying and re-keying of frames, mutual categorization of people as well as the situation, displays and feeling appropriate emotions, mutual signaling of the roles being played, mutual presentation of a self and identity, proper use of staging props, and assessment of the meaning of the demography and ecology of the situation.

3. The focused encounter is the nexus between the individual and larger scale social structures and cultural systems. Meso structures like groups, organizations, communities, and social categories such as class, gender, ethnicity, and age all impinge on the dynamics of an encounter, as do the larger social institutions that make up a society. Moreover, the embedding of an encounter in social structures also activates the culture of each structure and further constrains what can occur in the encounter. People can change social structures and culture from their actions in encounters, but change is never easy because of the weight and power of culture and social structures.

4. The unfocused encounter is essential to public order because it allows individuals to move in space without disrupting the flow of public behavior. Unfocused encounters are guided by rules about the territories of self, the use

of fixed equipment, the objects that can be appropriated, and the conversational preserves surrounding a person.

5. When these rules of public behavior are violated and the encounter becomes focused, rituals are used to signal apologies and to indicate that the person is competent and not a public threat; when these rituals are successful, the encounter ends or goes back to its unfocused state.

KEY TERMS

Categorization: Process of placing others in the appropriate categoric unit; of determining the appropriate level of intimacy or formality to be exhibited; and of determining the relative amounts of social, work-practical, or ceremonial content in the encounter.

Demography: Number of people present, the social categories to which they belong, and their movements in and out of an encounter.

Display Rules: Normative agreements about what emotions are to be displayed in a situation.

Ecology: Nature of the space, partitions in space, props in space, and the distribution of people in space during the course of interaction in an encounter.

Emotion Work: Efforts to display the appropriate emotions in a situation, even when these emotions are not felt.

Encounters, Focused: Episodes of face-to-face interaction revolving around an ecological huddle, focused talk, and solidarity.

Encounters, Unfocused: Episodes of mutual monitoring of people's movements without focusing attention on each other.

Feeling Rules: Normative agreements about what emotions should be, and are to be, felt in a situation.

Frames: Boundaries that are invoked by gestures signaling to others what is to be included and excluded from the interaction.

Keying/Re-keying: Interpersonal gestures, often ritualized, that establish a frame and that change the frame guiding an interaction.

Rituals: Stereotyped sequences of behavior that open, close, and structure the flow of interpersonal behavior.

Roles: Behavior of individuals occupying positions as well as the style of behavior that they exhibit.

Self: General conception and role identity about oneself that a person seeks to confirm in an interaction.

Self, Territories of: Space that people can claim around themselves in public settings and that others are not to violate.

Talk, Forms of: Use of the right form of speech in an encounter, with respect to the volume, tone, formality or informality, ritual address, and other aspects of talk that give it its form.

Chapter 11

Groups

The Power of Groups

He was lying on a couch in a large home on the beach of Santa Monica, CA in 1963. He would just lay there quietly while others in the house would come up to him and tell him to "hang in there" and "it will be okay shortly." The person on the couch had just walked in from the street, having come to the door of the house several times and been told to come back later. Finally, after jumping through hoops for several weeks, he was allowed into the house where he would try to kick his heroin habit of many years. But, contrary to the frequently reported agony of withdrawal, this man simply laid there. I asked how he felt, and he said "not too bad," and indeed he did not shake, sweat, groan, or do many of the other things that I had expected and, in fact, had seen in the temporary lock-up cells at the county jail. Why, then, was this person so calm? The answer was that he was in a place, long gone and somewhat disgraced when its original mission was transformed and scandal broke out, called Synanon House. This House was a sanctuary where drug addicts could come for recovery. The key to this man's calm was the social support of all those in the House who had gone through similar withdrawal. This instant set of encounters within the cohesive group of Synanon House had the power to reduce—indeed, virtually eliminate—most of the pain of withdrawal. What this man actually felt, at a biological level, was changed by the support of people who understood and knew what it was like to live a life of heroin dependency.

All groups have this kind of power. How we act, what we see, how we feel, what we say, and just about all aspects of our lives are shaped by the power of groups to regulate the flow of interaction in encounters. Imagine that you have signed up for an experiment in perception. You are in a room of several other students whom you do not know, and the experimenter indicates that you are to pick the longest lines from a set of lines on a card before you (Asch 1952). It is quite obvious to you that line A is the longest, and everyone appears to agree as they tick off their choices. But then a funny thing happens in subsequent rounds of the experiment: others in the group start naming what, to you, are obviously wrong choices. As your turn approaches, what would you say? About one third of the subjects went along with the incorrect choice. What you did not know is that everyone, but you, was in on the experiment and had been coached to make the wrong choice. You alone were the object of the study, and the goal was to see if you would feel the pressure of the group and go along with the others. Even a trivial group like this one where you do not know anyone can have power. Even if you indicated the right choice, you felt the pressure—even in such a contrived experiment. Groups where we have more at stake—our identity, income, prestige, sense of belonging—will have even more power.

There are many examples of the power of groups. For instance, "war heroes" who do extraordinary things in the heat of battle are generally not exceptional persons, but the tight-knit groups emerging in combat where people depend on each other push people to risk their lives to save a "buddy." Police in most areas of the country will bend the law to complete important arrests or to protect each other from scrutiny. Police work is dangerous and often unappreciated by the broader public; as a consequence, powerful cultural beliefs and norms that, ironically, often require them to bend if not break the law emerge in many police forces. Thus, the power of the police subculture and groups can force the police to break the very laws that they are required to uphold. In a classic study that created quite a stir in its time, each police officer in a Midwestern city was asked if they would report a partner who took money from a drunken prisoner and if they would testify in court against their partner. Almost everyone indicated that they would not report the offense; in fact, only one officer said that he would report the incident and testify in court—and he was a rookie cop (Westley 1956). The police stick together because they have to; and so, it is not surprising that they develop a subculture that assures they are not exposed to public scrutiny.

Even what we see can be influenced by group affiliations. In an interesting study conducted long before soccer became popular in America, youth raised in Mexico and the United States were given images on a screen that simultaneously flashed very briefly two pictures superimposed on each other—one of a baseball game and another of a soccer game. The Mexican children overwhelmingly "saw" only the soccer game, whereas the American kids saw the baseball game (Bagby 1957). Although this may seem like an obvious and trivial outcome, imagine a lifetime of group affiliations where your perceptions are shaped by encounter after encounter in a particular culture; your perceptions—what you actually see out there in the world—will be shaped by experiences in these encounters. The world out there is not an objective reality that imposes itself on our perceptions; it is very much a product of your perceptions that are heavily influenced by your biography of group affiliations.

Perhaps the most famous experiment documenting the power of roles in groups was conducted by Philip Zimbardo and his colleagues (1972). Today, I should add, this experiment would be illegal under "human subject" laws and would have never passed review committees set up at all universities to review the potential harm of experiments on subjects. In the study, normal college students were recruited for a study of prison life. Students, who were carefully screened for their emotional maturity, respect for the law, and health, were randomly assigned to the role of either prison guard or prisoner. The prison was made as realistic as possible. The guards wore uniforms; carried nightsticks, handcuffs and whistles; and wore reflecting glasses. The prisoners were stripped of their past and were forced to follow orders from the guards. Within days, the guards were abusing their power and treating the prisoners very badly. The prisoners began to develop emotional problems; soon, the experiment had to be terminated because the guards had gotten out of control and because the prisoners were suffering both physical and emotional abuse. How could middle class kids go "bad" so fast? The role of prison guard is well-known, as is the role of prisoner; and so, it was easy to play the role when an "authority figure" like a university professor says that it is acceptable. And so, as the guards assumed their roles in a new group, the normative expectations and roles typical of this group simply took over, erasing for a time the effects of previous group affiliations where such behavior would not be acceptable.

Thus, just about every aspect of your being—perceptions, feelings, identity, and behavior—is constrained by the groups to which you belong. As we engage in encounters, many of these are embedded in larger social structures. When you meet friends at school, these may be part of friendship groups embedded in a fraternity or sorority; and both are embedded in an organization—your college or university—that, in turn, is embedded in the broader institutional system of education organized across the entire society. At each level of social structure, the culture of the structures at this level—your friendship group, fraternal organization, university, and institution of education as a whole—imposes itself on you.

The *most immediate influence* is generally the greatest, however. As you role-take with others in the encounter, perceive their expectations, receive their evaluation of you, plug yourself into the culture of the group, and understand how to play roles, your thoughts, perceptions, emotions, behaviors and identity will be influenced by these immediate others and groupings. This is why the college kids in the prison experiment could go bad so fast; they were isolated from their normal encounters in groups and made into prison guards. To go against what is expected of you invites sanctions that are painful, causing a person to experience negative emotions like shame; and so, people generally go along to avoid breaching the interaction. If you doubt this power of the group in which you are currently engaged, deliberately breach the interaction by breaking a rule, talking inappropriately, asking the wrong question, or otherwise making a nuisance and fool of yourself. Your reluctance to initiate such a breach should tell you something about the power of groups.

We can define **groups** as relatively stable networks of status positions, regulated by norms about how individuals in positions are to behave in their roles. Ultimately, groups are constructed from encounters that are repeated over time among the same people; most of the time, groups are lodged in larger social structures such as organizations, categoric units, communities, and institutional systems. Groups are thus the conduit by which the culture of larger structures is often brought to bear on encounters of face-to-face interaction.

Primary and Secondary Groups

Effects of Group Size

When groups are small, they are pretty much coextensive with an encounter. Everybody is focused on a similar topic, each is able to respond to the others, and the group acts as a whole in a cohesive way. But once the number of people in the group increases, the dynamics of the group change. If you have ever been to a party where you were among the first to arrive, you and others probably sustained a common focus marking one encounter, but as more party-goers entered, the party group began to break down into separate encounters of face-to-face interaction, and people perhaps began to migrate around from encounter to encounter. Any professor who has to teach both small and large classes is aware of the effects of size. When I teach introductory sociology, the class is large and the entire dynamics of the group change. I will often have to stare down impromptu encounters among students who become sidetracked from lecture, or worse, I will have to internally groan as a cell phone rings and, what is even worse, is answered by a student who proceeds to talk. How, then, does group size influence what occurs in the group?

The key dynamic is that as size increases, the ability to sustain face-to-face interaction is soon lost. There are simply too many people to be able to respond to them personally. Related to this demographic problem is the fact that the number of potential relationships exponentially increases. For example, in a group of 2 people, there is relationship possible; in a group of 3, 3 relationships are possible; in a group of 4, 6 relationships are possible; in a group of 5, 10 relationships are possible; in a group of 6, 15 relationships are possible; and in a group of 7 (still pretty small), 21 dyadic relationships are possible. As is evident, the number of potential relationships is increasing at an exponential rate. If each relationship requires a person's attention through role-taking and role-making, it soon becomes difficult to sustain the intimacy that comes with direct face-to-face interaction.

Size and the Changing Structure of the Group

Groups are often labeled primary and secondary. This distinction follows from the effects of increasing the number of members in a group (Hare 1992). As more people are added to a setting, it becomes increasingly difficult to know everyone or to interact directly with them. The result is that **secondary groups** become less cohesive and less intimate; they become more formal with explicit norms; and they become difficult to sustain for long periods of time (imagine, for instance, being stuck in a large sociology class all day). Such groups are thus created for some relatively short-term purpose, such as giving a lecture or watching a concert. In contrast, **primary groups** are smaller, and thus, they have the potential for greater intimacy and cohesion because their members can interact face-to-face and get to know one another. Intimacy is not inevitable, however, especially if members of a small group do not spend much time together. Hence, a primary group emerges when rates of interaction and feelings of intimacy have been given time to develop—as is the case for your family and close friendship cliques.

Many groups are somewhere between primary and secondary—work groups, friends in a dorm or sorority, or a small class. These are relatively small groups, and one can often sense the movement to a more primary pattern. But equally often, this movement does not go all of the way for lack of duration, or because the activities of the group (e.g., competition for promotions, for grades, for popularity, etc.) get in the way—a fact that conflict theories always emphasize. We have no name for these in-between groups, except their designation as groups. But the growing size destroys the possibility of a great intimacy, and even when size does not get in the way, the nature of the larger organization in which the group is lodged frequently inhibits intimacy, closeness, and cohesion. Table 11.1 delineates some of the key differences between primary and secondary groups.

The Respective Power of Primary and Secondary Groups

The more a group reveals a primary profile, the greater is its capacity to influence behavior along many dimensions. One line of influence is our self-conception because we see ourselves reflected in the gestures of others who are important to us. Another is our values and beliefs because we tend to take on the cultural symbols of groups in which our sense of self and identity is implanted. Still another is our role behavior and motivations because we conform to the norms of primary groups and because we take on their values and beliefs and, as a consequence, adjust our general role-playing style and demeanor. Yet another line of influence is our feelings because our emotional states will tend to ebb and flow with our experiences with those who have become important to us.

It is perhaps disturbing to recognize that groups have this kind of power—especially in a society where cultural values emphasize self-reliance, self-determination, rugged individualism, and personal autonomy. But if we are honest with ourselves, the point is obvious: self-conception, values and beliefs, moods and emotions, motives, demeanor, and role-playing style are dramatically influenced by group affiliations. Take any group in which you feel some closeness to its members and think about your self-feelings, emotional states, demeanor, beliefs, motivations, and values. These will be greatly shaped by your membership in this group, although your past group memberships (e.g., family and close friends) will also have exerted considerable power over you. Thus, we are not interpersonal chameleons; we do not change every aspect of our being with each new group because our present group affiliations will have to overcome the cumulative effects of our past affiliations or, as is more often the case, blend into these effects of past group attachments.

Table 11.1   Differences between Primary and Secondary Groups

Basic Properties of Groups	Primary Groups	Secondary Groups
Size	Small (2-12 people)	Larger (up to several hundred)
Cohesiveness	High	Lower
Formality of norms	Informal and implicit	More formal and explicit
Personal involvement in role	High	Lower
Intimacy of relations	Moderate to high	Low to moderate
Permanence	Longer lasting	Short-term
Goal-directedness	Moderate to low	Moderate to high
Clique formation	Low to moderate	Moderate to high

Group Dynamics

Leadership

Groups that must get something done tend to develop two types of leaders—what Robert Bales (1950) termed task leaders and socio-emotional leaders. At times, of course, the task leader is appointed by virtue of the larger authority system (a Teaching Assistant, for example, if you are in a sociology course with discussion sections). **Task leaders** seek to direct others in the group and to coordinate their activities to achieve the group's goal. But task leaders also create tensions, and so, **socio-emotional leaders** emerge to ease the tension—some with a joke, a wry comment, or soothing words when feathers get ruffled. At times, a particularly adept leader can play both roles, being a task master and, at the same time, able to ease tensions and keep emotions under control. This process of leadership formation becomes readily apparent once we are looking for it. Observe what occurs in a study group, a dorm meeting, a work meeting, or any situation where the group is trying to get something done; chances are this division of leadership along task and socio-emotional lines will be very apparent.

Decision-Making

We might think that leaders would make bolder decisions than the group as a whole, but in fact, collective decisions by the group tend to be more decisive than those by an individual (Janis 1972; Kogan and Wallach 1964). The reasons for this phenomena are twofold: First, when an individual alone must decide, fears about making a mistake or being wrong invite caution, whereas a group decision deflects responsibility to more individuals, thereby making them bolder. Second, in cohesive groups, members often withhold criticism of each other, and as a result, they may be less critical of bold suggestions, thus leading the group to act more decisively.

Indeed, this latter process often leads to what has been termed **groupthink** (Janis 1972, 1982), where individuals reinforce each other so much that they lose touch with reality and become too bold or grandiose. For example, many of Adolf Hitler's mistakes in World War II can, I suspect, be seen in groupthink terms as close advisors keep reinforcing each other's pronouncements to the point that strategically bad decisions were made. Much of America's continued involvement in the Vietnam war was, no doubt, the result of groupthink processes among top-level military brass and advisors to the president; they simply lost touch with the reality of the war and the strength of the Vietcong. Many of the disastrous economic decisions made in American corporations during the 1970s and 1980s were also driven by groupthink rather than the external realities of an ever more competitive world economic system. And perhaps, some of the optimism of how Iraq would immediately fall into a pro-American political democracy was the product of groupthink at the highest levels of the American government.

Whether bold or timid, decisions within a group tend to go through a sequence of events. Initially, information gathering occurs; next, evaluation and assessment ensue; tensions begin to rise as members line up on one side or the other; a decision is then made; and finally, efforts to restore harmony by socio-emotional leaders become prominent. If you have ever been in a decision-making group, you will have noticed the sense of euphoria, joking, and other tension-release processes at the end of a meeting. Much socio-emotional work smooths over tensions and creates a more pleasant atmosphere if the group must meet again.

Cohesiveness and Solidarity

Groups vary considerably in how much attachment members have to each other and the group. In cohesive groups, where people feel solidarity, members are more secure and are more likely to conform to the norms of the group. What conditions produce these effects (Kellerman 1981; Shotola 1992)? One is small size because solidarity is created by high rates of face-to-face interaction that are only possible with smaller numbers (Collins 1975). Another is a sense of threat from the outside, for people band together when they feel besieged (Simmel 1956). Yet another force is the similarity in backgrounds of members because it is far easier to develop strong attachments to those who are like you and belong to the same categoric unit(s). And a final force promoting solidarity is a high rate of positive sanctioning (as opposed to negative sanctions) for conformity to group norms; if people experience rewards for conformity, positive emotions are aroused, leading people to develop emotional attachments to those offering these rewards (Coleman 1991).

Think about any group in which you experienced solidarity, and it will be evident that these forces are at work. An athletic team, a fraternity or sorority, a close set of friendships, or a family all tend to reveal at least some of these forces, and as a consequence, they reveal cohesion and solidarity. Such groups have the most power over us because our membership in them is so rewarding.

Free Riding

When groups have a task to complete, the members of the group must coordinate their actions to accomplish the goal. There is always a tendency, however, for some members to avoid doing their share in achieving the goal; and yet, they enjoy the benefits of having completed the task. This is the problem of **free riding**, whereby one or a few get a free ride to benefits earned by others. Of course, if everyone free rides, nothing will be accomplished; and so, norms emerge to limit free riding. People always monitor the contributions of others to the group and make assessments if they are doing their fair share. We might let a bit of free riding go, but if it goes too far, we experience negative emotions such as anger and are likely to sanction free riders, trying to bring them into line. In social groups, where the point of the group is to have fun, free riding is less of a problem but even here we all know people who do not pick up their fair share of the tab or reciprocate to contribute to the good feelings of sociality. Free riding will, when it goes too far, break the group apart; and so, people are highly observant of whether or not others are contributing their fair share to ongoing activity in the group.

For rational choice theorists, the problem of free riding is central. It is always "rational" to let others do the work and still enjoy the products of their labor. How is social order to be created and sustained, however, if everyone free rides? When free riding gets out of hand, it becomes rational to create norms directing individuals' behaviors and, then, to monitor and enforce conformity to these norms. Social order is thus created rationally when the harm of widespread free riding threatens the viability of collective activities.

Still, for many situations in complex societies, it is difficult to prevent free riding. For example, people can still watch public television shows without making a "pledge" of support for public television (and national public radio as well). "Pledge drives" employ two strategies to overcome the propensity of viewers to free ride: moral persuasion and gift-giving for those who "call in now" to make a pledge. Large social issues—such as public concern over the environment—can also be viewed with the logic of the free rider problem. For any given individual, it is "rational" to avoid the costs of engaging in environmentally responsible actions, but if everyone free rides and pollutes, the environment will be spoiled for all. Thus, laws must be enacted to force people to engage in environmentally responsible behavior; and in many nations, moralistic social movements try to make the environment a moral question, vilifying polluters as morally suspect.

Clique and Subgroup Formation

Groups often break down into subgroups, or in network terms, **cliques** (see Box 11.2 for how to determine clique formation in a group). The subgroups are still part of the more inclusive group, but members of the clique interact more with each other than with members of other cliques. Subgroups are more likely to form as the group gets larger because it is increasingly difficult to know and pay attention to everyone in the group; and so, people gravitate to cliques. Cliques can create tension in the group, however, as people come to view members of the other clique with suspicion. And indeed, if members of cliques develop what network theory terms highly *dense ties* (with everybody in cliques interacting with each other to the exclusion of ties with other people), the group's overall solidarity and cohesion is undermined, often to the point that the group breaks apart into separate groups.

Expectation States

When members of a group play their roles in a particular way, these performances create expectations that future role behaviors will also be enacted in this manner (Berger, Conner and Fisek 1974). We can feel these expectation states by the looks and anticipation of others, or by their disappointment if we do not live up to their expectations. This pressure pushes us into continuity in role performances, and it is one of the great points of power in groups.

But we do more than create expectations inside the group as a result of our actions and interactions; we always bring with us to a group characteristics from outside (Berger, Fisek, Norman, and Zelditch 1977; Berger, Rosenholtz, and Zelditch 1980; J. Turner 2002; Webster and Foschi 1988). These characteristics often generate expectations about what a person can, or cannot, do in the group, as well as how much prestige and influence a person should have in the group (Berger, and Zelditch 1985; Berger, Wagner, and Zelditch 1989). These are sometimes termed our **diffuse status characteristics** and include such fea-

Box 11.1: Constructing a Sociogram

Below is a hypothetical sociogram constructed in the following way: (a) Each person is asked to write the names of the persons that they like most and second most. (b) The reports are sorted in terms of who names whom. (c) Through a sorting process, the network of first and second choices is plotted in a way that reflects the friendship cliques in the group. This illustration has been simplified to indicate only the first-choice network.

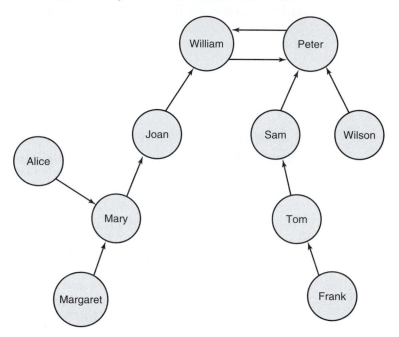

A sociogram like this tells us a great deal. First, the group is divided into male and female cliques, with William and Joan being the key link between males and females. Peter is the leader of the males and probably of the group. Mary tends to dominate the females. Tom, Frank, Alice, and Margaret are at the periphery of the group. Almost any group can be diagrammed in this way. The structure would be more complex if it introduced second choices, because it would then involve more connections among group members, but that would not change the logic of the sociogram: it visually represents the network of attachments in a group. This information provides a great deal of information about leadership, normative conformity, interaction patterns, decision making, and other dimensions of the group.

tures as age, sex, race/ethnicity, level of education, appearance, perceived intelligence, and other highly visible characteristics that members of the group can use to guide their responses. Membership in a categoric unit, as described in Chapter 6, is a diffuse status characteristic. Thus, when a group is embedded in categoric units, these diffuse status characteristics generate expectations and evaluations of others. For example, men and women have very different expectations leveled on them in groups, as do older people, minorities, and others who can be clearly distinguished. If you doubt this, examine a group embedded in categoric units where individuals carry different diffuse status characteristics and, then, ask what your reaction would be if the women started to play roles like the men, or vice versa, or if any of the participants began to act out of character. Your reaction should reveal your expectation states for these individuals. Indeed, if you doubt the importance of embedding in categoric units, breach an encounter in a group by acting as if the expectation states of another social category were directed at you. For example, if you are a woman, take on a man's demeanor by talking, standing, touching, and use phrases typical of men; or, and this may be more difficult, if you are a man, take on the demeanor typical of women, and see how others' respond to you. The difficulty of this role reversal underscores the power of diffuse status characteristics as they follow from membership in categoric units.

Referencing and Reference Groups

As mentioned in Chapter 7 on social structure, groups serve as a frame of reference or **reference group** for us, providing a perspective for orienting our thoughts and actions. This process operates not just for a group in which we are presently interacting, but also for groups in which we are not interacting, or even for groups in which we have never been members. In fact, most of the time we employ the norms, values, beliefs, and other cultural symbols of several groups simultaneously in a situation. We are, for example, aware of the norms and other expectations of the group we are in, but at the same time, we may also invoke the symbols of other groups, such as our family, close friends, or groups to which we aspire.

To understand our behavior, then, it becomes necessary to know the configuration of reference groups we are invoking (Kelley 1958; Merton and Rossi 1957). Our large brains and corresponding cognitive abilities (Piaget 1948) allow us to role-take with others far removed from the present, using our attachments or hopes for attachments to these others as guidelines for our conduct (Mead 1934; Shibutani 1955). Thus, reference group processes greatly expand the nature of membership in a group and the processes by which groups exert influence upon us. If you take any group situation, and ask yourself about which groups are serving as a frame of reference, you will be surprised, I think, that more than immediate others are exerting pressure on you. The power of distant reference groups, then, is always there, subtly pushing on thoughts and behaviors.

In using other groups as a frame of reference or perspective for guiding conduct, we can orient to these reference groups in a variety of ways. One obvious way is to be an actual member of a group. But even here, the relationships can be complicated. If you perceive that your membership in a group is beneath your dignity, you will often act in ways to signal this fact. Rather than embracing the norms of the group, you exhibit role distance and communicate through behaviors and words your distance from the group. A related orientation to a reference group is negative. A person is not a member of a group but reacts against the values, beliefs, and norms of the group. For example, those who are pro- and antiabortion not only abide by the ideologies and norms of their groups and the organizations, but they also react against the other group. Indeed, the behavior of members in one group is not fully understandable without reference to their negative orientation to the ideology of the "enemy." Yet another way of orienting to a reference group is to aspire to membership and guide one's behavior in the present to attaining membership in a particular group whose ideologies, norms, positions, and roles serve as a frame of reference. For instance, a Teaching Assistant's behavior can partially be understood by recognizing his or her orientation to becoming a faculty member of a department and university. Still another orientation is to identify with the ideology, norms, and roles of a group without being a member. In the 1960s, during the student rebellion, students would often dress in work clothes like those worn by farmers, but in fact, hardly any of them had ever gotten their hands dirty, much less farmed (or even mowed the lawn). Similarly, youth today often dress like groups to which they will never belong. For instance, many college students dress and affect some of the interpersonal demeanor of "boys-in-the-hood" and "gang bangers" but have never been part of a gang; indeed, gang membership would terrify them. Or, the young dress and act like members of their favorite sports team.

Thus, because humans have big brains, they can think about others, groups, and the attendant cultures who are not present and use these elements of other groups as a perspective that structures thought and action. In fact, a reference group need not be a group at all; it can be a complex organization; or it can even be imaginary as is often the case with schizophrenics who use as a frame of reference for their conversations people and groups that do not exist, except in their minds.

Virtual Groups

Over the last two decades, the internet has created an entirely new kind of group: the virtual group. All over the world individuals are part of chat rooms, blogs, games, and other activities with others whom they are unlikely to meet face-to-face. Yet, participation in these cybergroups can be enormously influential on a person, often becoming a major reference group directing behaviors from afar. I once asked one of my "Gothic" students where she first learned about this style of dress and demeanor (I had in mind TV reruns of "The Adams Family").

She indicated to me that she had learned the style on the internet and still used her cyberfriends as a sounding board not only for fashion but also for more substantive matters like beliefs and values. She told me that in the small southern California town where she grew up, there were no "Goths," but she felt the need to express herself in "different ways." And so, she plugged into new reference groups via the internet. Later, in college, she could reinforce this subculture style with face-to-face interaction with fellow "Gothics."

Thus, the cyber world opens up an entirely new domain of group activity, potentially expanding the diversity and reach of group influences on individuals. This influence increases when individuals can reinforce the perspective of cybergroups with face-to-face interactions with others who share a world view.

Bottlenecks

Groups organize much human activity but there are limits to how much they can do. For most of human history, people carried out their daily activities in relatively small bands that approximated primary groups, or if the band was larger, relatively small secondary-like groups with cliques and subgroups. But as populations grew and the tasks to be accomplished increased in scale, simply replicating more groups was not enough to do what needed doing. Groups are limited by several constraints, because they create what the German sociologist Niklas Luhmann (1982) called *bottlenecks*. These bottlenecks stem from the fact that, in a face-to-face group, only one topic can be addressed and only one person can speak at a time. If you doubt this, just watch what happens in a group where several people try to talk all at once, each introducing a new topic; chaos is the usual result, until someone reins everyone in ways that limit the topic and that allow speakers to take turns. The necessity for sequential interaction in small groups means that there are severe restrictions on how much groups can accomplish and on how fast they can proceed in performing tasks. As long as tasks are simple, groups are sufficient for organizing people.

But, as the scale of tasks magnifies, how are the inherent limitations of groups to be overcome? The answer resides in connecting groups together in some way so that each performs a limited range of tasks that are coordinated with tasks performed by other groups. What emerges from such efforts are *complex organizations*, the subject of Chapter 12. It is for this reason that groups are often embedded in organizations and operate as conduits for the ideology, norms, and other cultural elements of the organization. The coordination of groups is accomplished by instilling in them a common culture and by regulation with external authority. In this way, larger goals can be accomplished, but at a price: the activities of the group are constrained by the demands of the organization. Sometimes we are very aware of this constraint from above, as is the case when you study for examinations in your classes (a group) or work with immediate others (another group) on an assembly line; you are indeed aware of the constraints imposed by the more inclusive organization.

SUMMARY

1. Much behavior and interaction occurs within a social structure or organized networks of positions, norms, and roles.
2. Depending on their size, groups can range from primary to secondary. Primary groups are more intimate and cohesive, involving more conformity to norms than secondary groups.
3. Groups have power over people, constraining and constricting the perceptions, images of self, values and beliefs, emotions, motives, and role-playing style of their participants.
4. Groups are highly dynamic structures, revealing a number of basic processes: (a) leadership and the emergence of task and socio-emotional leaders; (b) decision making and development of consensus and groupthink;

(c) cohesiveness and solidarity as these emerge from high rates of interaction, similar backgrounds of members, and external sources of threat; (d) problems of free riding; (e) expectation states or the use of external characteristics of members or past performances to anticipate what individuals are to do in the group; (f) clique and subgroup formation; and (g) referencing or the use of outside groupings as a frame of reference for guiding thoughts and responses in a particular situation.

5. Groups are limited, however, in how much activity they can organize. All groups reveal bottleneck problems as tasks get more complex and as the number of people to be organized increases.

6. As the scale of society gets larger and the tasks become more complex, groups are connected together to create organizations that, as we will see in Chapter 12, reveal formal roles, a clear division of labor, hierarchies of authority, control of emotions, technical competence of incumbents, organizational control of offices, and career movements up the hierarchy.

KEY TERMS

Cliques: Division of group members into two or more subgroups of dense ties.

Diffuse Status Characteristics: Membership in a categoric unit that generates evaluations and expectations for how those in a social category are to behave. These expectations are carried into any group as diffuse status characteristics.

Free Riding: Tendency of group members to avoid making their fair contribution to group goals while still receiving the benefits of this activity from other group members.

Group: Small social structures composed of only a few different status positions, relatively small numbers of incumbents, relatively dense ties among positions, and clear cultural expectations about role behaviors.

Groupthink: Process in group decision making in which members reinforce each other to the point that the decision does not bear a close relationship to the realities of the situation.

Primary Group: Small, face-to-face groups in which people feel more involved, more intimate, and cohesive.

Reference Group: Perspectives of groups, both those in which one is participating and those that are remote, that are used as a frame of reference for self-evaluation and for guiding conduct.

Secondary Groups: Larger groups where face-to-face interaction among all members is not possible, with a corresponding decrease in intimacy, cohesiveness, and duration.

Socio-Emotional Leader: Individual who seeks to smooth out tensions that arise as the members of the group seek to realize the group's goals.

Task Leader: Individual in groups who directs and coordinates other members' activities to accomplish the group's goals.

Chapter 12

Organizations

Early human populations organized themselves in a very simple way: a few nuclear families (composed of mothers, fathers, and children) moving about in a band, gathering and hunting. Most activity in these simple societies was conducted by individuals alone, or in the family unit. And so it was for most of human history (Maryanski and Turner 1992; Nolan and Lenski 2004; J. Turner 2003). As people began to settle down between 8,000 and 12,000 years ago, their numbers increased greatly. Small groups cohabiting in small bands were no longer sufficient to organize the increased numbers of people, and so nuclear kinship units were connected together to form larger family units that, in turn, were linked into ever larger systems often termed lineages (see Chapter 18 for more detail on how this was done). Then, as the scale of society increased, lineages were used to build clans (of connected lineages) that could, if necessary, be linked together into moieties (sets of connected clans).

You can easily see what humans were doing: they were taking their basic group unit—the nuclear family of parents and their offspring—as the building block for more complex patterns of social organization. Using blood and marriage ties in this way, it is rather amazing how many people can become organized into a society—perhaps as many as a few million but more typically a few thousand. However, around 5,000 years ago, at the earliest, the limit to organizing people only by blood and marriage ties was reached. There were simply too many people and too many tasks to organize by connecting members of nuclear families into ever larger kin units. If societies were to get larger and more complex, a new form of social organization would need to be invented. And so, by fits and starts, formal or complex organizations began to appear in the middle east and Asia, and later, in Europe and parts of northern Africa. A **formal or complex organization** connects individuals together not by their place in a kinship system but by specialized status positions that carry specific obligations and skills and that are linked together into a hierarchical system of authority. We often call formal organizations by the name **bureaucracy,** usually with a slight sneer. Once people discovered how to build bureaucracies, however, human societies were never the same. Huge armies could now be put into the field; political systems capable of governing large territories could be established; large-scale public works projects like roads, ports, canals, and buildings could be undertaken; religious temples of enormous size and grandeur could be constructed; and so it went, once this new kind of structure—formal or complex organizations—was invented.

Max Weber's Ideal Type of Formal Organizations

The German sociologist Max Weber (1922), who was one of the founders of modern sociology, constructed an "ideal type" of *rational* bureaucracies. He recognized, of course, that this ideal type was a kind of fiction, but it could serve as a common yardstick for measuring different types of formal organizations. Here is what Weber saw as the underlying features of rational bureaucracies: First, all bureaucracies have an explicit division of labor, with each position or office having a delimited set of responsibilities. Second, the norms governing behaviors for any position, as well as for relations between positions, are explicit, clear, and codified in writing. Third, different positions are ordered hierarchically, with those positions and offices higher in the authority ranks supervising those below them. Fourth, role enactment by incumbents in positions is emotionally neutral and disinterested, with individuals repressing emotions and passions as they play their assigned roles. Fifth, people are assigned to positions for their technical competence rather than personal considerations. Sixth, positions and offices are not owned by their incumbents but by the larger organization. And seventh, employment constitutes a career in which individuals move up the hierarchy in terms of some combination of merit and seniority.

It sounds a bit cold and impersonal when stated this way; indeed, Weber worried about this aspect of bureaucracy and its effects on social life in modern societies where bureaucratization was a clear trend. Weber probably worried too much because people usually find a way to make life more bearable and pleasant within bureaucratic structures (Maryanski and Turner 1992). But still, given their formality and impersonality, why did humans create bureaucratic structures? Why "cage" oneself, to use Weber's metaphor, in this world of hierarchy, constraint, and impersonality?

Functional theorizing provides perhaps the best answer. As noted earlier, when populations get large *and* begin to engage in large-scale tasks, such as public works, military defense, or conquest, and internal political administration and control, needs or requisites for more complex organizational structures emerge. How could the great pyramids in Egypt be built? How could Roman legions conquer most of Europe and Northern Africa, and much of the Near East? How could thousands of workers be organized into corporations? War was perhaps the biggest impetus to the creation of bureaucracies as large armies were mobilized, but large-scale public works and governance of vast territories and big populations were also crucial. For large-scale activities to be undertaken by people, then, new structures beyond the group became essential. For most of human history, however, social activity occurred in relatively small bands. And even as kinship was used to create larger social units, there were limitations to *how* large-scale collective action could be. With advanced horticulture and agrarianism (see Prologue), the big steps were taken to an entirely new kind of social formation. These steps were not possible without two key innovations.

These two innovations involved (Weber, 1922): (a) the development of money and (b) the expansion of markets. Once workers can be paid by a reliable currency, sell their labor for money in a market, and use their income in other markets to buy goods that they can no longer produce for themselves, the stage is set for bureaucracies—*if* there is a need for large-scale mobilizations of people for various tasks. With money and markets, new nonkin structures could be constructed to expand the scale of human activity.

The late Talcott Parsons (1966, 1971), the preeminent functional theorist of the last century, argued that societal evolution and development depended upon the creation of bureaucratic structures. At first these structures did not resemble Weber's ideal type because family ties and other personal considerations often outweighed technical competence in the selection and promotion of individuals. Until this obstacle to "rationality" could be overcome, full modernization was not possible. Indeed, in much of the world today, many critical aspects of Weber's typology cannot be realized, with the result that societies remain arrested at a pre-modern phase.

Types of Formal Organizations

Amitai Etzioni (1961, 1964) once provided a useful typology of formal organizations in modern societies. One type is **voluntary organizations**, in which members can freely enter and leave the organization. Members in such organizations are not paid, although when the organization gets large there is a salaried professional staff that is organized bureaucratically. In America, voluntary organizations are highly visible, pulling members into their fold for a wide variety of reasons—for example, as a way to organize leisure time activities; as a means for pursuing a social or political cause; as a special interest group (e.g., National Rifle Association and Sierra Club); as an adjunct to another organization (like the PTA is for schools); as a way to facilitate communication and perhaps economic/political action among those in a social category (e.g., the NAACP or National Organization for Women); as a means for bestowing charity (the United Way, a skid row mission); and so on for many other needs, interests, and goals.

Another organizational type in modern societies is the **coercive organization** that separates members from the society and tightly regiments their activities under the ever-present threat of physical coercion. Prisoners, patients in mental hospitals, or draftees in an army are all part of a coercive organization whose professional staff is organized bureaucratically. Such organizations are usually very hierarchical, with clear lines of authority for regulating activity and, if necessary, for administering coercion.

A third major type of organization is the **utilitarian organization** where people enter the bureaucratic structure for some practical reason and where, in rational choice theory's terms, they have calculated the costs of entering with the rewards to be received. Private corporations, universities, unions, and government agencies are the most common type; in a post-industrial society, they dominate our lives.

This typology of three organizational types—voluntary, coercive, and utilitarian—is a kind of ideal type itself. There are often elements of the two other types in any one. For example, elementary and secondary schools are coercive in the sense that students are required by law to attend, but they are increasingly utilitarian; as individuals go up the educational ladder, they calculate the benefits of more education. Or, to take another example, voluntary organizations (e.g., a religious sect) can become highly coercive of their members once they have joined. And, there can be an element of voluntarism and utilitarianism in coercive organizations, as is the case when one joins the armed services or checks themselves into a mental hospital. Etzioni's typology, then, just gives us a rough sense for variations in the kinds of bureaucratic organizations that are used to organize people. We might now ask: What accounts for the prevalence of any one type, or different forms of a given type? An answer to this question resides in the ecology of organizations.

The Ecology of Organizations

All ecological theories emphasize that social actors compete for resources within various resource niches (see Chapter 3). Thus, from an ecological perspective, organizations occupy a resource niche consisting of members, customers, clients, government subsidies, or any resource that allows an organization to survive. In fact, organizations can be distinguished by the resources that they need to sustain themselves. For example, all schools occupy a resource niche funded by tax dollars and, at times, tuitions; all trade unions occupy a resource niche of workers in profit-making corporations or government agencies; all newspapers occupy a resource niche of subscribers and advertisers; all retail stores occupy a niche of customers, and within the broad base of customers, specialized niches for particular types of customers like car customers, clothing customers, sports customers, and so on. Rarely is there only one organization in a resource niche; there are typically several, and they soon find themselves in competition for resources in the niche. Indeed, whole *populations* of organizations, much like a species in the biological world, can emerge to exploit a resource niche. Yet, as the population of organizations increases, some die or at least decline in numbers when the niche is overexploited (Hannan and Freeman 1977, 1984, 1986, 1987, 1988, 1989). For example, the number of labor unions and membership in them grew when workers in America opposed the abusive practices of many companies (the pool of disgruntled workers being the resource niche of labor unions), but as labor-management relations became less confrontational and as the economy shifted to a more white collar profile, the resource niche of labor unions shrunk, with the result that the number of unions and the percentage of workers who belonged to unions decreased in America, and dramatically so. At one time, there were many American car companies; now, from domestic and international competition there are only two or three. In general merchandise sales, there used to be many big companies, many of which are now gone because of the competition—for instance, Montgomery Ward, White Front, Gemco, Fedco, Grants, and the like (if you have not heard of these, then they are really dead). Now we have Wal-Mart as the 600-pound gorilla making life difficult for the few stores of this kind that still survive—stores like Sears and Kmart (the latter ironically killed off many other general merchandise department stores, only to be severely wounded by Wal-Mart, which simply used Kmart's formula and executed it better). Now, Sears and Kmart have had to merge to compete against Wal-Mart. The same processes are seen, from an ecological view, to operate for all types of organizations—schools, hospitals, clinics, newspapers, retail stores, colleges, and the like.

An important part of ecological analysis is the notion of **niche density**, which denotes the total number of organizations in a niche relative to the resources in this niche. When density is high—that is, when there are many organizations trying to secure resources of a certain kind—competition in the niche increases and some organizations "die" or are folded into more successful organizations. For example, at one time there were many different labor unions that competed so intensely that, eventually, some died and most merged into large confederations like the AFL and CIO or other larger unions like the Teamsters. Take again the example of retail stores; here, the competition among large department stores has been intense, with many disappearing or moving to a new resource niche. JCPenney, for instance, used to sell everything from lawn mowers, furniture, and appliances to underwear and dresses, but it found that it could not compete effectively with Sears, Kmart, Wal-Mart, and big discount stores. So, it moved to a more upscale niche, abandoning general purpose retailing for an emphasis on middle level clothing and home accessories.

Thus, competition increases with density. Out of this competition some organizations survive and others will die, or be forced to seek resources in different niches. This process occurs not just with retail stores, but other types of organizations as well. For example, potential members are a resource niche for voluntary organizations; as their density increases and as more organizations seek members with a certain level of income, education, and other characteristics, some will have to move to a new niche consisting of members with different levels of income, education, and other features (McPherson 1981, 1983, 1988, 1990). For instance, community service clubs like the Lions, Rotary, and Optimist have had to move to a new niche and seek new kinds of members who, 50 years ago, would have had little chance of "getting in" these organizations. Competitive pressures even operate on agencies in government that seek resources from tax revenues; if too many agencies compete for resources of a given kind—say, those dealing with health—some will die or be consolidated with others.

The total level or amount of resources in a niche is also important. If resources increase, then competition will decline until more organizations move into the niche and increase its density. If resources shrink, competition will be intensified and some will die or move to new niches. A good example is the defense industry in America after the collapse of the Soviet Union in the early 1990s. For a time, until the recent run up in military expenditures in the aftermath of September 11, the total level of resources for military hardware decreased, forcing many companies into bankruptcy, into new niches (geared to nonmilitary domestic production), or into consolidation with more successful companies.

Ecological analysis thus views a society, and the world economic system for that matter, as a series of resource niches consisting of money, members, clients, customers, or any resource that can sustain an organization. High levels of resources in these niches allow new organizations to be born, until their density increases competition, causing some to die or seek new niches. Hence, the distribution of organizational types in a society reflects the number of resource niches, the density in these niches, the level of competition for resources in a given niche, and the rates of death for organizations. If there are a lot of governmental agencies, for example, this means that there are high taxes directed at public works and public welfare that can support these agencies (as is the case in France); if there are many newspapers, there is a large reading audience and a set of retail merchants to buy advertising; if there are many stores for teenage fashion, there are a lot of teenagers with money in their pockets; if there are large bookstores, there is a large reading public (or a public that likes to hang out in big-box bookstores and buy coffee); and so on. Thus, the number and types of formal organizations that exist in a society very much depend upon the level of resources in the niches they occupy and the competition among organizations in these niches.

The Internal Dynamics of Organizations

Ecological analysis tells us much about why different types of organizations come into existence, but it does not explain with any detail what goes on inside organizations. Whether or not organizations survive is, to a great extent, tied to how they operate. We should, therefore, review some of the internal dynamics of organizations.

The Informal System

As symbolic interactionist theories would emphasize, people construct social relations, even when there are severe bureaucratic constraints. Humans are not robots or cogs in cold, impersonal, bureaucratic machines; they develop friendships alongside, and often in defiance of, the formal structure of the bureaucracy. This process of generating a set of more personal and informal relations is often termed the **informal system** (Roethlisberger and Dickson 1939).

At times the informal system works to the advantage of the organizations, as is the case when employees bypass cumbersome rules that impede efficiency. At other times, the informal system works against organizational goals by creating networks of informal ties that keep people from doing their jobs. For example, we have all encountered people in organizations who seem to be too busy chatting or gossiping with each other to pay much attention to their jobs, but perhaps equally often we have found employees who use their informal networks in an organization to assist us and to cut through a lot of "red tape."

The structure of an organization, then, is much more than the positions and lines of authority on an organization chart. Superimposed on this formal structure are informal relations that supplement and, at times, supplant the formal system of positions, norms, and authority. To appreciate how an organization is actually structured and operates thus requires an understanding of both its formal and informal systems.

Authority

Authority and Conflict. All conflict theories stress the significance of inequality in generating tensions and confrontations (Collins 1975). Because organizations are hierarchies of authority, there should always be conflict because power is distributed unequally. In fact, the informal system is often fueled by resentments of people in lower level positions against those with authority (Dahrendorf 1959). In a sense, the informal system becomes a way to preserve one's personal dignity (and self-conception), while enabling one to resist quietly or get back at people in higher level positions.

Differences in authority also create conflicts over "turf" within an organization. Those who have certain responsibilities and authority resist giving them up to those who might take them over. Indeed, a great deal of infighting occurs in organizations as people and offices make claims to authority, only to find themselves in conflict with others making similar claims. We have all probably been caught in such a battle as different people assert their "rights" to deal with our problems; or we may have found ourselves in a situation where one person has encroached on another's job and has been reprimanded. One can just feel the tension in such situations, indicating that positions and formal rules do not always eliminate conflict. Indeed, they often aggravate it; and so, it is in the nature of authority hierarchies that conflict should take up a considerable amount of time and emotional energy of those working in an organization.

Tasks and Authority. The nature of an organization's tasks and the kinds of technology it must use greatly influence the nature of its structure, especially the levels of hierarchy (Perrow 1967, 1986). As a general rule, when tasks involve machines and workers, hierarchy increases because workers and machines need to be tightly coordinated. Yet, too much supervision can create resentments of workers against their supervisors, as was the case with the automobile industry in America until better efforts were made—as in Honda and Saturn automobile plants—to decrease levels of supervision *and* better coordinate machines and workers. Conversely, the more that tasks require the coordination of skilled workers to produce a unit item (like a custom yacht), as opposed to a mass produced item (like a small car), the more informal is the coordination of workers and the less need there is for supervision. The greater quality of such "craft" production is the motivation behind the effort by larger mass-manufacturing firms to use "teams" of workers who informally work together without close supervision by a foreman to produce units (like transmissions or engines for cars) that are then inserted onto the assembly line.

When service is the task of an organization rather than a physical good or product, hierarchy is reduced because moment-by-moment supervision is less essential. Instead, supervision involves the review of paper and information after it is produced, just to make sure work was done correctly. As a result, authority hierarchies are, to a degree, reduced.

Control and Authority. In addition to its tasks, the type of organization—whether a voluntary, utilitarian, or coercive type—greatly determines how control of its members occurs (Collins 1975). If an organization is a utilitarian one, using only wages and salaries to motivate workers, then considerable supervision is necessary to assure that workers "earn their money." However, if commitments of workers come from a sense of professionalism, supervision is less necessary because "pride" in work is a good substitute for authority and supervision. Voluntary organizations, as well as work involving a high degree of skill and training (medicine, law, university teaching, etc.), can usually dispense with much supervision because of worker commitments to their jobs. Efforts to couple unskilled wage labor with a sense of professional commitments to norms indicating what constitutes "a good job" have not always been successful, as the struggles in the last decades of the U.S. auto industry have illustrated. But if it can be done, then less hierarchy and supervision are necessary.

In coercive organizations, however, considerable hierarchy and supervision are always essential to assure that people are doing what they should, because in such organizations—such as prisons and mental hospitals—conformity to rules must be forced with the threat of coercion. Such organizations are never very effective, although armies can become efficient "fighting machines." In the case of an effective army, though, it is the building of informal commitments to norms and the pride of the soldiers (not the authority hierarchy or threat of a court martial) that make them effective on the battlefield.

Organizational Culture

The nature of tasks, authority, and control greatly influences the culture of an organization, or the symbol systems (values, beliefs, and norms) guiding role behaviors (Pondy 1983; Smircich 1983). If workers resent supervision and are motivated primarily by wages, then the culture of an organization will emphasize "just doing one's job" without great emotion or commitment to the organization. In contrast, if commitments to the goals of an organization motivate workers, then the organizational culture will stress worker efforts above and beyond their specific task. Or, if members simply try to avoid coercion by figures of authority, then it is likely that two cultures will emerge, an authoritarian one guiding the efforts of those who supervise to get conformity to their dictates and a subversive one emphasizing doing just enough publicly to avoid coercion but a great deal privately to subvert the efforts of an organization. Prisons are a good example of this last type of culture where the guards and administrators have an entirely different culture than the inmates who have a vast system of informal practices, norms, and beliefs that defy authority.

The culture of an organization has become a prominent issue because of foreign competition with American corporations. U.S. manufacturing firms, for example, have a long history of antagonistic relations with workers, fostering a culture of "just doing one's job" among workers who have few commitments to the organization and who, as a result, perform shoddy work. Changing this culture has proven difficult, although American manufacturing corporations must if they are to survive. Yet, rather than change the way it does business, a corporation often just exports its jobs overseas to foreign factories where workers are more docile. In contrast, among high technology companies, American corporate structure is most effective because it creates strong commitments of workers to the goals of the company, thereby securing extra effort and high quality work while reducing the need for supervision and too many levels of authority.

Problems of Personnel

Parkinson's Law.   Workers always try to appear busy to justify their jobs, even if such efforts are merely wasting time (Parkinson 1957). This situation becomes a source of vast inefficiency for an organization because it must often pay people to do unnecessary work. But, there is always the dilemma of how to determine what is necessary and unnecessary, especially when workers will go to great lengths to justify what they are doing. Thus, Parkinson's law states that "work expands to the time available for its completion." This fact poses a dilemma in determining *how much* time is needed for various tasks. The operation of Parkinson's law is often what makes large bureaucracies—whether governmental or corporate—so cumbersome, inefficient, and wasteful; and yet, it is always difficult to define *which* positions are unessential and whose jobs should be eliminated. This dilemma genders a great deal of political rhetoric about "eliminating waste" but just *where* and *how* to do so is always more difficult than the rhetorical promises of politicians and corporate managers would indicate.

The "Peter Principle".   Another source of inefficiency in organizations stems from the tendency of organizations to promote people to "their level of incompetence" (Peter and Hull 1969). If a worker does a good job at one level, he or she is usually promoted to a more demanding job (and, of course, a better paying job); at some point in this process, workers are moved to a position whose demands exceed their competence. Yet, rarely is this incompetent person demoted back to a job within his or her level of competence. If this process occurs again and again across a wide range of workers, the organization can become loaded with incompetents. By itself, this creates inefficiency, but often, organizations have to hire new people to "work around" or "assist" the incompetent—a practice that only burdens the organization even more.

Ritualism.   Because formal organizations have explicit rules guiding worker performance, they tend to encourage rigid conformity to these rules, even when such conformity subverts the goals of the organization. Such "ritualists" tend to be older employees who have done their job, day in and day out, in a certain way for a long time; as a result, they become so accustomed to their routines that they lose sight of the goals of their organization and blindly conform to the rules (Merton 1968). They go "by the book," revealing a trained incapacity for flexibility and innovation; if the informal system in an organization is dominated by such ritualists, then the organization becomes inefficient, ineffective, and if you have to deal with it, maddening and frustrating.

Alienation.   Many jobs are, let's face it, repetitive and boring. They do not need or require our creativity or innovation. We stay in the job for the money and little else. Such work is alienating, and bureaucratic organizations are by their nature structures in which a great deal of routine, repetitive work must be done—whether shuffling paper or sitting in front of a monitor on a computer. It is often difficult to make work less alienating because of its very nature; and thus a problem for all large-scale complex organizations is to keep too many people from being disaffected, putting in just enough effort to pass the grade but little else.

The Changing Structure of Formal Organizations

The organizations of modern life are changing in some dramatic ways. Part of the reason for this change is to get around the personnel problems examined above, but much more fundamental are changes associated with the use of technologies and machines and with the globalization of economic activity.

Pressures from Technology

Often in response to lower wage labor in other parts of the world, the application of technology has created industrial robots that can now do much of the dull, repetitive work in manufacturing. As a result, organizations can give manual workers potentially more interesting jobs, although much labor will remain dull and repetitive; or as has often been the case, organizations simply eliminate workers' jobs. Over the last 20 years, new applications of technological knowledge have created new kinds of jobs revolving around information and servicing. As an outcome, much of the labor force sits in front of a computer terminal or wears a phone set. These jobs are, however, often as boring as the manufacturing jobs in factories that they have replaced. In America, they tend to pay less than older types of manufacturing jobs. Moreover, as fewer workers are needed in manufacturing, sales and services jobs have also increased, but their organization is often tedious. A sales clerk in a department store, or a worker in a fast food outlet, is probably stuck in a job that is as routine as those in factories but without the pay and benefits of the older industrial jobs.

Thus, it is not clear that technological changes have created organizations that are dramatically less bureaucratic than those in the past. At the high-technology end (e.g., computer programming, engineering, corporate research and development, medicine and biotechnology, university education and research, etc.) organizations clearly provide more interesting and challenging work; to the extent that more high-end sales and service jobs in organizations allow for initiative and creativity, they too are probably more gratifying. But the impetus to change from technology fueled by intense global competition has not, as of yet, changed the nature of much work for most people.

Efforts in a competitive world economy to restructure organizations—both corporate and governmental—have been as important a source of organizational change as technology. Better quality goods and services, delivered quickly and inexpensively, require that work be reorganized in ways that increase commitments to the organization while reducing excess levels of authority and the problems it engenders—alienation, ritualism, and conflicts. Thus, organizations of the future will seek to create a cohesive culture emphasizing pride in work to reduce direct supervision, and to encourage innovation and initiative. Whether or not this change will occur on a broad scale is difficult to know, but there are limitations on how far these trends can go because people will still have to work with machines and provide menial services.

Pressures from Globalization

Another major change in organizations comes from the effects of globalization. Those who own and manage companies always seek to reduce costs, especially when they are in competition with other companies. One way to reduce costs is to use technology rather than people to do jobs. Still another is to export jobs to nations with lower priced labor pools. Since the 1980s, for example, manufacturing jobs in shoes, electronics, clothing, appliances, and other products were exported overseas where labor costs are much lower. The result, of course, is that these well paying blue collar jobs have become lost to American workers. More recently, white collar service and professional jobs have also been exported to lower priced professionals overseas. For instance, if you need to call the trouble shooter for problems with your computer, you are likely to be talking to someone in India; if you need to have a claim processed by your insurance company, it may well be done overseas; if you need a radiologist to read an MRI or a complex x-ray, it may well be someone in India or the Philippines; if you require drafting or other graphics work, it is may be done by someone in Budapest, Hungary; if you have a complex tax return, it is likely farmed out to one of the big accounting firm's foreign subsidiaries; if you need structural engineering, it can be done in India; and so it goes for an increasing number of what used to be middle class and professional jobs. For most of the latter half of the last century, it was the working class that had to deal with the effects of technology and the export of their jobs. But for the first time, upon college graduation you may confront the exportation of a wide range of jobs overseas—jobs that were once sure-fire ways to earn a living.

In general, competition among organizations at a global level is dramatically altering the structure of organizations, both service and manufacturing firms. Competition places a premium on lowering costs to squeak out profits; and there are two basic ways to lower costs, use technologies that eliminate labor costs (wages, salaries, retirement, and medical benefits) or export some tasks or entire production facilities to countries with a lower cost labor pool. Organizations are thus becoming truly global, moving jobs and production around the globe in search of lower priced labor. Only those domestic jobs that cannot be exported easily or that resist machine technologies may, in the not-too-distant future, remain in the United States. These jobs are found in organizations that need low-pay service workers (e.g., fast foods and retail sales), in manufacturing that is too complex to perform overseas (very high technology, or large products like cars that can be mass produced domestically), in manufacturing and trades that must be done "on site" (e.g., construction and agriculture) and in public work organized in governmental bureaucracies.

As organizations become increasingly global and as they rely upon information processing technologies, they do not necessarily become less bureaucratic. A certain amount of autonomy may be tolerated in far-flung divisions around the world, but tasks farmed out all over the world need to be coordinated; and information processing machines cannot do this task alone. There will need to be hierarchies of authority that coordinate and control. As long as these needs persist, so will formal, bureaucratic organizations.

Hyperrationality

As organizations, particularly multinational corporations, become global, they often standardize their products and engage in mass production of the same commodity in the same way all over the world. George Ritzer has called this trend "McDonaldization" because this fast food producer serves the same product, in the same way, all over the globe. Indeed, this kind of standardization enables organizations to rationalize production because the manufacturing process is the same, despite the diverse cultures in which these products are sold. This is a rationality that connects far-flung organizations into a common predictive template that increases efficiency (and profits). Of course, standardization is just that: it takes away diversity and uniqueness. Indeed, fast food restaurants like McDonalds often destroy smaller family enterprises. Thus, as organizations seek rationality and efficiency on a global scale, they often do so in ways that undermine indigenous enterprises that offer unique products reflective of a particular culture.

As Wal-Mart goes global, it often does to family-run small businesses in foreign lands what it does in America: it destroys them by offering standardized goods at a low price. The result is for retailers offering unique goods to be driven out of business by Wal-Mart and its highly rational system of squeezing wholesalers and distributing standardized goods at low prices.

SUMMARY

1. As the scale of society gets larger and the tasks it performs become more complex, groups are connected together to create complex organizations that reveal formal rules, a clear division of labor, hierarchies of authority, control of emotions, technical competence of incumbents, organizational control of offices, and career movements up the hierarchy.

2. There are various types of organizations: (a) voluntary organizations where people freely join to pursue certain goals and interests; (b) coercive or organizations where individuals are physically forced to remain separated from the rest of the population; and (c) utilitarian or organizations where members rationally calculate the costs and benefits of being a member.

3. One key dynamic of organizations is ecological: organizations exist in a resource environment and must often compete with other organizations for resources leading to patterns of growth and decline in various types of organizations in a society.

4. Another set of dynamics is internal, revolving around a series of processes: (a) development of informal ties within the formal hierarchy; (b) conflict stemming from inequality in the distribution of authority; (c) task activities as these reflect the technologies and products produced; (d) control and authority revolving around patterns of external supervision and worker commitments; (e) cultural processes in which values, beliefs, and norms create a particular "ethos" in how work is to be done; (f) personnel problems stemming from "Parkinson's law" or the expansion of work to fill the time allo-

cated, the "Peter Principle" or the promotion of workers to their level of incompetence, ritualism or the performance of work without consideration of the goals of an organization, and alienation arising from dull and routine work tasks.

5. The nature of organizations has, in recent decades, changed enormously under the impact of technology and world economic competition, causing the loss of many manufacturing jobs and the increase in lower paying sales and service jobs.

6. As corporations become global, they also become hyperrational, using the same production and distribution processes in very diverse cultures. As they do so, they undercut local business, thereby reducing the production and distribution of unique goods and services.

KEY TERMS

Coercive Organizations: Those bureaucratic structures in which members are forced to remain isolated from the society.

Formal Organization/Bureaucracy: Goal-directed social structures revealing hierarchies of positions, linked together by authority and clear norms, with increasing numbers of incumbents at the lower levels of the hierarchy.

Informal System: System of ties that people develop within the formal structure of an organization; such ties often supplant but always supplement formal lines of authority.

Niche Density: In organizational ecology, the total number of organizations of a given type seeking the same or similar resources.

Utilitarian Organizations: Those bureaucratic structures that people enter on the basis of calculations of costs and benefits.

Voluntary Organizations: Those bureaucratic structures in which people freely enter or leave the organization.

Chapter 13

Communities

Sometime around 8,000 to 12,000 years ago, a momentous set of events occurred. Humans who had been hunter-gatherers for perhaps as long as 150 millennia began to settle in one place. They settled near water and simply extracted the fish, while continuing to hunt and gather. Once sedentary with a stable supply of food, populations began to grow and, at some point, these settled peoples began to run out of food to gather. They were forced to take up gardening to generate enough plant life to supplement the fish and kills from the hunt. As they eventually ran out of game to hunt, they also began to herd animals for food. As these events unfolded—slowly at first—humans had created a new social form: community. A **community** is a physical place where people settle and where basic institutional activities—economic, familial, religious, political, legal, medical, and recreational—are conducted. Before humans settled, there were only bands of wandering hunter-gatherers who would stay in one place for only a short period and then move on to a new encampment in search of animals to hunt and plant life to gather. But, hunter-gatherers understood the connection between seeds and plant growth, and they knew how to herd animals where such animals existed, but they avoided gardening and herding for a simple reason: It is too much work. When the few remaining hunter-gatherers that survived into the twentieth century were asked why they did not take up gardening, they generally replied that they did not want to work so hard.

Thus, the price of community and the larger population that it could support was a dramatic increase in the amount of work that people had to perform to sustain themselves. The larger the communities became, the more specialized were the activities of individuals, with only some actively engaged in food production and ever more involved in the trades, services, and crafts. Today, you and I as members of even larger communities must constantly work to support ourselves—a far cry from the simple life of our ancestors who worked, at most, 15 hours per week. True, hunter-gatherers did not have homes, stereos, cars, and the many hallmarks of urban life, but they also did not have to worry about how to pay and maintain all of the material things that people in urban centers now possess. Of course, people in many urban areas in the world, including the United States, often live in great poverty and must worry about simply finding a place to live and staying alive, something that hunter-gatherers rarely had to ponder.

Urbanization

Urbanization is the process whereby an increasing proportion of the population lives in **cities**. Up to the twentieth century, most people still lived in rural areas in small communities, but by the end of the century and now into the twenty-first century, the vast majority of the population in the developed world resides in urban areas composed of a core city and its surrounding suburbs.

Agriculture and Urbanization

Urbanization cannot occur without the capacity to produce enough food to feed all of those who do not harvest the land. Some cities in Asia became rather large using just horticultural technologies without the benefit of the plow. The same was true in Meso and South America. Still, cities numbering several hundred thousand residents could not emerge without movement from horticulture to full-fledged agriculture using the plow and nonhuman sources of energy from animals, wind, and water. These communities built from an agricultural base first emerged in what is today Iraq and spread throughout the Middle East. By today's standards, of course, these were not large cities (Chandler 1987), as can be seen in Table 13.1 where the size of the largest cities in the year 100 A.D. are listed. Babylon, for example, was only a little over three square miles; even by the time the Roman Empire had reached its peak, Rome itself was around 340,000 inhabitants. Beijing at the peak of the Mongolian empire—the largest empire of contiguous land ever created—was never very large. And throughout Europe after the fall of the Roman Empire, very few cities were over 50,000 inhabitants.

There is some debate as to what caused the rise of large cities. Clearly, some cities, like many of those in Meso and South America, were created as places of religious worship; others throughout the world were primarily trade centers. Still others were the seats of governmental power and most were a combination of trade, religious, and governmental activity. Thus, the creation of religious, trade, and governmental

Table 13.1   Approximate Size of Largest Cities in the Year 100 AD

City	Number of Residents
Rome	450,000
Luoyang (Honan), China	420,000
Seleucia, on the Tigris, Iraq	250,000
Alexandria, Egypt	250,000
Antioch, Turkey	150,000
Anuradhapura, Sri Lanka	130,000
Peshawar, Pakistan	120,000
Carthage, Tunisia	100,000

Source: Chandler (1987)

centers encouraged the expansion of the economy to feed and support the thousands of people in these cities, while advances in the economy allowed for the building of larger cities. Large cities, even those of relatively modest size of the past, depend upon dramatically expanded economic production. There were thousands of people in cities who did not till or harvest the land, but they still had to eat and house themselves; and so, without agrarian production far exceeding the needs of the farmers themselves, urbanization cannot occur. Only societies that could produce an economic surplus to support religious and political functionaries, merchants, tradesmen, craftsmen, laborers, artists, and the many other specialized activities evident in cities were able to urbanize.

More than just producing enough food, however, is critical to urbanization. Urbanization also encourages new kinds of economic activity not directly related to food production. Someone has to construct boats, houses, streets, ports, canals, and buildings; trade creates new kinds of economic positions, from merchants through bankers and accountants to insurers; crafts trades continue to proliferate to meet ever increasing needs for goods such as pottery, silverware, tables and chairs, metal works, leather goods, clothing, shoes, and literally hundreds of other trades that meet the needs of the urban population; artisans emerge as permanent fixtures of urban life; and so it goes for many new kinds of specialized economic roles. Urbanization thus allows the economy to expand dramatically, as new kinds of goods and services are produced. And, as the economy grows, more people are attracted to the city in search of jobs and other opportunities to live better.

A critical feature behind this economic expansion and urbanization is the emergence of money and markets (Braudel 1977, 1982; Weber 1922). For most of human history, money did not exist; it was only with some degree of urbanization that money became a key part of economic exchange. Money allows something revolutionary to occur: it can be used to buy goods and services of *any* kind. This characteristic of money is so obvious that we often fail to realize what a revolution a stable currency represented in human affairs. For most of human history, people produced for themselves, shared, and bartered with hard goods (such as trading animal meat for woven goods). With money, an individual can express his or her preferences without needing a hard good to exchange in barter. Moreover, with money, markets can dramatically expand. And with market growth, people come to the city to live and sell their goods and services. As more people migrate to cities, markets must expand to meet their demands. Thus, once money exists, it acts like a supercharger on urbanization: Markets themselves attract people to urban centers to exchange goods and services; markets allow for the emergence of wage laborers who use their wages to create ever more demand in markets for consumer goods; markets generate needs for new services like banking and insurance; markets encourage the production of new kinds of goods and services that, in turn, bring more people to the city. Markets have thus been a highly dynamic force behind urbanization.

Even as urbanism stimulated the economy, and vice versa, most medieval cities were still dominated by religious and political structures at their core. The business district, as we know it today, filled in around these noneconomic functions of the medieval city. Indeed, today, the cores of the ancient cities that persist to this day in Asia, the Middle East, and Europe are still built up around large places of worship and governmental buildings. Industrialization, however, was to change the look and structure of urban communities.

Industrialization and Urbanization

Industrialization dramatically accelerates the effects of markets on urbanization. Industrial production uses nonanimate energy and fossil fuels to harness large numbers of workers to machines, thereby enabling the production of larger quantities of goods. Machines do the opposite to the agricultural sector: they replace the need for as much labor to produce food. As workers are displaced from agriculture, they migrate from rural areas seeking industrial jobs, thereby expanding the labor market. These workers must buy goods and services, thus expanding markets for housing, clothing, shoes, food, and other necessities of life; once markets expand, the industrial goods from factories can be sold in ever greater quantities and varieties. As the scale of all economic activity expands, needs for services like banking, insuring, advertising, accounting, and the like grow, thereby pulling more people to cities who in turn buy goods and services that expand markets even more. The industrial city thus becomes a "growth machine," expanding markets for the growing population and, at the same time, creating new opportunities for work that attract more people to the urban core. These dynamics are illustrated in Figure 13.1.

The city thus exerted enormous influence on the structure of human societies and, indeed, prompted the emergence of sociology as a distinct mode of inquiry. By the time the Industrial Revolution was 100 years old, sociology was beginning to penetrate academia as a specialized field. Given the power of the city to pull people from rural communities and to change so dramatically the way people lived, it is not surprising that the nature of city life and the dynamics of urban areas were among the first topics of sociological inquiry, especially in the United States where urbanization was so dramatic with wave upon wave of immigrants during the last half of the nineteenth century and first two decades of the twentieth century.

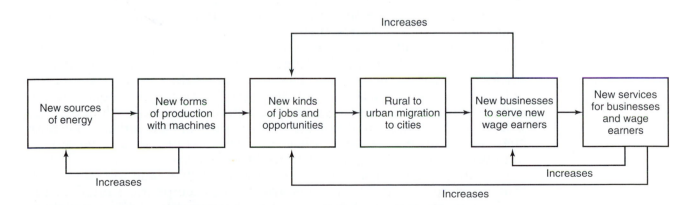

Figure 13.1   Industrialization and Urbanization

Box 13.1: Three Early Models of Urban Growth

These three models represent different attempts to understand patterns of urban growth and land use. Model 1 views cities as a series of concentric zones that are typified by certain activities and residential patterns. Such zones are the result of economic competition over how land should be used. Model 2 views urban growth and land use as a "pieshaped" process in which corridors of different activity are created. Such corridors are the result of how transportation systems—rails, highways, and waterways—develop. Model 3 stresses that cities develop distinct nuclei that are centers for specialized activities. Thus as cities develop, their distinct areas become even more specialized around particular types of activities.

Source: Adapted from Harris and Ullman, 1945.

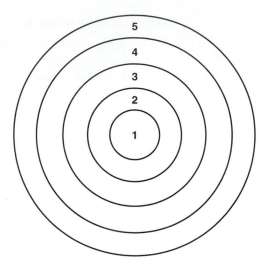

Model 1: The Concentric-Zone Hypothesis
1. Central business district
2. Zone in transition
3. Zone of working people's homes
4. Residential zone
5. Commuter zone

Source: Adapted from Burgess, 1925.

Early Studies of City Life

The Chicago School and Urban Ecology. The rapid growth of cities in the United States inspired the first generation of American sociologists at the University of Chicago. As a fast growing city, Chicago forced sociologists to explore the transformations that were all around them. These early sociologists and their students began by studying patterns of urban land use in Chicago. The first model of land use was developed by Robert Park, Ernest Burgess, & Roderick McKenzie (1925), who argued for a concentric zone pattern of land use around the central business district (see Model 1 in Box 13.1). Recognizing that this model was too simplistic, alternative models were presented, as shown in Models 2 and 3 in Box 13.1. These models were examples of ecological theory because they saw land as a resource niche that stimulated competition among various segments of the population—businesses, ethnic groups, industries, and government. More recent studies of urban land use still use elements of this ecological perspective, but the emphasis shifted to the analysis of interests and power of various segments of the population. Today, the structure of an urban community is the outcome of a complex

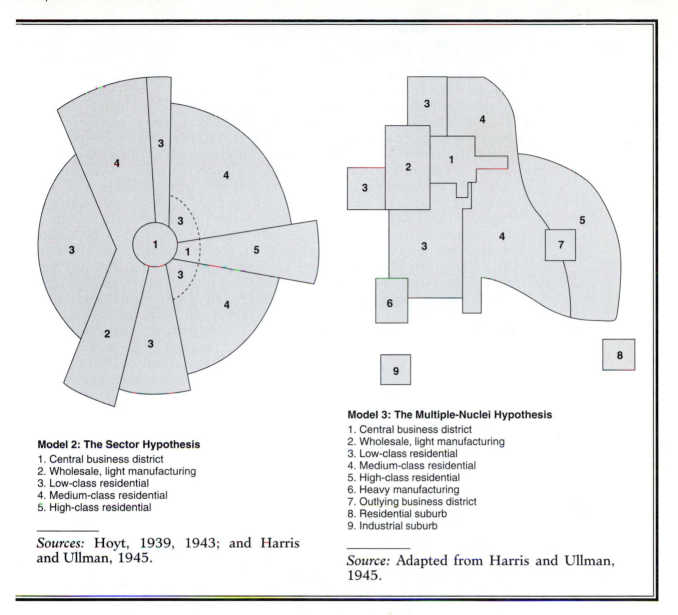

Model 2: The Sector Hypothesis
1. Central business district
2. Wholesale, light manufacturing
3. Low-class residential
4. Medium-class residential
5. High-class residential

Sources: Hoyt, 1939, 1943; and Harris and Ullman, 1945.

Model 3: The Multiple-Nuclei Hypothesis
1. Central business district
2. Wholesale, light manufacturing
3. Low-class residential
4. Medium-class residential
5. High-class residential
6. Heavy manufacturing
7. Outlying business district
8. Residential suburb
9. Industrial suburb

Source: Adapted from Harris and Ullman, 1945.

interplay among business interests, governmental goals, neighborhood and district political pressures, and broader citizen interests in police, transportation, parks, pollution abatement, and health services. Just how these play out in a particular community will vary, and so, the early Chicago models represent only a limited view of the urban landscape. In actual practice, the dynamics of cities are much more fluid and complex than portrayed in the Chicago School.

The Study of Urban Life.   From the beginnings of sociology, the lifestyles and living patterns of urbanites were fascinating to sociologists. In both Europe and America, a bias was evident in much of the early work on urban living: Life in the city was compared to a rather romanticized view of rural living where people were seen to have high rates of interaction and a sense of solidarity. Compared to this view of rural life, the perceived impersonality of the city was seen as problematic. The early Chicago School was hostage to these biases as it saw the city dweller as sacrificing close family, friendship, and religious ties; as a result, individuals were viewed as isolated, alone, and alienated. Georg Simmel in Europe added the notion that urban dwellers reveal a blasé interpersonal style to cope with the stimulation, noise, and complexity of urban life. In his famous article on "Urbanism as a Way of Life," the American, Louis Wirth (1938), echoed these biases in stressing that as communities are broken apart into districts and neighborhoods; and as people's daily lives are lived in diverse formal organizations like work and school, social bonds are weakened, with the result that it becomes impossible to have a sense of community-wide solidarity. Even the local small groups in which people participate lose their intimacy and their power to regulate social life, forcing reliance on formal sources of control like the police. Moreover, traditional institutions such as work, school, and church must now compete for people's time and energy, making it more difficult for people to give time to their families. Was this image of urban life accurate?

Later studies exposed these biases. There is a propensity of city dwellers, when in public, to "shut out" the noise and confusion around them, engaging in a kind of selective inattention. Yet, studies conducted later in the twentieth century revealed that city dwellers reveal strong family and friendship ties, have a sense of neighborhood and community, and have strong ties to fellow ethnics and to religious organizations (Fischer 1982, 1976; Gans 1962a; Greer 1956). People find a way, these data indicate, to form strong social ties and a sense of community.

Suburbanization

The Emergence of Suburbs

In many parts of the world, particularly in the United States, urbanization has been transformed into a process of **suburbanization** in which the large core city is now surrounded by smaller cities composed of extensive housing tracts, small central business and retail districts, large regional malls, and any number of "strip malls." Suburbanization is the result of both "push" and "pull" forces. Among the forces pushing people from the city are: (a) high taxes to support the larger city infrastructure (streets, health care, police, firefighters, mass transit, and government); (b) high crime rates; (c) decaying neighborhoods and, with a mass exodus of city residents, a declining business district; (d) noise and crowding; (e) declining quality of city services; and (f) environmental pollution.

Despite these push factors making people disposed to leave the city, suburbanization does not occur without changes in urban infrastructures. One change is in the transportation system; people have to be able to move out to the suburbs and, if their jobs are still in the city, to get back. Thus, without rail and road systems, suburbanization will not occur. Secondly, services and retail stores must also move to the suburbs. During initial phases of suburbanization, businesses were slow to move; now, businesses often move in anticipation of the spread of new housing developments, and in fact, malls often become the magnet for housing development. At some point in suburbanization, jobs must move out of the central city. Suburbanization, itself, creates jobs for the businesses that service the needs of suburbanites, but other economic forces make suburbanization more likely. One is the availability of comparatively inexpensive land for assembly line and other industrial work. Second is the lower tax rates that will attract businesses, especially if local governments offer tax incentives to businesses to locate in a suburban community and provide jobs for their residents. Another key force facilitating suburbanization is a large housing industry capable of building tracts of relatively inexpensive homes. Still another development is the movement of corporate headquarters or regional centers from cities to suburban "business parks," thereby creating white collar jobs outside of the city.

As these infrastructural capacities are set into place, they operate as "pull" factors, attracting people to the suburbs. The pull factors include (a) availability of larger houses with yards; (b) ability to commute to work in the core city; (c) movement of industrial and service jobs to the suburbs; (d) lower crime rates; (e) lower tax rates (at least initially); (f) better recreational facilities; and (g) reduced noise, crowding, and pollution.

Like the initial urbanization that created the large city, suburbanization changed the way people, especially Americans, live. An entirely new form of community emerged by the middle decades of the last century, and sociologists were anxious to study it. Yet, much like their earlier counterparts who compared the city to a rather idealized view of rural life, early studies of "suburbanites" compared their lifestyle against an overly romantic conception of city life.

Studies of Suburban Life

Early Studies of Suburban Life. Studies (Whyte 1957; Spectorsky 1955) of the emerging suburbs around Chicago provided an early view of suburbanites as careerists who commuted to the city and who were superficial conformists trying to "keep up with the Jones." Appearance was overly important, gossip was rampant, and life revolved around maintaining status. Family life was disjointed and extramarital affairs were a major preoccupation of residents. Was this portrayal accurate?

Later Studies of Suburban Life. This early image of the suburbanite was clearly biased, comparing suburban dwellers with "sophisticated and worldly" city dwellers or romanticized images of a rural life that never existed. The fact that people wanted to live in the suburbs is the first indication that life there cannot be so shallow. In fact, later studies showed that there was no great difference in behavior of city and suburban dwellers (Bell 1958; Berger 1960; Farley 1964; Gans 1962a, 1962b, 1967): family and friendship networks were important; commitments to community were strong; neighborhoods were important; involvement in civic and school life was equal or stronger than that evident in the city; and in general, it was clear that people live pleasant and happy lives in the suburbs. What was true at the midpoint of the last century is equally the case today, although life in the suburbs has changed because of the dramatic increase in women's participation in the labor force. Still, family, neighborhood, and community are important; and family life is the nexus of all other activities.

Thus, despite the early and rather biased negative evaluation of the suburbs by sociologists and social critics, people clearly like living in them. As a consequence, they have expanded dramatically over the last 40 years, especially in America. Yet, as more and more people move to the suburbs, many of the problems that pushed people from the city are recreated in older suburban communities. Noise, crowding, traffic congestion, pollution, rising crime, higher taxes, declining city services, blighted neighborhoods, and other forces that pushed people from the city become ever more evident in older suburban communities. As the problems of cities are replicated in the suburbs, the creation of **exurbia,** or communities that are located at some distance from cities, begin to emerge.

Exurbia

Some people continue to move out from the city but they jump over its suburbs, and many suburbanites look for places to live that are away from suburban communities. This movement is often facilitated by what are sometimes called "edge" cities composed of a business park or industrial firms moving far out where land is available, thereby pulling people from the city and suburbs to areas where daily commutes to the core city are no longer practical or desired. These communities offer all of the benefits that the early suburbs provided, and they are emerging all over the United States, England, and in some parts of Europe. For example, as the Japanese automobile industry has established manufacturing plants in the American south, these plants are often located in rural areas where cheap land, tax incentives, nonunion workers, government-financed infrastructures, and other incentives make these towns attractive. Of course, as these towns grow and as suppliers of factories are pulled into the area, these exurban communities become more like larger cities.

Metropolitan Regions

As the central core city, its suburbs, and even its exurbs have expanded, larger urban regions have been formed as the suburbs and exurbs of different core cities begin to bump into each other. These large metropolitan regions are sometimes termed **conurban** regions. For example, in California the metropolitan region around the San Francisco Bay comprises a huge metropolitan region with three core cities—Oakland, San Jose, and San Francisco—and a larger number of suburban governments. Increasingly, this region is moving toward what were once rural outposts such as Salinas. In the Los Angeles area, there are now several metropolitan regions that are converging, one from Los Angeles to Riverside-San Bernardino moving to the Palm Springs area, another from Riverside-San Bernardino to San Diego connecting a series of exurban communities, still another from Los Angeles-Long Beach through the exurbs of Orange County to San Diego, and yet another from Los Angeles through Ventura on its way to Santa Barbara. As the land across this several-hundred-mile expanse is filled in with contiguous suburban communities, a *conurban region* becomes a **megalopolis** because metropolitan areas are now blending into each other. Indeed, along the east coast, an even larger megalopolis from Boston through New York and Philadelphia to Washington, DC and Baltimore is emerging. Table 13.2 lists the largest metropolitan regions in the United States.

Table 13.2   Largest Metropolitan Regions in the United States, 2000

Region	Number of Residents
New York Area, including Long Island, northern New Jersey, and Connecticut	21.2 million
Los Angeles Area, including Riverside, Long Beach, and Orange County	16.1 million
Chicago Area, including portions of northern Indiana and southern Wisconsin	9.1 million
Washington-Baltimore, including surrounding areas in Maryland, Virginia, and West Virginia	7.6 million
San Francisco Bay Area, including Oakland, San Jose, and other cities extending out from the bay	7.1 million
Philadelphia, Wilmington-Atlantic City, including areas in Pennsylvania, Maryland, New Jersey, and Delaware	6.2 million
Boston Area, including surrounding areas in Massachusetts, New Hampshire, Maine, and Connecticut	5.8 million
Detroit Area, extending to Ann Arbor and Flint, Michigan	5.4 million
Dallas-Forth Worth and surrounding cities	5.2 million

Source: U.S. Bureau of the Census, 2003

Again, this trend is most evident in the United States; and wherever metropolitan regions exist, they pose a number of problems, including: (a) governmental regulation becomes very difficult across the entire region when so many cities and county governments and, in some cases, state governments must coordinate activities; (b) funding for infrastructures that all communities in the region use becomes extremely difficult; and (c) environmental, health and safety, police, fire, transportation, welfare, education, and other public service issues become particularly difficult to manage when spread across so many governmental jurisdictions. Added to these problems are patterns of residential segregation among ethnic groups, the poorest of whom tend to be trapped in the decaying neighborhoods of core cities and the most affluent of whom are in the suburbs (except for pockets of very wealthy people who have homes in the larger cities of metropolitan regions). The levels of segregation of select ethnic subpopulations from the non-Hispanic white majority are summarized in Table 13.3.

New Urban Trends

Resettlement of the Core City

The core city of a large metropolitan region often declines as its skilled workers, businesses, and tax base migrate to the suburbs and exurbs, leaving behind the poor who place heavy burdens of the social services of city government. Not all cities suffer this fate (e.g., San Francisco, New York, and Boston), and sometimes suburban growth actually fuels the rise of a large core city, as has been the case in Atlanta, Charlotte, Greensboro, San Diego, Dallas, Houston, San Jose, and other central

Table 13.3 Residential Segregation among Ethnic Populations in the United States

Segregation from Non-Hispanic Whites	Dissimilarity Indexes	
	Cities	Metropolitan Areas
African Americans	45	59
Asians	32	45
Latinos	35	43
Native Americans	39	59

Source: Frey and Myers (2003); U.S. Bureau of the Census

This dissimilarity index ranges from zero, which would mean that there is no segregation of an ethnic population from whites, to 100, which would denote complete segregation. The numbers also indicate the percentage of whites who would have to move into minority neighborhoods for the index to reach zero. These figures are averages for all cities over 25,000 inhabitants. In particular cities, indexes are much higher or lower. For example, the index for black-white neighborhoods is 87 in Chicago, 85 in New York, 81 in Philadelphia, and 76 in Boston.

cities whose suburbs have encouraged new development projects in the central city. Still, many once dynamic and prosperous core cities, such as Detroit and Cleveland, now have severe economic problems.

Often by conscious design, city governments have encouraged the resettling of the urban core through a combination of techniques: urban renewal of older housing and industrial space into attractive housing; subsidies to business for resettling in the core (thereby creating new jobs that can pull people back to the city); enhancement of cultural and recreational facilities; improvements in infrastructures; and efforts to reduce crime, pollution, and noise. The result has been for many cities to enjoy a migration of young and affluent people back into the core where the vitality of city life becomes an attraction. Some cities have been so successful in this strategy that housing prices are now so high that many cannot afford to move back. Yet, others such as Los Angeles, Baltimore, and Washington, DC have enjoyed only muted success in making city life at the core attractive to suburbanites.

Mega and World Cities

Another pattern of urbanization is the creation of giant cities or **world cities** of enormous size, surrounded by suburbs or, in less developed areas of the world, by large "shanty towns" of very poor people. In Table 13.4, the largest cities of the world are listed in rank order. Those in highly affluent countries reveal a more American pattern with relatively affluent suburbs surrounding the core city. In less developed countries, the large city is surrounded by very poor people living in shacks without adequate plumbing and other essential facilities. These cities with shanty towns around them are very much like many medieval cities that attracted the poor seeking escape from difficult conditions in rural areas but did not have the ability to employ or otherwise improve the lives of

Table 13.4   Largest World Cities, 2003

City	Number of Residents
Mumbai, India	11.9 million
Buenos Aires, Argentina	11.2 million
Seoul, Korea	11.3 million
Karachi, Pakistan	11.3 million
Manila, Philippines	10.1 million
Sao Paulo, Brazil	10.1 million
New Delhi, India	10.0 million
Istanbul, Turkey	9.2 million
Shanghai, China	8.9 million
Jakarta, Indonesia	8.7 million
Mexico City, Mexico	8.6 million
Dhaka, Bangladesh	8.6 million
Moscow, Russia	8.4 million
Tokoyo, Japan	8.2 million
New York City, United States	8.1 million

Source: World Atlas.com (2004)

migrants parked at the city's gates. And like their medieval counterparts, world cities pose severe problems of disorder as those without resources become restive over their plight.

The mega cities of the world are increasingly interconnected (Castells 1998). Corporations charted in one country often have offices in another large city; the money and stock markets of large cities are increasingly connected to each other; and capital flows around the banks, insurance companies, holding companies, and other mechanisms for amassing money at a very rapid speed as it chases sources of profit. And, even labor migrates from city to city in search of new job opportunities. Thus, the economic interdependencies so evident in the modern world system (see Chapter 25) revolve around networks of relations of corporations, governmental officials, and individuals living in the world's mega cities.

SUMMARY

1. For most of human history, communities did not exist. Somewhere between 8,000 and 12,000 years ago, people began to occupy permanent settlements, creating the first communities. Communities are thus structures organizing activities in geographical space.

2. Urbanization is the process whereby an increasing percentage of a population lives in ever larger communities. Large urban communities were not possible without advanced horticultural and agrarian production; with industrialization, larger cities began to emerge.

3. Suburbanization is the emergence of communities around a large core city, forming a metropolitan region.

4. Early studies of both cities and suburbs were biased by comparisons of urban life to idealized visions of traditional communities. More recent studies document that people in both cities and suburbs are actively engaged in neighborhood and community, while evidencing strong friendship networks and family ties.

5. As suburbs mature, people begin to move further from core cities into exurbia; and as suburbs and exurbs begin to flow into each other, a conurban region or megalopolis is created.

6. Aside from the creation of conurban regions, new urban trends include the resettlement of the large core city in many metropolitan regions, the formation of world cities all over the globe, and the extension of network ties among world cities as the process of globalization proceeds.

KEY TERMS

Cities: Communities in which a comparatively large and concentrated population lives and works.

Community: Organization of geographical space so that basic institutional activities can be conducted.

Conurban, Megalopolis: Merger of suburbs and exurbs to form a continuous urban region between two or more core cities.

Exurbia: Areas of urban settlement beyond the suburban areas.

Metropolitan Region: Urban area consisting of a core city and its surrounding suburbs.

Suburbanization: Movement of people from the city or from outlying areas into communities surrounding a core city.

Urbanization: Process whereby an increasing percentage of the population lives in cities and suburbs.

World Cities: Very large cities surrounded by suburbs or shanty towns in which a great deal of world economic activity is conducted.

Part IV Types of Social Structures: Stratification of Categoric Units

Categoric units are created when individuals are defined as distinctive in some way and are then evaluated and treated differently by virtue of being put into a social category. Because members of a social category are evaluated in diverse ways, this differential evaluation often leads to discrimination, whereby the members of a categoric unit are not given the same level of valued resources as those in other categoric units. Thus, categoric units often become key dimensions by which a society is stratified, with members of some categoric units receiving more of the resources that people value—income, prestige, power, health care, education, housing, and the like—than members of less valued categoric units. There are potentially as many dimensions of stratification as there are categoric units, but in actual reality, human societies tend to stratify around just a few of these. In Part IV, we explore three social categories that, more than any others, stratify a population. Class stratification denotes putting people into distinctive classes on the basis of their income, wealth, power, and prestige. Then, once people are so classified, they tend to stay within a particular class. Ethnic stratification occurs when people are defined as different because of their ethnicity, and, on the basis of belonging to a distinct ethnic category, they are subject to prejudice and discrimination. Gender stratification occurs when members of one sex or gender category are discriminated against by members of other sex and gender categories.

Because stratification revolves around the production and perpetuation of inequalities, it is one of the most volatile forces in human societies. People rarely accept the fact that they have less than others, and particularly so when they perceive that they have been subject to discrimination.

Chapter 14

Class Stratification

Some months ago, I witnessed the following scene on a street in Riverside, CA: An elderly homeless woman was pushing her supermarket cart, filled with a variety of things from cans and plastic bags to what looked like a sleeping bag, down the street that leads to my university. It was raining that day, and as she moved along on the side of the road, a big black BMW shot buy, hitting a puddle and splashing water on the old coat that this sad person was wearing. This indignity was probably one of many this woman has had to endure in her life, but to be dowsed by a fancy car underscores an important fact of social life: inequality. Some social categories of individuals consistently get more of what is valued in a society than other categories. Valued resources—power, material wealth, prestige and honor, health, educational credentials, housing, and other resources—are rarely distributed equally. Some have more than others, and their respective shares of resources help maintain their distinctiveness and visibility as members of a social class category. This homeless woman is a member of the poverty class because she has no resources. In fact, she has so few resources—a supermarket basket, the now-dirty clothes on her back, and a few other items—that she has no easy way to get out of poverty. She is trapped and must endure the indignity of being splashed by the affluent—as if being poor in an affluent society were not enough.

The plight of this old woman is only a dramatic marker of inequalities that pervade virtually every aspect of social life in complex societies. By virtue of belonging to categories (e.g., gender, ethnic, social class, and age) people will get varying levels of resources; and their respective shares of resources will perpetuate both perceived and real "differences" among members of distinct categories. Men and women, for instance, are "different" not only because of variations in their biology (which tend to be exaggerated), but also because of their varying shares of resources that can magnify or at least confirm perceived biologic differences. Ethnic subpopulations are "different" not just because of their cultural traditions but also because of their varying slices of the resource pie. Manual, unskilled workers are distinct from skilled white collar workers not just because of the nature of their work but also because they receive different amounts of critical resources. Poor people look poor because they do not have enough resources to look otherwise—just like the old woman walking down the street in Riverside, CA.

You are, of course, acutely aware of these divisions in a society. You sense the frustration and anger of those ethnics who do not have much, and you avoid places where you will stand out. If you are a woman, you may experience a quiet rage at the advantages men have in the labor market and in the houses of power, to say nothing of micro encounters between men and women where men try to dominate the conversation. If you are a man, you know that change in the distribution of resources is occurring and that you will have to share jobs, income, prestige, and authority more equally with women. And when you encounter individuals of a different social class, there is a tension beneath the pleasantries stemming from the fact that one of you has more resources than the other. Or, if you see a homeless person, you often look the other way to avoid having to face this reality. Inequalities, then, are an important dynamic in any society; and hence, they are worth understanding in more detail. In this chapter, we examine social class as a kind of categoric unit and the nature of class stratification in human societies. In subsequent chapters, we explore how ethnic and gender categories also lead to stratification.

Stratification

What is Class Stratification?

Stratification is the general term used to describe a society that distributes income, power, prestige, and other valued resources to its members unequally and creates distinctive classes of members who are culturally, behaviorally, and organizationally different (J. Turner 1984a). The *degree* of stratification is determined by *how* unequally resources are distributed, *how* distinctive social classes are, *how* much mobility occurs between classes, and *how* permanent classes are. A **caste system** like that in traditional India revealed a high degree of stratification because people born into a "caste" habitually received vastly different shares of resources than members of other castes and because it was difficult, if not impossible, to move out of the caste into which one had been born. An **open-class** system, like those in western democracies, is one where class boundaries are fuzzy and changeable and where some mobility from class to class is possible. Indeed, as a member of a society with a more open class system, you are now working to improve the class position given to you by your family, or you are trying to hang onto a class position. You work hard in school and worry about your performance because you know that educational credentials will determine, in large part, your job, income, prestige, and power in American society. The stakes are high, and this is why colleges and universities are tense and serious places beneath the surface frivolity.

Analyzing Stratification

Because stratification is such a central dynamic in human societies, it has been a topic of theoretical concern since sociology's beginnings. Let us see, therefore, how sociologists have sought to conceptualize stratification, starting with the conflict theories of Karl Marx and Max Weber.

Karl Marx on Stratification.   Marx presented a simple, and perhaps too simple, conflict theory of stratification (Marx and Engels 1848). In Marx's eye, those who own the means of production in a society (i.e., the resources and capital used to produce goods and commodities) are able to control the house of power, cultural symbols, work activities, and lifestyles of others. There is in all societies a basic tension between owners and nonowners—whether peasants and lord, or capitalist and workers. Because those who own or control the means of production have power, they are able to manipulate cultural symbols, creating ideologies justifying their power and privileges while negating the claims of others to property and power. And if need be, they can physically coerce and repress those who challenge their control. Yet, Marx argued that the basic **conflict of interests** between those with and without property and power would inevitably create the conditions for a revolution by those who had little control of their work activities, negligible property, and virtually no power.

How was a conflict of interest to become an open conflict that would redistribute resources and alter the nature of the class system (and, in Marx's naive utopia, do away with all class distinctions)? For Marx, the answer was this: those who owned and controlled the means of production would act in ways to "sow the seeds of their own destruction" by creating conditions that enabled the less advantaged to, first of all, become aware of their own interests in redistributing property and power and, second, to become politically mobilized to change the system (Marx and Engels 1848). For example, in his analysis of capitalism, Marx (1867) saw owners of the means of production—the **bourgeoisie**—as driven by their competition with each other in the pursuit of profits to act in ways that would raise the consciousness of their workers—the **proletariat**—and thereby enable them to see their true interests clearly. By lifting the veil of ideology propagated by capitalists, the proletariat would perceive their true interests and mobilize power to realize their interests in changing society. For example, the bourgeoisie were driven by competition to concentrate the proletariat in towns and factories, to make them alienated appendages to machines, to disrupt their routines and lives through layoffs, and to force them to live in squalor and filth by keeping wages as low as possible (Marx and Engels 1848). Under these conditions, workers could communicate their grievances and begin to break through the ideologies of the bourgeoisie (indeed, Karl Marx saw *The Communist Manifesto* as the decisive demystification of bourgeoisie ideology). Once workers were aware of their true interests, they could organize and take power from the capitalists.

Actual events never quite went as Marx predicted, but we should be careful in rejecting all of Marx's ideas because he had some basic insights. For Marx, stratification is to be understood in terms of economic organization, especially the relation of people to the means of production. Those who own and control property, especially the means of production, have power to determine the lives of others in disadvantaged classes. They can do so because they can use their money to buy power and to control the ideologies of a society such that their favored positions are maintained.

Yet, even though the power elite can control the playing field on which people compete for resources, class stratification inexorably generates conflicts of interests that often become the focal point for conflicts that redistribute money and property. The great revolution of the proletariat predicted by Marx did not sweep the industrial world, and in fact where revolution did occur it was more typically initiated by peasants than the urban proletariat. Obviously, class conflict did not produce the classless society that Marx assumed would emerge in the aftermath of the revolution. Still, there are very useful insights in Marx's analysis that should not be lost.

Max Weber on Stratification.   Weber (1922) was a lifetime critic of Marx, but he too proposed a conflict theory of stratification. The main difference between their respective theories was that Weber saw stratification as multidimensional. Inequality revolves around three dimensions: classes, status groups, and parties. **Classes** are created by people's relationship to markets—for jobs and income, for purchasing of consumer goods, and for creating a level of material well being. This notion is similar to Marx's ideas about classes being determined by the relation of their members to the means of production, but it is different in its recognition that many distinct classes can exist and that ownership of property is only one basis for generating a social class. Society does not, therefore, inevitably polarize into the "haves" and "have nots"; it can reveal a more textured and varied class system. **Parties** are the organization of power, but unlike Marx, these do not bear a direct relationship to property and the means of production. Members of a society can have power without great property, and vice versa; and power is often used for purposes other than the goals of the propertied classes (e.g., the military and its elite members are rarely owners of the means of production or holders of great amounts of property; the same is often true of influential politicians). **Status groups** are network ties among those who share similar cultural symbols, tastes, outlooks, and lifestyles, and who, as a result, can command a certain level of deference, honor, and prestige. Although status groups may reflect their members' shares of property or power, they are an independent basis of stratification (e.g., elite college professors often have group affiliations with powerful and propertied people, but they rarely have great amounts of property or power). Thus, for Weber, stratification involves more than hierarchies of classes that follow from the economic order; stratification also revolves around hierarchies of power and status group membership.

Yet, when analyzing conflict, Weber's theory is similar to Marx's (J. Turner 1991, 1993b). There may be constant conflicts within and between different classes, parties, and status groups, but when society-wide conflicts emerge, they are the result of: (a) a high correlation of membership in classes, parties, and status groups (i.e., elites in one are also elites in the other two), (b) great discontinuity in the resources of those who are high and low in these consolidated hierarchies, and (c) little change or opportunity for mobility to higher positions in these three hierarchies. When all these conditions prevail, a **charismatic leader** can emerge to articulate a revolutionary ideology and to mobilize the downtrodden to pursue conflict and redistribution of property, power, and prestige. Here Weber sounds like Marx, but with some important qualifications. First, high correlation of membership in classes, status groups, and parties is not inevitable, as Marx would have asserted, nor does great discontinuity of resource shares or low rates of mobility always occur. Second, even when all conditions are present (i.e., high correlation of membership, great discontinuity, and low mobility), a revolution does not necessarily follow. Chance and fortuity are important in determining whether or not a charismatic leader can emerge and be successful.

The Functional Theory of Stratification.   Marx and Weber both saw stratification as creating tensions and, at least potentially, producing conflict between those with various shares of resources. There is, however, another way to look at stratification: as an integrative force in society. For Kingsley Davis and Wilbert Moore (1945), as well as other functionalists (Parsons 1953), inequalities can be related to critical functional needs or requisites in society.

The famous and often criticized "Davis-Moore hypothesis" argues that if a position in a society is functionally important *and* difficult to fill because of the skills required, it will receive greater resources—money, power and influence, and prestige—than those positions that are not functionally important or hard to fill (Davis and Moore 1945). Both conditions—functional importance and difficulty in filling the position—must be present. For example, the position of garbage collector is functionally important (just imagine a world without garbage collectors) but unskilled and easy to fill; therefore, it will not receive a great many resources. In contrast, a doctor is both a functionally important and a high-skill position; hence, according to the Davis-Moore hypothesis, it must be highly rewarded. Inequality is, therefore, a way of motivating qualified people to undergo the training and sacrifice necessary to do functionally important and skilled work in a society.

Functional theories have, however, been resoundingly criticized for an obvious flaw: they make the existing inequalities in a society seem correct and legitimate, as if those with resources always deserve them because of their skill and functional importance. In fact, critics argue, people gain resources by luck, abuse of power, corruption, tradition, inheritance, and other processes that have little to do with functional importance or talent (Tumin 1953, 1967). Indeed, for many critics, the functional theory sounds like an ideology propagated by the powerful and rich to justify their privilege.

Evolutionary Theories of Stratification.   Some more recent theories have tried to understand stratification in a more long-term historical perspective, going back to hunters and gatherers and, then, moving forward to ever more complex societies. Gerhard Lenski's (1966) theory argues that stratification is the result of increasing economic production that creates a surplus of wealth beyond subsistence needs. As surplus grows, the ability to support nonproductive individuals increases; some are able to mobilize power to usurp this surplus, thereby creating privilege for themselves. Thus, privilege and power are connected: those with wealth can mobilize power to enhance their wealth. On the other side of this equation, those with power can use their power to extract surplus to gain wealth and prestige. But with industrialization, this long-term historical process is reversed, at least to a degree. Those without privilege in industrial societies begin to mobilize and oppose the abusive use of power and the hoarding of economic surplus (much as Marx would have predicted); they force the organization of power to be more democratic, often without a great revolution (as Marx would not have predicted). The result is for some redistribution of wealth through a progressive tax system that places higher taxes on the wealthy (or at least tries to do so, but the wealthy always try to weasel out of this burden). These revenues are then used to provide education, health, welfare, and job opportunities for the less privileged. But this process only goes so far because people fight against taxes and manipulate public opinion to convince the less privileged that high taxes are not in their best interests.

Class Systems

Inequality in the distribution of valued resources generates a set of social classes. It is tempting to view social classes as like layers on a cake, with clear lines of icing separating and marking each distinctive social class, from the highest layer down to the bottom. In some societies of the past and even into the present, this imagery is not too far off the mark, but in industrial and postindustrial societies, the hierarchy of classes is not as discrete and linear as the layers on a cake for several reasons. First, the dimensions that can be used to stratify people are not always correlated with each other, as Max Weber would have emphasized. One's income from work, the prestige of the work, and the power that comes with work can vary enormously. For example, a fully employed construction worker will often make more money than a schoolteacher, but the construction worker will be "blue collar" and the teacher will be "white collar," with the result that the teacher will have more prestige than the construction worker. Which one, then, is more *middle* class? Similarly, a high-ranking general does not have high income compared to many other professionals but can enjoy both power and prestige that far exceed many with higher incomes. Second, if families are viewed as holding a given class position, how do you classify the family that has a low-salaried male worker in a low-prestige and low-power job who is married to a higher-salaried doctor in a high prestige profession? Total family income might be one way to establish a social class position, but in this example, the male's low prestige poses a problem of just where this family belongs in the class system.

Thus, we will always have some trouble in finding the class position of an individual or family, especially in the middle classes between the very wealthy and very poor. Wealth alone carries prestige and, if desired, can be used to buy power or garner it through network ties among the wealthy and powerful (as Weber would have argued is often the case for people of a given *status group*). At the other end of the spectrum are the poor who have no wealth, power, or prestige, making their place in the system very clear. It is for all those classes in between the very top and absolute bottom that there is considerable ambiguity about a person's or family's actual place in the system. Yet, even if we cannot rank them in a linear hierarchy with certainty, classes still exist because the resources that people have do indeed influence how they behave, how they think, how they talk, how they dress, how they recreate, and how they spend their money. Thus, we can categorize someone as working class and middle class on the basis of lifestyle, behavioral demeanor, and other characteristics besides income alone. Indeed, we do this all of the time when we encounter people and interact with them. We look at their dress, their demeanor, their speech patterns, their teeth, their face (e.g., for signs of exposures to the sun), their grooming, their car, and just about any cue that is visible. On the basis of these cues, we *classify* others, often implicitly, into a class category. And then, on the basis of this *class*ification, we proceed to interact with them in a particular way. Thus, even though drawing boundaries around social classes can often be somewhat illusive, the reality of class is always present when we observe others and when we interact with them.

The older image of classes clearly ranked from top to bottom no longer quite fits reality. We can rank individuals and families on any one dimension, such as total family income, prestige of the jobs that they hold, or power that they have themselves or can garner through proxy organizations like a union or professional association. But, such a ranking does not capture what makes classes so important: People in different social classes often live in somewhat different worlds. They see the world differently, they spend their money differently, they behave and talk differently, they often live in different neighborhoods, they recreate differently, they acquire different possessions, and they enjoy different things.

One way to visualize how classes are created is represented in Figure 14.1. At the far left, people secure resources, such as income and prestige from work and education, and perhaps some power. Then, on the basis of the *amount* and particular *types* of resources that people can secure, they build a lifestyle consisting of their interests, attitudes, spending patterns, behavioral demeanor, and other ways that they use the resources they have. In general, people find it easier to interact and be with those who share a similar lifestyle; the old adage that "birds of a feather flock together" is not too far off the mark. As rates of interaction with those living similar lifestyles increase, a distinctive culture emerges, consisting of beliefs, norms, forms of talk, styles of dress, and other symbols that guide how people see and act in the world. A shared culture reinforces how people interact and their lifestyles, which only serves to make others with similar lifestyles and sharing a common culture more attractive as friends. And, as the young are socialized into this culture, they find interaction with those who share this culture and who want to pursue a similar lifestyle more attractive as they grow up, leading them

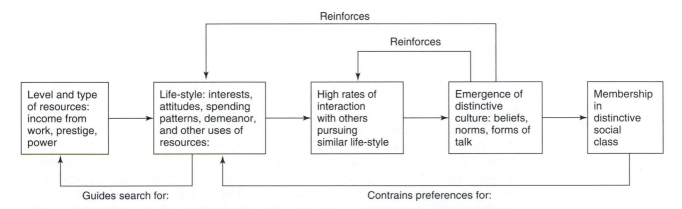

Figure 14.1 Resources, Lifestyle, Interaction, and Class Membership

to select marriage partners who support culture and the lifestyles typical of a social class. As these cycles of lifestyle, rates of interaction (including socialization and marriage), and emergent culture reinforce each other, people become distinctive in the way that they behave and organize their activities, with the result that they can be categorized as belonging to a particular social class. Once a member of a social class, as reinforced by interaction and culture, people seek resources that can allow them to sustain their lifestyle or, if they are young, to pursue this lifestyle as they grow up.

To break out of these reinforcing cycles often requires extra effort. If individuals desire to be upwardly mobile, for example, they must often abandon the people, lifestyle, and culture of their social class of origin and begin to adopt the culture of the social class to which they aspire, often before they have the resources to move into this new, higher social class. Given the power of socialization, interaction, and culture to constrain people's views and behaviors, it is not surprising that most people stay in the social class to which they were born. Social mobility always involves some costs, if only having to live in two worlds consisting of the social class in which one was raised and the new one to which one has moved.

Even if one does not move up, or down, the class hierarchy, moving to *any* new social class is difficult. People still must shift their lifestyles, adopt new friends, and incorporate a new culture, even as they maintain relations with those in another social class, such as parents and siblings who do not move to the new social class. Indeed, for those of you who were raised in the middle and upper middle classes—to say nothing of elite classes—adjustment to college life is relatively easy because the culture and structure of higher education are so much a part of the lifestyles of people in your social class. You know how to orient yourself, act, talk, and otherwise perform in this system. If, however, you are the first member of your family to go to college, as is the case with many at my university, it is a much more difficult adjustment because you have to learn a new culture, new patterns of interaction, new forms of talk, and otherwise engage in learning a new culture.

Figure 14.2 tries to represent the general profile of the class system in postindustrial societies. The dotted lines indicate that the boundaries separating classes are not hard; solid lines indicate that the boundaries are more difficult to traverse, whether one is leaving a social class or trying to get into another. The vertical dimension of the classes listed underscores that there is an implicit ranking involved, moving from least desirable at the bottom to most desirable at the top. People at the top will have more income, education, power, and prestige; those at the bottom have very few resources of any kind. Those in the middle classes will have varying levels of income, education, prestige, and power. Sets of these classes at more or less the same place in the hierarchy (e.g., upper blue collar and middle white collar or lower white collar and lower blue collar) have a sum total of resources—income, education, prestige, power—that is more or less equal, but this total comes from possessing different configurations of resources. Thus, for instance, elementary teachers will have more prestige but less income than carpenters, with the result that they, on average, are at about the same place in the hierar-

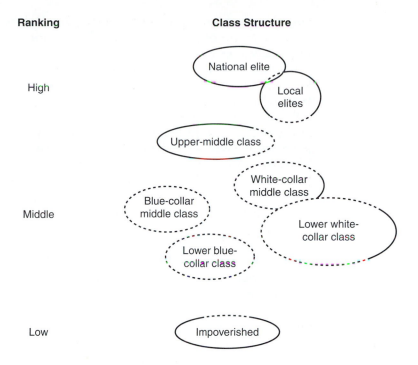

Figure 14.2   Class System of Postindustrial Societies

chy of classes. But, they live in different classes because their lifestyles, friendships, and culture are likely to be very different. Similarly, a successful college professor will have very high prestige but less income than a successful business person who will have less prestige than the professor, putting them at about the same place in vertical ranking of classes (upper middle), but again, they will generally live in very different worlds with different interests, tastes, friends, patterns of behavior, and culture.

Thus, those at the very top and bottom of the class system are generally clearly ranked; those in the middle are not so clearly ranked, but high income alone usually pushes people up the hierarchy, regardless of the source of the income (unless illegally gained). Thus, there is a bias in industrial and postindustrial societies toward valuing those who make more money than others. Income is generally correlated with education in postindustrial societies because educational credentials increase a person's earning power over the life course. This is not always the case, of course, but in general, a significant proportion of high-income individuals are highly educated professionals. Their income, per se, places them high in the hierarchy and brings them prestige, but their education alone also gives them additional prestige and, ultimately, is the reason for their high incomes. A successful business person may or may not have as much education (and the prestige that comes with education), but if this person is wealthy, this wealth alone pushes this individual up the stratification system and, with wealth comes prestige that pushes the person up a bit more, unless they are *de-classe* and crude. Thus, the upper middle classes, just below the national elites, are often the highest ranking people in a local community, especially if they also participate in local elite social, economic, and political circles. Below the upper-middle class are several blue collar and white collar "middle classes." Blue collar work is generally less prestigious than white collar work, but the income levels for these two types of workers can vary widely. Many white collar jobs are low paying, even when they require education that brings some prestige, whereas many blue collar jobs pay rather well. As a result, it is difficult to rank people unless we specify the dimension—money, education and prestige, or power—on which we base the ranking. In general, these individuals will reveal important differences in behavior, interests, and lifestyle, but one class is not clearly "above" the other in the overall system of ranks, although white collar workers will generally be ranked somewhat higher than blue collar workers with equivalent incomes because of the greater likelihood that the white collar worker will have educational credentials (that bring an extra measure of prestige).

Pierre Bourdieu's Analysis of "Distinction"

The French sociologist, Pierre Bourdieu (1984), proposed before his recent death an interesting twist in class analysis. He argued that members of different social classes carry of different amounts of varying types of **capital**. There are four basic types of capital: One is **economic capital**, which ultimately boils down to money that can be used to purchase goods and services. Another type is **cultural capital** consisting of education, interpersonal skills, habits, manners, linguistic styles, and tastes. A third type is **social capital** revolving around the positions in groups and social networks that people have. And the fourth type is **symbolic capital** or ideologies that can be used to legitimate the possession of the other three types of capital. People in different social classes carry varying amounts and configurations of these four types of capital. On the basis of the specific configuration of capital, they will have different world views, demeanor, tastes, speech, perceptions, and ways of thinking.

Bourdieu's analysis becomes particularly provocative when he divides the class system into three basic levels—(a) dominant class, (b) middle class, and (c) lower class—that can be distinguished by the overall levels of these four types of capital. Thus, the dominant class has more economic, cultural, social, and symbolic capital than the middle, with the middle having more than the lower classes. But then, he adds an interesting twist: within each of these three classes (i.e., dominant, middle, and lower) there are three **class factions**: the dominant faction, the intermediate faction, and the dominated faction. Table 14.1 summarizes his basic argument. Let's take the dominant class, which has three factions: The dominant faction of this top class has a lot of economic capital that can be used to buy other forms of capital such as cultural capital or social capital. The intermediate faction has less economic capital than the dominant faction but has moderate levels of cultural, social, and symbolic capital. The dominated faction has much less economic capital but high levels of cultural and symbolic capital. This pattern is repeated for the middle class and the lower class. The dominant faction has the most economic capital that can buy at least some of the other forms of capital; the intermediate faction has less economic capital but moderate levels (for this class) of the other forms of capital; and the dominated faction tends to have more cultural and symbolic capital than any other form of capital.

Table 14.1   Classes and Class Factions in Industrial Societies

Dominant Class: Richest in all forms of capital

Dominant faction: Richest in economic capital, which can be used to buy other types of capital. This faction is primarily of those who own the means of production (i.e., the classical bourgeoisie).

Intermediate faction: Some economic capital, coupled with moderate levels of social, cultural, and symbolic capital. This faction is composed of high-credential professionals.

Dominated faction: Little economic capital but high levels of cultural and symbolic capital. This faction is composed of intellectuals, artists, writers, and others who possess cultural resources valued in a society.

Middle Class: Moderate levels of all forms of capital

Dominant faction: Highest in this class in economic capital but having considerably less economic capital than the dominant faction of the dominant class. This faction is composed of petite bourgeoisie (small business owners).

Intermediate faction: Some economic, social, cultural, and symbolic capital but considerably less than the intermediate faction of the dominant class. This faction is composed of skilled clerical workers.

Dominated faction: Little or no economic and comparatively high social, cultural, and symbolic capital. This class is composed of educational workers, such as school teachers, and other low-income and routinized professions that are involved in cultural production.

Lower Class: Low levels of all forms of capital

Dominant faction: Comparatively high economic capital for this general class. Composed of skilled manual workers.

Intermediate faction: Lower amounts of economic and other types of capital. Composed of semi-skilled workers without credentials.

Dominated faction: Very low amounts of economic capital. Some symbolic capital in the form of uneducated ideologues and intellectuals for the poor and working person.

The portrayals in this table are inferences from Bourdieu's more discursive and rambling text. The table captures the imagery of Bourdieu's analysis. However, because he is highly critical of stratification research in America, he would probably be critical of this "layered" portrayal of his argument.

The next interesting twist is that the members of different factions within the three classes (i.e., dominant, middle, and lower) often have more in common with each other than with members of their own social class. For example, the dominated faction of the dominant class in a society is often composed of intellectuals, artists, and writers who have cultural and symbolic capital but much less economic capital than those factions above them. Because of their greater amounts of cultural and symbolic capital, they have an outlook on the world that is very different than members of those factions above them. They do not see the world the same way as industrialists or successful business persons; rather, they have more in common with the dominated factions of the social classes below them who also have cultural and symbolic capital. Thus, for instance, a successful college professor is in the dominated faction of the dominant (top) social class in a society, but this person may have more in common with school teachers in the dominated faction of the middle class or even the rag-tag street intellectuals of the dominated faction of the lower social class. Similarly, a small businessman in the dominant faction of the middle class has some economic capital, but he may feel much more kinship with Bill Gates in the dominant faction of the top social class than he does with clerical workers and teachers in the intermediate and dominated factions of his own social class.

Thus, in Bourdieu's analysis, social classes and the factions within them are formed by the varying amounts of the four basic forms of capital—economic (money), cultural, social, and symbolic. Depending upon the configuration of these forms of capital, people have something in common, even though they may occupy positions in different social classes. Or, they may have very little in common, even though they belong to the same social class. For example, I often find myself in the company of successful business elites, at least at the local level (in endless fund-raising efforts by my university). Even though we belong to the same social class, I belong to a very different faction of this class (the dominated), which is made all the more real to me by my efforts to solicit funds from more dominate factions of my social class. But more is involved—I simply do not have a lot in common with these members of my social class, except our shared interest in making the university better. The reason for this feeling is that we live in different social worlds; have different friends, tastes, speech patterns, and demeanor; and in so many ways are different from each other. I always feel much more at home interacting with school teachers and other segments of the dominated faction of the middle class.

Perhaps this emphasis on the factions of different classes is overdrawn, but it does capture a reality. The resources that people have or, in Bourdieu's terms, the types of capital that they possess shape how we all think and act. Depending upon the particular configuration of capital—how much money, how much education and culture, how many social ties, and how many and what kinds of symbols can be invoked to legitimate activities—people's outlooks, perceptions, tastes, preferences, goals, needs, dress, speech, and behavior will vary.

The Class System and Public Behavior

At one time, public behavior and class position were very much in line. High-ranking individuals could walk in public places and receive deference from low-ranking people—a tip of the hat, standing back to let pass, and other signs of deference. The reason for this kind of deferential behavior resided in the fact that, before industrialization and even during each phase of industrialization, there was linear hierarchy from the poor to elites, with each grade of person enjoying a certain level of income and prestige that located them in the hierarchy. This pattern—much like the layers on a cake—was easy to observe less than 100 years ago in Europe and, to a lesser extent, in the United States. Those of high rank commanded the public sphere and could expect deference from their inferiors. Behavior at the micro level of social organization (i.e., at the level of the encounter) mirrored and reproduced the structure of the macro level of reality—the hierarchical class system.

This connection between the macro class system and the micro encounter has broken down in postindustrial societies. Indeed, it is often the lowest social classes who dominate the public sphere through aggressive behavior, and the elite can no longer expect automatic deference from the less elite. Thus, as the hierarchy of classes has become less well-defined and linear, its power to dictate public behavior has declined.

Unfocused encounters in public are now often dominated by those who otherwise would be of low status—youth, unemployed, homeless, and members of disadvantaged minorities. Think of just about any public place that allows members of all social classes to congregate, and it becomes immediately evident that boom boxes, loud talk and demeanor, skateboarding, and aggressive walk and talk will often control the public space. It is the elites and upper middle classes who must give way—something that would not have occurred 100 years ago. Thus, at the level of the encounter, the social class system breaks down and, in many cases, becomes curiously inverted (Collins 2001).

Class Stratification in America

Let us recall our definition of stratification: the unequal distribution of valued resources and the creation of social classes or categories of people who, by virtue of their shares of these resources, reveal distinctive cultural symbols, demeanor, tastes, and lifestyles. And let us also remember that there are degrees of stratification in terms of how unequal resources are distributed, how distinctive class categories are, how permanent these categories are, and how much mobility between them occurs. With these considerations in mind, we can construct a brief picture of stratification in America.

Inequalities of Resources

Although "money isn't everything," a cynic might conclude that "what money isn't, it can usually buy." Although status group membership and the mobilization of power can operate somewhat independently of money, a rough indicator of the degree of inequality in a society is its **wealth distribution.** In the United States, this distribution is calculated by, in essence, (a) taking all people with money or property that can be converted into money; (b) rank ordering all persons from highest to lowest in terms of how much money they have; (c) dividing this ranking into equal size statistical categories, usually the top 20%, the second 20%, the third 20%, the fourth 20%, and the bottom 20%; and (d) then asking this question: how much of all the total wealth in a society does each of these ranked 20% categories, or *wealth fifths* as they are usually called, have? Calculating these figures is complicated, but the answer frequently comes as a shock to Americans. As Table 14.2 reports, the top 20% of wealth holders have most of all wealth in society—cash, stocks, bonds, houses, cars, jewelry, or anything that can be converted into money; the next highest 20%, or the second fifth, has some of the wealth; the third

Table 14.2   Distribution of Wealth in America

		Percentage of Total Wealth Held By		
		Bottom 80%	**Next 19%**	**Top 1%**
	1998[a]	16.6%	45.3%	38.1%
			└─── 83.4 ───┘	
	1989[b]	15.4%	47.6%	38.9%
Year				
	1983[b]	18.7%	47.6%	33.6%
	1962[c]	24.0%	┌─── 76% ───┐	

Source: [a]Errucci and Wysong (2003, 13)
[b]Wolff (1995, 1996, 2002)
[c]Turner and Starnes (1976)

Note: More recent data are not available because the Federal Government does not consistently publish the full distribution. Thus, it is often necessary to wait for secondary analyses of the data.

fifth somewhat less; the fourth fifth very little; and the bottom fifth virtually none. Thus, 20% of Americans have most of the wealth; the rest have little wealth—perhaps a house (which is mortgaged) and a pension fund if one is lucky. And, as a recent government report on wealth distribution documents (Federal Reserve System 2003), the top 1% of wealth holders has a net worth greater than 90% of the population *combined*. We have many of the props of wealth—cars, stereos, phones, TVs, and perhaps a home of our own. But in reality, at least half of all Americans have little; they can borrow on their future wages to buy comfort, but this does not lead to the accumulation of much wealth.

Income **distribution** is somewhat more equal, as can be seen in Table 14.3. The top 20% controls almost half of all the income in a given year (which is then used to accumulate wealth year after year). The second income fifth receives about one fourth of all income, the rest goes to the remaining 60% in the proportions listed in Table 14.2. These data are easier to collect (right off IRS tax forms) and, hence, are reported every year (U.S. Bureau of the Census, 2003). The last decade has seen the largest jump in the share of the top 20% in the history of the government reporting of these figures, as can be seen in Table 14.3. Inequality thus increased in America during the 1980s and 1990s to the proportions now evident.

Prestige is also a valued resource and like any resource, it too is distributed unequally. Table 14.4 reports the prestige rankings of various occupations in the United States. As is evident, occupations receiving high income and requiring high levels of education are the most prestigious. Those in such positions can thus command deference and honor from others.

Power is another valued resource because it gives some the ability to control, or at least influence, the actions of others. Yet power is a very elusive resource because those who have it often use it subtly and quietly. Moreover, power is often lodged in organizations, such as unions,

Table 14.3   The Distribution of Income in the United States

Year	Percent of Total Income Held By				
	Bottom 20.0%	4th 20.0%	3rd 20.0%	2nd 20.0%	Top 20.0%
2002	3.5%	8.0%	14.8%	23.3%	49.7%
1999	4.2%	9.7%	14.7%	21.3%	50%
1997	4.2%	9.9%	15.7%	23%	47.2%
1990	4.6%	10.8%	16.6%	23.8%	44.3%
1977	5.7%	11.5%	16.4%	22.8%	44.2%
1973	5.5%	11.9%	17.5%	24.0%	41.1%
1961	4.8%	11.7%	17.4%	23.6%	42.6%

Note: The share of the top 20% of income earners has been increasing over the last 30 years, whereas that for the other 80% has been declining. Income inequality is thus increasing.

Source: U.S. Census Bureau, Current Population Reports Federal Reserve, Survey of Consumer Finances.

corporations, and interest groups; as a consequence, the actual hold of individuals on power is more ambiguous and indirect. Thus, we cannot construct a table outlining the distribution of power, as is possible for wealth, income, and prestige. Power is much more difficult to measure, and finding it has been the subject of great controversy in sociology (Alford and Friedland 1985). Some argue that there is a *power elite* controlling much power (Domhoff 1967, 1978, 2002; Mills 1956) and using their power behind the scenes to influence major decisions. Others argue for a more *pluralistic* view and see power as dispersed across many diverse individuals and organizations (Dahl 1961). Such controversy exists because, once again, power is often hidden or diffused in ways that make it difficult to know who has how much power. But in general terms, those who have wealth, who control large organizations, and who are represented by large organizations will have power (Turner and Musick 1985; Turner and Starnes 1976).

Table 14.5 tries to offer a description of what enables members of a social class to exert power. On the left of the table are the variables that influence how much power the poor, the middle classes, and the rich can mobilize. At the bottom is the total power for each of these classes. The poor have very little power, primarily because they do not vote (thus neutralizing their larger numbers), have few organizations, have virtually no financial resources, have no lobbying tradition, and few influence channels. It is no surprise, therefore, that politicians do not pay attention to the poor, except during periodic episodes of collective guilt. The rich exert great power because, even though their numbers are small, they have resources, organizations, lobbying traditions, and influence channels. The middle classes have large numbers (who vote), various union and professional organizations that can represent their interests, some financial resources, lobbying traditions, and influence channels. Politicians pander to middle classes if they want to win elections, but the middle

Table 14.4 Prestige Rankings of Occupations in the United States

Rank	Prestige Score[a]
Physician	86
Lawyer	75
College teacher	74
Chemical engineer	73
Dentist	72
Clergy	69
Pharmacist	68
Secondary school teacher	66
Registered nurse	66
Accountant	65
Athlete	65
Elementary school teacher	64
Police officer, detective	60
Editor, reporter	60
Financial manager	59
Actor	58
Librarian	54
Social worker	52
Electrician	51
Funeral director	49
Mail carrier	47
Secretary	46
Insurance agent	45
Bank teller	43
Farm owner	40
Automobile mechanic	40
Restaurant manager	39
Sales counter clerk	34
Cook	31
Waiter and waitress	28
Garbage collector	28
Janitor	22
Parking lot attendant	21
Vehicle washer	19
News vendor	19

Source: "On revising prestige scores for all occupations." National Opinion Research Center; General Social Surveys.

[a]The highest score for an occupation is 90, the lowest is 10.

Table 14.5   Distribution of Power in the United States

Variables Influencing Power	The Poor (Bottom Income Fifth)	The Affluent (Middle Income Fifth)	The Rich (Portion of Top Income Fifth)
(1) Size of population	Large	Quite large	Relatively small
(2) Distribution of population	Rural and urban, large mass in urban cores	Urban, large mass in suburbs of large cities	Rural and urban, relatively high degree of dispersion
(3) Level of organization	Low, fragmented	High: unions, professional associations, corporations, and trade associations	High: corporations and trade associations
(4) Type of organization	Fragmented, decentralized, loosely coordinated national confederations	Highly centralized, tightly coordinated national confederations	Highly centralized, overt and covert confederations
(5) Financial resources	Meager	Great	Very great
(6) Supportive ideas	Value of humanitarianism to support welfare	Values of activism and achievement	Values of achievement, coupled with prestige from being wealthy
(7) Nonsupporting beliefs	Series of unfavorable stereotypes about poor	None	Mild conflict with Work Ethic and values of activism, achievement, and freedom
(8) Lobbying tradition	Short	Long	Long
(9) Established influence channels	Few	Many	Many
Total power	Very low	Moderate	Very high

classes do not have the level of power of the rich who quietly go about exerting political influence, often out of sight of the public and media.

Class Formation

How many classes are there in America? How clear are their boundaries? How much mobility from class to class occurs in a lifetime, or between generations? And how enduring are the classes? Answers to some of these questions are easier than others to provide. Let us take them in order.

How many classes are there? An answer depends upon how fine-tuned we want to be. A rough approximation would distinguish the following: elite (wealthy, powerful, and prestigious), highly affluent (accumulated wealth and prestige from high income professions or businesses), upper middle white collar (high salaried professionals or successful business persons who have accumulated some wealth), solid middle white collar class (respectable income, some wealth in pension funds and home equity), lower white collar middle class (modest income, few accumulated assets, perhaps home equity), upper blue collar class (respectable income, some wealth in pension funds and home equity), middle blue collar (modest income, few accumulated assets), lower blue collar service workers (with low income, prestige, and no accumulated assets), and impoverished (low income, unemployed, unemployable with no assets). As an important note, this last class of impoverished people is the largest of the postindustrial world—numbering 35 to 50 million people and engulfing 12% to 16% of the American population (Ropers 1991; Sherraden 1991; J. Turner 1993a; U. S. Bureau of Census 2003).

The differences in these classes revolve around several factors: one is whether one works with their hands (blue collar) or does nonmanual work (white collar); this factor is very important, and we can see rather easily the differences in white collar and blue collar people's demeanor, lifestyles, and other characteristics. Another dividing point is level of income and the capacity to accumulate assets from one's income; people who have assets act and think differently than those who do not. And the less money you have, the greater is the difference between you and those with some assets. A final point of division is how much power and prestige one has as a result of income, education, or work. People with power and prestige act and think differently than those without these assets.

These class lines are fuzzy, indicating that there is no hard divide or discontinuity between them. This observation answers the second question posed earlier and leads us to the third question; there is some mobility between these classes, but few great leaps up the hierarchy. Statistically, you are most likely to be mobile to the next adjacent class—either up or down—if you are mobile at all. If you start in the lower middle you might expect to make it to the solid middle or move to an upper blue collar job. If you start in the blue collar classes, you can move to the middle white collar classes with the acquisition of educational credentials. But if the economy is in recession and if government cuts programs back, then you are likely to stay where you started or even fall back down the stratification ladder. Most Americans remain in one social class during their entire lifetime; and if they are mobile, it is not very far—despite a lot of hoopla about those who have gone from "rags to riches."

An answer to our final question posed earlier emphasizes that classes in America are not completely stable because of broader changes in the economy that are altering the profile of jobs from manufacturing to service. Thus, the proportion of people engaged in blue collar work has decreased, whereas the percentage of people in white collar work has increased. Equally significant, there has been a dramatic increase in low-wage service jobs (e.g., fast food employees). Elite classes remain fairly stable, with some fluctuations in the composition of the highly affluent and upper middle classes. As you read these words you probably seek to stay in these last two classes, or to get into them. If you started nearby, you have a chance (if you get the right credentials, and a lot of them). But, the changes in the economy that increase the number of low-wage service and clerical jobs, while decreasing the higher wage skilled and semiskilled blue collar jobs, place you in a frightful situation: much of the white collar work available is not highly skilled, nor does this work pay well; and hence, realizing a more privileged class standing will be difficult and involve lots of competition. Moreover, it is now clear that there is a dramatic trend to "outsource" overseas many of the high-salaried and professional white collar jobs to professionals in poor countries willing to work for less. For example, radiologists in India can now read X-rays and CT scans for much less than American doctors; architects in Hungary can draw plans for much less than those in America; structural engineers in the Ukraine will provide analysis at much less cost than engineers in the United States; accounts in the overseas offices of the big accounting firms work for half what they do in the United States; and so on for an increasing number of what were once safe, high-salaried positions. Thus, in the future, it is conceivable that the size of the upper middle classes could decline.

Poverty in America

Poverty rates over the forty years are summarized in Table 14.6. By these official statistics, around 12% of Americans now live in poverty but this figure is low because it does not fully reflect the costs of living. But even if this figure is accepted, it signals that 33 million people live below what is an acceptable standard of living in the United States (see, Schiller 2004, for a thorough review of the economics of poverty). These individuals and families do not have adequate incomes, health care, housing, clothing, nutrition, and other resources. The existence of such a large poverty sector adds considerable tension to the class stratification system. We all sense that those who are poor are potentially dangerous because they are often angry over their plight; add to this anger other pathologies such as drug use and crime, and we have good reason to be fearful.

The social category of being poor overlaps with other social categories: the young and various ethnic minorities, as is summarized for select ethnic populations in Table 14.7. Children and their mothers are the most likely to be poor and growing up poor can seal individuals' fate in life: Those born to poor parents are likely to be poor when they grow up. The darker a person's skin color in America, the more likely they are to be poor, thereby adding an ethnic dimension to the tension of class stratification. When members of minority categories are overrepresented in the very bottom rungs of the class system, a double source of anger emerges: anger over being a minority targeted for discrimination and extra anger for the results of this discrimination: poverty.

Table 14.6   Poverty Rates over Time

Year	Percentage of Individuals Who are Poor
2003	12.5
2002	12.1
2000	11.3
1995	12.3
1990	12.0
1985	12.6
1980	11.5
1975	10.9
1965	15.8

Source: U.S. Bureau of the Census, 2004.

Table 14.7   Rates of Poverty among Ethnic Subpopulations

Ethnic Category	Percentage in Poverty in 2003
Non-Latino Whites	8.2
Latinos	22.5
African Americans	24.4
Asian/Pacific Islanders	11.8
Native Americans	20.0

Source: U.S. Bureau of The Census, Current Population Survey, 2004.

Poverty always creates dynamic tensions. Over the last decade in the United States, very little has been done to alleviate these tensions. The welfare system was "reformed" in 1996, limiting the amount of welfare that individuals can receive in their lifetime to five years, thereby forcing the chronically poor to survive without much help. For a time, jobs were available as the economy grew in the 1990s, but in the first decade of this new century, low-skill jobs are fast declining, leaving the poor relatively few options. When desperate, people do desperate things—joining violent youth gangs, using drugs, committing crimes, engaging random acts of violence, and otherwise posing threats to members of society.

Unemployment or episodic employment is one reason that people are poor. They have few job skills or they have other problems such as drug dependency. Many jobs at the unskilled end of the spectrum pay very little, with the result that even if a person works full time, his or her total income is inadequate to even a basic standard of living. The minimum wage is just under $7.00 per hour; and so, if a person works 40 hours a week, this individual's total weekly income comes to $280 per week or $1,120 per month. Subtract day care, food, rent, transportation, and Social Security and Medicare taxes; the result is that there is not enough money to live on in an urban area. And, medical and drug costs have not been factored into this budget. Thus, as long as wages cannot sustain people above the poverty line, widespread poverty is inevitable in America.

What accounts for poverty, above and beyond low wages? Why are some people poor, whereas others take advantage of their opportunities and get ahead? There is no definitive answer. At one time "culture of poverty" arguments held sway (Lewis 1965). When people are born into poverty and must live their lives in poverty, they make adjustments and develop cultural beliefs that opportunities do not exist and that it is a waste of time to try and get out of poverty—thereby sealing their fate. In turn, they subtly communicate this despair to their children who do the same to their children in a cycle that is difficult to break.

This "culture of poverty" argument is not wholly wrong, but it is incomplete. Other factors need to be added. First, the number of entry level and low-skill jobs is declining in America, thus depriving people of those first employment opportunities that can serve as a stepping stone to better paying jobs. Second, schools in rural areas and inner cities where the poor live are not very good; they are underfunded, over-crowded, and poorly equipped, thus making them unpleasant and alien places. Third, the local street cultures of many inner cities discourage academic achievement and, instead, offer other temptations: distributing illegal drugs, gang activity, and crime. Fourth, poor families are often broken and headed by a single parent, thus increasing the likelihood that children are left unsupervised if the parent must work and undisciplined if the parent is exhausted and depressed about what life has dealt. Finally, poor families have members who are poor models because of domestic violence, criminal activity, and drug use.

One outcome of being really poor is that you become homeless. No one knows just how many homeless people there are on a given night in America, but it is probably well over a million. Once homeless, it is difficult to find work, go to school, or do anything that is normal because you have no clean clothes, no easy way to take a shower, no money to buy toiletries, and no way to do what is necessary to go to a job interview or to school. And, if there are other problems—like drug or alcohol dependency—it is doubly difficult to find a way to move back into the mainstream. Because there has been a clear increase in the number of homeless families, the young in these families will have difficulty getting the education that they need to move out of poverty.

The debate over poverty is intense, but a sociological perspective forces us to look beyond people's motives and drives to the social and cultural forces that shape people' behaviors and that provide opportunities or impose constraints on their options. Just what the future holds for a society with such a large poverty sector remains to be seen. But, Americans should expect problems when over 30 million people cannot secure enough resources to live adequately and have little hope for mobility out of poverty. Some people are poor for only a short time; others are in and out of poverty sectors depending upon their ability to find low-skill work; and still others are chronically poor and have little hope of escaping their plight. But all of these individuals represent a potential lightening rod in American society as their frustrations and anger build. High levels of inequality always generate trouble for a society, and the United States is not an exception to this rule.

SUMMARY

1. Inequality in a society revolves around the differential distribution of valued resources to various categories of individuals—class, ethnic, and gender being three of the most important.
2. Class stratification exists when income, power, prestige, and other valued resources are given to members of a society unequally and when, on the basis of this inequality, various subpopulations become culturally, behaviorally, and organizationally distinctive.
3. The degree of stratification is related to the level of mobility between classes and the permeability of class boundaries.
4. There are several approaches to the study of stratification: (a) the Marxian approach emphasizing the ownership of the means of production as the cause of class stratification and mobilization to conflict and change in patterns of

stratification, (b) the Weberian perspective stressing the multidimensional nature of stratification (revolving around not just class, but party and status groups as well), (c) the functional approach arguing that inequality operates as a reward system for encouraging individuals to occupy functionally important and difficult-to-fill-positions, and (d) the evolutionary argument that the long-term trends toward increases in inequality after hunting and gathering have been reversed somewhat in modern societies.

5. The ranking of social classes from high to low is complicated by the middle social classes who possess varying configurations of resources. The middle blue collar and white collar classes are, however, distinctive because people in them have different lifestyles, tastes, and behavioral demeanors. The differences among people in the upper, middle, and lower social classes are highlighted by Pierre Bourdieu's analysis of class factions. Moreover, members of similarly located factions in different classes can have more in common with each other than with members of their own social class.

6. The breakdown of a clear linear hierarchy of classes (save for those at the very top and very bottom) is reflected in changes in public encounters among members of social classes, where it is the lower social classes who often dominate what transpires in encounters.

7. Stratification in America is marked by high levels of inequality with respect to material well-being and prestige. Inequality in the distribution of power is more ambiguous. Fuzzy boundaries between adjacent social classes exist in America. Mobility is frequent, but most people do not experience great mobility in their lifetime.

8. Particularly problematic for American society is the large poverty sector that must live in a society where affluence is abundant.

KEY TERMS

Bourgeoisie: In Karl Marx's analysis, those who own and control the means of production in capitalist societies.

Capital: Pierre Bourdieu's term for the kinds of resources that individuals have in varying social classes and factions within classes.

Caste System: Stratification system with clearly marked class divisions, in which people are born and have little chance for mobility to a different class.

Charismatic Leader: Max Weber's term for those who, by virtue of their personal qualities, can mobilize subordinates in a system of inequality to engage in conflict with superordinates.

Classes: For Max Weber, those who share a common set of life chances and opportunities in markets; for Karl Marx, the divisions in a society reflecting ownership of the means of production; for more general analysis, the differences among subpopulations by virtue of their respective share of valued resources.

Class Faction: Existence within each social class of a dominant, intermediate, and dominated sector, or faction. Members of similar factions in different social classes often have more in common with each other than with members of their own class.

Conflict of Interest: Karl Marx's term for the basic tension and incompatibility of goals between those who control resources and those who do not.

Cultural Capital: Amount of education, knowledge, taste, skills, manners, and linguistic styles possessed by individuals.

Economic Capital: Amount of money from productive and economic activities that individuals possess.

Income Distribution: Percentage of total income held by different percentages of the population, usually calculated in terms of income fifths.

Open-Class System: Stratification system with less clearly demarcated classes and with opportunities for mobility from class to class.

Parties: For Max Weber, the organization of power as a distinct basis for inequality and stratification of individuals who bear varying affiliations and access to organizations holding or seeking power.

Proletariat: Karl Marx's term for those who do not own the means of production in capitalist society and who must, therefore, work for those who do.

Social Capital: Nature and extensiveness of networks and social relations possessed by individuals.

Status Groups: Max Weber's term for subsets of individuals who share similar lifestyles; who form ties because of shared culture, tastes, and outlooks; and who, by virtue of these, can command a certain honor and prestige.

Stratification: Structures revolving around (a) the unequal distribution of valued resources to the members of a society and (b) the distinctive categories thereby created by virtue of the shares of resources held by different subpopulations in a society.

Symbolic Capital: Symbols or ideologies that individuals can mobilize to legitimate their possession on economic, social, and cultural capital.

Wealth Distribution: Percentage of total wealth held by different percentages of the population, usually calculated in terms of wealth fifths.

Chapter 15

Ethnic Stratification

Everywhere we look in the world today, diverse ethnic groups are trying to kill each other. Bombings, mass killings bordering on genocide, coup d'états by leaders of one ethnicity over another, ethnically aligned armies standing ready for battle, and as Americans saw on September 11, acts of terrorism that can kill thousands at a time are possible. Ethnicity is thus one of the most volatile forces in the social universe; people come to hate each other with a passion that is often difficult to understand. For example, why would Hitler kill millions of Jews? Why would ethnic cleansing become a state policy in the old Yugoslavia? Why would Catholic and Protestant Irish engage in mutual car bombings? Why do so many Arabs hate Jews in Israel? Why would Tutsi and Hutus in Rwanda and Burundi kill each other on a massive scale, numbering into the hundreds of thousands? And so it goes for almost any part of the world. Violence of a most intense kind is evident everywhere, and much of this violence is connected to ethnicity. Why is ethnicity such a volatile force in human affairs?

The answer to this question ultimately resides in patterns of inequality. Systems of class stratification often have an ethnic component in this sense: Members of particular ethnic subpopulations are over- or under-represented in certain classes; and when the lower social classes of a society are disproportionately populated by people with a particular ethnic background, class-based tensions are transformed into ethnic conflict. Ethnicity acts like a turbo charger on inequalities, taking them from conflicts over money and power to conflicts about people's identities, heritage, and culture.

Interwoven with class stratification, then, is ethnic inequality and ethnic tension, if not outright conflict. You can sense this fact every day, as you move about and deal with people from different ethnic backgrounds. You may see yourself as a tolerant and fair person, but you cannot help but feel a subtle tension between you and members of other ethnic populations. This tension is not just the result of cultural differences (e.g., languages and beliefs), variations in behavior (speech styles, ways of carrying oneself), and organizational differences (diverse patterns of group affiliation); it is also the result of differences in money, power, and prestige that become associated with these cultural, behavioral, and organizational differences. If you are low in these because of your ethnic background, you may show a subtle hostility and carry a chip on your shoulder; if you are high, you sense this hostility and perhaps you even deny a distant sense of fear. Because so much of our lives in

American society involves ethnic relationships and conflicts, we need to know more about this phenomenon.

Race and Ethnicity

Race as a Social Construct

The term **race** is used to denote what are perceived as biological differences, such as skin color and facial configurations. But we mean more than just biology; if we did not, we would make racial distinctions between the tall and short races, the gray- and brown-eyed races, and similar rather trivial biological differences. In fact, we should probably never use the term "racial" group because it has no scientific basis. Where, for example, is the cutoff line in terms of biology between being "black" or "white," Asian or Caucasian?

When we use the term "race," then, we really mean **ethnicity**, or those behavioral, cultural, and organizational differences that allow us to categorize members of a population as distinctive (Aguirre and Turner 2004). Yet, when ethnic distinctions are associated with superficial biological features like skin color or eye configuration, they become convenient "markers" of ethnicity. And they often become a basis for escalated prejudice and discrimination that, in turn, increases **ethnic stratification,** or the disproportionate allocation of various ethnic populations to particular social classes.

Prejudice and Discrimination

Prejudices are beliefs about members of an ethnic group who are perceived to possess undesirable qualities (Allport 1954, 1979). Think of ethnic epithets, and the connotations they carry, as good indicators of prejudicial beliefs: "nigger," "whop," "pollack," "beaner," "chink," "buddha head," "spick," "coon," and so it goes. Prejudicial beliefs are, therefore, a prominent part of American culture, as well as the cultures of other societies.

Discrimination is the differential treatment of others because of their ethnicity, and most particularly, the denial of members of an ethnic population equal access to valued resources, such as housing, jobs, education, income, power, and prestige. Prejudice often fuels discrimination, and acts of discrimination are frequently justified by prejudices. Yet, a one-to-one relation between prejudice and discrimination is often hard to discern. For example, in a classic study during the height of prejudice against Asians in the period around World War II (La Piere 1934), hotel and motel owners were asked if they would rent a room to an "Asian," with a high proportion indicating that they would not, but in fact, they had rented a room to an Asian couple. This kind of disjuncture between prejudice and discrimination led Robert Merton (1949) to distinguish among (a) the "all-weather liberal," who is unprejudiced and does not discriminate; (b) the "reluctant liberal," who is unprejudiced but in response to social pressures will discriminate; (c) the "timid bigot" who, like the hotel and motel owners, is prejudiced but in response to social pressures will not discriminate; and (d) the "all-weather bigot," who is prejudiced and discriminates. In America, there has been a clear movement over the last 40 years away from the all-weather bigot toward the "all-weather liberal," but the "reluctant liberal" and "timid bigot" may still make up the majority of the population.

You might now ask yourself: which one am I? The answer is probably more complicated than Merton's typology. You may hold some prejudices, but try not to discriminate because of them. And you may inadvertently discriminate without prejudice or because of unacknowledged prejudices.

People's prejudices and behaviors are, of course, more complicated and subtle than Merton's typology would suggest. Individuals may hold attitudes that they do not see as prejudicial and never discriminate. Or, people may inadvertently discriminate not out of prejudice but from insensitivity to, or ignorance about, members of an ethnic category. The critical point here is that people's perceptions, feelings, attitudes, and behaviors bear complex relationships to each other, especially with respect to ethnic relations. For many individuals in multiethnic societies, there is a tension among their beliefs, emotions, and behavioral dispositions toward members of other ethnic categories.

Although individual prejudice and single acts of discrimination are interesting to observe and think about, especially with respect to our own thoughts and behaviors, what is sociologically more interesting is **institutionalized discrimination**, in which there is a consistent and pervasive pattern of discrimination, legitimated by cultural beliefs or prejudices, and built into the structure of a society. At times, institutionalized discrimination can be explicit and obvious, as has been the case for the African-origin population during and after slavery. For African-origin members of society, there was a clear denial of access to citizenship rights like voting, jobs, education, health, and housing that was legitimated by highly prejudicial beliefs. The Civil Rights Movement and the Civil Rights Acts of the 1960s were the culmination of efforts to break down such institutionalized discrimination, but today such patterns persist in less obvious form. That is, institutionalized discrimination is now more subtle and complicated. For example, blacks suffer today in crime-ridden and drug-infested ghettos because of the past legacy of discrimination, but they are now blamed by many whites (a prejudice) for not escaping these conditions; moreover, they are seen as getting preferential treatment for jobs through affirmative action, which has led to pressures for reducing affirmative action and other policies designed to help minorities, especially African Americans. The end result is that many blacks remain poor, subject to white prejudices about the "lazy, welfare dependent poor" who do not deserve assistance. Such prejudices are then used to legitimate cutbacks in formal assistance while encouraging informal discrimination. You may hold these more subtle and complicated prejudices, but you should recognize them for what they are. Thus, institutionalized discrimination today has become more complex, and is a pervasive feature of American society and, for that matter, *all* societies with distinct ethnic groups.

Dynamics of Ethnic Stratification

The central dynamic of ethnic stratification is, therefore, discrimination by one or more ethnic groups against targeted ethnic groups. But this simple observation begs several important questions: How does one ethnic population come to have the power to discriminate? And why do its members want to discriminate? The answer to these questions forces us to examine the interrelation among a number of crucial forces (J. Turner 1986b; Turner and Aguirre 2004): (a) the *relative resources* of ethnic groups, (b) the *identifiability* of ethnic groups as targets of discrimination, (c) the *level* and *type* of discrimination, (d) the *intensity* of prejudicial beliefs, and (e) the *degree of threat* posed by one ethnic group to another. Let's examine each of these forces.

Relative Resources of Ethnic Populations

Ethnic groups possess different amounts of resources—money, power, prestige, work skills, and educational credentials. These differences are, of course, often the result of past discrimination, as is the case for many African and Native Americans today. Differences in resource levels are also due to other forces—for example, the history of an ethnic population in another society and the demographic profile of those members who migrate to another society.

In general terms, the more resources an ethnic group has, the better equipped it is to fight off the full effects of discriminatory efforts by a more dominant group. Thus, when Africans came to America as slaves, they had few resources to fend off their continued enslavement, whereas today many Asian immigrants come with money, entrepreneurial skills, pooled family labor, credit associations among fellow ethnics, and educational credentials that are used to achieve access to valued resources, even in the face of discrimination. In being able to secure access to resources—say professional jobs and successful family businesses—these immigrants can eventually come to acquire other resources, such as housing in integrated neighborhoods and community political power (Turner and Bonacich 1980). In contrast, those who have few financial, educational, or political resources are less able to begin this process of ratcheting up their resources. Many African Americans and Native Americans in the United States experience this plight; they lack an initial resource base with which to overcome the legacy of past discrimination as well as the persistence of subtle, informal discrimination in the present (Turner, Singleton, and Musick 1984).

Identifiability of an Ethnic Population

To be a target of discrimination, you must be visible and distinctive in some way. If members of an ethnic population look different in terms of surface biological features, such as skin color and an eye fold, they are easier targets of discrimination. Thus, it is easier to target dark-skinned and Asian ethnics than other ethnic populations. In contrast, European-origin immigrants to America had a great advantage over other ethnic groups because they could learn English and blend into the population within one or two generations.

Cultural characteristics such as language and religious beliefs, behavioral demeanor, and organization into distinctive kinds of groups can also make people targets, especially if associated with some physical distinctiveness. Thus, Mexican Americans in the southwest, Puerto Ricans in the northeast, and to a lesser extent, Cubans in Florida can become targets of discrimination because of language and perhaps Latin cultural demeanor, plus some distinctiveness in their skin color.

Once victimized by discrimination, biological distinctiveness is maintained because of intra-ethnic marriage and reproduction, whereas distinctive cultural, behavioral, and organizational patterns are sustained by high rates of intra-ethnic interaction and ghettoization in particular neighborhoods and by a general defensiveness against a society in which one does not feel welcome. The ironic result, of course, is for ethnics to remain easily identifiable and, hence, targets of further discrimination. This cycle can become truly vicious, especially for ethnics who have few resources other than their common plight with which to fight off the consequences of discrimination. It should not be surprising, therefore, that those ethnics in America who are easily identified, who lost most of their financial resources or never had them to begin with, who had their cultural heritage stripped away, and who possess few organizational structures in which to take refuge have been the most likely to remain in this vicious cycle.

Level and Type of Discrimination

The level of discrimination has varied enormously in the history of human societies, from **genocide,** where ethnics are killed off through expulsion and, when these extreme forms of discrimination are not possible, through segregation in a ghetto and a narrow range of jobs. Jews in Germany, Native Americans in the United States, and Indian populations in meso America have all suffered from efforts at genocide. More typical, however, is discrimination involving the physical segregation and economic isolation of a subpopulation. This is possible only as long as members of a population remain distinctive and identifiable.

One type of ethnic minority is lower class. Here disproportionate numbers of a population are isolated in slum housing tracts and pushed into the lowest paying occupations such that they are in the poverty class of a society. African Americans have suffered this fate in the United States, although in recent decades many African Americans have been able to escape poverty and move into the middle classes. Another type of ethnic minority created by discrimination is a *middleman minority* where members are segregated but, at the same time, allowed to occupy a narrow range of entrepreneurial and professional economic positions that give them some affluence. For example, Jews in feudal and early modern Europe often occupied a high proportion of positions in banking and finance; or many Asian immigrants in America today have moved into small business niches such as convenience stores.

What determines which type of a minority an ethnic population will become? One important condition is the resources—money, entrepreneurial know-how, educational credentials—that a population can mobilize. When ethnics have some resources, they can more readily move into middleman minority positions and live a more middle class lifestyle. But resources are not the only factor; another is the absolute size of an ethnic population. A small minority with resources can more readily find middleman niches than a large one, for the simple reason that there are not enough small business positions for a large population. A large ethnic population will, therefore, be pushed to lower classes, especially if

their resources are limited and, as a result, their ability to fight off discrimination will be low. African Americans have suffered this fate because this population is too large to fill middleman minority positions
and has insufficient resources to overcome discrimination (Turner and
Bonacich 1980). Some members of a large minority who can mobilize resources, such as securing educational credentials, can move into middle
class positions, but they leave behind their fellow ethnics. For example,
many blacks in America have made dramatic strides in moving to the
middle classes in the post Civil Rights era of the 1960s, but the fate of
the vast majority of blacks in the lower classes has remained the same, or
worsened over the last 35 years. Thus, the African American population
is now divided by large class differences (Wilson 1987).

Degree of Threat Posed by an Ethnic Population

Whether large or small, why would one group bother to discriminate?
Are humans just brutes who do not like others who look and act differently? Part of the answer to this second question may be "yes," but a
more significant part is that discrimination is stoked up by fears,
whether real or imagined. If one ethnic population sees itself threatened
by another, it will discriminate. The basis of the threat can vary: loss of
jobs or high wages because others will work for less, loss of cultural traditions, loss of political power, loss of neighborhoods and housing, and
so on. When a population feels economically, socially, and politically
threatened, it discriminates; and the more threatened it feels, the more
intense and severe is the discrimination.

A large, identifiable ethnic group is more threatening than a small
one because it can "overrun" jobs, schools, politics, and housing. African
Americans were kept enslaved probably beyond the economic viability of
the Plantation System because their numbers came close to equaling
those of whites in the deep south (Singleton and Turner 1975); hence,
white blue collar and farm workers feared for their jobs, politicians their
power, and all their "southern way of life." In the late nineteenth century
and early parts of the twentieth century, each wave of new white immigrants to America threatened the previous wave who had just begun to
feel secure; and so, Germans discriminated against the Irish, the Irish
against Italians, Italians against Poles, and all white ethnics against
blacks when the latter began to migrate to the northeast in the early
decades of the twentieth century. Today, immigrating Mexican Americans have similarly generated fears among Anglos as their numbers have
grown. These kinds of fears about the effects of an ethnic group on another may or may not be accurate. Fears typically are inaccurate, and
they are often fueled by political leaders for their specific purposes—as
did Hitler with Jews in Germany, or as some American politicians have
done with respect to African Americans and Latinos.

Prejudicial Beliefs about an Ethnic Population

When fearful, people erect negative stereotypes about those who pose or,
more typically, are perceived to pose a threat (Feagin 1991). The greater
the fear, the more negative the stereotypes. African Americans, for example, have had to endure incredibly vicious stereotypes as less than
human, childlike, foolish "Sambos," sexually aggressive, welfare cheaters,

and so on. To a lesser degree, each wave of European immigrants suffered from negative stereotypes—dumb Pollacks, greasy and dishonest Italians, corrupt and drunk Irish, and so on—but they all had the advantage over blacks of being white and, hence, less identifiable once they shed some of their European culture.

Negative stereotypes escalate fears that, in turn, justify more intense discrimination. Thus, cultural beliefs are an important dynamic because they codify a subpopulation's sense of threat and, at the same time, intensify this sense of threat, while legitimating acts of discrimination. Of course, other beliefs can operate as a counter force against prejudicial beliefs, as has been the case in America where beliefs in "equality of opportunity" have always posed a challenge to prejudicial beliefs and negative stereotypes of ethnics.

A Model of Ethnic Antagonism

We are now in a position to pull these elements of ethnic conflict into a more general view of the dynamics of ethnic discrimination. Figure 15.1 outlines the elements of a model. Let's start at the end of the model, on the far left side. The processes operating in the model produce this outcome: A system of social classes where members of targeted ethnic subpopulations are pushed into a particular social class or classes by virtue of discrimination by a more powerful ethnic subpopulation. If an ethnic population has been pushed to the lower social classes, this fact will inevitably create tensions in a society; these tensions will often erupt into violence between the propagators and victims of discrimination.

The key dynamic is discrimination, and all of the arrows in the model in Figure 15.1 flow into and out of this force. The fuel behind discrimination is threat. When people feel threatened, they will discriminate. Threat comes from two sources: (a) the size of a population and (b) its resources. If a targeted ethnic population is large, people often fear

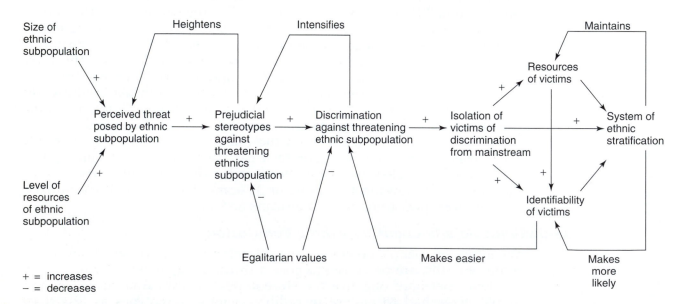

Figure 15.1   Dynamics of Ethnic Antagonism

that its members will overrun a society, taking jobs, assuming political power, integrating neighborhoods, and changing the culture. The most intense discrimination is typically reserved for members of a large ethnic group because size intensifies feelings of threat. A small ethnic minority, then, poses less of a threat, although in a particular community its members can loom large. But at a societal level, a small ethnic group generates far less threat than a large one. The resources that a population brings with them, or acquires, can also increase threats. If an ethnic population has money, educational credentials, capital, and other resources, it can present a threat to those who do not have these resources. Generally, resource-rich ethnic groups are comparatively small in numbers, but they create a sense of threat to members of specific occupations and to particular communities where they are over-represented.

When threatened, people develop prejudicial beliefs and negatively stereotype the targeted population. Of course, when portrayed in such negative terms, these stereotypes only intensify the threat and, hence, the likelihood of more intense discrimination. And so, the more people can negatively stereotype their targets, the more they feel justified in discriminating against such "undesirable" people.

Stereotyping as it fuels threat and discrimination maintains the identifiability of the targeted population. When confined to a particular social class, they will exhibit the features of this class because they will interact with only members of this class (see Figure 14.1 for how these class processes operate). But more is involved. Ethnics who are victims of discrimination will tend to live in the same neighborhoods (because of housing discrimination); have the same level of economic resources (because of job discrimination); have the same level of power and relations with police (because of political and police discrimination); and in general live in close proximity, interact, marry, and procreate. The result is that if there are biological features marking them—such as skin color or an eye fold—this feature will be passed down from generation to generation. But, more fundamentally, the culture, demeanor, tastes, preferences, language, speech patterns, and other markers of ethnicity will be retained because members of an ethnic group have lived together, interacted with each other, and socialized their young within an ethnic enclave with a distinct culture. As a result, even if there are no clear biological markers for discriminators, there will be sociocultural markers that discriminators will pick up on, negatively stereotype, and use as the basis for discrimination.

As ethnics sustain their identifiability, they confirm the negative stereotypes about them, fuel the threats of their tormentors, and remain easy targets of discrimination. The result is for members of an ethnic population to be over-represented in a particular social class in the system of class stratification.

A key feature of the model in Figure 15.1 is that virtually all of the arrows connecting the forces in play are positive; they increase the values of other forces. Threat fuels negative stereotyping and discrimination, and discrimination intensifies prejudices; discrimination sustains identifiability, and identifiability makes members of ethnic groups an easier target of discrimination; social class position in the ethnic stratification system sustains identifiability and, hence, discrimination, and vice versa, and so on for all the paths connecting the arrows in the figure. It is this cyclical and self-reinforcing nature of ethnic discrimination that makes it hard to break apart once it gets going. This cycle can become not only self-reinforcing, it can escalate as the effects of each force raise the level of the others, and vice versa, to the point where people are willing to commit truly horrible acts of violence against a population. Often the targets of violence will fight back, which only fuels threat and leads to more violence. Eventually, this cycle of violence and threat can lead the more powerful ethnic population to commit genocide. It is this potential for escalation of the forces in the model in Figure 15.1 that makes ethnic stratification so volatile.

Ethnic Discrimination in America

We now have the conceptual tools for analyzing ethnic stratification in America. Those most disadvantaged ethnics—that is, those disproportionately in the lower and poverty classes—have been the most biologically distinct, the lowest in most crucial resources, the victims of the most intense discrimination, the most threatening because of their large size, and the subjects of the most negative stereotypes and prejudices. Those ethnics who have been able to move into the mainstream have been less identifiable, have possessed resources, have been small in numbers, have posed less threat, and, as a result, have been subject to less vicious stereotyping.

When there is a correlation between membership in a class and a distinct ethnicity, the potential for ethnic conflict increases. Those members of ethnic groups who do not have resources are resentful, whereas those who have them fear those who resent their privilege. To some extent, if the poor in lower social classes can be upwardly mobile and have hope for a better future, some of the intensity of resentment is mitigated. Recall Table 14.7 where the poverty rates for various ethnic categories were reported. Non-Latino whites have a poverty rate of around 8% poor, whereas Latinos have a rate of almost 23% poor, African Americans have over 24% poor, Native Americans 20% poor, and Asian/Pacific Islanders have around 12% of their members in poverty. The figures for all of these minorities are disproportionate; they are over-represented in poverty, which means that they have not had access to resources to the same extent as non-Hispanic whites. There is, then, an ethnic stratification system in America—one that generates tensions among diverse ethnic populations.

Take any ethnic population in America—Poles, Jews, African Americans, Mexican Americans, Cubans, Native Americans, Vietnamese, Koreans, Japanese, Chinese, and so on—and study each with respect to the forces of identifiability, resources, threat, prejudicial beliefs, and discrimination. If you do this, you will be able to see why you and others stand at particular points in the class system in the United States. It is an exercise worth performing because with the collapse of the Soviet Union in the 1990s, the United States is now the most ethnically diverse society in the world. Hence, so much of your life will be entangled with these dynamics of ethnic discrimination and the resulting system of ethnic stratification.

Table 15.1 summarizes the relative size of various ethnic subpopulations in the United States today and the projections for the future. As is

Table 15.1   Changing Ethnic Mix in America (in %)

Relative percentage of various ethnic subpopulations	Year		
	2001	**2025**	**2045**
Non-Latino Whites	71.0	62.0	54.5
African Americans	12.2	12.9	13.2
Asian/Pacific Islanders	4.0	6.2	8.4
Latinos	12.1	18.2	23.1
Native Americans	0.7	0.8	0.8

Source: Aguirre and Turner (2004, 56).

evident, some dramatic changes are underway. Some of these may pose a threat to the declining white majority and thus rekindle discrimination. The biggest change is in the size of the Latino population, which will constitute 23% of the population by mid-century. The relative size of the African American population will remain about the same, at 13%. Asian Americans will be a little less than 9%. What is striking about the profile of ethnicity is that by mid-century, European-origin whites will drop from over 71% of the population to just over 54%, a small majority. Native Americans will remain a very small proportion of the population at less than 1%. If these growing ethnic populations continue to be over-represented in the poverty class, then ethnic tension in America will increase.

Native Americans

We may celebrate Christopher Columbus' discovery of America, or even give Leif Ericson some credit, but the real founders of the Americas were those migrants who crossed the ice bridges connecting the Asian and American continents or who used primitive craft to navigate the cold waters between Asia and the North American continent. These migrants came thousands of years before Europeans and settled the entire Americas, and so they can rightly be called Native Americans. Europeans practiced what can only be considered genocide on the native population. It is difficult to estimate the size of the indigenous population in North America at the time of European contact, but the best guess is that the population was between 2.5 and 5 million inhabitants. By 1850, however, the size of the population had declined to around 200,000. The decrease occurred because of massacres and war, but also from the introduction of European diseases to which the indigenous population had no immunity. Over the last 150 years, however, the population has recovered and grown to what it was at about the time of European contact, although some of the increase may be the result of people's self-reports on their ancestry.

Many of those Native Americans who survived were put on Indian reservations, and even to the present day, much of their lives is governed by the Bureau of Indian Affairs. The reservation system allowed whites to gain access to the best lands and the resources on and below the ground, thus depriving those on the reservation of any real possibility of economic self-governance. The effects of dependency on the government were profound: Until very recently, this population was the most impoverished, the least educated, the least likely to hold managerial and professional jobs, the poorest housed, and along with African Americans, the most likely to die early. For just about any valued resource, then, Native Americans were disadvantaged and at the bottom of the class system.

This discrimination was justified by negative stereotypes ranging from "savage redman" ready to kill white settlers (the reverse was more typically the case), to the "silent sidekick" of a white hero as portrayed in many western movies, to fat cat capitalists who earn money from the minerals or casinos on reservation lands. These stereotypes have been sustained by the use of Native Americans as mascots for sports teams, a demeaning activity that whites cannot seem to understand.

These stereotypes and the discrimination that they justified were in response to perceived threats that the indigenous population posed for whites. This threat was intensified to justify the land-grabs and killings of Native Americans; although they fought back and thus escalated the sense of threat, the real threat was to the ability of whites to take control of the continent. Those who wanted to control the land and its resources had a vested interest in making sure that the native population was seen as threatening.

The discrimination that ensued was highly institutionalized. Through the Bureau of Indian Affairs and restrictive laws, the federal government regulated conquered "nations"; schools on and off the reservation sought to destroy native cultures and "Americanize" Native Americans; economic resources that might serve as a new basis for prosperity were taken from tribes in a variety of land-grabbing schemes; and confinement to reservations isolated Native Americans from the mainstream but did not give them a viable way to prosper on the reservation, while those who left the reservations were subject to white violence and job discrimination.

It is now clear that at least some white Americans have a sense of guilt about Native Americans; although casino revenues offer hope to some Native Americans, many others far removed from urban areas must continue to live in poverty. Four hundred years of discrimination cannot be easily undone in a few generations, and so, the descendants of the original Americans will continue to suffer in the immediate future.

African Americans

African Americans, along with Native Americans, have the highest poverty rates, the lowest incomes, and the shortest life spans (Aguirre and Turner 2004). Some progress has been made in education and jobs, where many African Americans have been able to secure enough education to pursue middle and upper middle class professions. Still, a vast poverty sector has been left behind in decaying slums where housing, schools, public safety, and other amenities are in short supply. Moreover, even affluent African Americans must live with the uncertainty of whether or not others will treat them as equals or view them suspiciously and make racist remarks. One recent study confirmed that middle class African Americans are still subject to abusive treatment and offensive remarks (Feagin 1991). Moreover, in another study (Van Ausdale and Feagin 2001) of a preschool, young children could be heard making racist comments to blacks, thus confirming that along with the Three Rs of reading, 'riting, and 'rithmetic is a fourth R: racism. Most non-blacks cannot imagine what it would be like to *never know for sure* whether or not you will be judged by your skin color.

At different historical periods, African Americans have always threatened white Americans. The large slave populations in the Plantation System of the south posed a threat along many fronts: fears by working class whites that freed slaves would take their jobs; fears that slaves would lust after white women; fears that if given the right to vote, they would dilute white power; and fears that freed slaves would go on a rampage of violence in retaliation to enslavement. These fears translated into massive discrimination. Slavery itself is, of course, an obvious form of discrimination, but when Reconstruction ended after the Civil War, African Americans were denied about every right imaginable: they were segregated into separate schools, they were denied by white violence and intimidation the right to vote, they were denied employment in every sphere save for the most menial work, they were subject to constant white harassment and violence such as murder and lynching, and they were forced to display submissive demeanor in the presence of whites.

As African Americans began to migrate out of the south in the decades around World War I, they posed fears to white immigrants who were just making economic gains and who were trying to unionize. Indeed, desperate blacks were recruited from the south by northern industrialists as strike breakers, thus escalating white fears (Bonacich 1976). The result was for whites to violently attack blacks, to segregate them into the worse housing, to segregate schools, to put up obstacles to voting and to gerrymander districts to dilute the voting power of those who did secure the vote, and to confine blacks to the lowest ranking job classifications when they joined unions. Up to the 1960s, African Americans endured housing, job, legal, educational, and political discrimination. The Civil Rights and Voting Rights Acts of the 1960s broke most of the legal barriers to blacks seeking housing in white neighborhoods, blacks seeking to vote, blacks seeking job opportunities, blacks seeking a decent education, and blacks seeking political office. Informal discrimination remains, however; and so, probably more than any other ethnic group in America, African Americans must still endure subtle and informal discrimination.

Discrimination is legitimated by beliefs and black Americans have been subject to the most vicious stereotypes. They have been viewed as "subhuman," as "animals," as childlike "sambos," as "sexually aggressive," as "culturally deprived," as "welfare dependent," as violent gang members, and more recently, as beneficiaries of reverse discrimination against whites through "affirmative action" (Turner and Payne 2002; Turner and Singleton 1978; Turner, Singleton, and Musick 1984). These beliefs could be mobilized to discriminate, and even today, as the public turns against affirmative action, the one tool that has been instrumental to African American mobility into the middle classes is under attack. The situation for many African Americans has improved over the last 40 years in incomes, jobs, office holding in government, educational attainment, and housing (Turner and Payne 2002). Yet, a large proportion of the African American population still lives in slum enclaves with few prospects.

Latinos

Latinos constitute the fastest growing population. The largest subpopulation is Mexican American, followed by Puerto Ricans, Cubans, and others from Central and South America as well as the Caribbean (Aguirre and Turner 2004, 19). Although some Mexican Americans were in what became the United States after the war with Mexico, most Mexican Americans and Latinos migrated to America. Mexican Americans came as workers for agro-business for much of the last century; Cubans came in the 1960s in the aftermath of the revolution led by Fidel Castro (although more recent, dark-skinned Cubans of African origin came later in the 1980s); Puerto Ricans began to immigrate in large numbers in the 1950s and, by the mid-1970s, half of the island's population had immigrated to the United States; and other Latinos from central and south America, coupled with African-origin Latinos from the Caribbean and other islands, have come mostly during the last three decades in response to political turmoil and difficult economic times in these regions.

Mexican Americans.   Immigrants from Mexico have been subject to much discrimination. Much like African Americans, early workers were denied citizenship and voting rights through literacy tests and harassment, they had their neighborhoods gerrymandered to dilute their local political power even when their numbers were high, they were forced into segregated schools of inferior quality, and they were subject to constant harassment by the Border Patrol and police. The large influx of illegal immigrants from Mexico in recent decades has increased the sense of threat that fuels discrimination. Moreover, Mexican origin residents have been subject to prejudicial stereotypes, ranging from simple peasants who cannot participate in the American mainstream through "Frito Bandito" images of dishonest and tricky cheats to aggressive urban Chicanos to Latino "hordes" who threaten the jobs of whites (and blacks) and burden the welfare, medical, and social service systems. All of these portrayals of Mexican origin residents have justified discrimination and abusive treatment of both immigrants and U.S. citizens. Because Mexican Americans are identifiable by their language and culture, they are relatively easy targets for abusive acts by police and other authorities like the Border Patrol; coupled with the intermingling of those who are here legally and illegally with those who are citizens, efforts to reduce immigration often lead to treatment of American citizens *as if* they were undocumented immigrants. Since most enforcement of immigration policies has failed to stem the tide of immigration, the sense of threat, especially in the southwest where Hispanics will someday constitute half of the population, has intensified as whites and other minorities see the "Latinization" of their communities. Some people, of course, embrace this change as inevitable, whereas others who are less economically secure are fearful and become the storm troopers supporting discrimination.

Puerto Ricans.   Between 1950 and 1975, large numbers of Puerto Ricans came to New York City and other larger cities in the northeast. This rapid and concentrated immigration aroused fears in many communities.

Because Puerto Rico was a commonwealth nation, most of the immigration was legal, thereby limiting the use of police and immigration officials as the front line of discrimination. The fears revolved around Puerto Ricans flooding local labor markets with cheap workers who would undercut white wages, overburdening public facilities, and draining the welfare system. Discrimination revolved primarily around housing segregation (and hence school segregation) and differential treatment in the labor market. As a result, Puerto Rican neighborhoods are often next to, and indeed intermingled with, African-American ghettos; like black neighborhoods, they have often been gerrymandered to reduce Puerto Rican political power. The result has been for Puerto Ricans to be over-represented in low-paying jobs and under-represented in the halls of political power and higher education.

Cuban Americans.   In contrast to other Latinos, Cuban immigrants were defined as refugees from an oppressive communist regime. The result is that they enjoyed special protections and privileges from Congress and other agencies of government, such as the Small Business Bureau who gave low-interest loans to these "refugees of communism." Cubans settled mostly in south Florida; because so many of the early immigrants were well-educated professionals and businesspeople, they were able to penetrate the business and political communities without arousing the sense of threat to the point where highly negative stereotypes and blatant discrimination prevailed, as had been the case for other Latinos. Moreover, as sons and daughters of the educated, Cuban children were able to perform well in school and, like their parents and grandparents, secure higher paying jobs than any other Latinos. The boatlifts of the 1980s that brought black Cubans changed the dynamics of south Florida. President Castro clearly let many prisoners and mental patients leave Cuba; as African-origin Cubans of lower socioeconomic backgrounds with drug, criminal, and mental problems began to arrive in Florida, the reception was much more abusive. Most were put into stockades for a time; and as they sought housing and work in the community, they were subject to the same discrimination that African Americans have endured. Still, Cuban Americans are over-represented in the middle classes compared to other Latinos.

Asian Americans

Asian Americans began arriving in the United States at the turn of the last century. Table 15.2 lists the relative numbers of the larger Asian subpopulations in America. Early immigrants were Filipino, Chinese, and Japanese, whereas later immigrants in the last century to the present have tended to come from China, Korea, India, Laos, and Vietnam. Though still comparatively small, the Asian population is growing; if illegal immigrants are counted, the population is growing much more rapidly than census bureau statistics would indicate. Still, it is predicted that the Asian population will be only 9% of the population by mid-century. Early Asian immigrants suffered job discrimination, confinement to Asian ghettoes, educational discrimination, and religious persecution if they held non-Christian beliefs. The fact that Japanese Americans were interned into concentration camps during World War II, while German

Table 15.2   Relative Numbers of Asian Ethnic Subpopulations, 2000

Subpopulation	Number
Chinese	2.3 million
Filipino	1.9 million
Japanese	.8 million
Asian Indian	1.7 million
Korean	1.1 million
Vietnamese	1.1 million

Source: U.S. Bureau of the Census (2002).

Americans were not, underscores the ease with which whites could discriminate against Asians. Much of this discrimination was fueled in Hearst newspaper articles about the "yellow peril," and so, for the first half of the twentieth century, Asians were subject to intense discrimination and, as is the case today with Latinos, many were deported whereas others, who were citizens, were not allowed to bring their wives and children to join them.

The early stereotypes that legitimated discrimination revolved around notions that Asians were "clannish and cared little about America," that they were not going to adopt the American way, and that they had little loyalty to America. Some of these stereotypes persist, but for Japanese in particular, these stereotypes have almost disappeared. For Filipinos and Chinese, however, they have not diminished as much because of new waves of recent immigrants from these countries. Koreans came as "middleman minorities" with resources to penetrate small business niches, but they suffered the fate of most middleman minorities and were viewed by rivals as "aggressive and pushy," as "driving whites out of business," as exploiting people in minority communities, and as generally not blending into the American way. Refugees from Vietnam and surrounding countries also came with resources and suffered much of the same stereotyping as Koreans: "clannish," "aggressive," and not willing to "assimilate." But, like their Cuban counterparts, Vietnamese and other immigrants from south Asia have often brought entrepreneurial and professional skills that have led them to push their children to do well in schools; and so, it should not be surprising that Asians have higher median incomes than even whites. Yet, Asians are often still viewed suspiciously as "clannish" and are subject to informal discrimination in jobs, housing, and even education.

White Americans

Successive waves of white ethnic immigrants to America during the period between 1840 and World War I were all subject to discrimination and vicious stereotyping. Those already here feared the changes that millions of new immigrants would bring to their communities and the country as a whole. The original English-German settlers feared the first wave of European immigrants and portrayed these new arrivals in very negative terms that, in turn, legitimated their confinement to slum housing and low-paying jobs. However, the American public school system was established during this period to "Americanize" the new immigrants, with the result that as the nineteenth century turned into the twentieth century, an increasing proportion of sons and daughters of immigrants could receive an education that would be the key to their subsequent mobility up the class system. The general pattern was for those immigrants who had just begun to move up the stratification system to fear the latest pool of immigrants, to discriminate against the new arrivals, and legitimate this discrimination with very negative stereotypes. For example, in one political cartoon, the Catholic Irish immigrant was portrayed as the "missing link" between apes and humans. Thus, the Protestant Scots-Irish feared and discriminated against the Catholic Irish who came later; the Catholic Irish feared and discriminated against Italians who did much the same to the "dumb Pollacks"; and all discriminated against African Americans as they began to migrate north during the first two decades of the twentieth century. Jews, a good portion of whom came from Russia and later Germany, were also subject to intense discrimination and stereotyping as "Christ killers" (conveniently ignoring the fact that Jesus was a Jew and that it was the Romans, not Jews, who crucified him), as "clannish," as "too shrewd businessmen," and "as controlling too much monetary activity." Yet, because of their long history as targets of discrimination, Jews knew how to adapt; because of their entrepreneurial skills and emphasis on education, Jewish Americans are over-represented in the upper middle classes, although they are still subject to discrimination in housing, memberships in private clubs, university fraternities if not the university itself, and even in sectors of the economy. This discrimination is subtle and informal, making it invidious and difficult to overcome.

The United States as a Multi-Ethnic Society

Ethnic dynamics are always volatile because one ethnic group will often perceive another as a threat to its well being. The United States is now one of the most ethnically diverse societies in the world; indeed, much of the vitality and energy of the society has come from immigrants anxious to work and build a better life. At no time has immigration of new ethnic groups to the United States been peaceful, although over the long haul, some degree of assimilation and integration among ethnic populations has occurred. Still, even as tensions among white ethnics have declined, the dilemma of how to overcome the effects of slavery and fully institutionalized discrimination on African Americans for 400 years has not been resolved. The current flash point is over affirmative action, but the underlying problem is that the playing field cannot be level as long as large numbers of African Americans must grow up in slums and attend inferior schools. The effects of genocide and the reservation system on Native American's ability to enjoy an affluent life have not disappeared, even though gaming on reservation lands offers improved prospects for some. Thus, the lasting effects of discrimination for those who were here and those brought here as slaves will be with Americans through this century.

If we add to these long-standing problems the dramatic demographic changes that are occurring with Latino and Asian immigration, coupled with comparatively high birth rates for Latinos, the ethnic mix today promises to become a pressure cooker in the future. Any time the relative proportions of ethnics change rapidly in a society, those who are losing ground—whites, African Americans, and Native Americans—will feel threatened by those who are gaining in numbers—Latinos and Asians. Whether these threats translate into mean stereotypes justifying blatant discrimination remains to be seen, but as long as ethnic division and social class division are correlated, tension in society is inevitable.

SUMMARY

1. Inequality in a society revolves around the differential distribution of valued resources, such as jobs, income, housing, and education, to various categories of individuals including categories demarked by ethnic distinctions. When there is a correlation between social class and ethnicity, ethnic tensions inevitably increase in society.

2. Ethnicity is the identification of a subpopulation as distinctive in terms of surface biology, resources, demeanor, culture, and organizational patterns; ethnic stratification exists when some ethnic subpopulations consistently get more of the valued resources in a society than other ethnic subpopulations.

3. Ethnic stratification is created and sustained by discrimination, which is legitimated by prejudicial beliefs. Discrimination and prejudice are fueled by the (economic, political, social) threat that a target ethnic group is perceived to pose, while being sustained by mutually reinforcing cycles revolving around ethnic identifiability, threat, prejudice, and discrimination.

4. The United States is one of the most, if not the most, ethnically diverse countries in the world; each ethnic group that has immigrated to America has been implicated, as either a victim or active discriminator, in discriminatory dynamics creating and sustaining an ethnic stratification system.

5. White immigrants have been able to overcome these dynamics after several generations. African and Native Americans have not been able to overcome discrimination because of their easy identifiability and because of the extreme and long-term nature of the discrimination. Latinos and Asians have also been subject to intense discrimination, but Asians have been able to find niches where they could prosper while some Latinos have been able to move up the class system. Still, because so many new and poor Latino immigrants arrive each year, many are just beginning the several-generation climb from poverty.

6. The demographic profile of the United States is changing, with Latinos and Asians increasing as a proportion of the population and with European-origin, African Americans, and Native Americans decreasing. These changes in the relative size of various ethnic subpopulations will increase threats, the ultimate fuel behind discrimination and ethnic stratification.

KEY TERMS

Discrimination: Differential treatment of others, especially those of an ethnic group or a gender category, so that they receive less valued resources.

Ethnic Stratification: Situation where members of particular ethnic groups are disproportionately over- and under-represented in particular social classes.

Ethnicity: Those behavioral, cultural, and organizational characteristics that distinguish subpopulations in a society.

Genocide: Systematic killing of larger numbers of members of an ethnic subpopulation.

Institutionalized Discrimination: Patterns of systematic discrimination against an ethnic subpopulation that are legitimated by cultural symbols, that are carried out informally and formally, and that are built into the structures of a society.

Prejudice: Beliefs about the undesirable qualities of others, especially those in an ethnic group.

Race: Perceived biological distinctiveness for categories of individuals.

Chapter 16

Gender Stratification

Sex and Gender

Humans are either male or female, although a few people carry some of the sex organs of both males and females. The sexes evolved by natural selection to increase genetic diversity by mixing the genes of two different organisms, thereby limiting the effects of harmful genes. **Sex** thus refers to the biological differences between males and females; for most species, biologically based **sexual differentiation** directs the behaviors of men and women. For a long time, people thought the roles that men and women play in society were destined and directed by the biology of men and women, or their sex. Even hunter-gatherers, who displayed the most equality of any known societal type, probably assumed that it was somehow "natural" for women to gather and men to hunt. Yet, even as they divided the labor, hunter-gatherers did not assign more worth and value to men and women based upon their different work roles. Things changed, however, as humans settled down and adopted horticultural and, later, agrarian technologies (see Timeline at the beginning of the book); soon, the equality between men and women evident among hunter-gatherers was replaced by inequality: men had more power, material wealth, and prestige than women. Why did this happen? And why did it take thousands of years, right up to the last century, to mount serious opposition to what can only be described as sexual inequality in which men get more of what is valued in a society than women?

No one has a clear answer as to why sexual inequalities increased once humans left hunting and gathering. Part of the answer resides in the fact that people obviously categorize each other by sex—as either male or female—and that this categorization also brings extra baggage: cultural definitions of how men and women are "different" and how these differences dictate appropriate roles, dispositions, and identities between the sexes. The more sexual differences—which denote only what is biologically distinct in males and females—are elaborated by cultural definitions, then the more these perceived sexual differences become elaborated into **gender differentiation**. Because inequalities in resources come from the positions that people have in society, the roles that they play, the identities that they acquire in socialization, and the social structures to which they belong, sexual differences have become elaborated into gender differences. And, as one gender gets more of the valued resources that a society has to offer, gender differences are codified into a system of gender stratification.

Thus, **gender stratification** is the situation whereby members of one gender category consistently receive more valued resources than members of another gender category. The most obvious gender categories are male and female, but there are other gender categories, such as gay and lesbian, transvestites, or hermaphrodites (people born with elements of both sex organs). In this chapter, we focus on **stratification** revolving around distinctions between men and women.

The distinction between sex and gender is not so easily separated in the public's eye because much of what a population comes to see as the "natural" biological propensities of the sexes are culturally defined and enforced through sanctions. The only clear biological differences between men and women are genetically caused differences in hormonal secretions and their effects on the development of the sex organs and other anatomical features (skeletal size, percentage of body fat, distribution of hair, and musculature). There may be other genetically based differences, but there is no unambiguous evidence for these. Moreover, even the most unambiguous differences become so elaborated and impregnated by cultural beliefs and norms, as well as roles and practices within social structures, as to make the line between sex and gender unclear.

The socially constructed basis of sex is dramatically illustrated by cases where the biology of a person's sex is ambiguous. For example, in one study, children born with the organs of both sexes (hermaphrodites) took on the gender characteristics—attitudes, demeanor, and sexual preferences—that reflected their socialization by parents as either male or female (Ellis 1945; Money and Ehrhardt 1972). In another illuminating case, a young and seemingly normal girl who had the external sex organs of a female and who had been raised as a female underwent a voice change at puberty; a closer medical examination revealed that "she" was chromosomally a male. Informed of this, she "went home, took off her girl's clothing, and became a boy, immediately beginning to behave like other boys" (V. Reynolds 1976, 125).

From a sociological view, then, we should concentrate on gender as a social process revolving around cultural and social forces that affect the positions occupied and the roles played by men and women. I concentrate on gender as it generates a system of stratification because it is a topic that directly affects all of our lives.

Explanations for Gender Stratification

Sociobiological Theories

Sociobiological theories emphasize that the genes seek to survive in the gene pool. Those behaviors and social structures that enable genes to be passed onto the next generation are fitness enhancing, and thereby, are likely to be retained. From this point of view, many kinds of arguments about the behavioral differences between men and women, as well as the structural outcomes of these behavioral propensities, can be developed, although all of them are highly speculative. The basic theme of all of these arguments goes as follows: natural selection favored behavioral propensities and social structural arrangements that allowed parents and their offspring to survive and, as a result, pass on their genes. The emergence of the sexual division of labor in nuclear family units organized into hunting and gathering bands, and the elaboration of sex-based roles into culturally defined gender distinctions about the nature of men and women, represented a successful strategy that enhanced fitness. The sexual division of labor, the nuclear family, and the band are all "survivor machines" for genes; this adaptation proved highly successful for humans and their ancestors right up to a few thousand years ago.

For hunters and gatherers, this kind of argument has some merit, but it does not explain how the sexual division of labor became elaborated into an often oppressive system of gender stratification. Hunters and gatherers did not have stratification, and so, how can stratification be seen as an efficient machine for survival when it generates so many tensions and conflict? Clearly genes are not pushing for stratification, and so once we leave a hunter-gatherer society, sociobiological theories cannot adequately explain the scale and persistence of gender stratification in human societies.

Functional Theories

Functional theories generally make an argument that is very similar to the one that a sociobiologist might offer. These functional theories emphasize that a sex-based division of labor was more likely than any alternative to meet the survival needs of early human populations. It is more efficient, and hence more adaptive, in a simple society to have women perform activities around childrearing and domestic activity, while having men leave the camps to hunt for game and, later, to fight in conflicts. Women must bear and nurse the children, and their domestic activities would seem to flow "naturally" out of this biological "fact" of human life. In contrast, men cannot nurse and are, on average, about 15% to 20% bigger than women; thus, it is more "natural" for them to leave camps to hunt and perform other tasks that cannot be done by nursing females. Once this division of labor existed, it became elaborated and expanded, eventually leading to inequality between the sexes when humans settled down.

Like sociobiological theories, there is some merit in this argument, but it is seriously flawed. First, women in many traditional societies do most of the heavy work *and* raise children (Nolan and Lenski 2004). Once the nomadic hunting and gathering way of life is abandoned and people settle down, there is no reason why men cannot do the same and use their talents for raising children and performing domestic chores. Second, if women's roles are so functionally important, why do they command less prestige, power, and wealth in the post-hunting and gathering era? Thus, we need to look elsewhere for a more complete understanding of why gender stratification has persisted.

Conflict Theories

One place to look is conflict theory, where the emphasis is on power (Collins 1975; Collins and Coltrane 1991). Because men are somewhat larger and stronger than women, at least on average, they have created and sustained a gender-based stratification system through coercion. Thus, over the long course of history, men and women have competed for scarce resources, with men ultimately holding a decisive coercive edge.

A similar theory argues that the maintenance of a gendered stratification system is the outcome of men having coercive power over women (Chafetz 1990, 1984). What, then, increases the coercive power of men over women, above and beyond the strength differences between the sexes? The coercive power of men increases when:

1. The division of labor in society is already gendered (women do one kind of activity, and men another).
2. Women are confined to certain jobs that affirm gender stereotypes, as is the case when women are in "nurturing" occupations like nursing, social work, and teaching.
3. The gendered division of labor gives men more income than women, allowing them to assert their superiority.
4. Men control the elite positions of economic and political power that determine the societal level policies in the economy and political-legal arena.
5. The perceived differences between men and women are accepted by members of society, including women, and when these differences are emphasized in ideologies or beliefs about (a) differences between men and women, (b) norms about how men and women should behave, and (c) actual practices in face-to-face encounters.
6. Women themselves accept the advantages of men through (a) gendered divisions of labor in the family, (b) gendered adult role models for children, and (c) gender-biased socialization.

Another kind of conflict theory emphasizes women's control of economic resources (Blumberg 1984). When women can control economic resources, they gain power and can limit the level of gender stratification. Conversely, when they cannot control economic resources, they lose power and can be coerced physically, politically, and ideologically. Women's economic power is thus the key as to whether or not gender stratification exists. Women who can participate in the economy, who can perform jobs that are indispensable and important, who can control their own income, and who can hold property are able to resist discrimination and, thereby, subvert the gendered stratification system. Historically, women have often worked but they did not have control of their incomes, thus making them dependent upon men; it is no coincidence that the modern-day women's movement against gender stratification began as women became a larger part of the labor force and, as a consequence were able to control their incomes and own property. Under these conditions, women can lobby against domestic violence, elect those sympathetic to their interests, and change gender ideologies.

What these conflict theories share is the view that men control power when women do not have the economic resources to make claims to gender definitions that promote equality. As long as men control (a) the political arena, (b) the highest level positions in the economy, and (c) the media and sources of cultural ideologies about men and women, women will be at a disadvantage. They will not be able to secure jobs or control of income, power, and symbols that enable them to push for more equality.

Women have, no doubt, been quietly angry with their subordinate position throughout history, but the lack of economic, political, and ideological resources, coupled with socialization and forces of social control (e.g., ridicule and coercion), have often worked to blind women to the vast inequalities or to keep them from protesting too much. Indeed, it is only in very recent history as women entered the labor force and gained control of economic resources that the cultural mask has been pulled off, leading to a growing social movement in much of the industrial world to redress the inequalities between men and women.

Interactionist Theories

Interactionist theories all emphasize the importance of face-to-face interaction, especially the effects of people's self-conception and identity. For interactionists, individuals learn through interaction with others the cultural definitions of how boys and girls and, later, how men and women, are supposed to behave. As they are learning these broader cultural definitions from parents, friends, and media, they are also developing a conception of themselves revolving around a sexual identity that will incorporate many of these broader definitions about the nature of men and women, and how men and women are supposed to behave. As a result, male and female youth will play gendered roles to affirm gendered identities, and they will seek out those positions in social structures that enable them to play roles successfully. They will find attractive gendered roles that enable them to affirm their gender identities. Later in life, women may come to realize how their identities have been shaped in ways that support gender stratification, and they will have to fight against the gendered identity and the cultural scripts associated with this identity. What interactionists emphasize, then, is that gender is learned and becomes part of a people's conception of themselves; and that in each and every interaction, people are guided by their identities and by cultural scripts about how men and women are to behave. Thus, it is often difficult to break the hold of culture and identities that implicitly support a system of gender stratification.

A General Model of Gender Stratification

We are now in a position to examine the dynamics of gender stratification in more detail. The theories summarized above give us some clues, but we need to add much more detail to the general picture laid out in these theories. We can begin with the idea that gender stratification has something in common with other forms of stratification: certain categories of people are victims of discrimination because they are identifiable. Sex is obvious, and as sexual differences get elaborated into cultural definitions about the nature of men and women, women stand out even more—in dress, in hairstyle, in demeanor, and in all those ways that make women "feminine." But why would men and, at times, women discriminate? As is the case with ethnic stratification, women pose a threat to male jobs, to male dominance, to male privileges, to male political power, and to the higher prestige that men enjoy. And, because women constitute a majority of most populations, the threat to male dominance is that much greater. When threatened, individuals will discriminate. Discrimination is justified and legitimated by cultural beliefs. Unlike the often vicious stereotypes against members of ethnic groups, the stereotypes about women are, on the surface, more benign but no less powerful. Thus, women are by "nature" more emotional, more nurturing, more family oriented, more domestic, and less aggressive than men; as a result of these differences, they should play the homemaker roles in the family and, if they must work, they should seek the "pink-collar" jobs that support men (like secretary) or nurturing jobs like elementary school teacher, librarian, and social worker—all of which carry less income, power, and prestige. Also, because women must bear children and are assumed to be naturally more attentive to children than men, it is often assumed that women rather than men must interrupt their careers when they "hear the clock ticking"; this belief discourages employers from seeing women as career professionals, and women themselves from entering or staying in "fast track" careers in the executive arena. Thus, like ethnic stratification, (a) male fears as well as female fears among those women who "buy into" the traditional gender ideologies lead to (b) beliefs that stigmatize women in their ability to compete with men in the economic and political arena that, in turn, (c) justify discrimination in jobs and politics. Together, these forces work to generate a system of gendered stratification. Women can be readily identified, and so, as they are forced into homemaker roles or into the "pink-collar" labor force; they confirm beliefs about gender that justify discrimination. As a result, women receive jobs carrying lower levels of income, power, and prestige than those held by men.

There are, however, some important differences between gender and ethnic stratification. One of the most obvious is that unlike an ethnic minority or even a particular social class, women cannot be shuffled off to a ghetto and forgotten; they must live side by side with men each day, and as a result, they must constantly adjust to male dominance. Indeed, each moment of interaction in the household recreates the gender system. Second, women cannot easily assemble around their common interests because they are isolated as individuals in their families where domestic obligations limit their ability to raise each other's conscious awareness over the inequities in the gendered stratification system. Third, women have been socialized into gender identities, have played gendered roles, and have learned gendered definitions from infancy. The result is that it is often difficult to change and abandon identities and investment in roles that have been a part of people's lives since they were born. Fourth, even when women work, they have a domestic burden that is greater than men's. Even when they work, women are expected to shop, clean, cook, wash, nurture, and do domestic chores to a far greater extent than men. Numerous studies document what is often called "the second shift" of household and domestic chores that women must take on when they come home from work (Hochschild and Machung 1989;). This double domestic and work burden often discourages women from staying in the labor force, thereby affirming gendered beliefs that legitimate discrimination.

Figure 16.1 summarizes these dynamics in graphic form. Like ethnic discrimination, these forces are all positively related to each other: one force raises the values of others, and vice versa, in a series of vicious cycles culminating in a system of gendered stratification. Let us now use this model to review gender stratification in the United States.

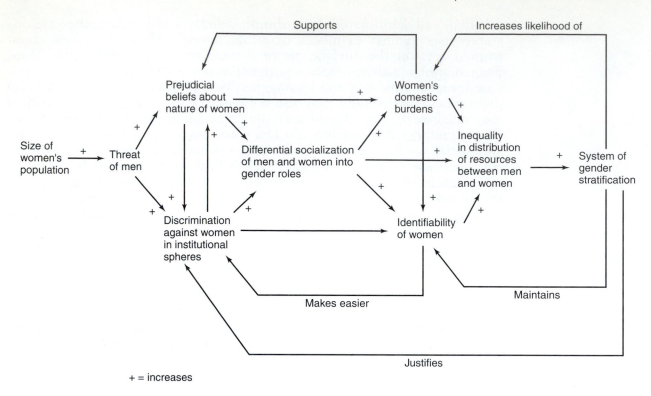

Figure 16.1   Dynamics of Gender Stratification

Gender Stratification in America

The Cycles of the Gender Stratification System

The size of the population of women always poses a threat should they enter the male domain in great numbers. Men experience threat, which at a cultural level, leads to formation of beliefs against women, emphasizing their nurturing and domestic character (J. Turner 1977). Such beliefs have been translated into normative expectations about the proper positions (domestic) and role behaviors (passive, supportive, nurturant) for women. Such cultural symbols persist because the young are socialized by their families, schools, peers, and media to accept them. When a baby is born, its sex is the first thing the parents wish to know because it dictates how they will respond to the child and what they will expect. Girls will, for example, be channeled into a "soft" demeanor, boys into "hard" and more aggressive behavioral modes; girls will be encouraged to practice in their play activities "female" roles (mother, nurse, and housewife), whereas boys will be encouraged to adopt masculine roles (imagine the consequences for a boy who wants to play with a doll or learn how to sew). With this channeling into play activities, definitions of what it means to be masculine and feminine are communicated.

These not-so-subtle messages about masculinity and femininity are reinforced by peer interactions and experiences in schools. Peer interactions reinforce school and family socialization, as does the media (books and television). The end result, as interactionist theories would stress, is that boys and girls (and later men and women) come to define them-

selves in masculine and feminine terms and to seek out positions in social structures that reinforce these definitions. Such efforts are reinforced by the broader institutional (economy, government, religion)
structure in America and elsewhere in the industrial world.

The end result of having internalized cultural beliefs about gender
and having developed a gendered identity is for women to be caught in a
conflict between their domestic roles (childbearing, childrearing, cooking, shopping, and etc.), on the one side, and perhaps a desire to play
roles in the economy that are the same as those available to men. And,
even when women do work, they are subject to these expectations and
must take on the "second shift" of domestic chores. On average, married
women who work spend about 13.2 hours on household work compared
to their working husbands who devote 8.2 hours to household labor
(Stapinski 1998). It is clear, then, that women do much more of this domestic labor than men—thus putting women in a constant conflict between work and home, while at the same time exhausting them to the
point where they often drop out from the labor force.

However, women have become increasingly involved in the labor
force, as Table 16.1 documents. Now, around 60% of women work; and
for those who have families, they must work extra hard when they get
home and take on the "second shift" (Hochschild and Machung 1990).

Even as more and more women enter the work force, however, they
are over-represented in the lower-paying, lower-prestige, and lower-
power jobs, such as secretary, phone operator, nurse, social worker,
teacher, dental hygienist, day-care worker, child care, receptionist, maid,
and stenographer. There is, then, what is often termed a "split labor market" for men and women. This split is not only evident in the large percentage of women in particular "women's occupations" but also in the

Table 16.1   Percentage of Women in
Labor Force

Year	Percentage Working or Looking for Work
2002	59.8%
2001	60.1
1990	57.5
1980	51.5
1970	43.3
1960	37.7
1950	33.9
1940	25.4
1930	22.0
1920	21.4
1910	21.5
1900	18.8

Source: U.S. Department of Labor (2003).

comparatively low percentage of women in traditional men's occupations, such as executive administrators of larger corporations, many professions such as engineering, and higher paying manual labor (e.g., carpentry, electricians, plumbers). Such "occupational ghettos" for women exist in virtually every society, but they are surprisingly evident in societies like the United States where beliefs favor gender equality (for comparative data, see Charles and Grosky 2004).

This split in the U.S. labor market results in women earning only about 75% of the wages paid to men, as is reported in Table 16.2. Moreover, even when women are *in the same occupations* as men, this percentage does not change dramatically. As conflict theories would predict, this lack of economic parity with men works against women in the micro-politics of the household where men can still claim to be the "principle" breadwinner, forcing women to make up the difference between their wages and their male counterparts through unpaid (and generally unappreciated) domestic work. It should be emphasized, however, that the gap between women's and men's wages has been slowly closing and that women have entered traditional male occupations at increasing rates. Thus, change is occurring; perhaps in the future, women will be on economic parity with men, thereby giving them power to renegotiate their domestic burdens.

At the more macro level of power, women are still under-represented at just about every level—state legislators, members of the U.S. Congress, cabinet positions in the Executive branch of government, and judicial appointments in the federal courts. This under-representation at the macro level of power influences women's power at the micro, interpersonal level because the culture of political decision making still has a male bias. For example, women's reproductive rights, protection against male violence, maternity leave policies, job discrimination by sex, and many other issues that women face in their daily lives are very much influenced by macro-level political decisions where the "woman's voice" is not heard in proportion to their numbers in the society. Again, change is

Table 16.2 Women's Wages as a Percentage of Men's Wages, 1951–2002

Year	Women's Wages as Percentage of Men's Wages
2002	76.0%
2000	73.0
1990	71.6
1980	60.2
1970	59.4
1960	60.7
1951	63.9

Source: U.S. Women's Bureau and the National Committee on Pay Equity (2003).

occurring. Over the last three decades there has been a significant increase in the proportion of women in positions of macro-level power.

Still, the resource shares of women are less than those of men, and they are disproportionately confined to the "pink-collar" work force, which only sustains the identifiability of women as the "feminine sex." Moreover, the continued pressure on women (from socialization into gendered identities and internalization of gender stereotypes, as well as male and societal expectations) forces women to play gendered domestic roles that often make them ambivalent about their work roles. Should they pursue a career and not have children? Should they stay home? When should they interrupt their career? Men rarely have to ask these questions, with the result that women will be more likely than men to sacrifice or compromise careers to bear and raise children—all of which works to maintain their feminine identity that confirms gender stereotypes and legitimates both blatant and subtle discrimination in the workplace.

The Feminist Movement

The rise of the feminist movement in the late 1960s and 1970s coincides with the rise in women's participation in the workplace, as women increasingly challenged the traditional gender stereotype of women as "homemakers." As women's economic power increased, ideological spokespersons emerged to articulate an alternative ideology that challenged the view of women's traditional roles. This ideology was, of course, threatening to men and to women who had internalized the traditional culture of women's place as in the home and as an adjunct to male careerism. The movement has been extremely effective in changing cultural beliefs and laws about discrimination; yet, it has not achieved the goal of equality between males and females in the economic, political, and domestic arenas. The very fact that the Equal Rights Amendment could not receive the necessary two-thirds support from state legislatures signals that macro-level power is still aligned against the feminist agenda, the main elements of which are summarized in Table 16.3. Feminism threatens the status quo and the system of gender stratification, with the result that it will be resisted now and into the immediate future.

Table 16.3   Elements of Feminism

There are several versions of feminism, but all feminists would argue on the following:

(1) The current system of gendered roles must change.

(2) The cultural ideology that defines what men and women *should* be like and what they *should* do must be changed.

(3) The system of gendered division of labor must change, giving women the same choices as men in domestic, work, political, and community roles.

(4) Male violence against women must end; not only is it wrong, per se, it supports male domination of women.

(5) Women should have autonomous control of their sexual behavior and reproduction.

(6) Women and men should have more choices about their sexual activities, careers, and domestic activities.

SUMMARY

1. Inequality in a society revolves around the differential distribution of valued resources to various categories of individuals—class, ethnic, and gender being three of the most important.

2. The gender dimension of stratification is sustained by mutually reinforcing cycles of socialization, gender identity, and gender-related beliefs that, in turn, become the basis for discrimination and prejudicial beliefs fueled by men's sense of threat.

3. Despite significant gains over the last three decades, women are still under-represented in those positions that bring income and power, while being burdened with domestic chores, even when they work. Moreover, women still receive on average only about 75% of the income of men.

4. Gender relations are changing in America, as the mutually reinforcing cycles of the gender stratification system are being broken by women's participation in work and politics and by assaults on gender beliefs that place women at a disadvantage.

KEY TERMS

Gender/Gender Differentiation: Process of culturally defining the appropriate positions, roles, and demeanor for men and women.

Gender Stratification: Situation where the positions typically occupied by men and women habitually receive different levels of valued resources.

Sex/Sexual Differentiation: Biological differences between men and women.

Stratification: Structures revolving around the unequal distribution of valued resources to the members of a society, leading to the creation or accentuation of distinctive categories whose members share similar kinds and levels of resources.

Part V Institutional Systems

As societies become more complex, distinctive institutional systems emerge. These systems are ultimately built from micro encounters and meso-level structures like groups, organizations, and communities, as well as from distinctions among social categories. However, once they exist and operate, they constrain what occurs in those meso structures from which they are built. Institutions tend to develop their own culture, and they dictate certain types of encounters, groups, organizations, communities, and categoric units. Thus, to understand how a society operates, it is essential to study the institutional systems. These are macro structures because they cut across an entire society; when a society has relations with another, it is the institutional systems of each society that form relationships, as is the case with the economies in world markets or with governments in various political alliances. Moreover, almost any encounter of face-to-face interaction is embedded in an institutional system, with the culture of this system influencing how people relate to each other. In this section, we examine only some of the key institutions of human societies—economy, polity or government, kinship and family, religion, and education. There are other institutional systems, such as science, medicine and health, and sports, for example. Like all other social structures in human societies, each institutional system represents a distinctive subfield within sociology.

Chapter 17

Economy

If people do not eat, they die, and society dies with them. Thus, a truly fundamental problem for humans is securing resources from the environment, converting these into usable commodities, and then distributing them to the members of a society. From a functional perspective, the economy resolves one set of problems facing the species: securing resources, converting them so that they can be consumed, and then distributing them so that all members of a society can survive. And thus, because the **institution of economy** is so fundamental to life, it should not be surprising that all other institutions will be greatly influenced by its structure and dynamics. Without the energy that comes from food and its distribution, nothing else can occur. Encounters cannot be sustained, groups cannot be formed, organizations cannot be built, communities cannot function, and other institutions from kinship to religion cannot operate. What is true of food is also the case for any material resource that humans extract from the environment and distribute to each other; without these resources, society is not possible.

It is for this reason that many sociologists have argued that the economy is the prime mover of society. The nature of the economy determines the kinds of groups, organizations, communities, classes, social categories, and other institutional systems that are possible as well as their structure and culture. This view of the economy as *the* prime mover may be an exaggeration, but it is not an exaggeration to recognize that the economy shapes just about everything else that goes on in human societies.

Basic Elements of all Economies

All economies operate in terms of some very basic elements (J. Turner 1972, 1997, 2003): technology, labor, capital, and entrepreneurship. Ultimately, an economy is built from these, and so, let us pause briefly to see what these elements are.

Technology

Technology is knowledge about how to manipulate the environment. We often think of technology as the products of this knowledge, but we are better off viewing technology as simply knowledge that can be used to control some aspect of the environment. Technology is thus symbolic and part of culture; to a very great extent, the level of technology will influence the content of the values, beliefs, ideologies, and norms that guide conduct and social organization. Ultimately, technology determines how much access to resources a population can have, how these resources are converted through production into goods and commodities, and how these resources are distributed.

Labor

Labor is simply human effort, but the nature of this effort varies enormously from using a digging stick to break the soil to pushing a button on a computer to activate the machine. Thus, technology influences the skills and expenditures of energy by people as they gather, produce, and distribute products. Moreover, labor can be viewed in the aggregate along several dimensions, such as how large the total pool of labor is, how skilled it is, how old or young it is, how gendered it is, and so on for other dimensions. At times, labor is denoted by the term **human capital,** and when this is done, it can be measured like money and other forms of capital by its quantity along some dimension such as education or skill.

Capital

Capital is the term denoting the tools or implements that are used to gather, produce, and distribute. As with labor, technology influences the nature of capital. People with a very low level of technology will have simple levels of capital formation, such as bows and arrows, spears, digging sticks, and perhaps grinding stones and cooking pots. These are the implements to get at the environment, find resources, and convert them so that they can be used and distributed to others. A people with a high level of technology will have a vast array of implements, such as machines, factories, trucks, roads, boats, airplanes, and many other devices that can extract resources, produce goods, and distribute these products. Moreover, liquid capital or money and credit also emerge in higher-technology societies. Here, capital is a potential that can be spent, when needed, to buy the machines, tools, and services needed for gathering, producing, and distributing.

Entrepreneurship

Entrepreneurship is the way in which the other elements of an economy are organized—that is, how technology, labor, and capital are interrelated with each other in gathering, producing, and distributing. As the scale of an economy gets larger, organizational problems inevitably escalate, leading to the creation of new kinds of mechanisms and structures to organize technology, labor, and capital. At first in human history, entrepreneurship was accomplished by small families in small bands of hunter-gatherers; today, markets, legal systems, factories, vast bureaucracies, governmental regulatory agencies, corporations, and many other structures operate as entrepreneurial mechanisms, coordinating technology, labor, and capital in ever more complex ways.

Types of Economies

Hunting and Gathering Economies

A majority of the 150,000 to 200,000 years that humans have existed as a species were spent in a hunting and gathering economy, where small bands of 30 to 50 individuals wandered over a territory gathering indigenous foods and hunting game. The technology was simple—people had a knowledge of plants and animals; capital consisted of spears and perhaps a bow and arrow; labor was divided by gender with women gathering and men hunting; and entrepreneurial functions were performed by families in the band, or by individuals working alone. Such economies did not produce much, but neither did people work very hard—perhaps 15 hours a week. As noted in the Prologue, the anthropologist Marshall Sahlins (1972) once called hunters and gatherers "the original affluent society" because life was relaxed and leisure dominated over work.

It is clear that hunters and gatherers of the past also knew about planting with seeds because they would often throw some seeds out when breaking camp with the hope that they could later "harvest" the food when returning months later. But, for most of our history as a species, humans avoided settling down on the land. Why? I suspect the answer has always been the same: who wants to work that hard turning soil, planting seeds, weeding gardens, harvesting the crop, storing what one can, and then doing it all over again year after year (Maryanski and Turner 1992)?

Horticultural Economies

At some point between 8,000 and 12,000 years ago, some humans began to work this hard. Horticultural economies emerged, consisting of knowledge about seeds, plants, and cultivation (technology); digging sticks, grinding stones, and other hand-held implements (capital); gardening and harvesting, mostly by women (labor); and organization by kinship and village (entrepreneurship). Horticulture is distinct from agriculture because gardening is conducted without the aid of a plow and other non-human sources of energy, like beasts of burden and wind or water power. It is not fully known why humans took up this labor-intensive economy, but let me offer a best guess (Maryanski and Turner 1992).

Humans first settled down, at least for a time, near rivers because fish and lush plant life around rivers were plentiful. Why move about if the staff of life is there for the plucking? With the extra food and a more sedentary life, the population began to grow; people began to exhaust local plant life and to hunt out game animals because they did not move on and let resources replenish themselves. Eventually, these settled populations were too large to move in the old way, and so, they began to practice horticulture. They had made a decisive step, though, because once settled the nature of human society changes dramatically. When populations grow, new structures are required—elaborated kinship and political authority—to coordinate and control activity; and territories now have to be defended, creating needs for political authority to mobilize military activity. The beginnings of the end for the original affluent society were thus initiated. In a few thousand years, hunting and gathering would be gone forever.

There are variants of horticultural societies, such as herding societies where people live by tending livestock. There are also fishing societies where village and kinship rules organize deep-sea fishing. These societies are all similar in that they rely mostly upon human power, while being organized by kinship rules and small village communities.

Agrarian Economies

Agrarian economies represented a significant technological break from horticulture because they possess knowledge of how to harness animal power and inanimate energy (water and wind) to basic economic processes. This breakthrough, in turn, stimulated further technological development—knowledge of metallurgy and smelting being two of the most important. As a result, capital accumulation in a more productive economy could be greatly extended. Money became widely used; and metal tools, shops, milling facilities, roadways, canals, transportation using the wheel, and a host of implements became common. Labor was ever more specialized, and new kinds of economic positions and roles—merchant, shopkeeper, artisan, banker, and other specialties—emerged. Entrepreneurship changed dramatically because village and kin alone were no longer adequate organizing forces and were successively replaced by markets, feudal political structures, merchant houses, guilds, law and contract, organizational units that began to look like the modern corporation, and larger urban communities where goods and services could be exchanged in markets.

Industrial Economies

Industrialization is the process of harnessing fossil fuels to machines attended by labor in a factory. This process was initiated just a few hundred years ago, but it has transformed the world. Industrial economies have vast technologies about how to manipulate and control the environment (indeed, they can destroy it), and they constantly develop new knowledge. Capital formation involves money and numerous new ways of accumulating money (e.g., stocks and bonds) to buy the implements of production; the number and variety of tools and implements are, as we all know, astounding. Labor becomes highly specialized and increasingly skilled; and it sells itself in a market, like any other good or commodity. Entrepreneurship is accomplished by highly complex arrangements: the state and law, large-scale and complex market systems, bureaucracies and factories, and corporations as a way of pooling capital, labor, and technology in the pursuit of profits.

This transformation of the economy is often viewed as an Industrial Revolution, with capital letters, because it fundamentally changed the organization of not only the economy but all other social structures and the content of culture. The revolution began in England when James Watt introduced the steam engine, which was hundreds of times more powerful than human and animal power. With this new source of energy, machines could be driven. In turn, machine-driven factories pulled workers into urban communities to sell their labor power for money (but not much) in a labor market. With factories, machines, and labor could come mass production of so many more goods and products that generated so much wealth (and poverty for workers), that the old landed aristocracy lost much of its hold on power. The result was for government to move toward a more democratic profile, especially as the new merchant classes and industrial workers began to demand some influence on political decisions. With more to produce and distribute, more services were needed, which, in turn, expanded education. As more diverse kinds of economic activity unfolded, specialization increased as workers found ever smaller niches of employment. And with more wealth, needs for education, democracy, and complexity, government expanded; over time, new institutions like science and education grew and others like religion changed. All of these dramatic transformations occurred in the last 250 years; and so, it is not surprising that industrialization was seen as a revolution.

Growing out of industrialization was a quieter process, but a process no less revolutionary in how it influences people's lives. This quieter revolution is often termed post-industrialization.

Post-Industrial Economies

Post-industrial economies, like the one in which you and I participate, represent a shift in the nature of work. As technologies increase and are used to build new forms of capital like robotics, labor is increasingly organized around technological expansion, services, market activities, and decreasingly around manual labor. Hence, white-collar jobs come to outnumber blue-collar work; and once this threshold is passed, a society is **post-industrial.** With post-industrialization, markets and money become more dynamic and volatile, accelerating at a dizzying pace the flow of goods and services on a world scale. Urbanization and suburbanization increase as work is organized into bureaucratic structures that pool workers, and in the process, create new markets for service organizations that pull more workers in urban areas. The state and government increase their functions to control and regulate the complexity of the economy. Education expands as professional and technical credentials are needed for the new service-oriented white collar jobs. This shift in the nature of work can be seen in Figure 17.1 where the relative percentage of works in farm, blue-collar and white-collar jobs is summarized for the last century and in Figure 17.2 where the decline in manufacturing jobs is reported the last decades.

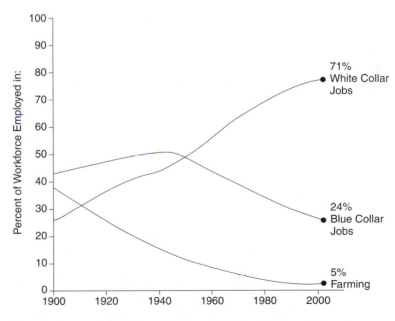

Figure 17.1   Relative Percentages of Labor Force in Farm, White-Collar, Blue-Collar Jobs in the United States
Source: Statistical Abstracts (1999, Table 677) and (2003, 579).

Some have argued that another revolution is now occurring, the Information Revolution made possible by the computer and technologies that can store, retrieve, send, and array information at incredible speeds. Yet, from another perspective, information technologies only accelerate the employment of people in nonmanual and professional white-collar jobs, and so, they can be seen as part of post-industrialism. Of course, 50 years down the road when I am gone and you are old, we may look back and see the invention of the computer as more revolutionary.

Another way to view post-industrialization is in the shift in the amount of capital and work force devoted to the **primary sector** revolving around extracting resources and raw materials from the environment, the **secondary sector** that converts raw materials from the environment, and the **tertiary sector** that involves the provision of services to members of a population. In a sense, the evolution of the economy has gone from the primary through the secondary to the tertiary sectors. The key point is that more and more of the labor force is employed in the tertiary sector during post-industrialization.

Trends in Post-Industrial Economies

Reorganization of Production

The hallmark of the industrial economy was the factory system where machines and labor were coupled to produce a commodity. The factory does not go away with post-industrialization, but it does become more automated through the combination of computers and robotics. Fewer workers are needed in such factories, which is one reason that the proportion of blue-collar workers declines. This decline has important consequences for class stratification because these well-paying blue-collar jobs cannot serve as the first stepping stone for people who try to move up the class system; there simply are not enough jobs available for all those who need them. Moreover, as labor costs increase in post-industrial societies, along with taxes and governmental regulation, factory work is often exported to poor nations whose work force is docile and desperate and whose governments are willing to tolerate workplace abuses and environmental degradation. As a result, fewer high-paying factory jobs remain for the workers of post-industrial societies.

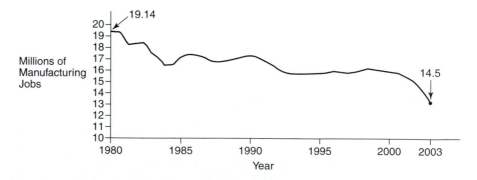

Figure 17.2   The Decline of Manufacturing Jobs in the United States, 1979–2003
Source: Department of Labor Statistics (2003).

Factories have increasingly become places where modules made in other factories are put together into a final product. For example, more and more of a car is being made by sub-contractors who build platforms, sheet metal panels, seats and dashes, electrical grids, and other features of a car; these are shipped "just in time" to a larger factory where they are all put together by computer-guided machines with human attendants. Moreover, although the big factory still exists for large and complex items like a car, an increasing number of factors are small and use high technology, making either components for larger factories or products for relatively small niches, such as finished rolled steel, electronic materials, furniture, and various specialty items that cannot be produced in a cost-effective manner by a large factory.

Production of Services

What distinguishes a post-industrial economy, however, is not just the changes in the factory system but the increasing production of services, such as educating, administering, banking, brokering, insuring, accounting, advertising, managing, repairing, moving, distributing, wholesaling, and many other services. These services (a) allow workers to acquire the skills they need; (b) enable computers, machines, and people to work together; (c) facilitate the organization of other productive activities; (d) sell and distribute products; (e) create new technologies; and (f) provide many other services needed to extract resources, covert them to goods and commodities, and sell them in markets.

In post-industrial economies, government becomes a larger employer because it is necessary to coordinate and control activities in a complex society through police, laws, courts, and a larger number of regulatory agencies. It is also necessary to create and staff public school systems. The result is that the proportion of the workforce providing services in government increases.

The bureaucratization of activities in other institutional systems also increases the production of services and, hence, the white-collar workforce. Schools—from primary through universities—need teachers and administrative support personnel, as noted earlier. But other institutional systems such as medicine, science, sports, and religion are organized to provide services; the larger the organizations providing these services become, the more administrators and support personnel are needed to organize production and distribution.

Leisure time, recreation, and sports all expand as forms of economic activity in post-industrial societies. All of these products are heavily skewed toward service workers of various kinds. Add to these products those of the entertainment industry—from movies and computer games to Broadway shows and television—and the production of services expands by millions of workers in a society as large as the United States.

Complex economic activity dramatically increases the level of professionalization. Education becomes a "big business" in providing knowledge and credentials for those who will be key players in diverse institutional spheres—lawyers and judges in law, doctors and nurses in medicine, researchers in science, teachers in schools, priests and other professionals in religion, and so on for virtually all kinds of activity that involves the production and distribution of a service. The production of services thus increases the rate of professionalization that, in turn, increases the production of services.

At times it almost seems as if people do not make things any more. They provide services in larger organizations that produce other services or that produce hard goods in factories driven by computers and machines. Yet, factories still need workers; many jobs—from housecleaning and janitorial work to taking orders and cooking hamburgers in fast food outlets—must be done by manual labor. The big change is that much of the manual labor in post-industrial societies now pays very little, thereby increasing inequality for those who get stuck in these low-end blue-collar jobs.

Expansion of Markets

We are so used to markets using money and credit that it is easy to forget what a recent revolution they represent. Markets are only a few thousand years old, and the first ones revolved around barter. But, over the last 3,000 years, money and credit became part of markets, allowing people to express their preferences with a medium—money—that could buy any good or service, provided one had enough. Credit slowly eased its way into market transactions, allowing people to buy when they did not have all of the money. And today, the credit card or "plastic" drives the economy as people mortgage their future earnings by buying on credit.

Once an economy is freed from the constraints of barter, where one good (like a chicken) is exchanged for another (like a candle), the expansion of the economy can begin to accelerate. In barter, one must find a producer (let's say of candles) who needs another good (say, a chicken); this matching up of what people have to exchange is inherently limiting. But, with money and credit, this limitation is blown away; people can now express their preferences for any good that, in turn, creates demand for producers who seek new niches where they can sell products. As a result, not only does the volume of goods produced increase, but the varieties of commodities increase. In post-industrial societies, demand in the market place (as it stimulates the production of a greater number and variety of goods) is manipulated by advertising so that people's needs for goods never wane. Thus, people come to want more and more as their appetites are stimulated by slick advertising, with the result that these new appetites translate into demand, causing an increase in production.

With post-industrialism, markets become global. Trade among nations has always existed, ever since there were nations. But the nature of global markets has been transformed with new transportation and communication technologies. Money can now move in seconds in financial markets to virtually any place in the world. Vast quantities of goods can be shipped in containers and offloaded by computer-driven machines in hours rather than days. Indeed, the container is what makes the import of goods from China and other low costs producers so profitable because the container can be stacked on a ship, moved across the ocean, and unloaded by a computerized inventory system attached to a crane in just a few days. People can fly about the globe in hours rather than months, selling, buying, and providing services. And computer networks make all phases of business—from accounting, warehousing, and keeping inventory through advertising, selling, and buying to designing and financing—almost instantaneous on a global scale.

Now virtually anything can become a commodity, as postmodernists have emphasized. Any thing, person, physical object, piece of information, or symbol can be bought and sold in a market. In a sense, nothing is sacred; if enough people with money or credit want it, it can be extracted, packaged, marketed, and sold. There is, then, a **commodification** of the world occurring right before our eyes. We can buy the symbols of another culture, such as its sacred texts or clothing; we can buy any object from plutonium to Harley-Davidson motorcycles in just about any place in the world; we can buy any service from prostitution to computer servicing; we can buy people, from overseas adoptions to marriage partners, just about any where; and we can buy information in most places. Just how far this trend goes is hard to guess, but in just 50 years, global markets and commodification have transformed the societies of the world.

Hyperdifferentiation

It is obvious that activity in the economy and elsewhere is becoming more specialized. We occupy specialized positions in specialized organizations within a specialized niche in the economy. This partitioning of social life has, postmodernists would argue, a counterintuitive outcome: a dedifferentiation. How can **hyperdifferentiation** create its opposite? The argument goes like this, and I will leave it to you to see if it resonates with your experience. The idea is that the more the world is partitioned, the less powerful are the boundaries between specialized activities. In simpler societies, differentiation imposed often impenetrable boundaries—a peasant did not become a lord, a mason, a priest, or an artisan a blacksmith because these divisions meant something and entrance into them was jealously guarded. But, these days anyone can proclaim themselves a religious leader and get a following; people enter many professions with an online degree from a virtual university; people can move from social class to social class and, indeed, the goal of life is to better one's class position; and so on for the weakened partitions of a complex, post-industrial society.

Hyperrationality

The hallmark of bureaucracies is rationality: activities are organized to coordinate them in an efficient manner to get something done, from winning a war to making a product. Recall Max Weber's "ideal type" of bureaucracy reviewed in Chapter 11. This kind of rationality has penetrated just about all spheres of activity in post-industrial societies. Concern is with speed, efficiency, cost-benefits, and profits—often to the exclusion of other criteria, such as morality, human dignity, or community. Moreover, **hyperrationality** depersonalizes the world and leads to what George Ritzer (2004) termed the "production of *nothing*" by which he means standardized, centrally controlled, and mass produced goods that lack any uniqueness or individuality. In contrast, the production of *something* involves locally produced goods that are unique. Fast food is perhaps the best example of the production of nothing because the food is the same the world over, but everywhere one looks, it is possible to see rationalization taken to the extreme so that unique, individually produced, and local manufacturers are blown out of business. For example, Wal-Mart is a chain of big box stores that look the same wherever you go, selling mass produced goods; despite having a "greeter" at the entrance and requiring that employees always ask if "you need help," Wal-Mart sells goods in a rather impersonal way (but also at a cheap price). Wal-Mart is, in fact, perhaps one of the most rational companies on earth—with its sophisticated inventory systems, just in time warehousing, rapid distribution system where goods come in on one side of a warehouse and go out the other, and in so many other innovative ways. It is also driving local business and retail outlets to bankruptcy. When what we buy is depersonalized in this way, people become—so many postmodernists would argue—zombies, going to their big box store and buying the same goods in the same way. The fact that people like this shopping experience can, depending on your point of view, be either a good or bad thing.

One irony of hyperrationalization is that it is often irrational. That is, efficiency can break down. For example, a fast food restaurant, designed to get you in and out rapidly and efficiently, is hardly rapid or efficient at the lunch hour when long lines can develop. Wal-Mart is no fun on a busy Saturday. Thus, trying to make organizations super-efficient can often lead to inefficiencies because the organization only knows "one way" of doing things and cannot be sufficiently flexible when its environment changes.

Post-Industrial Economies: An Overview

What, then, can we predict as the trend toward post-industrialization continues. First, globalization will continue with the gathering of resources, production of goods and services, and distribution involving interrelations among nations. Second, the production of services will continue to accelerate, with the production of goods and commodities moving outside a country's borders in search of the lowest-priced labor. Third, the production of services will also move outside the more mature and high-salaried countries to developing nations like those in eastern Europe, China, India, and other parts of south Asia. Third, mass marketing and retailing will continue driving smaller businesses into insolvency, but at the same time, create niches for businesses that can meet people's needs for unique goods and services. Fourth, the hierarchies of traditional bureaucracies may break down into more horizontal structures among educated professionals who need flexibility to meet corporate needs. Hierarchy will remain and be supplemented by the control of computer-driven machines in factory work. Fifth, large corporations will continue to operate globally and will increasingly be out of the reach of governmental control and regulation in the nation in which they are chartered. Sixth, labor and capital will continue to move about the world rapidly. Capital will seek low-priced labor, whereas labor will try to migrate where capital has been invested in manufacturing facilities. Migration, both legal and illegal, will thus accelerate. Seventh, the labor force will increasingly be split between the better-educated, higher-skilled, and better-paid sector, on the one side, and the less educated, lower-skilled, and poorly-paid blue-collar worker on the other. As a result, inequalities within post-industrial nations will thus increase. And finally, because of the interconnectedness of the world economy, the potential for a global economic meltdown in production will put pressures on corporations and governments to find new, world-level forms of economic governance of markets, corporations, and governments.

The American Economy

The American economy is post-industrial; hence, its labor force is increasingly non-manual. And, as you know, there is a credentials race—indeed credential inflation—for individuals like you trying to become certified as competent to do certain kinds of non-manual jobs (Collins 1979). College students are, in essence, getting ready to sell themselves in a highly competitive labor market. Conflict theories would emphasize that this fact of life sets up an inherent tension among people, as they fight and compete for credentials and jobs in companies that seek their services for as low a wage or salary as possible.

Such jobs are located in profit and nonprofit corporations as well as governmental organizations, all of which are organized to varying degrees as bureaucratic structures. Relatively few of you will be in a family business, or working alone; you will be lodged in groups within complex organizations of some sort. Corporations in America are private, owned by families or more commonly by stockholders and, unfortunately in many cases, by anxious creditors. They compete with each other within local, regional, national, and increasingly, world markets. One's fate in corporations—whether as a blue-collar worker or white-collar employee—will depend on how the corporation performs in these markets. With the dramatic expansion of world economic activity and the movement of corporations to all parts of the world, economic life for most individuals will be insecure because of the intensity of the competition. If a person works in government, or perhaps as a paid professional in a voluntary organization, his or her security will depend upon either tax revenues or contributions, both of which are tied to the success of corporations in domestic and international markets as well as on the taxable income of workers in these corporations. Because the need for government services is constantly expanding, despite ideological preachings against inefficient government bureaucrats, a significant portion of the workforce is involved in providing government services. Yet, for the foreseeable future, the majority of the American workforce will not be employed in either large corporations or in government but, rather, in small businesses that are particularly vulnerable to both domestic and world system competition and economic cycles. Certain trends are clearly evident in this mix of organizational structures (Turner and Musick 1985).

Oligopoly

One trend is toward **oligopoly** where a relatively few corporations produce a particular good or service and control the market for this good or service. Corporations try to control their environments so that they will not be hurt by competition over prices that, in turn, will lower profits. Karl Marx predicted that there would be a "falling rate of profit" as companies competed with each other to the point that they could not make a profit, thus sending capitalism into an economic tailspin that would lead to a revolution. Corporations often avoid this problem by buying out their competition, or by merging, in ways that allow them to control a large segment of a market and, thereby, set prices that increase profits. For example, in the major industrial sectors, such as automobiles, aluminum, chemicals, steel, accounting, stocks and bonds, advertising, radio and television, entertainment, and big box mass retailing, relatively few corporations control the market. This trend is likely to continue, as corporations in key markets become larger and more dominant.

Multinationalization of Corporations

Corporations are increasingly becoming **multinational**, seeking to maximize profits by using the capital and labor of foreign countries and by selling goods and services in these countries. Conversely, foreign corporations sell many goods and services in the United States and, in some industries like automobiles, have set up factories in the United States. Although such factories provide wages for workers, the profits are sent back to their country of origin and do not circulate in the domestic economy. Moreover, by setting up factories in the United States, foreign companies are in a better position to outcompete domestic companies, especially because these corporations tend to hire non-union workers.

Even if a foreign company does not set up a factory in the United States, many domestic markets are becoming dominated by companies chartered in other nations. For example, consumer electronics (outside of computers), such as television, cameras, video equipment, and video games are very much dominated by foreign companies. As a result, domestic companies have trouble entering these markets, forcing workers who might have jobs in these industries to look elsewhere.

Table 17.1   Estimated Numbers of High-Skill Jobs Moving Offshore[a] from the United States

Type of Economic Activity	Number of Jobs	
	2005	**2010**
Life sciences	3,700	37,000
Art, design	6,000	30,000
Legal/law	14,000	75,000
Sales	29,000	227,000
Architecture	32,000	184,000
Management	37,000	288,000
Business operations	61,000	348,000
Computers	109,000	473,000
Office support	295,000	1,700,000
Total loss of jobs	588,000	3,3000,000

[a] To India, Mexico, China, Taiwan, and the Philippines.
Source: Business Week, August 24, 2003, 38.

Although American companies do a significant amount of business overseas, the tendency is to outsource to other countries many administrative, engineering, and marketing services to nations with lower priced labor. The result is that many white-collar and professional jobs are being exported. Moreover, manufacturing corporations—from shoes and apparel to most electronics—now use inexpensive foreign labor to produce goods that are marketed under American brand names in the United States. Thus, jobs are exported for the production of the very goods that domestic workers must buy.

Declining Union Membership

As the proportion of workers in white-collar jobs has increased, union membership among blue-collar workers has declined. This dramatic trend, as documented in Figure 17.3, is the result of more than the shift from blue to white-collar service jobs in a post-industrial economy. It is also the outcome of the trends summarized earlier. Foreign corporations often seek to avoid hiring unionized workers. Domestic corporations are outsourcing manufacturing jobs to other countries. And, corporations can threaten to outsource work to other countries as a way of breaking a union or as a bargaining ploy to achieve wage concessions. All of these forces combined have made companies, and often workers themselves, reluctant to be unionized. The result is for wages and benefits for union workers to go down, except in a few select industries.

Professionalization

As a post-industrial economy, many jobs have become professionalized in America, requiring specific levels of education and credentials to per-

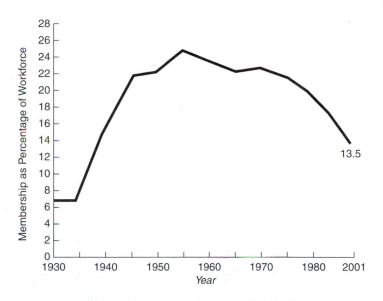

Figure 17.3   Union Membership 1930–2000
Source: U.S. Department of Labor, *Handbook of Labor Statistics,* (Washington, DC: U.S. Government Printing Office, 1983), p. 137. Statistical Abstracts (2003, Table 630).

form certain kinds of work. Increasingly, however, professional work is being bureaucratized in larger corporations, with the result that professionals must at times compromise their "professionalism" for corporate bottom lines. For example, Health Maintenance Organizations (HMOs) have changed the way doctors and hospitals work. When an HMO actually owns a clinic or hospital, it operates as a business, assessing care against cost; even if the HMO only operates as an insurer, it will provide only so much money per procedure, thus forcing compromises in health care. The accounting scandals of the last decade in corporate America—Enron and Worldcom being the best examples—are the result of big accounting firms compromising professionalism in the name of profits. Even universities must now compete for corporate dollars in ways that often bias their research and teaching missions. Thus, professionalization will continue but professionals will not be as free to use their expertise as more and more professionals work in large, profit-oriented corporations.

Government and the Economy

Despite powerful ideologies arguing for free and unregulated markets, government will always be involved in regulating many aspects of the economy. A capitalist economy is oriented to profits, with the result that controls on environmental pollution, worker safety and health, and other "costs" will be avoided unless government steps in and forces the issue. Moreover, accounting practices, fraud, volatile stock markets, misrepresentations, price gouging by oligopolies, and other inevitable outcomes of free markets must be regulated in some way. Similarly, the supply of money and credit must be regulated to control inflation or deflation. Thus, a large complex economy requires external regulation by the state; this is one of the main reasons that government becomes so large in post-industrial economies.

As government increases in size, individuals and corporate actors must be taxed to pay the salaries of governmental employees. Taxation is always a hot-button issue in a society, particularly the United States, with the result that economic actors almost always push for laws relieving them of some taxes and for cutting back governmental agencies that regulate them. The result is a cycle in which regulation is pushed back, only to have abuses and problems emerge that force re-regulation. This kind of cyclical dialectic between actors in government and the economy is inevitable.

Growing Inequality

As we saw in Chapter 13, inequality in income has been increasing over the last decade. Much of this increase is the result of the splitting of the labor force that, increasingly, is composed of a larger, low-wage sector and a higher-wage blue-collar and white-collar sector. Coupled with a large poverty sector, the gap between the affluent and less affluent is growing. The result is that a very large proportion of the American population must work for low wages without benefits like health care and retirement. This segment of the labor force will not only pose a problem today but as they age, they will create additional burdens in the future as they seek income and medical care in their declining years. This problem is particularly noticeable in the United States because of: the relatively low levels of taxation on corporations and individuals (compared to other industrial and post-industrial societies), the decline in union membership where workers would have higher wages and benefits, the export of jobs to cheaper labor pools that once provided good wages and benefits, and the general lack of sympathy of the affluent for the poor.

Increasing Risk for Workers

Another trend evident in the American economy is the increasing assumption of risk by workers. As corporations are squeezed to reduce their costs in competitive markets, they increasingly seek to unburden themselves from managing retirement systems and health care for their workers. Defined-benefit retirement systems, where workers are guaranteed certain income levels and health benefits based on their job classification and years of service, are rapidly disappearing. And the few industries that still have them—older legacy airlines, automobile companies, and some steel companies—are seeking to reduce benefits. Indeed, the costs of these programs now threaten the survival of many companies in a market where their competitors do not have to pay defined retirement benefits. In fact, some companies have deliberately gone into bankruptcy to shed their retirement and health care obligations. In 1979 for example, almost 40% of workers had some kind of defined benefit retirement program; by 2001, only 20% had such retirement programs. The result is for workers to assume greater risks for their future retirement and health care. Many companies simply outsource jobs to other companies that do not provide health care or retirement benefits beyond Social Security (which will go bankrupt itself within 40 years); other companies create various matching retirement accounts in which employers and employees each contribute a certain amount, with the management of the account left *to the worker* rather than the company. If workers do not put enough aside during their working years, they will be hard pressed when they get older; and if the Medicare program becomes too costly for government, retirees may not have adequate health care as they get older.

Accompanying this increased risk is a decline in real wages for many workers. In constant dollars, the minimum wage was $7.48 per hour in 1978 (in its actual purchasing power), whereas it is $5.15 per hour today. Virtually all of these workers, if they make any contribution at all to retirement, do so through the Social Security system (many work "off the books" and, hence, make no contribution to Social Security). At $5.15 per hour, it is impossible to save or to take out health care insurance; and so, all of these workers assume much greater risks now and in the future when they retire.

There has been political pressure in recent years to "privatize" some portion of Social Security, giving workers the right to manage some of their Social Security contributions. But, given the relative ignorance of most Americans about financial investments, privatization could lead to more financial difficulty down the road. Even when privatizing is labeled with highly appealing phrases like "the ownership society," it involves a large transfer of risks from government to individual. Thus, as both government and industry shift risks to individuals, people's futures will be more uncertain as they take on more risk. And, to the extent that global competition forces companies in all societies to reduce costs to remain competitive, both government and industry may be forced to continue transferring risks to workers.

SUMMARY

1. Social institutions are congeries of positions and social structures that seek to resolve fundamental problems of humans as a species, especially as a species that must rely upon culture and social organization to survive in its environment. Because of their importance, most of the general norms guiding behavior in institutional structures are well known and infused with values and beliefs.

2. The economy is the institution that organizes technology, labor, and material capital for gathering of resources from the environment, converting these resources through production into usable goods and commodities, and distributing these goods and commodities to members of the society. Hunting and gathering, horticulture, agrarianism, industrialism, and post-industrialism are, thus far, the basic forms of economic organization during the course of human history. The historical trend has been for the distribution of labor to shift from the primary sector (gathering) to secondary sector (producing) and, finally, to tertiary sector (servicing) of the economy.

3. During post-industrialization, production is reorganized in new kinds of factories that use computers and machines to make goods and commodities; services become an increasingly important product; markets expand the volume, variety, and scale of distribution; hyperrationality or the concern for efficiency and profit maximization increases; hyperdifferentiation or the partitioning of activities into ever greater specialties accelerates; and commodification or the conversion of more and more objects into marketable goods increases.

4. The American economy is well into post-industrialism and reveals a number of trends: the formation of oligopolies where a few corporations dominate a market, the growth of multinational corporations chartered here and spreading overseas as well as foreign corporations doing business in the United States, the use of government to regulate the economy in key areas, the growing inequality in the incomes of the labor force, and the increased assumption of risks by workers.

KEY TERMS

Capital: Implements of economic production and the money used to purchase these implements.

Commodification: Process whereby any object, person, or symbol can be converted into a good that can be bought and sold in a market.

Economy, Institution of: Organization of technology, capital, and labor into structures for the purpose of gathering natural resources, producing goods and services, and distributing these goods and services to members of a society.

Entrepreneurship: Organizational forms and capacities that coordinate technology, capital, and labor.

Human Capital: Another way to designate labor as an element of the economy.

Hyperdifferentiation: Increasing specialization of all activities into more narrow sets of activities.

Hyperrationalization: Increasing emphasis on efficiency, speed, and cost-benefit concerns.

Industrialization: Process of harnessing fossil fuels to machines attended by labor for the purpose of gathering resources, producing goods, and distributing commodities.

Labor: Persons performing economic activities.

Multinational Corporation: Company chartered for business in one country that does business in other countries.

Oligopoly: Domination of a market sector by a few dominant companies.

Post-Industrialization: Change from an industrial economy where a majority of the work force is employed in the manufacturing of hard goods and commodities to one where the majority of the work force is employed in providing services.

Primary Sector: That portion of the economy involved in gathering resources from the environment.

Secondary Sector: That portion of the economy devoted to the conversion of raw materials into goods and products (production).

Technology: Systems of symbols organized into knowledge about how to manipulate the environment.

Tertiary Sector: That portion of the economy involved in providing services.

Chapter 18

Government

Emergence of Polity

For most of human history, bands of hunter-gatherers wandered a territory without the need for leaders who could tell others what to do. At times, perhaps, leaders would emerge if there was conflict with another band or if other problems arose that required close coordination of people. The few bands of hunter-gatherers who survived into the last century were reluctant to give anyone too much authority. They might give another prestige, but not the power to tell them how they had to act; and indeed, they would ridicule anyone who thought they were better than others. A few hunter-gatherer populations, such as the Australian aborigines, did have political leaders and, in fact, engaged in conflict with bands in neighboring territories. Conflict clearly is a condition that generates needs for leaders who can coordinate others to fight, although some argue that aborigines represent former horticulturalists who brought conflict and leaders with them when they migrated across the land bridge that once connected New Guinea with Australia. Still, with the exception of aborigines in Australia, most hunter-gatherers do not appear to have had even the rudiments of government. Thus, for almost all of human history, government or polity did not exist.

Why would people subordinate themselves to leaders who would wield power over them? The answer is simple: they had little choice as their numbers grew. As populations began to grow, social life could no longer be organized informally or around kinship relations in small bands. Leaders who could tell others what to do were necessary to coordinate activities and, if necessary, control deviance and conflict. Once this step was taken, government was born; and there was no looking back to the generally noncoercive relations among hunters-gatherers (Carneiro 1970; Fried 1967; Lenski 1966; Lenski, Lenski and Nolan, 1991; Maryanski and Turner 1992; J. Turner 1972, 1997, 2003).

Basic Elements of All Polities

All political systems are based upon the consolidation and application of **power,** or the capacity of one set of actors to direct the behaviors of others. This power is lodged in **leaders** who make binding decisions on members of society and who direct societal activity. Leaders are on top of an *administrative structure* that carries out the decisions of leaders and that monitors as well as enforces conformity to directives. Thus, at its most basic core, government consists of the mobilization of power by leaders who direct activities in a society through an administrative structure.

Bases of Power

At the most general level, there are four **bases of power** (J. Turner 1995, 2003): (a) the use of *coercion* or physical force, (b) the use of *symbols* and ideologies, (c) the organization of *administrative* controls, and (d) the *manipulation of material incentives*. Let me elaborate on each of these here.

1. Coercive Base of Power. Political leaders always seek to gain the ability to coerce or physically force others to do what they want. Actual coercion is often unnecessary because the threat of physical force is often sufficient to get others to act. Coercion as a base of power can be very effective in the short run, but if leaders rely too much on coercion, resentments build and eventually people will begin to fight back. Moreover, once coercion is the primary base of power, it costs a great deal to keep it going: people must be constantly monitored, a standing force loyal to leaders must be supported, and administrative structures must be elaborated to keep tabs on who is doing what and to imprison or kill those who fail to conform. Still, Joseph Stalin killed perhaps as many as 20 million people in Russia over decades with little fear of retaliation; and it took an invasion of the United States to remove the leader of Iraq, who based much of his power on coercion. Thus, coercive power can work for many decades.

2. Symbolic Base of Power. People can be moved by symbols organized into ideologies. When the symbolic base of power is used, leaders make appeals to cultural traditions, religious beliefs, history, laws, constitutions, emblems like flags, and virtually any symbol that has the power to move people. Often, leaders who use symbols effectively are *charismatic* in their ability to mobilize people's passions with ideologies. For example, in Iran after the revolution of 1979, the clerics very effectively mobilized religious symbols to legitimate their hold on power; and it is only recently that this hold seems to be eroding. Similarly, if the United States did not have forces in Iraq, there is little doubt that the clerics would use religious symbols to take power.

The symbolic base of power does not, however, have to be part of a revolutionary scenario. Political leaders are given *legitimacy* by symbols that assert, in essence, their right to make binding decisions on others. These legitimating symbols can be much more low key than a religious belief system, as is the case when constitutions and law give leaders the right to regulate the conduct of others. For leaders' hold on power to endure, then, they must cultivate symbolic power and be seen as having the legitimate right to lead.

3. Administrative Base of Power. Control of others can occur through administrative structures. When leaders set up structures for carrying out their orders and for monitoring conformity, this power to monitor and control greatly enhances their power. They need not use power themselves; rather, functionaries in the administrative system exercise power for them; once a large-scale administrative structure is in place, the ability to rule a society is dramatically expanded. Large projects can be undertaken; taxes can be collected; police and military can be organized; agencies for specific tasks can be created; and in general, the ability to do more things is enhanced.

Not only does an administrative structure become a useful tool for leaders to implement their decisions, but once in place, the structure itself also becomes a source of power. The administrators become powerful because they have a structure that can tell others what to do and that can monitor conformity, often without the knowledge of the top leaders. This power can be abused, but often the administrative system is the only source of political stability in societies that undergo periodic revolutions, as was the case for France in the eighteenth and nineteenth centuries or as it has been during the chaotic aftermath of the breakup of the old Soviet Union.

4. Material Incentive Base of Power. People can be encouraged to do what leaders desire through the manipulation of material incentives. If orders are followed, material rewards are offered; if they are not followed, material resources are taken away. All leaders ultimately begin to tax their population, taking their surplus resources and, then, selectively giving them back to induce conformity. Of course, a great deal is skimmed off the top to support elite privilege, but leaders will almost always try to bestow or withhold material benefits to control members of a population.

In contemporary societies, incentives are usually offered as subsidies to encourage certain kinds of activity; or as tax incentives (i.e., tax breaks) to do the same thing. Or, often government purchases products from certain producers to subsidize their operation—as is the case when the government chooses one defense contractor over another. Thus, through a variety of means, government increasingly relies on incentives to get people to do what it wants.

These four bases of power are all used by governments, but in different proportions or configurations. When coercion is used, this base of power is usually accompanied by an extensive administrative bureaucracy that organizes coercive force, that monitors conformity to dictates, and that punishes those who do not conform. **Totalitarianism**, for example, relies heavily on the coercive and administrative bases of power. A more democratic polity will still have coercive force and a large administrative structure, but it will rely much more on legitimating symbols (as enshrined in a constitution and laws) and on manipulation of incentives (tax breaks and subsidies) to get people and organizations to voluntarily "choose" to do what government wants.

Rise of the State

Ultimately, as government grows it becomes bureaucratically organized, and when this transformation has transpired, we can speak of the *state* (Weber 1922). The state is thus the most visible manifestation of the administrative base of power. At first, the bureaucracy was merged with kinship, but as more effective and efficient administrators were needed, if only to collect taxes, and as more efficient police and armies were required to maintain order and defense, pressures built for bureaucratic structures resembling Weber's ideal type portrayal, in Chapter 12.

Once the state is large, bureaucratic, and able to support itself, it can do more. It can construct more public works, engage in long-distance war, and administer more territory. And as a result, the scale of governmental activity increases and is limited only by two forces: the capacity of the economy to support it and the willingness of the population to accept it. Again and again in history, the state has bankrupt itself through patronage to elites and military adventurism (Goldstone 1990; Skocpol 1979), thereby making itself vulnerable to conquest by another, more powerful state or to an uprising by those angry with how they have been treated.

The *state* begins the bureaucratic organization of decision making. At first, the state apparatus—tax collectors, administrators, military, and police—is under a hereditary monarch whose power is typically legitimated by religion. This form of state is not a "rational" bureaucracy in Max Weber's terms because family ties and patronage are still prominent. It is the form of government in agrarian societies.

The modern, bureaucratic state emerges with industrialization, recruiting its members for their skill and expertise and, increasingly, democratically electing its key decision-making members. Religion recedes as the dominant legitimating symbols, being replaced by laws and, in most cases, a constitution as the principle bases of symbolic power.

Modern states vary along a number of important dimensions. One is the degree to which its bureaucracy is *rational,* recruiting and promoting people in terms of skills and performance. Another is the degree of **centralization** of power and decision making. In some states, power and decision making are concentrated, whereas in others power and decision making are more decentralized and dispersed. Still another variation is the extensiveness of state *intervention* into social life, with some states intervening in most spheres of social and economic life, as was the case with old communist societies of the last century where the state owned most property and set production quotas and prices for goods and services. In contrast, other states allow considerable autonomy to social and economic actors, as is the case in the United States; still other states fall between the American and old Soviet extremes, using state power to regulate much social life and, at the same time, not owning nor overly regulating economic units.

A critical point of variation in modern states is the degree of **democracy,** or the extent to which regular and free elections determine who are to be decision-making leaders, and for how long. In some societies, such as those in the old communist bloc countries and in some of their old members, democracy is at its early stages of development. By way of contrast, the degree of democracy is so high in many western European nations and in the United States that there is apathy about voting (especially among younger age groups).

Related to the degree of democracy is the *division of power.* All modern states have separate executive, legislative, and judicial branches of government, but the *autonomy* of these branches to make binding decisions varies. In some, the legislature and judiciary are heavily influenced by leaders in the executive branch, often being little more than rubber stamps. In others, there is more autonomy with elected legislatures and judges in the judiciary having independent powers to check and balance the executive branch and each other.

Still other variations in states are the degree of legitimacy and the need to resort to *coercion.* These two factors tend to be related: state systems with low legitimacy or a weak base of symbolic power must rely on

coercive force, or the threat of force, whereas those systems high in legitimacy can usually—though not always—achieve compliance by appeals
to symbols and by manipulation of material incentives. But force is often
necessary even in highly legitimate state systems when particular decisions are defined as illegitimate by some—as has been the case in America over issues such as school integration, busing, abortion, and other
issues on which the population is polarized. Thus, states vary in what we
might call generalized or *diffuse legitimacy* where the basic structure and
operation of the state is considered appropriate, even when there is disagreement with particular decisions by the state.

Trends in Governmental Organization

Once humans created government, there was no turning back. On the
negative side of government is the control and regulation that ensues.
Moreover, as all conflict theories emphasize, power is used to extract the
resources of the many for the privilege of the few. As power became consolidated in the evolution of human societies, inequality increased, at
least up to the current industrial and postindustrial eras (Lenski 1966).
On the positive side, government enables a society to do more things
that often improve standards of living. As government expands, so does
its capacity to encourage new kinds of economic outputs, build schools
and generally expand education, finance medical care for the masses,
build transportation and communication infrastructures, provide welfare
to the poor, subsidize housing, and do many things that are not easily
done without government.

As government has expanded with industrialization and postindustrialization, some trends are evident. These are not universal or even inevitable, but if we look at governments around the world, there are
nonetheless some common events occurring in the organization of the
four bases of power: (a) the growing scale of the administrative base, (b)
the bureaucratization of the administrative base around rational-legal authority, (c) the centralization of the four bases of power, (d) the use of
law as a symbolic base of power, (e) more reliance on material incentives,
(f) somewhat less reliance on coercion, and (g) democratization. Let me
briefly review these trends, again emphasizing that they are only trends
rather than inevitabilities.

Growing Scale of Government

As the population, economy, and territory of a society grow, so does government. There is more to regulate, control, and coordinate; and so, it is
inevitable that the size and scale of government will increase. Although
people often resent this growth in government, especially paying taxes to
support government officials, there is no alternative to a large-scale government. There are simply too many problems that need to be addressed,
and government is the only way that humans can deal with these problems. Let me offer a partial list of problems requiring government: crime
and deviance; building of roads, ports, and airports; financing of education; monitoring of professional ethics in professions such as medicine
and law; providing support for the poor; building up national defense;
making sure that contracts are enforced; regulating potential abuses in

markets, labor-management relations, factories, and health care facilities; monitoring and controlling environmental degradation; and so the list could go for several pages. There is no real alternative to government if this abbreviated list of problems is to be addressed. Like it or not, government will continue to grow.

Bureaucratization of Government

To organize large-scale activities, bureaucracies had to be invented; and it was in the realm of government that many of the first bureaucratic organizations appeared (although large-scale religion was also instrumental in creating bureaucracy). Winning wars, collecting taxes, funding and building public works, policing, developing a court system, and many other tasks simply require more people who are organized to administer more tasks. Max Weber's portrayal of bureaucracies as the ultimate form of what he termed "rational-legal" domination is not far off the mark because governmental activities are increasingly organized in structures that reveal clear lines of authority, that have specialized functions and offices with a clear division of labor, that keep elaborate records, that have formal rules, that require technical competence, and that constitute careers for governmental employees. True, in some societies, family ties or religious affiliations intrude on the march of rational-legal authority; people's ethnicity, gender, and class background also can distort rationality; or their political and ideological leanings can also determine who will be allowed into the administrative bureaucracy. Still, as the tasks of government become more extensive and complex, there is a clear trend toward recruiting and promoting people on the basis of education and skill rather than on family, class, religion, ethnicity, gender, and other considerations. Even in highly totalitarian societies where nonrational considerations are important in who is at the top of the bureaucracy, more rational criteria (skill, education, and competence) guide the selection of personnel and the implementation of policies in the majority of positions of the state bureaucracy.

Centralization of Government

Even as government extends its influence into more and more activities, it is clear that there is a trend toward centralization of power. Increasingly, the executive branch of government directs activity in industrial and postindustrial societies, even those like the United States with a constitutionally mandated separation of power and a federalist system that decentralizes much power to states, counties, and communities. The reason for centralization is that some tasks simply need to be controlled from the top levels of the administrative base of power: military defense, funding of infrastructures, coordination of economic policy, financing of schools, welfare, healthcare, and other tasks. Of course, in more repressive regimes like China or Russia, power has been centralized for a long time; in these more totalitarian societies, there might actually be less centralization of power down the road. Yet, even as more totalitarian regimes loosen their grip on power, their bureaucracies will remain centralized and other branches of government (e.g., legal and legislative) will be coordinated by the top-level executives of a regime. And in more decentralized federalist systems like the United States, more power has shifted to the Executive Branch of the federal government over the last 75 years.

Importance of Law

As societies become more complex, problems of coordination and control escalate dramatically. There is simply more activity to coordinate, more conflicts to resolve, more people and organizations to control, more deviance to manage, and simply more activities requiring rules to regulate and courts to adjudicate. Indeed, without a well-developed legal system, societies can never become very large or complex. As law has become so essential to the operation of societies, it takes on more importance as a symbolic base of power. Rule by law rather than blatant coercion becomes essential if complex societies are to be dynamic. As a consequence, the most general legal tenets, often crafted into a constitution specifying rights and duties of government and citizens, become the principle source of legitimacy for the state. Leaders rule less and less by Divine Rights, except in a few Islamic societies, than by legal rights; and in being given the legal right to lead, these leaders must also honor obligations specified in the legal system. The legal system specifies the procedures by which leaders are to assume power (increasingly through elections), the limitations on their use (and abuse) of power, and the obligations that they have by virtue of having power. Leaders are given the right to rule as long as they abide by the rule of law; in this way, law legitimates their power, while providing the mechanism by which much of the actual coordination and control of activity in a society is carried out.

Increasing Reliance on Material Incentives

With industrialization and postindustrialization in capitalist systems, government does not try to micromanage economic activity, or even to own the means of economic production. Even in societies with a history of government ownership of companies, there is a clear tendency in the new global economy for governments to "sell off" their stakes in ownership, relying upon private sources of capital to fund the operation of companies and markets to determine the fate of companies. However, governments do seek to manage economic activity in a more macro sense along several fronts. They always attempt to regulate the money supply, especially those structures like banks and financial markets that influence the supply of money. Moreover, governments always have goals of productivity and economic growth that they seek to realize. And, governments have projects—from defense through health care and education to pollution control—that they finance with tax dollars. To regulate money, to achieve economic goals, and to implement projects, governments increasingly employ material incentives to get people and organizations to do what they want. They offer a tax break (or loopholes); they selectively spend money; they provide direct subsidies (to schools, airports, trains, defense contractors, and other actors); and in general they seek to guide activity in a certain direction by manipulating incentives. Material benefits go to those who move in the direction desired by government; penalties and other disincentives are placed on activities that are not considered desirable. The reason for this increasing reliance on incentives is that the complexity of activity in a society is simply too great to manage directly with administrative structures; and those societies in the industrial era that have sought to do so have paid the price of bloated and repressive governmental bureaucracies, economic stagnation, and restive populations.

Decline in Coercive Repression

Coercion is everywhere we look in the world—the middle East, China, south Asia, Latin America, and of course, right at home in the United States. Coercion is not going away because it is essential. But increasingly with postindustrialization, where the rule of law prevails and where material incentives are often sufficient to get actors to do what is desired, the constant application of coercion by a repressive state apparatus is less essential. Strategic and selective use of coercion rather than a constant repression is increasingly more evident, although coercion is still widely practiced in many societies. But, when coercion, coupled with the large administrative structure necessary to carry out coercive repression, is overused, societies become less dynamic. Productivity declines, resentments escalate, and fiscal crises become chronic, especially in an emerging global order.

Democratization

There are, of course, many repressive regimes where leaders are not elected or, if elected, the outcome of the election is a foregone conclusion. Yet, there is a slow and halting trend toward democracy evident in industrializing societies and in virtually all postindustrial societies. Those who make laws and who direct the administrative or executive branches of government are increasingly selected by competitive elections. Part of the reason for this trend is that capitalism with open and free markets allowing people to express their preferences and to choose what they will buy generates an ideology of choice, not just in markets but in the political arena as well. Also, capitalism cannot be highly dynamic without freedom from governmental constraint, a fact that works against totalitarian political regimes in the long run. Another part of the reason for democratization is that advanced postindustrial societies and their agents of development, such as the World Bank and International Monetary Fund, constantly put pressures on less developed regimes receiving loans to "democratize." Still another factor in the sporadic trend toward political democracy comes from the education of the population; as more and more people become educated and literate, they also become critical of political repression and desirous of more choice in their lives, although a highly oppressive regime can often educate and still repress criticism, as the Soviet Union and China did for so long or as many Islamic countries do right now. Still, education does broaden horizons that make people more interested in having some say in who governs them. Yet another force of democratization is globalization, at all levels. The Internet has made repression less effective, while opening new horizons to many in the world. The dynamism of world markets forces governments to loosen domestic markets if they want to be a player in the world economy. Economic development within repressive societies seeking to enter world markets requires the expansion of education that, in turn, increases pressures for democracy.

There will, no doubt, be countries that remain less democratic or that slide back into a more repressive regime. There is perhaps no "end of history" where democracy and capitalism prevail, but in the present, there is clearly a trend toward more democracy. People are having more and more say in who leads them.

Government in America

Government in the United States is, obviously, a modern bureaucratic state. The bureaucracy is rational, despite all of our grumbling about the inefficiencies of government bureaucrats. Power is relatively decentralized, although as we will see there has been a clear trend in the movement of power from local communities to the state governments, from state governments to the federal government, and within the federal government from the legislative and judiciary to the executive branch. State intervention in the economy is probably the lowest of an industrial or postindustrial society. Government is highly democratic, although special interests who finance campaigns and voter apathy are eroding the level of democracy. The division of powers among executive, legislative, and judiciary is still great, though declining. Diffuse legitimacy is high and enshrined in emotionally charged cultural symbols (e.g., the flag and the Constitution), though great controversy rages on particular issues. Reliance on coercion is low, although dissent on particular social issues as well as high rates of crime have forced the use of coercive force. Use of incentives through tax codes and other forms of subsidy is high. And, although the administrative structures of government are extensive, as they are in all industrial and postindustrial societies, they are not as extensive as in most other postindustrial societies.

Structure of American Government

As you all know, the United States is a *federalist system* with a division of powers among the Executive, Legislative, and Judiciary branches. This tri-part division exists at all levels of government: federal, state, county, and city. All offices in the legislative branches of government—from city councils and county boards of supervisors through state assemblies to the federal Congress are elected—whereas only some of the positions within the executive and judiciary branches of government are put to competitive voting. The highest level executives at the state and federal levels of the executive branch are elected—governor and various state-wide officers as well as the President at the federal level. At the local level, some mayors are elected, but others are appointed, and city managers are hired without electoral inputs; some judges at the city and county level are elected, although at the state and federal level they are appointed with approval from legislative bodies. Most heads of key agencies of government—the administrative base of power—are appointed by the executive branch, with approval from the legislative branch; and most of the bureaucrats under these appointed heads are career government workers.

Like governments all over the world, American government at city, county, state, and federal levels is growing as new problems and issues emerge. The system of government is more bureaucratized and centralized than 50 years ago. Key agents in the bureaucracy have more educational credentials and are more professional than they were a half-century ago. And, in general, there is less political corruption than in previous generations. Yet, despite these improvements in the efficiency and honesty of government, some enduring dilemmas persist.

Growth in Government

Most Americans believe that government has grown too large, and they perceive that it is the federal government that has grown the most. In fact, the opposite is the case: as is reported in Table 18.1, state and local governments have grown while the federal government has shrunk, as measured by the number of people employed by various levels of government. For example, the number of people at all levels of government increased by 20% between 1980 and 1999. Of course, the population also increased by about this much, and so, government employees as a percentage of the population that these employees serve has not increased very much. But, the number of federal employees declined from 2.9 million in 1980 (and 3.1 during the 1980s) to around 2.7 million employees in 1999, whereas state government employees rose from 13.3 in 1980 to 17.5 in 1999 and local governments (city, county municipalities) grew from 9.6 in 1980 to 12.7 million employees in 1999. This growth at the state and local level occurred in all political climates, whether Democratic or Republican. At the federal level of government, however, government declined under Democratic administrations and increased during Republican administrations—a fact that contradicts the political ideologies of the two parties.

Government and Taxation

Many Americans believe that they are "overtaxed." Indeed, any politician who proclaims a need for a "tax increase" is dead politically. But, few ask the question: Do Americans pay more in taxes than people in other economically developed countries? The answer is clearly "no" as is revealed in Table 18.2. These data were compiled by the Organization for Economic Cooperation and Development, one of the better sources of comparative data.

Table 18.1   Number of Employees in Government (in millions)

	Levels of Government		
Year	Number of Civilian Federal Employees	Number of State Employees	Number of Local Employees in City, County, and Municipal Governments
1999	2.7	17.5	12.7
1995	2.8	16.6	11.1
1990	3.1	15.3	10.1
1985	3.1	13.7	9.7
1980	2.9	13.3	9.6

Source: Statistical Abstracts (2003, Table 449).

Table 18.2 Total Tax Revenues to Government
in Developed Countries as a Percentage of
Gross Domestic Product

Sweden	52.0
Denmark	49.8
Finland	46.2
Belgium	45.9
France	45.2
Austria	44.4
Norway	43.6
Italy	42.7
Netherlands	41.0
Canada	37.4
United Kingdom	37.2
Germany	37.0
New Zealand	35.2
Switzerland	35.1
Ireland	32.2
Australia	29.9
United States	28.9
Japan	28.4

Source: Organization for Economic Cooperation and
Development (OECD; 2000, 67–68); see also Campbell
(2004, 140).

Table 18.2 rank orders the developed countries of Europe, plus
Japan, New Zealand, Australia, and the United States, on tax revenues
as a percentage of Gross Domestic Product (GDP), which is the best
way to compare the tax burden on a population. Because all of these societies have high levels of productivity and high levels of per capita income, taxes as a percentage of gross production is a good way to get a
sense for the relative tax burden on members of a society. As is evident,
the United States is second from the bottom on overall tax burden, just
above Japan but below all other developed countries in Europe, New
Zealand, and Australia.

Thus, Americans are not taxed more than other citizens in economically developed countries. It may still be that Americans do not want to
be taxed as much as others, and indeed, such appears to be the case. Yet,
without taxes, public services suffer; and so, Americans must accept that
if they do not want to pay taxes at the same rate as most other people in
developed countries around the globe, they will have few public services—
health care, transportation, welfare, police and fire protections, government jobs, libraries, quality schools, and other services that are funded
from tax revenues.

Problems and Dilemmas in American Government

Is There a Power Elite?.   At each level of government, it is clear that those with money and those who are well-organized exert more influence on political decisions than the poor and less well-organized. There is considerable debate within sociology and political science over whether or not decision making in America is dominated by a power elite or is more pluralistic. Let us start with the pluralism argument.

Pluralism argues that power is dispersed rather than concentrated. Power is concentrated in the hands of diverse interests, but these groups often have different goals. Moreover, their power is limited to the capacity to *veto,* or stop those political decisions that might hurt their interests. At the national level, such diverse interests as labor, oil, coal, steel, auto manufacturers, environmentalists, and national associations (like the American Medical Association and the National Rifle Association) organize to bring pressures on the president, heads of executive agencies, and members of Congress on particular issues that affect them (Kornhauser 1961; Rose 1967). This diversity of interests assures that no one power elite can dominate decision making. For example, the auto industry may not want to meet federal air-pollution standards, but the auto manufacturers will always face opposition from environmentalists.

At the community level, the same view prevails: diversified interest groups are meant to check and balance each other in influencing political decisions, thus making the political process pluralistic.

In contrast, **power elite** advocates argue that relatively few elites disproportionately control political decisions. In the 1950s, the late sociologist C. Wright Mills (1959) codified the elitist point of view by postulating a *power elite* at the national level of government. Mills visualized three interlocking elites that have common interests in what he called "military capitalism." These three elites included top military personnel, executives of large corporations, and powerful members of Congress. The power elite, he felt, is drawn from three sectors of the society— military, economic, and political.

Mills argued that the interests of these elites converged rather than diverged. Top military personnel, for example, have an interest in a large defense establishment; America's large corporations enjoy doing business with the Pentagon through lucrative defense contracts; politicians enjoy contributions from executives of corporations and profit from the prosperity created by military installations and defense industries in their districts.

However, more than common interest is involved, Mills argued. These elites circulate and establish many informal contacts. For instance, retired generals often go to work for defense contractors. Politicians become corporate lobbyists or executives. Administrators of regulatory agencies and cabinet officers go back and forth between government and industry. These elites thus know and come to depend upon each other. As a result, they are able to exert enormous political influence. Decisions in government, Mills believed, reflect the common interests and informal liaisons of these power elites.

Scholars such as William Domhoff (1967, 1978) have sought to extend Mills's analysis by exploring the way a small group of elites maintains its political power. Domhoff has sought to document how the social, economic, and political lives of the elites are interwoven. Marriage patterns, club memberships, common directorships on corporate boards, and residential proximity all operate to maintain the privilege of an upper elite that, in his words, "rules America."

At the community level, studies have questioned findings about a pluralistic decision-making process. Domhoff (1978), for example, found networks of elites that have a disproportionate influence on decision making. Similarly, in the 1950s Floyd Hunter (1953) examined Atlanta, GA and concluded that a group of about 40 "influentials" operating behind the scenes influenced political decisions.

Figure 18.1 summarizes the basic arguments in this long-term debate over "who rules America." In a very real sense, both lines of argument are correct. There is no doubt that there is an elite of wealthy people who own or manage America's large corporations and who, in concert with military leaders and key members of Congress, exert a disproportionate influence on political decision. At the same time, the interests of these elite individuals do not always correspond, often putting them in competition with each other. Moreover, there are other interest organizations that exert considerable political influence—some unions, professional groups like teachers associations and lawyers, environmental organizations, associations of government employees, gun owners, and others who are not elites, either as individuals or as corporate units. There is often a serious contest over influence between these groups that does not pull elites into the fray, as is the case when environmental organizations fight against off-road advocates, as when control advocates

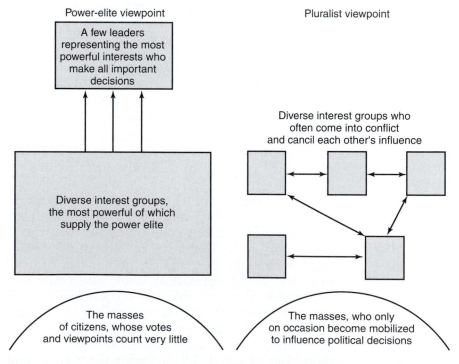

Figure 18.1   The Power Elite and Pluralist Viewpoint

battle the National Rifle Association, as when local developers come against preservationists or as when teachers confront local school boards. Many political decisions are not highly relevant to elites, and here we can see pluralism in action. When the wealthy and larger corporations have a stake in a political decision, however, they are likely to prevail, unless the generally docile public is aroused or a coalition of less powerful organizations can collectively exert power. Thus, automobile manufacturers have lost some battles over issues such as mandatory safety devices and emission controls against the combined organizational power of environmentalists. Similarly, at times large timber companies have lost to environmentalists. Still, on average, the larger corporate interests disproportionately influence political decisions, as power elite proponents would argue.

Voting and Political Power.   The political system in the United States is structured to have two parties for national and state elections, with political party affiliation being less important in county and city elections (although often significant in large counties and cities). At the national level, the electoral college system discourages third parties because the party with a plurality takes all of the votes for a given state. In fact, a third party almost assures that the party farthest from its agenda will win an election, as was the case with the Green Party in the Presidential election of 2000. Most Green Party voters would have voted democratic, but the 80,000 Green votes in Florida assured that the Republican (who could hardly be portrayed as an environmentalist) won over the Democrat, (who did have environmental credentials). At the state level, independents and third party candidates can win elections but without national party affiliation and financial backing, it is typically difficult for them to win. Thus, unlike most political democracies that have a parliamentary system, where minority parties can form coalitions to give a larger party the margin of victory (in exchange for influence and cabinet positions), the United States is dominated by two large brokerage parties that must appeal to broad and diverse constituencies; and in so doing, they dilute their agenda. As a result, more and more Americans are registering as Independents because they do not believe that the two major parties stand for anything.

   Another problem with the voting system in the United States is voter apathy. Fewer and fewer Americans are voting, with elections often being decided with less than half of the public voting. This low turnout reflects, perhaps, the sense that votes do not mean anything because large corporate interests dominate decisions anyway. Indeed, many disenfranchised voters are implicit power elite advocates—rather than making them mad, their implicit insight makes them apathetic.

   The apathy is most noticeable among the young and poor, both of whom have a big stake in elections. For the young, decisions are being made that will influence their financial future, especially over issues such as Social Security, workers compensation, medical care, and other issues that will determine the quality of their life in the future. Similarly, the poor, who have much to gain from government programs to help them, are the least likely to vote, thus assuring that their voice in politics will be virtually silent. Indeed, it is the collective concern (and guilt) of the more affluent that has more influence on the politics of the poor than the actual outcry from the poor themselves.

These patterns of voting give the affluent in society more influence than their numbers would justify. They also give the elderly considerable influence than their numbers would indicate over policies that will shape the lives of their children, grandchildren, and great grandchildren. Moreover, the affluent and elderly are well-organized, and so their influence extends beyond the vote with effective lobbying organizations who exert influence on legislators. Coupled with the power of elite organizations, those who most need government services now and in the future are the least likely to influence political decisions that affect their lives and well being.

Legislative Decision Making. It has become increasingly difficult at all levels of government, but particularly at the federal level, to make comprehensive, change-oriented decisions. As Figure 18.2 outlines, there is always an ad hoc coalition of interests that lobby against legislation that would force radical changes. The members of this coalition may have little in common except their opposition, but it is a foolish legislator who ignores the sentiments of organizations who have members, money, and influence. Also, legislators themselves have powerful ideological biases that may work against change, as do members of their constituency. The end result of the processes outlined in Figure 18.2 is for legislation to be killed, delayed, or compromised to such an extent that it will not change very much. Add to these dynamics the threat or actual veto by the chief executive, whether a governor or the President, and it is easy to see why radical change is difficult. In a sense, this conservatism in the legislative process can work toward stability and against rash decisions, but it also operates against making changes that need to be made before an unmanageable crisis emerges.

Centralization of Power. Americans are generally distrustful of highly concentrated power, but it is now clear that an increasing portion of funding for local and state programs—schools, welfare, prisons, health care—comes from the federal government, which gives it the power to set policies and make many decisions *for* state and local governments. This trend represents the centralization of power, becoming more remote from local needs, but it also works to equalize government benefits by not letting states and local communities be too restrictive. Which is worse: unequal and, hence, unfair treatment of people at local levels or increasing centralization of power at the national level and more equal treatment of people? A related issue is not only the trend of power moving to the federal level (because "those who pay the bills call the shots"), but within federal government toward the Executive branch. Increasingly, Congress *reacts to* initiatives from the President and top advisors rather than generating policies on its own. Similarly, the judiciary has become more conservative in interpreting the Constitution, although much of this is the result of the last decades of appointments (a trend that could be reversed in future decades). The dilemma posed is that, as the Executive branch initiates most key legislation and Congress can only react, while being split by public opinion and influence from special interests, decision making increasingly falls to one person, the President,

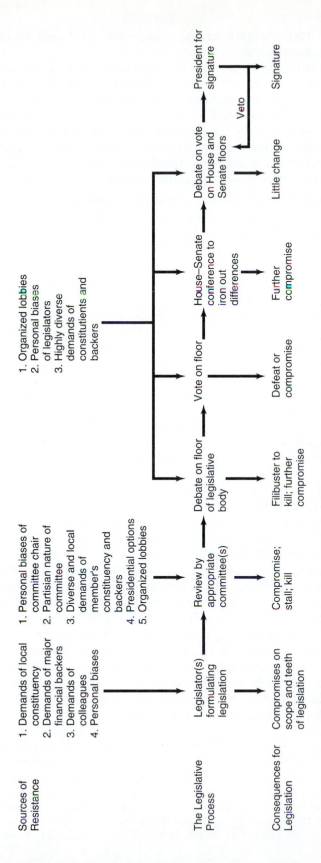

Figure 18.2 Legislative Roadblocks to National, Change-Oriented Legislation
Source: Jonathan H. Turner and David Musick. *American Dilemmas* (New York: Columbia University Press, 1985).

and the top advisors to the President. The end result is that power is more concentrated.

Another force promoting centralization of power as well as growth in the size of governmental bureaucracies is democracy. The phrase "democracy creates bureaucracy" has the ring of truth for this reason: As people express their will in elections and in public opinion polls, or as interest groups lobby legislators, they all want the government "to do something" about their preferences, needs, and interests. As the government responds, it expands the bureaucracy and, at the same time, centralizes power to meet the public's and special interests' needs.

Americans' Ambivalence about Government.   A final dilemma in government is America ambivalence about regulation by government. Americans pay comparatively low taxes, the lowest in fact of the modern industrial world (except for Japan); and we distrust the capacity of government to provide services in an efficient way. All political decisions as well as elections must confront this general distrust of government and this reluctance to pay taxes.

Yet, without government regulation, society as Americans know it would not be possible. Schools, police and fire protection, sound monetary policies, roads and other infrastructures, control of crime, delivery of health care, regulation of abuses in markets, environmental protection, worker safety, enforcement of contracts, and so many activities that make society possible can only be provided by government. Alternative ways of organizing activities, such as markets, simply cannot perform these kinds of functions. But, despite this fact, Americans are distrustful and resentful of government.

Moreover, the governments of America's competitors in the world economy heavily intrude into both the social and economic spheres, coordinating economic and social policies. And they all use tax revenues to redistribute significant wealth and, perhaps more important, to encourage technological development and capital formation in selected areas within the economy. The United States has no coordinated economic policy, and it lags behind all industrial nations (save for perhaps England) in using tax revenues to subsidize technology and capital formation in key industries (defense being the only exception here). Without such subsidies American industry is less competitive, but to create them would involve raising taxes—a strategy that Americans are generally unwilling to accept even as their well-being is threatened by world economic competition.

These are some of the dilemmas faced by American government and they are ones about which we all have well-formed opinions. What is necessary is for each of us to rethink our opinions in light of not only personal biases but also in relation to trends in the modern state and, most especially, in the new world economic order.

SUMMARY

1. Social institutions are congeries of positions and structures that seek to resolve fundamental problems of humans as a species and as a species that relies upon culturally mediated patterns of social organization. Because of

their perceived importance, most of the general norms guiding behavior in institutional structures are well known and infused with values and beliefs.

2. Government is the institution that uses power to set goals for a society and to mobilize resources for achieving these goals. All polities reveal the consolidation and use of power, the emergence of leaders to make decisions, and the existence of an administrative structure to implement decisions by leaders.

3. Governments all mobilize four bases of power: coercion, administrative structures, symbols and ideologies, and material incentives. Depending upon the configuration of bases mobilized, the structure of the government will vary.

4. When power becomes bureaucratically organized, a state can be said to exist. Modern states vary with respect to the rationality of their administrative bureaucracy, the centralization of decision-making power, the extensiveness of state intervention into domestic affairs, the level of democracy in the selection of leaders, the division of power among the judiciary, executive, and legislative branches, and the level of legitimacy attributed to government.

5. World trends in the organization of government include the growing size and scale of government, the increasing bureaucratization of the state, the centralization of power in the state, the reliance on law as the symbolic bases of power and a corresponding decrease in the use of the coercive base, and increasing democratization in the selection of leaders.

6. Government in the United States is a relatively decentralized federalist system, although there is a clear trend towards more centralized power in the Executive branch of government. There is considerable debate among sociologists over the extent to which a power elite disproportionately influences political decisions, some arguing that a small group of elites controls power and others contending that a more pluralistic pattern of political influence operates. Voting has become a large problem in America, with fewer people exercising their right to vote in elections.

KEY TERMS

Administrative Base of Power: Use of administrative structures to regulate and control members of a population.

Coercive Base of Power: Use of physical force in social relations.

Centralization: Concentration of power in the hands of fewer and fewer individuals and agencies in government.

Democracy: Reliance upon free elections to place incumbents in leadership positions of government.

Leaders: Those who can use power to make binding decisions on a population and who, as a result, direct societal activities.

Material Incentive Base of Power: Use of incentives by political leaders to encourage and discourage various lines of conduct among members of a population.

Pluralism: Argument that decision making in government is influenced by competing interest groups.

Power: Capacity to direct the behavior of others.

Power, Bases of: Varying ways that power can be mobilized to direct the behavior of others. The four basic bases are the coercive, administrative, symbolic, and material incentive—all of which are mobilized to varying degrees to exert power.

Power Elite: Existence of a small group of corporate leaders and wealthy individuals who, in conjunction with key members of the military and the legislative branch of government, disproportionately influence the direction of political decisions.

Symbolic Base of Power: Use of symbol systems, such as ideologies, laws, religious dogmas, accounts of history, and the other ideas to legitimate the power of leaders to direct behaviors among members of a society.

Totalitarianism: Governmental form that relies on the extensive use of coercion and the constant monitoring by administrative structures to control members of a population.

Chapter 19

Kinship and Family

Children grow up, fall in love, have sex, and marry—perhaps reversing the sequence of sex and marriage. So it has been since humans emerged as a species. The nuclear family unit of parents and offspring was probably the second structure organizing human activity, proceeded only by the hunting and gathering band of individuals wandering a territory to gather plant life and hunt animals. At some point, the band became populated by men and women who developed enduring bonds as they bore children and raised their offspring. Thus, the **institution of kinship**—or relations among individuals by virtue of blood and marriage ties—is almost as old as humans, and indeed, bands of hominids or prehumans may have revealed early family structures. Why was the family one of the first social structures in human societies?

Explanations of Kinship

Sociobiological Explanations

As natural selection worked on the ancestors of humans, it forged bonds between men and women that endured. The pressures for these bonds came from the fact that infants are not sufficiently developed to survive without a prolonged period of care and protection, and the best way to assure that this care occurs is to have the partners who created a child stay together and collectively work to assure that their offspring survives. A sociobiological perspective would emphasize that, in staying together and protecting their child, parents assure that at least one half of their genes stay in the gene pool. Thus, kinship promoted fitness by creating a stable pair bond between parents to protect immature infants and, hence, their genes.

Functional Explanations

Functional theorizing asks the question of what need or requisite a social structure meets. And so, in addressing the question of why kinship systems connecting people by blood marriage ties would emerge, the answer is a list of needs that kinship fulfills. From a functional perspective, then, kinship and family relations meet certain basic survival requisites (J. Turner 1972): (a) regularizing sex and mating, thereby avoiding much of the potential conflict and tension over this most basic activity; (b) providing for the biological support of each member of the society, and especially the newborn and young who are a society's future; (c) creating a stable unit of socialization so that the young can acquire the culture and role-playing skills essential to adult life; (d) supplying an atmosphere of emotional and social support for the young and adults alike; and (e) regularizing and systematizing the placement of young adults into crucial productive (economic) and reproductive (child bearing, rearing) positions of the society. For functionalists, if these needs are not met, the survival of the species becomes problematic; and in the simple societies of the first humans, blood and marriage ties represented the easiest route for building viable social structures.

A functional argument can be phrased in more biological terms: those pre-humans and early humans that could not develop a stable structure for regularizing sex and mating, biological support of their children, socialization of their children, emotional support, and social placement would be less likely to survive than those bands that did develop such stable structures. The most efficient route for assuring the stability of this structure was to form pair-bonds, revolving around affection and sex, among adults who would protect and raise their young. Thus, functional theorizing can invoke an argument similar to that of sociobiologists without having to assume that natural selection created behavioral propensity for marriage in order for each partner to maximize his or her fitness, or ability to keep genes in the gene pool.

Kinship is universal among humans, and so, there must have been heavy pressures—perhaps biological but equally likely sociological in nature—for family structures as the most viable way to assure that the human species could reproduce itself, and thereby, survive. Once created, however, social and cultural forces could alter the elementary nuclear unit of parents and their offspring.

Basic Elements of Kinship

Kinship is a system of norms about some very fundamental matters, and because adherence to these norms is crucial for the survival of humans, they are infused with strongly held values and ideologies. The rules of kinship always carry special significance for the members of a society. There are several key rules, and once these are known, it becomes possible to describe diverse kinds of kinship systems.

Marriage Rules

One cultural norm is about **marriage rules,** which are after all, what creates and sustains family and kinship systems. In many societies, when and whom to marry have not always been a matter of free choice. In many kinship systems, marriage must occur outside of a larger kin unit or community (a rule of **exogamy**) and at times into another specific group (a rule of **endogamy**); and always, marriage has been guided by **incest rules** forbidding sexual relations and marriage between parents and offspring, between siblings, and between other close relatives (Murdock 1949, 1965).

Descent Rules

Another kinship rule that has a great impact not only on marriages but also on virtually all other aspects of kinship is **descent rules**. The rule of *descent* specifies whose side of the family is to be more important. Three basic options have existed in the history of human societies:

(a) **patrilineal descent** where the male's side of the family is more important, with wealth and authority passing through the male line (son-father-grandfather-uncles, etc.); (b) **matrilineal descent** where the woman's side of the family is more important, and where property and authority pass through the woman's *male* relatives (not the woman herself or her female relatives); and (c) the one with which you are most familiar, **bilateral descent** where both sides are equally important and, at the same time, neither has great influence. This last form of descent is what typified the few remaining hunting and gathering populations, and so, we can infer that this was the first descent rule in human societies.

Residence Rules

Another set of kinship rules revolves around where and with whom the married couple will live after marriage. These are termed **residence rules** with several patterns dominating the history of kinship: (a) **patrilocal rule**, where the couple lives with or near the male's family; (b) **matrilocal rule**, where the couple resides with the woman's relatives; (c) **avunculocal rule**, where the couple lives with the husband's uncle on his mother's side; and again the one with which you are familiar, (d) **neolocal rule**, where there is free choice about where to live. In general, descent rules determine residence rules, but not always, with the result that matters can become awkward when power, property, and authority (the descent rule), on the one hand, do not correspond to where people live (the residence rule), on the other. Still, over 70% of the societies that have been known were patrilocal (Murdock 1949), although most hunting and gathering societies—the original society of humans—were neolocal and allowed married couples to choose which band they would join when married.

Rules of Family Size and Composition

In all kinship systems, there are rules indicating who is to be a member of the family unit. The first hunter-gatherers had rules similar to those in the postindustrial world: the **nuclear family unit** consisting of parents and offspring was to be the primary unit, with other relatives excluded. Indeed, today it is considered unfortunate and a burden if another relative, such as a "mother-in-law" or an "aging parent," must reside with a couple. Between hunting and gathering at the beginning of societal evolution and the present day, however, very different rules have prevailed. After hunting and gathering, many societies allowed **polygamy,** or the taking in of multiple wives or husbands. When a male can marry more than one wife, this arrangement is termed **polygyny,** and when a wife can have more than one husband, this situation is denoted by the term **polyandry.**

An even more important set of rules on family size follows from the descent and residence rules. Nuclear family units in many traditional societies are linked together to form larger family units. The descent rule will indicate through which side of the family the linkages are to occur; and so, in a *patrilineal system,* the families will be connected along the male line with a male's nuclear unit being connected to the nuclear units of his male kin (brothers, father, uncles, and cousins), whereas in a *matrilineal system,* the linkage will occur along the female's side with nuclear units of her kinfolk. These families will often reside in a large family compound or have somewhat separated units in a small village, but they are treated as a distinct unit by others in the village.

Rules on the Division of Labor

In all kinship systems, there are rules about who is to do what tasks in the household. Generally, men and women in the household unit are assigned different activities; while these can vary enormously, they have historically favored men. Even hunter-gatherers, who displayed more equality than any other human society, divided labor with women doing much more work than men, although there was not very much household work to do anyhow. But, after hunting and gathering, women were increasingly assigned a considerable amount of work within the household (cooking, cleaning, child care) and, in many societies, outside the home in the garden plots of horticulturalists or the larger fields of agrarian farmers. It is only recently that this extra burden on women has been challenged. And we are in the midst of a rewriting of the rules about the division of labor in postindustrial societies, although even when women work, they must often take on the "second shift" of domestic chores after work, such as preparing meals, washing dishes, doing the laundry, and cleaning the house (Hochschild and Machung 1989).

Rules of Authority

Kinship systems all have rules specifying who has authority over whom and over what activities. Among hunter-gatherers, there was relative egalitarianism in that no one had authority over another. After hunting and gathering, however, the rules dramatically favored males, with males having more authority over women within household units. Even in matrilineal systems, where the female line is important, it was the female's male relatives like her brother or uncle who would have the power. Thus, after hunting and gathering, **patriarchy** or the control of women by men emerged in kinship systems; indeed, in some societies women were considered "property" and had few rights. The fact that women could only vote in the first part of the twentieth century in the United States underscores that patriarchy was very much a part of industrial America and lingers to this day.

Rules of Dissolution

All kinship systems have rules for ending a marriage. These rules can be as simple as a wife putting her husband's belongings at the front door or as complex as having to go to trial and prove fault. Traditional societies after hunting and gathering made divorce more difficult, particularly for women who often did not have the right to end a marriage—a sure sign of patriarchy and the treatment of women as property. Even today, in traditional parts of the global system, dissolution of a marriage is virtually impossible for women.

Historical Trends in the Structure of Kinship

From Relative Equality

The first societies of hunters and gatherers had a very simple system, much like the one we know in the United States (Maryanski and Turner 1992): bilateral descent with no elder or relative having any authority over the couple; neolocal residence where people are free to choose the place and persons with whom they will live; incest prohibitions as well as exogamy (usually specifying that you had to marry outside your band); and at times endogamy (indicating into which other band you would marry); clear division of labor (men hunt, women gather and prepare food); relatively egalitarian authority (both men and women have equal authority, or shared authority); small family size of just mother, father, and offspring; and easy dissolution of the marriage.

Toward Growing Inequality and Patriarchy

When human populations first began to grow during horticulture and, for a while, in early agrarianism, rules of kinship were *the* most important organizing principles, and they made family and kinship a much more complex phenomenon. Kinship became, in essence, the functional equivalent of bureaucratic organizations; thousands upon thousands of people— indeed in some cases, millions—could be organized by a descent rule as it dictated the nature of other kinship rules. Most of these horticultural societies were not so large, although they could become so with kinship rules. In broad strokes, here is how one builds a larger social structure with kinship rules: the descent rule, along with marriage and residence rules, allows for the building of more inclusive kinship units, starting with the married couple and their children (the *nuclear unit*), moving to the **lineages** that link together several nuclear units, then to the **clan** consisting of linked lineages, and finally to the **moiety** that groups clans together and divides the society in half (into two moities). There are many subtle variations and most societies were not as neat and clean as this scenario implies. However, kinship can be used as the organizational backbone of a society when its members cannot construct bureaucratic social forms.

Max Weber (1922) once worried about the constraints of "the iron cage" of rational bureaucracy on the human spirit, but it is unlikely that this modern cage is anything like the cage of kinship (Maryanski and Turner 1992). Just imagine getting married, moving in with your husband's parents (patrilocality), and being under the authority of all elder male kin in the lineage and perhaps clan and moiety (patrilineal descent), with authority residing with males and with the division of labor forcing all females, who have been thrown together from other descent lines, trying to get along and work together at gardening and domestic chores while the males go off to war or do various handicrafts. Sounds like a nightmare to me, at least if you are a woman, and humans got out of this kind of system as soon as they could, even if they had to subordinate themselves to the state and political authority.

A Conflict Perspective on Family

It is in the more elaborate forms of kinship that the greatest inequalities can be found; as conflict theorists would emphasize (Collins 1975; Collins and Coltrane 1991), the differences in power and authority of men and women would create tensions that could periodically erupt into conflict. However, this conflict potential was more often controlled by powerful norms and beliefs about "the women's place" in the family, by the potential for male (and his relatives) coercion, by day-to-day interpersonal sanctions, and by rituals. In such a situation, women have few resources to mobilize, especially if surrounded by her husband's relatives (as in a patrilocal system). Things are better if she can be around her relatives (as in a matrilocal system) because she can draw upon them for support. One resource women have is sex, which they can deny to men or ritualize in ways that gains them resources or at least limits the power of men (Collins 1975). Another crucial resource for women is cultural symbols that have often been used to create "mystique" about the nature of women that, in turn, can be used to control husbands (Collins 1975). But throughout human history, ever since humans left the relative equality of the hunting and gathering way of life, women have been at a disadvantage. And we live with the legacy of this disadvantage today, as was reviewed in Chapter 15 on gender stratification. Female resentment of their subordination has always been present, though repressed and submerged by cultural beliefs and sanctions. But, as women have begun to work in great numbers in the labor force and acquire material resources, these resentments are coming out and forcing a rebalancing of power relations in the households of the postindustrial world (Blumberg 1984; Chafetz 1990).

However, patriarchy is not easy to stamp out because it has been ingrained in family relations for thousands of years. Even as women work, their labor is "discounted" and not valued as much as male labor; despite some control over economic resources, women are at a disadvantage in negotiations over who is to do what tasks, who is to interrupt a career to raise children, and who is to have ultimate authority. Part of this disadvantage resides in cultural ideologies that privilege men; another part resides in women's internalization of these ideologies and their sense that they should raise children, cook, and do domestic chores; and of course, part of the disadvantage is that men do not want to give up their power and privilege. Men are never caught in the moral dilemma about jobs and raising children, whereas women are often conflicted between whether or not they should interrupt their careers or give up work for the sake of children. As women struggle with this moral dilemma, men are able to sustain their control of macro-level economic and political resources that, in turn, gives them more power at the micro-level negotiations that occur in the family.

Still, change is occurring in many postindustrial societies. Women are demanding that men do more household and child-related labor and that they too sacrifice some aspects of their careers for the family. But, as we saw in the chapter on gender stratification, men still are at an advantage in these negotiations, even as the culture of gender relations is changing.

Kinship in America

The Basic Structure

Perhaps the above history of kinship seems remote, but it is relevant to understanding kinship in America today. Structurally, our kinship system is bilateral, neolocal, and nucleated, with considerable ambiguity over authority and the division of labor between men and women. This structure of a relatively isolated unit with changing and ambiguous norms about the division of labor and authority is inevitably going to reveal conflict and increased rates of dissolution (J. Turner 1977). Let us examine this situation in more detail.

Industrialization completes the renuclearization of the family that began during the agrarian era. Large extended families revolving around lineages and clans were never particularly pleasant, despite all of the romanticism about "the old days"; and so people got out of them whenever possible. Agrarianism began the process; industrialization completes it because extensive kinship ties are a hindrance in an industrial system where people move about, leave their homes to be educated, pursue independent careers, and try to enjoy the good life.

Romantic Love and Marriage

The isolated nuclear family faces a number of dilemmas. One is the expectations that guide the formation of this family unit in the first place. In the United States, powerful beliefs about romantic love dominate mate selection (J. Turner 1977, 72–78): one is supposed to marry on the basis of mutual attraction and compatibility (rather than fecundity, money, family ties, and other less romantic considerations); such attraction extends to love and sex, with the couple becoming an emotionally bonded pair; and this compatibility is to persist, even in the face of problems, because "love conquers all." Of course when this **romantic love complex** is stated in this way, it is easy to snicker. But, if we are honest with ourselves, some version of these ideas has guided, or is now guiding, mate selection.

Thus, American couples enter marriage with expectations—typically very unrealistic ones—about what will occur. Moreover, living together before marriage does not appear to help the future stability of the marriage. For example, in a study in Sweden where living together is common, women who cohabited with their spouses before their marriage were 80% *more likely* to get divorced than those who did not live with their husbands before marriage (Bennett, Blanc, and Bloom 1988). A similar finding emerged in a recent study in the United States. Now, obviously something is amiss here, and it is this: those who live together without marrying are often afraid of commitments and have other doubts about marriage; and so, we might expect them to get divorced more often. Yet, those who do not live together before marriage will tend to enter the marriage with unrealistic expectations, setting the stage for dashed hopes and anger.

These romantically-in-love couples must confront the full weight of ambiguous norms about authority and the division of labor. And if children enter the picture, this normative confusion becomes even more unclear, especially if the wife has career aspirations or if she must work to make ends meet. Who does what in the care of the child? Who has the say, and over what issues? These questions are not easily answered because norms are contradictory and influx, and they become increasingly paramount when the wife is working or when she sacrifices/interrupts her career to raise children. Add to this mix concerns over finances, fatigue from work, and accumulated resentments in trying to make things run smoothly, and what is likely is marital tension leading to divorce.

There are other factors affecting divorce. One is that women are less dependent on men for income than they were 50 years ago. As the percentage of women who work has increased, so has their ability to support themselves when they decide to leave a marriage. A second factor is that divorce is no longer as stigmatizing as it once was. A divorced woman in the 1950s in America carried a quiet stigma, a fact that kept many women from leaving unhappy marriages. Today, as divorce rates increased during the 1970s, the stigma associated with divorce has virtually vanished. A third factor is the women's movement, which raised the consciousness of women (and, to a much lesser extent, men as well). Women came to realize that they did not have to stay in marriage and that their self-worth is not defined solely in terms of being mothers in intact families. And finally, divorce laws changed in the 1960s and 1970s, making it much easier to get a divorce. Before these laws were changed, one party had to prove another "at fault," whereas today, marriages can be terminated by mutual agreement or by one party simply citing "irreconcilable differences" with his or her spouse. Higher divorce rates are, therefore, inevitable. But how high, and is the institution of kinship in America collapsing?

Divorce and Dissolution in American Families

Divorce rates are difficult to calculate, for the simple reason that, to do it accurately, one would have to let people live their whole married lives before knowing for sure if they will get divorced. Thus, the figures often bantered in the media—50% of couples get divorced!— are very problematic, if not just plain wrong. The reason this figure is misleading is that it simply divides the number of marriages in a given year into the number of divorces for that year, and in recent years, there have been around 50 divorces for every 100 marriages. But these two figures have nothing to do with each other because the divorces in a given year are the outcome of *past* marriages, not those in the present; and hence, they cannot predict the future for those who are just getting married.

Another way to get a sense for whether or not divorce is increasing is to tabulate the number of divorces per 1,000 members of a population. In 1960, there were 2.2 divorces per 1,000; in 1980, this number had jumped to 5.2 divorces per 1,000 people. But, after 1980, the figure went down to 4.3 divorces per 1,000. Unfortunately, the government no longer collects and reports data on divorces and marriages, but it appears that divorce is declining. Yet there are problems with these data. For one thing, the demographic profile of the population will influence the number of divorces; when the proportion of young adults in the population is high, divorce will increase because there are more people getting married and divorcing, whereas when there are fewer young adults as a proportion of the population, as is the case today, fewer people get married and, hence, divorced. Thus, the rise in divorces per 1,000 people from 1960 to 1980 may have been due to the larger percentage of young people in the population at that time.

The best way to accurately assess divorce is to follow people after they get married for the rest of their life to see if they get divorced, but such a figure would say little about your chances for marital success today. Of the marriages occurring in 1923, for example, 19% ended in divorce, while for weddings in 1975, the estimated projection (based on divorces that have already occurred and estimate of the rates of divorce for middle-aged adults), 50% will get divorced. Projections for more recent years suggest that divorce will occur in about 40% of marriages (Coltrane and Collins 2001, 130–132). But, these data do not tell us what the chances are for marital success or divorce for all those getting married *today*. It appears to be the case, however, that divorce is declining somewhat, but it is difficult to know if this downward trend will continue.

Who gets divorced? And when? The Center for Disease Control (2002) collected data on almost 11,000 women between ages 15 and 44, asking questions about their family history. On average, 20% of marriages ended in the first five years, with the rate jumping to 43% by 15 years. Table 19.1 summarizes some of the findings for different ethnic, income, religious, and age groups.

Single-Parent Households

Eighty percent of those who get divorced remarry, and so, people want to be married in a nuclear family unit. But there is a fluctuating trend in one-parent families, partly as a result of divorce but also significantly

Table 19.1   Percentage of Women Whose First Marriage Ended in Divorce

Characteristics	Percentage Who Divorced after 15 Years
All women	43
Income	
High	31
Medium	40
Low	65
Ethnicity	
Asian	23
Latino	42
Non-Latino White	42
African American	55
Religion	
Catholic	37
Conservative Protestant	40
Non-Christian	40
Liberal Protestant	44
No religion	55
Age at Marriage	
25+	35
20–24	36
18–19	49
Less than 18	59

Source: Centers for Disease Control (2002).

among unmarried mothers. About 30% of all babies born in America are to women who are not married (Coltrane and Collins 2001, 131). These children will grow up under difficult circumstances, as their mothers seek to cope with the stresses of supporting and raising children. Add to this number the children in step-parent families and divorced single-parent households and we can see that children and their parent(s) must deal with a great deal of strain in their households—as perhaps some of you may have experienced first hand. Virtually every study of these households reports terrible strain on both parent(s) and children.

Rates of single parenthood vary by ethnicity. More affluent whites and Asians have the lowest rates, whereas Latinos and African Americans reveal the highest rates, with the African American rate approaching 70% (Coltrane and Collins 2001, 131). For the less affluent, economic strains always supercharge family relations and destroy the myth of romantic love, whereas for the more affluent, they can afford to buy help to relieve domestic strains. But, social class position alone is not the sole determinant of these differences in ethnicity; cultural traditions such as religion and family structure (such as extended kinship ties among Asians and Latinos) are also very important in explaining these differences.

Family Violence

Stressful marriages are often violent. The stress may cause the violence or vice versa, but violence is now a part of many families. Much violence occurs against women. It is difficult to get an accurate account of how much violence against women occurs because so much goes unreported. The U.S. Justice Department estimates that well over 800,000 women are victims of violence each year, and 20% of the homicides against women come from their spouse or ex-spouse. Well over 1,000 women a year die from domestic violence. Until relatively recently, domestic violence was regarded as a "private matter," a situation that obviously favored abusive men. Today, the law is changing as states are increasingly enacting anti-stalking laws and marital rape laws, while the police are beginning to enforce assault laws against violent husbands and ex-husbands.

Women are not the only victims of violence. The U.S. Clearinghouse on Child Abuse and Neglect reports that over 1,000 children die from abuse each year, but millions more suffer from violence. Both men and women are likely to abuse their children, and the data show that they were abused as children. Thus, family violence is often passed down from generation to generation.

An Empty Nest Syndrome?

Parents in families report wanting to be away from their children and feel much happier when children are grown and gone (White and Booth 1985). Surprisingly, even steadily married couples experience a significant increase in happiness when their last child has moved out (White and Edwards 1990)— indicating that talk of the "empty nest" syndrome is greatly exaggerated, at least in most cases.

Emerging Alternative Families

Gay and Lesbian Couples.   Same-sex marriage is not legal in any state in America, although such marriages are now legal in parts of Canada. Some states such as Vermont and Hawaii have laws that confer benefits to the gay and lesbian couples. However, in 1996 Congress enacted a law banning homosexual marriage, indicating the prevailing sentiment against such marriages. The ideological and political battle for gay marriages is not likely to recede, however, because public attitudes have changed dramatically over the last 20 years.

An increasing number of gay and lesbian couples desire to adopt children or bear them through insemination. This movement has been strengthened by laws and court decisions that in many states have removed barriers to adoption, with the result that one can reasonably talk about a gay and lesbian nuclear family structure.

Cohabitation.   There are probably around two million gay and lesbian couples living together, and perhaps as many as 4.5 million unmarried heterosexual couples. Well over half of these couples do not stay together, but still, one half of the population from ages 25 to 45 reports having lived with someone for a period of time (Brines and Joyner 1999), indicating that "living together" is becoming a prominent life style in the United States.

Families without Children.   Although most people who marry have children, there is a clear increase in the number of couples who choose not to have children. Changing norms about the role of women and greater economic opportunities now allow women to have meaningful lives—indeed, often rather affluent lives—without bearing children. At times, bearing children is simply deferred, with women having children in later life, but for many couples a family without children is preferred.

Being Single.   An increasing number of people remain single for significant periods of time. "Being single" has become a much more prominent lifestyle, with over 26 million households reporting only one member (U.S. Census 2003). The proportion of young women who are single also has increased as they pursue education and careers before marrying. It is difficult to know how many single-person households will join together into a marriage, but it is clear that "singlehood" is increasing.

Future of the Family in America

As is evident, the American family is changing and dramatically so. Most people still aspire to be married and have children—a fortunate fact because without children in families, you and I would not exist. Still, the changes in the family evident today are likely to continue. Certainly the most dramatic change is that women are claiming authority in the family in response to older patterns of patriarchy, and especially so when they are working. Divorce rates will probably remain relatively high, but perhaps not as high as they were a decade ago. Single-parent households may increase, putting enormous economic and emotional strain on family members. The number of gay and lesbian couples may increase, and it is likely that single-individual households and families without children will increase.

SUMMARY

1. Social institutions are congeries of positions and structures that seek to resolve fundamental problems of humans as a species and as a species that relies upon culturally mediated patterns of social organization. Because of their perceived importance, most of the general norms guiding behavior in institutional structures are well known and infused with values and beliefs.

2. Kinship is the institution organizing relations around marriage and blood ties. Such organization is achieved through a series of norms guiding conduct with respect to marriage, descent, residence, authority, division of labor, family size and composition, and dissolution. These rules regularize relations in ways to resolve fundamental problems facing humans, such as sex and mating, biological and social support, socialization, and social placement.

3. After hunting and gathering and up until very recently, kinship systems have advantaged male power and authority while subordinating women. Patriarchy still remains in most family systems, but with postindustrialization, a more egalitarian pattern is emerging. This trend is the result of women's growing economic power, ideological changes that have occurred with the women's movement, increased political power of women, and new laws giving women options for divorce.

4. Kinship in America is dominated by isolated nuclear units in which romantic love determines mate selection and in which crucial norms, especially over authority and division of household labor, are ambiguous and rapidly changing.

5. Divorce is common in America but rates do not appear to have increased over the last decade. Domestic violence against women and children is common.

6. New family patterns are emerging in America. Single-person households are increasing. Marriages without children are increasing. Gay and lesbian partnerships are increasing, as is childrearing in these partnerships.

KEY TERMS

Avunculocal Rule: Residence rule specifying that a married couple and their children are to live with the male's mother's brother (or uncle on his mother's side).

Bilateral Descent: Rule of descent specifying that the male's and female's side of the family and kin network will be given equal importance.

Clan: Kinship structure created when lineages are linked together by a descent rule.

Descent Rules: Norms specifying whether the male's or female's side of the family and kin network are more important in terms of property and authority.

Endogamy: Rule specifying that individuals must marry within another kin group or community.

Exogamy: Rule specifying that individuals must marry outside a kin group or community.

Extended Family Unit: Kinship unit created when several nuclear units are joined in one household.

Incest Rules: Norms prohibiting sex and marriage among parents and offspring, and at times other closely related kin.

Kinship, Institution of: Organization of marriage and blood ties among members of a society into structures that, from a sociobiological perspective, allow adults to increase their genetic fitness and that, from a functionalist perspective, have consequences for regularizing sex and mating, providing for biological and social support, socializing the young, and placing the young into adult positions.

Lineage: Kinship structure created when several family units are linked together by descent and residence rules.

Marriage Rules: Norms specifying who can marry whom in a society, and when.

Matrilineal Descent: Rule of descent specifying that the woman's side of the family and kin network (especially her male relatives) are to be the most important in terms of property and authority.

Matrilocal Rule: Kinship norm specifying that a married couple and their children are to live with the female's family and kin.

Moiety: Kinship unit created when clans are linked together, dividing a society in half into two kinship units.

Neolocal Rule: Residence rule indicating that a married couple and their children have autonomy in deciding for themselves where to live.

Nuclear Family Unit: Family unit created by the married couple and their offspring.

Patriarchy: Situation where males control resources and dominate women in family relations and, more broadly, in relations outside the family as well.

Patrilineal Descent: Rule of descent specifying that the male's side of the family and kin network are to be the most important in terms of property and authority.

Patrilocal Rule: Kinship norm specifying that a married couple and their children are to live with the male's family and kin.

Polyandry: Marriage rule allowing females to have more than one husband.

Polygamy: Marriage rules allowing for an individual to have more than one spouse.

Polygyny: Marriage rule allowing males to have more than one wife.

Residence Rules: Norms specifying where married couples are to live and reside.

Romantic Love Complex: Set of beliefs emphasizing mutual attraction and compatibility as the basis for selecting marriage partners.

Chapter 20

Religion

With big brains humans can think about a world that they cannot see and touch—a sacred realm inhabited by supernatural gods and forces that have the power to change the world and people's lives. Not all hunting and gathering societies had religion but many did; so, it is likely that religion was the first institution to separate from kinship and band. To come so early in societal evolution suggests that religion is more than the byproduct of having a big brain that can ponder this unobservable realm of the sacred and supernatural. Other forces were at work, but what were they?

Functional theories can perhaps provide a tentative answer by rephrasing the question: What pressures were exerted on human populations to develop a system of ideas and practices directed at the supernatural? How did religion help humans survive in their environment? For functionalists, religion allowed humans to (a) reinforce important norms and (b) reduce anxiety. And in so doing, religion operates as an important mechanism of social control.

1. Taking the first function, one way to assure that key norms are obeyed is to view them as dictates from supernatural forces that are constantly monitoring conformity and sanctioning with bad luck and other negative outcomes a lack of conformity to norms. Thus, religion increases social control by assuring that people abide by critical norms.

2. Another function of kinship is to reduce anxiety and uncertainty. Religion can help alleviate anxiety by providing beliefs about the power of gods to make the world secure, while providing the rituals necessary to entice the gods to intervene in problematic situations. In having these effects on people, early societies would reveal more cohesion and control, making them more likely to survive in their environments.

At first religion was very simple, perhaps beginning with ancestor worship and slowly graduating to views of supernatural forces guiding all members of a hunting and gathering society. And if the functional explanation is correct, those hunters and gatherers who had to live with danger and uncertainty were probably the most likely to develop religion because it gave them a sense of solidarity and helped alleviate their anxieties. The nature of religion, however, began to change with horticulture, and later with agrarianism. Religion became a central institution in people's lives, specialized religious practitioners emerged, gods and supernatural forces became more powerful and numerous, and ritual appeals to these forces became more frequent and organized (Wallace 1966). Suddenly, in just a few centuries, the world religions of today—Christianity, Hinduism, Buddhism, Confucianism, and Islam—came to dominate, sweeping across great spans of territory and then displacing local religions (Bellah 1964). And today, a quick review of the front page of a newspaper informs us that religion is highly salient and volatile. Indeed, religion will remain a dynamic force in the global system of societies.

Basic Elements of Religion

All religions have certain elements in common. From its simplest to most complex forms, a religion reveals (a) a distinction between the sacred and profane, (b) a set of beliefs about the sacred and supernatural, (c) rituals directed at the supernatural, and (d) cult structures organizing people who share beliefs and emit rituals directed at the forces articulated in beliefs. Let me review each of these elements in more detail.

The Sacred and Profane

All religions make a distinction between the **sacred** and the **supernatural**, on the one hand, and the **profane** or secular, on the other. All religions impute special powers to objects, events, forces, and at times, persons who influence daily life, giving them a *sacred* quality. Thus, religions see a basic dichotomy in the universe between the everyday, mundane world that humans experience and the realm of the supernatural that has the power to influence events in the everyday world. Most religions also postulate a *supernatural* realm, beyond the everyday, mundane world where the sacred forces, beings, objects, and events exist and operate.

Beliefs and Values

Conceptions of the sacred and supernatural are part of more general sets of religious *values* and *beliefs*. **Religious beliefs** articulate the nature of the sacred and supernatural, often spelling out in detail diverse beings and forces as well as distinct realms of the supernatural. Descriptions of the sacred beings and forces in the supernatural realm often constitute a **pantheon,** a kind of organization chart and "who's who" in the supernatural. **Religious values** are statements, emanating from the supernatural, about what is right, wrong, good, and bad; while other values exist in a society, those enunciated by religion have a special quality because they are sanctioned and backed up by the sacred beings and forces in the supernatural realm.

Rituals

People become connected to religious values and beliefs through *rituals* (J. Turner 1972; Wallace 1966). A **religious ritual** is a patterned and stereotyped sequence of actions—bodily movements and positioning as well as verbal utterances—directed toward the supernatural, asking for its intervention in the secular, profane world. Rituals can be privately performed, but equally often, rituals are performed collectively in the presence of others who are typically part of a cult structure organizing ritual activities directed at the supernatural.

Cult Structures

A **cult structure** is the unit within which rituals are performed and these structures can vary from a gathering of aboriginals around a totem through a storefront church in America to the world Roman Catholic bureaucracy. Those who are members of a religious structure—whether big or small, permanent or transient, old or new—share religious beliefs and values, practice common rituals, and as a result, develop a sense of togetherness and "community."

The Evolution of Religion

Religion in Simple Hunter-Gatherer Societies

Before its disruption by Western people and government, the traditional Eskimo system provided an example of religion in a simple society (Wallace 1966). Although there was variation among Eskimo bands, their beliefs showed a common form. Beliefs in the supernatural centered around a pantheon of spirits and gods. Some of the lesser gods were simply prominent human beings and animals that had been accorded special status. Each individual, or a small group, had various minor spirits regulating behavior. A particular kin group, for example, might have its own ancestral spirits with whom to reckon. Higher up in the pantheon were two primary gods—the Keeper of Sea Animals and the Spirit of the Air. The mythology about the lives, history, and interventions into worldly affairs of these gods, however, varied from group to group. Moreover, the exact division of powers and hierarchy of control among these society-wide gods was somewhat blurred. Religious beliefs among the Eskimo divided the universe into different realms, graduating from mortal human beings through local spirits and ancestral souls to the two higher gods.

Ritual activity was conducted primarily within the family. Each Eskimo inherited "spirit helpers" through the patrilineal descent system— (i.e., from the father's side). These helpers guided individuals in their daily lives. The wearing of little talismans of walrus tusks, bags of pebbles, and small shells was required to secure the help of these gods. In addition, to get help, the person must refrain from killing the animals represented by these body adornments. A less individualistic form of ritual activity was required by the game-animal beliefs. People were required to observe certain taboos, such as not cooking land and sea animals together. Violations of taboos were to be confessed openly; if an individual persisted in violations, banishment from the community ensued.

The only formal religious practitioners were part-time shamans. Shamans were to serve as intermediaries in calling upon the spirit helpers for assistance. People suffering from ill health or bad fortune were assumed to have violated a taboo and offended a god. It was the shaman's job to find out which god had been offended or which taboo had been broken. Once the diagnosis was made, the shaman underwent a spiritual journey to rectify the situation.

Thus, the Eskimo had a form of religious organization that may have resembled that of our hunter-gatherer ancestors. Beliefs made only a few distinctions among supernatural realms and did not clearly specify relations among gods. Cult organization was coextensive with kinship and ritual activity was individualistic and only sporadic. A number of taboos were observed, but these were not extensive. From a functional perspective, such a religious system served the Eskimo well. It helped alleviate anxiety by assuring people that "helpers" guided their lives and that consultation with the shaman could eliminate misfortune. It reinforced kinship norms and provided certain taboos that, in many cases, represented sound medical advice. We can view the Eskimo religious system as a baseline. Other religious systems in more advanced societies reveal more complexity in their beliefs and in the organization of ritual activity.

Elaboration of Religion

There is a general trend in religious systems toward a more complex belief system denoting clear supernatural realms and evidencing an elaborate pantheon of gods, more extensive rituals conducted at specific times and places in clearly defined cult structures, and more clarity in those religious values dictating what is good and bad in human affairs. The complexity of religious beliefs and rituals appears to peak in traditional agricultural societies, after which a sudden reversal occurs: beliefs depict fewer gods, and rituals become simplified. Religious values remain explicit, however. Cult organization becomes highly complex, and by using new social technologies, it becomes bureaucratized. Most of the religions that now dominate the world—Christianity, Hinduism, Buddhism, Judaism, Confucianism, and Islam—emerged out of, or replaced, religious systems with more elaborate pantheons of gods, myths about their feats, extended rituals, and tight-knit cult organizations.

Trend Toward Simplification of Religions

The trend in religious development over the last 1,000 years has been toward monotheism, or the worship of one god. For example, Islam, Christianity, Judaism, and Confucianism clearly tend toward monotheism. Allah, God and the Trinity, and Tao, respectively, are the supreme powers in the supernatural realms of these religions. Hinduism and some forms of Buddhism, however, still have a more elaborate pantheon of gods or godlike beings. Religious mythologies have declined and are simplified in more contemporary religions. For instance, the myths concerning the activities of Krishna and Vishnu, the sequences of Buddhas, God and Moses, God and Jesus, Allah, the angel Gabriel, and Mohammed are very sparse compared to myths of earlier religions and to myths of religions in isolated pockets of traditional life. Compared to the jealousies, conflicts, rivalries, genealogies, and love affairs of earlier gods, the myths of the dominant religions of the world today (with the exception of Hinduism) are almost sedate.

Another critical difference between newer religions and those of the past is that, for the first time, beliefs emphasize that people have the potential for understanding the nature of both the everyday and supernatural worlds (Bellah 1964, 367). For example, Hinduism not only holds out the prospect of better reincarnation in one's next life but also the possibility of becoming a god. Christianity offers salvation after death. Islam postulates paradise after death. Conversely, places in the supernatural realm are provided for those who are morally unworthy: hell, a poor reincarnation, and so on.

Values remain highly explicit in newer religions, for it is through conformity to values that people are able to qualify for access to supernatural realms. Thus religious "codes of conduct" become a prominent feature of modern religions. The Ten Commandments, the sayings of Confucius, and the Noble Eightfold Path among Buddhists represent conspicuous examples.

Cult organization becomes more complex at the same time that pantheons, mythologies, and rituals are being simplified. The new social technology—bureaucracy (see Chapter 12)—is used to organize and extend religious influence. In nonindustrial societies, this bureaucracy is often a powerful political force, and conflicts between political and religious leaders can become acute. With industrialization, however, this conflict declines as the political bureaucracy grows in power and separates the church bureaucracy from political influence, except in some parts of the Muslim world.

The creation of religious bureaucracies opens up new possibilities for conquering and conversion. Bureaucracies can mobilize resources toward explicit goals, and one of the goals of most modern religions is expansion. The result is that the world becomes dominated by relatively few religions as bureaucratically organized cults invade and displace more traditional religious practices. Table 20.1 lists the worlds largest religions.

A Conflict Perspective on Religion

Functional theories provide one explanation as to why religion evolved in the first societies. Although religion may alleviate anxieties and sanction important norms, Karl Marx and Frederick Engels offered an alternative view of religion, once it was established in more complex societies. One of Marx's most famous phrases is that religion is "the opiate of the masses." What he meant by this phrase is that religion can be used by the powerful in society to blind people to the realities of inequality. If kings can rule by "divine right," their use and abuse of political power is legitimated by religious beliefs and by religious functionaries. The god or gods have, in essence, given certain individuals the right to control others and to usurp a society's riches. Because people live miserable lives, religion also holds out the possibility that, if they abide by religious mandates that keep them poor, they can have a better life in the supernatural

Table 20.1   World's Largest Religions

Religion	Number of Adherents	Percentage of World's Religious Population
Christian	1.9 billion	32.8
Muslim	1.2 billion	19.6
Hindu	762 million	12.8
Chinese Folk	379 million	6.4
Buddhist	354 million	6.0

Source: Time Almanac (2002; 433).

Note: Estimates for numbers of individuals in each religion are not exact, but the relative rank order of adherents is probably correct.

realm when they die. In this way, the poor and oppressed are kept from protesting because their suffering now will be rewarded after they are dead. Religion thus blinds people to the real cause of their misery—the powerful and elite—and keeps them in line. As a functionalist would argue, religion maintains social control, but from a conflict perspective it is control that generates inequalities and assures the privilege of elites.

There are some data that give support to Marx's argument (Swanson 1960). When societies are hierarchical and stratified, the pantheon of gods is also stratified, as are the levels of the cult structures that organize people's rituals directed at the gods in this pantheon. Because the structure of the pantheon and the structure of society mirror each other, and especially as the priesthood supports the existing distribution of power, religion legitimates the hierarchies in society, making them seem to be the natural order of things. Yet, even as religion operates to legitimate inequalities, religious organizations persist because they give meaning to people's lives. Marx probably overemphasized the obfuscating effects of religion; people are probably not the "dupes" that he portrayed them to be; and indeed, they are not always blinded to the real source of their misery.

Religion in America

The History of Religion in America

The first religions in America were, of course, those practiced by native Americans. The first European settlers on America's shores were members of small Protestant cults (Herberg 1955; Williams 1970; 356). They settled in a religious vacuum because there was no dominant religious system. Members of these cults were intolerant of other cults, despite the fact that they had often come to America to escape the very persecution that they were willing to practice on others. Because the cults were small and geographically dispersed, however, none could generate the resources and organization necessary to eliminate the others. The result was the acceptance of religious diversity—an acceptance that was eventually codified into law.

Although each of these Protestant cults revealed a somewhat different adaptation of Protestant theology, they did share one critical belief: there was to be a personal relationship between God and human beings; each person was to "make peace" with God. The church provided a place for common worship and ritual activity, but ultimately each person must actively come to terms with the supernatural. These beliefs reinforced such dominant American values as individualism and activism (see Chapter 5). Individuals must be free to actively pursue their interests and deal with the world around them. Thus the beliefs of the Protestant cults of early America reinforced those values that, in turn, stimulated industrial capitalism (Weber 1905).

The rise of capitalism and the resulting urbanization of the American population encouraged the growth of religious cults. Protestant cults became more bureaucratized on the national level, forming umbrella organizations for local church organizations. The expansion of industry also encouraged the migration of Europeans to this country in the latter half of the last century. With these European immigrants came the other two major religious groups in America: Catholics and Jews.

Although early immigrants were subject to all manner of economic, political, and religious discrimination, the begrudging tolerance of Protestant cults for each other and the codification of this tolerance in the Constitution allowed the Catholic and Jewish religious groups to flourish. Later immigrants bringing religions from Asia and the middle east similarly enjoyed legal protections, although tolerance of non-Christian religions has never been great in America.

The Ecology of Religion in America

The United States is overwhelmingly Christian, but several of the larger denominations, such as the Presbyterian Church of the United States, United Methodists, and the Episcopal Church, have revealed a decline in memberships. On the other side, some denominations are growing rapidly: Seventh Day Adventist, Mormons, Assemblies of God, Jehovah's Witnesses, Southern Baptist, African Methodist Episcopal, and Roman Catholicism. Most of these growing denominations were relatively small 30 years ago, and so with a small base of members, their rates of growth are very high. Table 20.2 summarizes the percentage increases and decreases in the membership of various denominations in the United States.

There is a pattern here: older, established, and somewhat staid denominations have been losing members, whereas evangelical religious denominations have been gaining members. This trend suggests a different kind of explanation than either functional or conflict theory can

Table 20.2 Relative Growth and Decline in Religious Membership in the United States

Fastest Growth	Percentage Increase, 2003
African Methodist Episcopal	58
Jehovah's Witness	48
Seventh Day Adventist	35
Assemblies of God	34
Mormons	32
Southern Baptist	16
Roman Catholic	12
Loss of Members	
Reformed	−20
Disciples of Christ	−14
Episcopal	−13
Presbyterian	−12
United Church	−9
United Methodist	−9

Source: National Council of Churches (2004).

offer. Ecological theory argues that organizations, such as churches, exit in a resource niche—those seeking religious meaning—and like any set of organizations in a niche, they compete for members. Many of the dynamics of religion in America are thus ecological in nature; the relative increases and declines in religious affiliations reflect competition among religious organizations carrying different messages.

Part of the competitive dynamic revolves around the tendency of older, established churches to "intellectualize" their teachings and, thereby, make them more secular, less immediate, and less emotional. This is because more affluent people begin to join successful religions, but unlike those who are less affluent, they do not require the emotional, evangelical spirit that may have started the religion; they are, after all, more secure and less worried about their lives. For many, this tendency takes away the appeal of religion, especially for the masses who need and want religion to "solve" their immediate problems and anxieties. And so, new religions appeal to them because they can become more evangelical, emotional, and immediate, while being less intellectual, cerebral, and secular. There is a class conflict dimension to religion in America, with older and less evangelical denominations appealing to the affluent, prompting the lower classes to look elsewhere.

Broader secular trends of the society in many institutional spheres, especially as fueled by the growth of science as an institution, are also part of the pattern of religious fracturing in America (Stark 1981; Stark and Bainbridge 1980). Society-wide secularization penetrates some religions, and in so doing, religion becomes less salient to many who want and need religion in an immediate and emotional way. The result is that a market for religious zeal emerges—a big market niche—and new denominations, often using the media very effectively, emerge and win converts. Many of these fail, but as the growth figures indicate, many succeed and dramatically so. When old faiths become too secular, then, they lose members to more evangelical ones; and so, we might predict that secularization of societies creates market niches for new denominations, leading to intense differentiation and competition among denominations (see Organizational Ecology in Chapter 12 for a review of the basic dynamics involved here, as organizations compete for resources).

Religious Conflict in America

Because Americans vary in terms of *how* evangelical they are and *how much* they want religion to penetrate their daily lives, conflict often emerges. Many of the major conflicts in America—prayer in schools, abortion, vouchers for church schools, faith-based social programs funded by government, a pledge of allegiance that mentions God, teaching Darwinian evolution in the schools—reflect this split in the cult structures, or denominations, in terms of how fervently evangelical or secular they are.

Religion and politics make for a volatile mix because those who hold religious beliefs view many political decisions as moral crusades about ultimate right and wrong. The fathers of the American Constitution were not particularly tolerant of other religions, but they proposed a separation of church and state because they recognized the potential for debilitating conflict. Over the last two decades, the more conservative and evangelical denominations in America have become politically active, with the result that the electoral process, the appointment of judges and administrators, and the legislation of social policy are heavily influenced by the religious convictions of a well-organized set of religious denominations. It is likely that political conflict will increasingly revolve around religious conflict, the very thing that the framers of the Constitution wished to avoid.

Religiosity in America

Competition among religions has the effect of increasing religiosity in the United States. As religious organizations compete with each other, they refine and target their message, often using the media to advantage. As they do so, they pull individuals into religious cult structures; as these individuals engage in the rituals directed at the supernatural, their emotions are aroused, and they become more religious. There is, of course, wide variation among Americans in the degree of religiosity, but all surveys show that most Americans are religious and that they see religion as an important part of their lives.

Compared to other postindustrial societies, this religiosity is the exception rather than the rule. But, in a society that never had an official "state religion" that dominated worship and, indeed, in a society that encouraged religious freedom, a large resource niche was created among all those who sought meaning in the supernatural, leading to intense competition among religious cults. The competition has led to more effective marketing of the message, pulling a large proportion of the population into cults and, thereby, increasing religiosity in America.

Social Characteristics of Religious Memberships

Max Weber (1904) was perhaps the first sociologist to explore the relationship between religious activity and people's place in society. He noted that urban artisans and shopkeepers of the eighteenth and nineteenth centuries, for example, were inclined to view the nature of the world much differently from the way farmers in the European countryside did. The market economy and its emphasis on the exchange of goods, contracts, and meeting one's financial obligations led urbanites to seek religious doctrines that emphasized control of events. Farmers' dependence upon the unpredictable forces of nature led them to rely upon magic and other appeals to supernatural realms.

This initial insight still concerns sociologists. What background factors influence people's religious affiliations? What are the social characteristics of those in different religious cults? Most research in this area is, unfortunately, much narrower than Weber's original analysis. In American sociology, emphasis has been placed on the occupational, income, educational, familial, political, and ethnic/racial correlates of religious affiliation. We can briefly summarize the findings of this research in the following manner.

Religion and Income.   In general, Jews are over-represented in higher income groups than Catholics in comparison to their numbers in the general population. On the whole, Catholics have higher incomes than

Protestants, although when Protestant groups are broken down, Episcopalians, Presbyterians, and Lutherans have higher average income levels than Catholics (but still less than Jews), and Baptists and Methodists earn less, on the average, than Catholics.

Religion and Education.   Because of the connection between income and education, the data on religion and education show much the same pattern as those for income and religion. Jews are over-represented, in comparison to their numbers in the general population, among college graduates; Catholics and Protestants are just under the national average for college graduates. When Protestant groups are broken down and examined, however, Episcopalians and Presbyterians are well above the national average. Lutherans and Methodists are just under the average at about the same level as Catholics. Baptists are considerably under the national level.

Religion and Family.   Religion appears to influence the selection of marriage partners. People tend to choose marriage partners whose religious beliefs and affiliations are close to their own. Divorce is influenced by religion: intermarriage across religious lines is more likely to result in divorce than marriage within denominations. Rates for each religious group tend to vary, with Protestants more likely to end marriage than either Catholics or Jews (Lenski 1963). Remarriage after divorce is higher among Protestants than Catholics.

Religion and Politics.   The relationship between religion and politics is somewhat confounded by social class. Protestants are about equally split between the Democratic and Republican parties, but the wealthier Protestants (e.g., the Episcopalians and Presbyterians) are much more likely to be Republican. Poorer denominations, such as Southern Baptists, are more likely to be Democratic. Catholics, who are predominately of ethnic origin and blue collar occupations, have clear preferences for the Democratic party. Jews present an inverse relationship between class and party affiliation because, although more likely to be affluent, they vote Democratic.

Race, Ethnicity, and Religion

In general, the largest single group of African Americans are Baptist, attesting to their southern roots. Blacks, however, have a wide variety of smaller church organizations that do not affiliate with the Baptist church. Hispanics, such as Mexican Americans and Puerto Ricans, are overwhelmingly Catholic. Asian Americans tend to affiliate with churches corresponding to their class position, and because this group is predominately in the middle class category, their affiliations tend to be Protestant *if* they are Christian. Many more recent Asian immigrants have often retained the non-Christian religion from their homeland. White ethnics, who migrated to the United States in the early part of this century from southern and eastern Europe, are overwhelmingly Catholic. Many from eastern Europe, of course, are Jewish. Most German, Swedish, Norwegian, and Danish immigrants are Protestant.

SUMMARY

1. Social institutions are congeries of positions and structures that seek to resolve the fundamental problems of humans as a species and as a species that relies upon culturally mediated patterns of social organization. Because of their perceived importance, most of the general norms guiding behavior in institutional structures are well known and infused with values and beliefs.

2. Religion is the institution that organizes ritual practices directed toward sacred and supernatural forces in the affirmation of certain beliefs. Religion probably emerged in simple human societies as a strategy for reducing anxiety and tension-reduction, while reinforcing critical norms and values.

3. Historically, from hunting and gathering to agrarianism, religion became more complex in its beliefs, rituals, and cult structures. Then, beliefs were simplified as the World Religions emerged, although bureaucratization of complex cult structures continued.

4. In more complex societies, religion has often legitimated the status quo and the unequal distribution of resources, such as power and wealth.

5. Religion in America is overwhelmingly Christian; and yet, it reveals a large number of denominations that appear to ebb and flow in terms of their capacity to attract and retain members.

KEY TERMS

Cult Structure: Unit organizing rituals and sustaining religious beliefs and values.

Pantheon: Set of religious beliefs specifying the inhabitants, as well as their relations and life histories, of the supernatural realm.

Profane: Denoting processes in the empirical world, in comparison with the sacred, which is of the supernatural world.

Religious Beliefs: Conceptions about the nature of the sacred and supernatural as well as the entities and forces in the supernatural realm.

Religious Rituals: Stereotyped sequences of behavior designed to make appeals to the forces of the supernatural realm.

Religious Values: Conceptions of what is right and wrong, as well as what should exist and occur, that are viewed as emanating from supernatural forces.

Sacred: Objects and forces having a special quality because they are connected to perceived supernatural powers.

Supernatural: Realm where gods and unworldly forces operate.

Chapter 21

Education

Reading this page emphasizes your involvement in education. You may not feel like reading today, but your eyes pass over the page; you underline words with a yellow marker (often converting a white page to yellow); you make mental notes; and if really ambitious, you take written notes. Such is the power of the educational system in which we have all been involved. It organizes much of a person's life until adulthood and it has profound consequences for what happens to all people for the rest of their lives.

This power is recent. Education, as we have come to know it, has only recently expanded its influence. For most of human history, formal education was unnecessary. Children learned what was necessary in their families or in play with other children. As the economic life of a society changes, however, kinship becomes inadequate to the task of imparting all those skills necessary for participation in the society. Education becomes formal and increasingly embraces a larger proportion of the population.

The Emergence of Formal Education

The beginnings of formal education can be traced to organized religious activity. Shamans, witch doctors, and other religious practitioners may have selected pupils for religious instruction. Much of the lore, tradition, and sacred customs of a society were imparted to these students, who in turn passed them on to other selected students.

Education was dramatically expanded with the emergence of state forms of governance (see Chapter 18). Governments require administrative specialists—people to do the bookkeeping, to organize state affairs, to wage war, and to collect taxes. Although early political leaders initially relied upon kin to conduct governmental activities, the need to recruit and train specialists increased as governments grew. Growth usually depended upon an economic surplus of an agrarian economy, and so, formal education of specialists probably did not occur until 5,000 years ago. By 4000 B.C., the Egyptians had formal education, not only for elites but also for selected peasants who showed "promise" and the ability to assist in the administration of government. Canals, irrigation and sewage-disposal systems, the pyramids, tombs, and cities of this early state government could not have been designed and built without some degree of formal education of those from outside elite groups.

Formal education may also have been acquired by the craftspeople and tradespeople as well as the shopkeepers of early cities. The creation of the larger trading centers of all the early empires probably required formally educating people to keep records and to administer other aspects of economic transactions. For significant periods of history in Asia and Europe, however, political unification and economic trade often disintegrated. The Dark Ages are "dark" not because nothing occurred but because there were few to keep records, except for isolated religious practitioners. Similarly, in Asia, literacy from formal education appears to have increased and then decreased according to political and economic trends (J. Turner 1972, 149–150).

Even under the best conditions, however, education was a "recessive" institution. It reached elites but few of the masses. With the coming of the Industrial Revolution, the need for literacy, for specialized skills, and for political control of people's minds increased dramatically. Schools were established to educate and indoctrinate industrial workers, tradespeople, and, increasingly, administrative specialists in industry and government. With advanced industrialism, education became an increasingly prominent institution. Thus, the power of education to shape people's lives is a recent development in the evolution of human societies.

Explaining the Dynamics of Education

A Functionalist Explanation

From a functional perspective, education emerges and expands to meet the needs of a society for literacy, skill, knowledge, control, and other requisites of an urban-industrial age. Once established, the institution of education begins to have at least five major consequences, or functions, for society: (a) cultural storage, (b) cultural expansion, (c) socialization, (d) social placement, and (e) social change.

Cultural Storage.   Human beings live in a world of symbols. We use many of these symbols—technologies, values, beliefs, and norms—to guide and organize our daily affairs. We store these symbols in our minds to guide us from within. As societies become more complex, however, it requires more than a single mind, or even the minds of many people, to store an entire cultural heritage. Written language permits the elaboration of culture to the point of requiring storage by specialists. Education serves this function. It keeps, maintains, and preserves the cultural system of a society.

Cultural Expansion and Change.   As only a repository of culture, educational structures might resemble a "museum of symbols." In actual practice, however, educational structures are usually involved in cultural innovation (i.e., cultural expansion and change). Research is a major task in universities and colleges. New technologies; new insights; and new interpretations of the present, past, and future are part of the goals of many structures of higher education. Indirectly, students are being taught to think, reflect, ponder, and create new insights at all levels of the educational system. One of the goals of primary and secondary schools, as well as of colleges and universities, is to impart the skills that enable people to expand the cultural storehouse in a wide variety of adult roles.

Socialization.   In schools, students learn not only substantive knowledge but also the skills necessary to play roles in the society at large, but more than intellectual substance and technique are taught. Individuals also learn how to participate in formal organizations, how to live with impersonality, how to compete, and how to subject themselves to just and unjust evaluations. Thus, schools teach many of the interpersonal skills and psychological dispositions necessary to participate in modern society. In the shadow of an academic curriculum, then, is a hidden one: learning how to "play the game of life" according to the rules of modern industrial societies (Drucker 1959).

Social Placement.   In societies lacking formal educational systems, placement as adults in the broader society follows kinship rules. Gender, birth order, and the rank of a family determine what children become and do as adults. In more developed societies in which a wide variety of alternative jobs exists, education increasingly assumes enormous importance in social placement (i.e., in determining what economic and social niches people occupy). The credentials acquired in the system of education become the main mechanism for hiring and promoting people. Education thus becomes "society's gatekeeper," sorting and allocating people to different positions in the broader society.

Social Change.   As a set of structures involved in storing and expanding culture, in socializing skills and attributes, and in placing people in social niches, education can serve as a vehicle for change. It grips the minds of the young and possesses the power to determine what they learn, how they acquire this knowledge, and for what purposes it is used. Aside from any innovations that the educational system may generate, education can meet political ends. It can create a "new citizen," undermine traditions of kinship or religion, or generate a work force with new skills. It is no coincidence, therefore, that totalitarian states often use education to mold the population in certain directions. Nor is it surprising that governments, totalitarian or otherwise, often initiate their economic and social development through the creation of new schools oriented toward the masses. Even in developed societies such as the United States, education fosters change in industry and government. Efforts to integrate schools racially and ethnically, the creation of federal land-grant colleges, the proliferation of community colleges, and the endowments of private universities by corporate interests all document efforts to change society in certain directions through the educational system.

The Conflict Theory Corrective to Functional Analysis

There are two basic conflict perspectives on education in modern societies, one inspired by Marx's analysis of capitalist society (Bowles & Gintis 1976) and the other by Weber's description of status groups (Collins 1979). Each emphasizes that the educational system in capitalist economies operates to sustain inequalities, but the underlying dynamic in the two approaches is very different.

In the Marxian version (Bowles & Gintis 1976), education operates to sustain the inequalities inherent in capitalist society. The existence of free public education—with its emphasis on open competition and achievement, grades, test scores, and "equal access" to opportunities—

operates as a mechanism to preserve the existing class structure. By emphasizing "objective" grades, achievement test scores, intelligence tests, ability "tracks," and other supposedly neutral means for evaluating students, the educational system convinces underachievers and their parents that the failure to do well in school and life it is their own fault. In schools that are integrated by social class, children from the lower classes of society experience difficulty doing well in a system dominated by middle class teachers, values, and curricula. Integrated schools often deny lower class students credentials necessary to get good jobs, giving the advantage to middle class children, thus maintaining their privileged position.

In schools populated by predominately lower- and working-class children, the emphasis is on obedience to rules, deference to authority, punctuality, and other traits necessary for lower class work. Conversely, in schools populated by middle class children, the system is much more likely to encourage independent work and creativity, to tolerate independent thought and action, to trust students, and to stress self-control. As a result, middle class students are better prepared to assume supervisory economic roles. The overall consequence is for the capitalist class structure to reproduce itself, using the schools as one of the central instruments of such reproduction.

The other conflict approach views the school system not so much as a direct instrument of the capitalistic class but as a tool for maintaining the cultural differences among individuals (Collins 1979). Groups of individuals compete with each other to gain and sustain prestige and social honor. Educational credentials are one of the main focal points of this conflict. Indeed, the functionalist's view that higher educational credentials are necessary in an economic system requiring increased skill and expertise is inaccurate. The actual skill levels required to perform many jobs can be learned rather quickly on the job and do not, in fact, require college and postgraduate education. Some very technical jobs may necessitate higher education, but increases in such positions cannot explain the rapid expansion of higher education. The expansion has been encouraged by the educational establishment to preserve its privilege and by employers who can use educational credentials to select "right thinking" workers. Together they have created an over-valuation of credentials. As more and more people seek higher education, these credentials become worth less and less. To make one's educational credentials "mean something," still further education is sought. As people scramble to acquire more education, the interests of the educational establishment are served. As employees demand credentials (even though they are not essential for actual job performance), they can use their "need for the best qualified" to keep lower class and minority groups out of jobs for which they are qualified but for which they do not have the "proper credentials." They can also sort out white middle class individuals who do not display the appropriate demeanor and lifestyle by averring that their credentials are "not quite what we needed." Credentials thus become a means of restricting access to desirable jobs and preserving prestige (and of course, income) differences among individuals.

Credential inflation is the outcome of these status processes. As credentials become the primary marker of "skills," people seek more credentials to "stand out" in a competitive labor market; and employers buy into this inflationary cycle because it is easier to use credentials than in-depth knowledge of a person in making hiring decisions. And, of course, the education establishment supports this inflation because it is good for its well-being. In the end, a population can become overeducated for the range of actual skills needed to perform routine jobs.

A Further Corrective from an Interactionist Perspective

Schools are agents of socialization, but they are in a sense double agents. They not only actively socialize, but they also react to the legacy of so-cialization in the family and, to a lesser extent, to peer groupings of the young. The effect of schools on the motives, self-conception, interper-sonal styles, and cultural directives of children, therefore, is influenced by many of the capacities that children bring with them into the school. If children bring achievement motives, a self-conception of themselves as able and capable of cognitive learning, a set of middle class interpersonal skills (speech, gestures, demeanor), and a profile of cultural symbols em-phasizing achievement, activism, and other dominant values, then the school reinforces these capacities. As children interact with the teacher, they receive messages that reinforce the interpersonal legacy of their so-cialization outside the school. Students also add to this legacy in ways that facilitate subsequent adjustment in the educational bureaucracy, in the job market, and in high-prestige occupations or professions. Teachers praise and parade children who have verbal skills, who have developed the capacity to mobilize energy in the classroom, workbooks, and home-work exercises, who bring with them value commitments for trying hard, who display the dress, speech, and gesture patterns of the middle-classes, who demonstrate a willingness to express themselves, and who show a desire to compete in cognitive exercises. They are labeled "good students." As a result, they develop a conception of themselves as able to do well in competitive intellectual and verbal arenas. They learn how to mobilize and channel their cognitive energies. They increase their verbal and interpersonal skills in bureaucratic contexts. And, as a result, they begin to acquire a dossier of good grades, high test scores, and honor roll classes. This dossier allows them access to college preparatory classes and eventually higher education.

Children who bring to the school a different legacy are labeled, at worst, "bad students" or "problem students" and, at best, "average stu-dents." A student with an ethnic accent, a harsh and grammatically sub-standard speech style, a physically aggressive demeanor, a self-concept revolving around noncognitive abilities, a set of motives emphasizing ac-tivity and achievement in nonacademic contexts, a profile of cultural symbols emphasizing obedience (or, conversely, aggressiveness) will, in the end, suffer in the school system. The teacher communicates in speech and gestures a clear message: school and academics are not your forte. As a result, children do not aspire to the verbal, interpersonal, and cognitive skills necessary "to do well" in the system. Their self-concept does not encompass confidence in their abilities to perform school work. Consequently, these students acquire a record of poor-to-average grades and test scores and a legacy of non-college-preparatory courses. These inhibit their easy transition to college and keep them from acquiring those credentials that can facilitate their chances in the job market.

The Structure of Educational Systems

Most contemporary systems of education are divided into three levels: *primary schools, secondary schools,* and *higher education.* Although there are wide variations in just how primary education is conducted, most societies have developed a *primary school system* for a majority of those between the ages of 6 and 12. Because this schooling may be all the formal education that people receive in poor nations, emphasis is on imparting rudimentary skills in reading, writing, and arithmetic. Political socialization to keep the masses loyal to the existing government is also a goal of the primary system.

In more affluent nations, primary schools prepare students for participation in the *secondary schools* that are to occupy their energies through adolescence. In most societies, a secondary school education is the last phase of the standard educational process. Comparatively few go further, and it is only in America that over half of the college-aged population is educated beyond secondary level. Part of the difference between American schools and those of other advanced societies is a result of differences in the structure of secondary schools. Most societies employ what is termed a *multiple-track system,* as opposed to the *single-track system (with multiple lanes)* in the United States. The differences between these two systems are shown in Figure 21.1.

In the **multiple-track system,** secondary schools train people for specialized jobs. Different schools usually specialize in their own distinc-

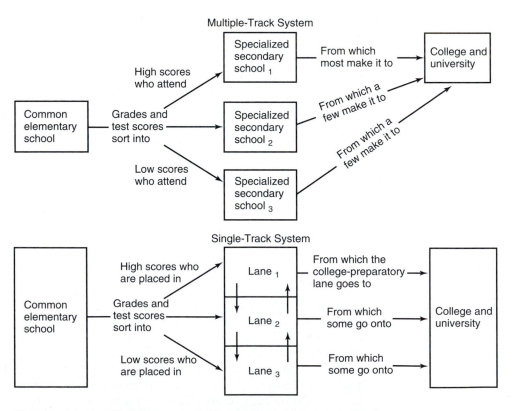

Figure 21.1   Multiple- and Single-Track School System

tive types of training. As a result, much of what is taught in professional and trade schools in America is part of the secondary curricula in other societies. In contrast, the American system has a **single-track,** for all must go to primary and secondary schools. Within the secondary school are *lanes* for directing students into vocational and college-preparatory courses, for example. Lanes have many of the same consequences as tracks in the multiple-track system: they sort and circumscribe the options that will be available to students upon graduation. They simply do it within one school.

In most societies higher education is reserved primarily for the sons and daughters of elites or for those who have shown exceptional ability in primary and secondary schools. The majority of citizens do not attend college, although it must be remembered that their secondary education is likely to involve considerable specialized training. In some societies, such as the United States, there has been "credential inflation" (Collins 1979), resulting in mass higher education as students seek more advanced credentials that mean less and less. Yet, with postindustrialization in multiple-track systems, the beginnings of credential inflation can be seen in other societies as a greater percentage of secondary school graduates begin a university education than was the case two decades ago.

Education in America

The Structure of Lower American Education

Mass Education.   Virtually every American receives a primary-school education and close to 90% graduate from high school. Illiteracy is now below 2%, although rates of "functional illiteracy" are much higher. Even college enrollments have increased dramatically, with over 50% of the population beginning some form of education beyond high school but with a much smaller percentage actually receiving four-year college degrees. For example, only 15.5% of the American population has a Bachelors degree, but another 21% has some college, and yet another 6.3% has an Associate degree from a community college (Chronical of Higher Education 2003). Education thus extends to all segments of the population. Mass education is a fact of social life in America.

Education and Democracy.   Mass education does not necessarily mean equal education. The quality of schools in America varies between rural and urban areas, urban and suburban cities, and from state to state. To attend school in a rural area of a poor state means accepting education that is of lower quality than that in the rural area of a wealthier state, or than in the suburban area of any state. To the extent that educational democracy means educational equality, there is far from complete democracy in the educational system in America, and this is an issue that is at the heart of many dilemmas confronting the educational system in America.

Decentralization.   The American educational system is the least centralized in the industrial world. At the lower educational level, individual schools enjoy some autonomy from each other but are subject to the district's authority. School districts have some autonomy from the state and federal administration, and each state establishes its own educational

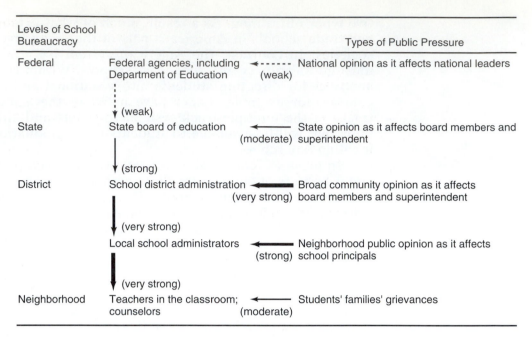

Figure 21.2   Decentralization in American Schools

Source: Jonathan H. Turner, *Patterns of Social Organization* (New York: McGraw-Hill, 1972). p. 176.

system within general guidelines laid down by the federal government. Figure 21.2 shows this pattern of influence and control.

As the figure shows, American schools are subject to strong community pressures. Local property taxes finance a large portion of school functions, school-board members are elected, and strong beliefs in "local control" dominate public debates about education. American lower education is thus highly decentralized with very little coordination and control at the national level (Pierce 1964).

At the higher education level, a similar pattern of decentralization is evident. Private schools enjoy considerable autonomy from the federal government. State colleges and universities are administratively separate, although each is subject to budgetary and policy constraints of a statewide administration. Community colleges are usually a part of the school district or a separate college district and are thus subject to some pressures by a school board and local community, although the state may also exert considerable control over community college districts.

Privatization.   Parallel to the public system of education in America is a large private sector. At the lower educational level, from kindergarten through high school, most private schools have religious affiliations, although elite secular private schools also exist.

Home Schooling.   Right up to the 20th century, a significant proportion of children were schooled at home, but by the midpoint of the 20th century, virtually all children were educated outside the home. In recent decades, however, new laws and court decisions now allow parents to educate children at home (following state-imposed guidelines); therefore, an increasing number of parents are involved in **home schooling.** This movement is a reaction against perceived deficiencies of public schools, coupled with a desire of parents to control their children's education. Computer technologies and an array of study-programs have enabled parents to provide more advanced instruction.

Critics of home schooling argue that parents are not professionals and, hence, that the education offered will be inferior to what is provided in schools. Moreover, critics contend that children become isolated from the diversity of society (class, ethnicity, gender) and do not learn skills about how to participate in bureaucratic organizations. Yet, whatever the merits of the critics' arguments, home schooling will continue to expand, although as a proportion of the total student population in America, home schooling teaches a tiny percentage of students.

Year-Round Education.   The summer vacation is a holdover from a time when children were needed to help harvest crops, although it appears to help some students rest and enjoy their childhood in creative ways. Crowding and financial pressures have forced many school districts to adopt **year-round schooling** with shorter "off time" breaks throughout the year. Year-round schools make more efficient use of school facilities because they do not sit idle during the summer, and they keep students focused on their work for the whole year, thereby avoiding the "fall off" in performance that comes with summer. Whatever the advantages and disadvantages, more districts are likely to move to a year-round system in America in the near future.

Higher Education in America

Scale of the System.   The United States has more colleges and universities than any other country in the world—by a very large margin. And, if community colleges are added to the mix, the scale of American higher education is even more dramatic. In any given year, over 15 million students are enrolled in some form of higher education (Chronical of Higher Education 2003, 16). Almost 36% of the 18- to 24-year-old population is enrolled in some form of college.

Diversity of the System.   The college and university system is not only large, it is diverse along several axes. First, there is the split between public and private universities and colleges. There are over 1,500 nonprofit four-year private and over 600 public colleges and universities. But, because private institutions generally have lower enrollments, only 3.2 million of all students are enrolled in private four-year colleges and universities, whereas 6.0 million are in four-year public universities. Second, there is a split between two-year community colleges and four-year schools. There are 1,085 public community colleges (135 nonprofit private and 490 for profit community colleges). The public community colleges provide the first two years of college at relatively low costs; and increasingly over the last decades, they offer a wide variety of more vocational programs (Brint & Karabel 1989). Third, there is a wide range of four-year colleges and universities: (a) small, four-year liberal arts colleges (mostly private) with few or no graduate programs; (b), very large four-year state universities with some graduate programs and with teaching-oriented faculty; (c) very large and elite state universities with many graduate programs and with a large research faculty; and (d) elite private universities of various sizes with strong graduate programs and research-oriented faculty. Fourth, there is a growing number of for profit universities (now some 318), generally with a combination of online and classroom courses, catering to those who work full time. And finally, there is a variety of extension programs affiliated with mostly public universities.

Research Mission.   Unlike many societies that fund research in national academies of science and technology, much research is conducted in the university. Indeed, in many research universities, funding from governmental agencies and corporate sponsors represents a greater portion of the university's budget than student fees/tuition and money from state legislators combined. Thus, research is big business for some universities, and there is now a growing concern that universities are so dependent upon external funding that pure research is giving way to "research for hire" (by government and corporations).

Students in the System.   Depending upon where you are in this complex and diverse system of higher education, your experiences will vary. If you are at a small private university, you will generally have small classes and much attention from professors, especially if this college is not research-oriented. You will still have smaller classes and receive attention at a research-oriented private university, but not as much as at a teaching-oriented school. If you are at either a large teaching- or research-oriented state university, your classes will generally be large, and faculty attention to you will decline. If you are online at a for profit university, you interact primarily with your computer. And, depending on its size, your experience at a community college will approximate a smaller private or state-funded college or a large public university.

Whatever your classroom experience, one fact seems to emerge: in classes large and small, relatively few students actually speak up. Students are generally passive, and therefore, relatively little classroom time in all types of colleges and universities is devoted to active classroom discussion and debate.

Enduring Problems and Dilemmas of Lower Education

Schools and Stratification.   Thomas Jefferson felt that schools "bring into action that mass of talents which lies buried in poverty in every country for want of means of development." There can be little doubt that mass public education has increased the skills of many Americans, but the educational system does not do so equally. This fact has important consequences. Because we live in a "credentialed society," people's chances for success are strongly influenced by their educational credentials; and thus, the extensive use of credentials forces the educational system to be society's gatekeeper. People who conform to the system's requirements receive credentials, whereas those having personal, cultural, and socioeconomic handicaps—or those who experience difficulty conforming for other reasons—may not obtain the credentials that assure them of well-paying jobs.

It now appears that some bureaucratic routines of public schools (emphasis on control, order, plans, schedules, and other organizational features) can inadvertently discriminate against non-middle-class children. For example, the formality of schools, with their concern for silence, the lesson plan, schedules, and the control of movement can work to the disadvantage of some children from the lower classes, in which physical assertiveness, noise, and spontaneity are more likely to be valued (Miller 1958). In middle-class-oriented schools, therefore, lower class children are more likely to become alienated.

Another source of discrimination comes from the teachers in public schools. Most are from the middle classes. As a result, they can communicate a subtle attitude or expectation that lower class or minority students will have learning problems. By expecting less of lower class students, teachers can potentially and unintentionally convince the students that they have "learning problems" (Rosenthal & Jacobson 1968; Silberman 1971, 83–86).

Seemingly objective and fair tests represent yet another form of discrimination against lower class children. Intelligence tests, national achievement exams, or in-class quizzes are competitive and timed. Such tests favor students from middle class backgrounds in whose culture the importance of test-taking and competition probably have been stressed. Moreover, most tests are written in standard English, and this fact gives middle class students, whose parents are more verbal than those in lower classes, a competitive advantage. In addition, national achievement and intelligence tests usually portray a world that is more familiar to middle class students.

Discipline and Violence. Over the last three decades, American schools have become more violent. Despite efforts at bureaucratic control, violence from the street and, all too often from the family, is brought in to the school. Dysfunctional family life, drug use, and gang affiliations all clash with the bureaucratic control system and the demand for achievement. The public wants more discipline, but there are limits to what can be accomplished, unless several conditions prevail (Gup 1992): (a) firm and consistent discipline in the school, (b) strong support from parents, (c) alliances with community organizations, (d) adequate counseling options, and (e) expelling of habitual trouble makers. It is often difficult, especially in poor communities and neighborhoods, to meet all of these conditions.

School Finances.   Because schools are financed at the local district and state levels, there is considerable inequality in school facilities, teacher qualifications, libraries and lab equipment, extracurricular activities, after-school programs, and many other facets of primary and secondary education. Affluent school districts in affluent states spend more than poor districts in poor states. Moreover, even in more affluent states such as California, schools are underfunded; the state simply does not spend as much money as is required for a high quality of education. As the ethnic diversity, the special education needs of disabled students, and the volume of students to be educated increases, most states need to raise the level of funding for education. But, because of existing tax formulas or political agendas against expanding government, it becomes difficult to increase the budgets of public schools.

Vouchers and School Choice.   Some states have experimented with a **school voucher** system in which parents are given the money from the state to shop around in the education market for a school of their choice—whether this be a public, religious, or for-profit school. Proponents argue that a competitive market will improve schools, whereas critics contend that vouchers would deprive the public system of needed resources, especially in poor areas where the money is most needed and where students (and their parents) have few options (Cohen 1999). Moreover, as for-profit schools enter the educational market, it is not clear that these schools would be as concerned about the quality of education as their financial bottom line. The debate over "school choice" will, no doubt, escalate as the problems of many public school systems mount in the decades to come.

Declining Academic Standards.   It is clear that high school graduates today are less prepared than they were two generations ago. Scholastic Aptitude Test (SAT) scores have been declining since the 1960s (although they rose slightly in 2003); and on the bases of other achievement and progress tests, student abilities in mathematics, reading, reasoning, and science have also declined (Sanchez 1998). Moreover, functional illiteracy—or the inability to read and write so as to live a normal life—is increasing. Indeed, 40 million adults read and write below an eighth grade level (United Nations 2000); thus, 21% of adults in America read only at the eighth grade level, a rate that is lower than any other English-speaking country, nation in western Europe, or Japan.

There is no clear answer to why academic standards and performance are declining. The answer probably resides in a mix of factors, including: (a) lack of parental supervision of their children's school work (which is related to increases in single-parent households and both parents working in intact homes); (b) social promotion in schools; (c) amount of time of students in front of visual media such as games and television; (d) anti-intellectual youth cultures; (e) increase in immigrants for whom English is a second language; (f) declining financial support for schools, especially in urban areas; (g) overcrowding in schools; (h) overuse of temporary teachers without full credentials; and (i) increasing drop-out rates, especially for minority children.

Enduring Problems in Higher Education

Credentialism.   Enrollments in universities are increasingly driven by students' needs to become "certified" for the job market. Learning and acquiring a breadth of cultural capital is increasingly taking a back seat to "getting the degree." This kind of orientation generates an anti-intellectual climate, and at its worst, encourages larger numbers of students to cheat on exams and term papers.

Credentialism also leads students to pursue more degrees, even when not absolutely necessary in terms of the skills required. But, as long as students must compete in labor markets, this *credential inflation* will continue (Collins 1976).

Funding.   Higher education is expensive because technology and laboratories must constantly be updated. The result is for fees and tuition to rise at rates much higher than the general rate of inflation. As costs to students increase, many cannot attend the college or university of their choice.

Teaching Versus Research. Most studies of teaching and research document that the best researchers are also among the best teachers. But, those actively engaged in research must have reduced teaching loads if they are to have the time to conduct research. The result is for classes to become larger because the faculty teach fewer of them. For students who pay high tuition or for state legislators who are more interested in faculty teaching than research, there is always a point of tension between research faculty and those who would like to see more teaching from faculty. In nonresearch colleges and universities, the problem works the other way: the faculty teach so much that they burn out from teaching and become less interested in students and learning.

Corporatization. Increasingly, many administrators within and politicians outside the university system appear to favor a "corporate model," which can mean several things. First, one model of a corporation is to organize the university like a business with accounting practices that highlight "profit" and "loss" centers. Second, another model is to solicit money from businesses by creating programs such as an Executive MBA or by having business fund research. This model sees the university marketing itself as any business trying to sell its products. A third model is to compete in an "education market" for student tuition dollars, once again marketing the university as a "total experience" (from student centers through sports to fraternities and sororities). Still another model is the "research park" that brings private corporations (mostly technology companies) to malls around the university and that encourages interaction and joint projects with faculty.

All of these models clash with the university as a place of learning, for its own sake, and as an entity engaged in pure research that is untainted by agendas from for-profit corporations. Given the high costs of higher education, however, some aspects of the corporate model will increasingly become a part of university life.

Affirmative Action, Diversity, and Equity. For several decades, colleges and universities have sought to diversify their student bodies by admitting under-represented minorities. To do so, it has been necessary at highly selective schools to admit some minorities whose record, though strong, is not as strong as that of some white students who are not admitted. There has been a number of celebrated court cases on this issue, especially at public universities, where white students have claimed "reverse discrimination." A recent U.S. Supreme Court decision in 2003 allows universities to consider ethnicity, as part of a whole package of attributes, in their admission policies. For those opposed to affirmative action, this decision has aroused opposition that, as in California, may lead to enactment of laws against using ethnic background in admission decisions. Private universities are less affected by any decision or law because they are private and can set their own admission policies, although blatant discrimination would make them vulnerable to a civil rights law suit and withdrawal of funds by the federal government.

Lost in much of the debate over "ethnic preferences" is social class biases at elite schools. Most students admitted to elite schools, including minority students, are from affluent backgrounds (Massey, Charles, Lundy, and Fischer 2003; Steinberg 2002). This bias reaffirms and reproduces the class structure of American society because it forces lower and working class students to attend less prestigious universities that do not offer a clear path to upward mobility (Brantlinger 2003; McDonough 1997).

The issue of how people can have "equal opportunities" will not go away in the near future. Efforts to "level the playing field" will be met with cries of "reverse discrimination." Yet, most students who meet the admission standards of a college or university—well over 80%—are admitted. Thus, the debate centers on elite private and public universities where there are far more qualified applicants than available positions.

SUMMARY

1. Education is a comparatively recent institution, differentiating from kinship with agrarianism and dramatically expanding with industrialization and postindustrialization.

2. Education expands because it provides new mechanisms for cultural storage, social and cultural change, and social placement of individuals. At the same time, education also operates to sustain the existing class system and status groups in this system.

3. Most educational systems in the world are divided into primary, secondary, and higher education. Most create a multiple-track system in which students of varying abilities and interests go to separate secondary schools, whereas some like the one in the United States have adopted a multiple-lane system in which students are put in lanes or tracks within the same secondary school.

4. Education in America is administered at the state and district level, and in most districts the majority of financing comes from local tax revenues. Alongside public education is a large system of private schools, extending from preschools to universities offering advanced degrees. Recent trends in the primary and secondary school systems include year-round education and an active home schooling movement.

5. Higher education in America is the largest in the world, educating in a given year over 15 million students who attend a variety of public and private colleges and universities. In the United States, universities conduct a good portion of the basic scientific research for the nation.

6. Within the American lower educational system, a number of enduring problems persist: inequality in schools and the effects of schools in maintaining the stratification system; increased problems of violence and discipline; problems in financing the schools, especially in poor areas; and problems in maintaining academic standards and performance. These problems have led to the advocacy of school vouchers whereby students can use state money to shop around for the best school for their children.

7. Within the higher educational system, several problems are evident, including: credential inflation, student financial aid as the costs of education continue to exceed the rate of inflation, the balance between teaching and research, corporatization of colleges and universities, and maintaining diversity of student populations.

KEY TERMS

Credential Inflation: Process whereby educational credentials are sought by more and more individuals, with the result that they become less valuable on the labor market, thereby forcing students to acquire more credentials.

Home Schooling: Social movement in which parents are increasingly teaching their children at home under guidelines set by state boards of education.

Multiple-Track System: Placement of students in different secondary schools depending upon their performance on standardized tests and grades in primary schools.

Single-Track, with Multiple-Lane System: Placement of students in different lanes or tracks within the same secondary school depending upon their performance on standardized tests and grades.

School Vouchers: Proposal to allocate to each parent state monies for them to shop around and choose the public or private school that they think is best for their children.

Year-Round Schooling: Increasing utilization of school facilities all year long, thereby eliminating the traditional summer vacation.

Part VI Social Change and Transformation

The history of human societies over the last five-thousand years reveals profound changes. By fits and starts, societies have become larger, more complex, more volatile, and more damaging to the ecosystem. In this group of chapters, we examine processes that are both a cause and outcome of change—social movements, revolutions, wars, terrorism, and globalization. Finally, it is essential to close with an understanding of how the growth of human populations, their organization into industrial societies, and the globalization of capitalism are affecting the world's ecosystem. Ultimately, no matter how complex patterns of social organization become, humans are still an animal who depends upon renewable resources for survival, and yet, human social organization threatens these resources and indeed the survival of millions of species on earth, including humans.

Chapter 22

Social Movements

Unruly crowds, riots, revolts, and collective violence are very much a part of human societies. We cannot read a newspaper or watch television without hearing about internal dissent and conflict within some society in the world, including our own. Dissent is a major force of social change in human societies. The more people are outraged about certain conditions, the more likely will these dissenters become a force of social change. Why, then, is dissent such a pervasive phenomenon?

To answer this question, we must enter the subfield in sociology called **collective behavior** that examines sudden transformations of culture and social structure. At times, dissent is largely symbolic, involving fads and fashions that violate the public's sense of decorum; at other times, dissent involves noisy crowds and protests; at certain moments crowds turn ugly, creating more violent riots; at still more intense moments, protesting crowds become larger and more focused and form a revolutionary force that can potentially topple those in power; at other times, crowds become implicated in a longer term social movement for change; and at those points in history when all else fails, protest can become organized into warring factions in a society-wide civil war. Thus, the form of dissent and collective behavior can vary in its scale and scope, its level of violence, and its effects on the organization of a society.

Preconditions of Social Movements

Dissent is protest against existing social arrangements, and so, collective behavior ultimately begins with people's perception that something is wrong and must be changed. These perceptions do not have to be explicitly formulated, at least at beginning stages; rather, individuals more often feel and sense a grievance or sense of dissatisfaction. The functional theorist, Neil Smelser (1963), has termed this initial condition *structural strain.*

What contributes to such strain? The most consistent force behind strain is inequality and stratification. As all conflict theories would emphasize, inequality in the distribution of resources is the underlying source of protest; when people begin to feel that this inequality is unfair and unjust, the level of structural strain increases. If power is too concentrated and arbitrary, if markets generate great differences in wealth and well being, and if honor and prestige are hoarded by a few and denied to most, then the level of structural strain will be high. Moreover, if inequality is associated with economic, political, and social domination of those without resources by those with them, then the level of structural strain is even higher (Stark 1992, 614). People resent being told what to do and having their lives controlled by others; they begin to get angry and perceive that something must be done.

Yet, structural strain can come from sources other than inequality. Segments of a population may be upset over certain conditions in society that need to be changed. For example, people may be concerned about the environment, abortion rights, drug use, immigration, gun control, and other issues making them susceptible to collective behavior.

Not all social movements emerge from structural strains. Some social movements address lifestyle issues, such as rebirthing, transcendental meditation, and psychological awareness. In these movements, individuals may be responding to strains in their personal lives but not to broader structural strains in the society at large. Other social movements can emerge as counter-movements against another social movement. For example, the antibusing movement emerged as a backlash to at least this part of the Civil Rights movement and the anti-abortion movement arose in response to that portion of the women's movement advocating abortion rights. Such movements are generally conservative, trying to preserve existing structural and cultural arrangements in society. Still other movements respond to particular issues, such as Women Against Drunk Drivers or efforts to ban assault weapons (which generated a counter-movement), that are less connected to patterns of inequality and the tensions it generates than to highly specific "problems" that can be addressed without redistributing resources in a society. They arise because people perceive that certain conditions are "not right" but rarely do they challenge the broader societal structure and culture.

Thus, there are many potential preconditions for the emergence of a social movement. All of these preconditions have one common theme: the desire to change some aspect of a society and its culture that is viewed as problematic. The success of a social movement varies enormously, depending upon a number of important factors.

Conditions Leading to the Emergence of a Social Movement

There are several macro structural factors that increase the likelihood that a social movement will emerge (Benford 1992). One factor is the nature of the political system in a society. A democratic society is more likely to reveal social movements as part of the larger political process, whereas a repressive political regime will generally seek to crush change-oriented social movements. Repression thus works against social movement, particularly if government is willing to use massive coercive force to put down an emerging movement (Tilly 1978). Even within political democracies, political opportunities for a social movement can vary. For example, the Civil Rights movement gained increased purchase only after the worst abuses had declined (e.g., lynchings of blacks in the south) and after considerable migration of African Americans from the south to the midwest and northeast had occurred. Under these conditions, political opportunities for a more concerted Civil Rights movement expanded (McAdam 1982).

Another key condition is the existence of existing organizations. If a society reveals many voluntary organizations, these organizations can serve as a base point for a new social movement (Morris 1984). The organization provides a ready constituency of movement participants, leadership, and financial resources to pursue efforts to change some condition in society. Even when existing organizations are not actively used to mount a social movement, the very existence of many organizations in a society creates a template for organizing a social movement, and especially so if government tolerates many diverse organizations. Conversely, if a society does not evidence many organizational structures outside of work and government, there are few models of how to organize voluntary activities, thereby making social movement formation more difficult.

Conditions Increasing Participation in Social Movements

Intensification of Dissent

When people begin to "share their grievances," the potential for dissent is increased (Smelser 1963; Turner & Killian 1987). The sharing of grievances is facilitated by several conditions, initially articulated by Karl Marx and Friedrich Engels (1848) and later incorporated into modern conflict theories. First, if potential dissenters have social ties and communication networks, these can be used to communicate their grievances; the mutual give-and-take of such communication often begins to arouse people's frustration and anger, while bringing into focus the sources of their grievances (Zald & McCarthy 1979). Second, leadership is essential, for people do not spontaneously focus their anger and mobilize; they must be led by others with the ability to articulate grievances and convince them that something must be done. Third, beliefs must be articulated so that people have symbols with which to unite and justify their grievances and potential actions (Smelser 1963). Fourth, the sense of grievance experienced by people must escalate, creating a gap between what they think should occur and what actually occurs; the more rapidly this disjuncture develops, the greater its effects on intensifying grievances (Davies 1962, 1969).

Social Networks and Recruiting Members

To recruit members, a social movement must have connections to potential recruits. For example, the Civil Rights movement could draw upon ties to African American churches as a source of recruits. Similarly, the antiwar movement during the Vietnam era could draw upon networks among students at American universities. Likewise, the unionization movement could draw from relationships among workers in industrial corporations. Social movements thus recruit a good portion of their participants from existing networks (Snow, Zurcher, & Ekland-Olson 1980). Individuals first attend a meeting because a fellow student, family member, or coworker asks them to come to a meeting. Networks can also work against a social movement, however. Sometimes membership in one set of networks (e.g., family and work) holds a person back from participating in a social movement because family members and work colleagues would disapprove. Thus, networks can work both ways in either providing a conduit for attracting members or setting up roadblocks to participation in a social movement.

Justifying Movement Participation: Beliefs and Frames

For people to become sufficiently mobilized to incur the costs of participating in a social movement, they must develop rationales for participation. Snow and Benford (1988) refer to "vocabularies of motive" that arise as individuals talk with one another, intensifying their beliefs about a problematic condition that needs to be eliminated. Indeed, effective leaders of a social movement often engage in active "framing" of the issues so that they will have appeal to particular audiences. As individuals talk about the issues and develop vocabularies of motives justifying their participation, they not only develop powerful beliefs and ideologies for their cause, they also deepen their commitment to the cause. Often, they may have to abandon older commitments to take up the cause of a social movement, and it is only through the give and take of interaction within networks of those pushing for a movement that they develop sufficient motivation and commitment to make the sacrifices to join a social movement, even if this means disapproval by others.

Resources and Social Movement Organizations

Beliefs justifying a social movement can be viewed as a symbolic resource that rallies individuals to a cause. But for a social movement to gain purchase, other kinds of resources are also necessary. One is an organizational base, or a **social movement organization** (SMO). For a social movement to be successful it must have an organization that can be viewed as "the command posts of movements" (McAdam, McCarthy, & Zald 1988). These SMOs provide leadership structure, a means for raising financial resources, a basis for recruiting new members, a means for lobbying the media and politicians, and a staff for carrying out the day-to-day business (mailings, printing, taking phone calls, etc.) that sustain a movement. Thus, for a social movement to have much effect it must be organized bureaucratically. Sometimes a social movement will have many—perhaps thousands—of SMOs all pursuing more or less the same goal, such as nuclear disarmament or environmental protection—whereas at other times a movement will have only a few large organizations.

SMOs often begin in a particular locale, with informal gatherings of individuals who have similar concerns or grievances. Over time, as more recruits and financial resources flow into the group, they set up an organizational structure composed of paid staff and volunteers. And, if the organization continues to be successful, it grows into a larger SMO and perhaps begins to merge with other SMOs pursuing similar goals, or if a complete merger does not occur, it forms alliances with other SMOs. Once a set of SMOs or one large SMO is in place, it has greater capacity to articulate its beliefs and interpretive frameworks (through the media), to recruit new members, and to attract financial resources.

Collective Behavior

Theoretical Approaches to Crowd Behavior

When the preconditions for dissent have been intensified by the forces discussed above, collective outbursts become more likely. SMOs can use various tactics, such as marches, sit-ins, teaching rallies, strikes, and boycotts. All of these fall under the rubric of *collective behavior*. Much of the subfield of collective behavior examines the dynamics of **crowd behavior**. Early **contagion theory** stressed that as people interact, they begin to bounce grievances and angry moods off one another, heightening their emotional mobilization. This process is circular and escalating because, as people mutually communicate their anger, the intensity of emotion in a situation is ratcheted up; when this occurs, the emotional arousal becomes more intense. As this process unfolds, people become highly suggestible to the responses of others, and as a consequence, a "mob" can suddenly move in a particular way, and people can do things that they would ordinarily never consider doing. Although a certain amount of emotional contagion is, no doubt, involved in crowd behavior, more recent theories stress additional factors.

Convergence theory emphasizes that people are not so much transformed and swept away by emotional contagion as they are self-selected to engage in certain lines of behavior. When people gather in a crowd, they do so because they have certain grievances in common and are *already* prepared by beliefs, leaders, and previous communications to act in certain ways (Cantril 1941). When students protested in the 1960s and early 1970s, for example, they were ready to do certain things; they were not overrun by a "mob mood," although some emotional contagion was, no doubt, involved. Similarly, in lynchings of blacks in the south during the early decades of this century, those who gathered were of similarly low economic background and were already prepared to vent their fears in this most heinous act (Cantril 1941).

In contrast, *emergent norm theory* questions the assumptions of both contagion and convergence theories. There is often a lack of initial convergence among crowd members' orientations and dispositions, and individuals are not just overwhelmed by contagious moods and emotions. Rather, as all interactionist theories emphasize, individuals are seen to look for and find meanings by reading each other's gestures, like any other interaction situation (Turner & Killian 1987). Out of such role-taking, they develop new norms and standards about how to behave. And, they interpersonally reward each other for conformity to these emergent norms. These norms can, of course, encourage violent behavior, from looting to lynchings, but such behaviors involve the same basic interaction processes as in noncrowd activities: co-presence, role-taking, emergent norms, and conformity to norms.

Interaction ritual theory emphasizes that crowd behavior is very much an interaction ritual (Collins 2004). People are co-present and mutually aware of each other. They have a common focus of attention. They begin to interact and actively raise their emotions. As their emotions are aroused, they increasingly have a sense of group solidarity. Their interactions take on a rhythmic flow and entrainment, which enhances the sense of solidarity. A crowd at a football game can have this kind of solidarity through each participant's interaction with those nearby, and when important events occur, the crowd rises as one and engages in various forms of cheering. Such crowd behaviors are very much like simple interactions that we have with others in our daily routines, but in the case of the crowd there are more individuals feeding off each other; and if circumstances are right, the crowd can turn ugly and violent as the focus of attention shifts to a target that is perceived to have imposed wrongs (such as the referee in a soccer game). As the rhythmic flow of the interaction and emotional mood are intensified, the emerging solidarity generates action against a target. Other kinds of crowds also reveal these same dynamics.

Types of Crowds

These theoretical approaches to crowd behavior are not contradictory. There is usually some self-selection of individuals into the crowd situation, usually in terms of shared grievances. There is also a certain amount of emotional charge and contagion, but this is controlled and channeled by rituals and emergent norms. The basic types of crowds reflect the interplay of these forces (Blumer 1978). A *casual crowd* is a collection of people who have little else in common besides their co-presence and stimulation by a common event, such as observing some highly visible stimulus like an automobile accident. A *conventional crowd* involves people self-selected and assembled for a specific purpose, such as observing a game. An *expressive crowd* is a self-selected gathering of people who intend to be influenced by norms, ideologies, rituals, and emotional contagion, as is the case at a religious revival, rock concert, or political rally. And, an *acting crowd* is people who are self-selected, emotionally aroused, and focused on aggressive acts, such as looting and rioting. As one goes from a casual to acting crowd, self-selection, emotional contagion, ritual solidarity, and emergent norms specifying violation of conventional norms all increase. This is what gives them such volatility, as well as the potential to change social structures.

But whether this potential is realized depends upon other social conditions. Rioters can be crushed or they can topple a government; mass rallies can fizzle or they can mobilize sentiments and prompt further action. Much depends upon the broader social and cultural context of a crowd's formation.

Context of Crowd Behavior

If crowd activities are part of a larger *social movement,* or a longer term and systematic effort to change particular conditions, then they tend to become expressive crowds that mobilize people's sentiments and emphasize grievances. Crowds thus become the strategy for exerting pressure for change. The mass demonstrations for Civil Rights in the early 1960s, for example, were a strategy of the larger social movement; they were used not only to call attention to the plight of African Americans, but also to force change in old patterns of white domination in politics, schools, economy, and public facilities.

Yet, crowds can still spark violence even when part of a well-organized social movement. Often the violence is initiated by those charged with social control (e.g., the police and army) or from those in a casual crowd, or self-selected expressive crowd, watching a demonstration. Suddenly, these crowds become an acting crowd, attacking members of an organized demonstration. Indeed, the strategy of crowd protests is to incite reactions to dramatize the plight of those for whom the demonstrators protest. For example, nonviolent protesters in the Civil Rights Movement often encouraged the police to attack them to demonstrate in the media the oppression of blacks by whites.

Social movements can also cause crowds to become violent indirectly, by arousing emotions and shared grievances of people who then engage in crowd behavior independently of the movement's organization and leaders. For example, most of the riots in America's black slums in the 1960s were caused by a casual crowd of people sitting and standing outside on a hot summer night watching a routine arrest by the police. Because the Civil Rights Movement had activated people's grievances and aroused emotions about the domination and abuse of black Americans, the casual crowd on a hot summer night quickly turned into an acting crowd, setting off a chain of events leading to a common focus and rhythmic interaction as well as emergent norms condoning looting and destruction of property. These crowd members shared what Smelser (1963) termed a "generalized belief" about their plight, and they responded with disproportionate emotion to a "precipitating incident" or event such as a routine arrest that sets an acting crowd into motion. Such motion is particularly likely when people's sense of deprivation escalates, as a result of rising expectations that cannot be met or as a consequence of a sudden downturn that increases the gap between what people have had in the past and what they now get. Such was the case in the Los Angeles riots of 1992, where the sense of deprivation of blacks suddenly escalated after the verdict in the Rodney King case, where the police who had savagely beaten King were acquitted by a white jury outside of Los Angeles county. Within hours people on the street in south Central Los Angeles were attacking whites, breaking windows, and looting. As more people poured out onto the streets, the crowds moved in many directions and spread the destruction. Thus, when people's sense of injustice and deprivation increases, they are prepared to act with only the slightest provocation.

Historically, crowds have at times erupted with such force that they have deposed political regimes. Such crowds usually emerge in the context of high inequality, emergent leaders, generalized beliefs, communication networks, and weakened political authority. The acting crowd in one area becomes the stimulus for crowd formation in other areas, soon creating such a strong wave of dissent that a **revolution**, a rapid and violent overthrow of a political regime, occurs. The French Revolution, the revolution in Iran overthrowing the secular shah and creating the current religious polity in that society, and the street demonstrations that brought down the Soviet Union document how rapidly crowds can destroy a regime, *if* it is politically weak and vulnerable (Goldstone 1990; Skocpol 1979). But events in China during the late 1980s, and elsewhere throughout the history of large societies, indicate that revolutionary crowds can be crushed when the regime is still in control of the means of coercion and when the crowds have few organizational resources of their own.

Social Movements and Change

As noted earlier, for crowd behavior to be successful in changing a society, it must be connected to a resource base of organizational structures (SMOs), leaders, networks of communication, ideologies, people, money, and at times coercive capacities (McCarthy and Zald 1977; Zald and McCarthy 1979). Most successful revolutions, or social movements, had organizations, leaders, generalized beliefs, some money, and coercive capacity; when the crowds erupted, they could be sustained or channeled toward the goals of the movement.

From a utilitarian theoretical perspective, **resource mobilization theory** stresses this point, arguing that social movements and other change-producing patterns of collective behavior emerge only when there are resources (Tilly 1978; Zald and McCarthy 1979). There are always grievances in a society, but most never generate collective movements for lack of a resource base. As a result, individuals calculate that the costs of failure far outweigh their current deprivation and they do not participate in a collective action (Oberschall 1973; Oliver 1984). But when the costs of deprivations and grievances are high and the rewards associated with protest are high, then people will join and participate *if* they calculate that their chances for success are high. What tips people's calculations? Resources: leaders, ideologies and generalized beliefs, organizational structures (unions, churches, secret societies, etc.), finances, communication networks, large numbers of potential recruits, and if needed, coercive capacities all increase people's perceptions that the movement can be successful. When resources can be mobilized, it is rational to incur the costs and risks of joining; when resources cannot be mobilized, it is rational to pass and continue to endure the costs of deprivations.

Again, context is important. If resource mobilization must face equally well-organized opposition, it is less likely to occur, or to be effective when it does occur. But if the opposition is weak or divided, then the mobilization of resources for dissent can proceed and people will think it rational to join in.

The Aftermath of Dissent

When dissent becomes widespread in a society, the forces of social control have broken down and the forces of disorder have increased. As a result, a society will never be the same—whether for better or worse. If episodes of dissent over inequality have been successful, patterns of stratification will change, as will the institutional structures sustaining the old patterns. Cultural beliefs will change in ways legitimating new structures. But there is often an ironical twist to these changes: power must often become more concentrated and abusive to implement changes and to stave off counter-social-movements or counter-revolutions in which advocates of the old order try to restore things to where they were. As a basic rule, the more violent the change-producing dissent and the greater the changes that dissent has ushered in, the more power will be concentrated to hold things together. And typically, such power becomes yet another source of inequality, domination, and rising grievances—a fact emphasized by most conflict theories. Indeed, the 70-year history of the old Soviet Union had all the elements of this sad story—a supposedly liberating revolution followed by more concentrated power to hold the new order together, that, eventually, caused grievances to rise to the point of forcing the Soviet Union's collapse. If dissent is unsuccessful, the same situation will prevail: power is concentrated to keep a lid on dissent, thereby escalating the grievances of individuals. Such is currently the case in many parts of the world, including the middle east, Indonesia, Iran, and even China, where concentrated power is used to keep a lid on a potential powder keg.

If dissent occurs in a democratic context, however, it can at times work to release tensions and increase the viability of a society—a fact emphasized by more functional theories (Coser 1956). Conflict need not force reactive repression, but instead foster accommodation. The Civil Rights Movement in the 1960s illustrates this fact because demonstrations eventually led to a series of civil rights laws that reduced discrimination. Similarly, in less democratic societies, the collective actions of blacks in the southern regions of Africa led to surprisingly peaceful transformations from white to black rule, although many black-white tensions still exist in this part of the world.

Thus, power and dissent always stand in a delicate balance. Too much coercion and domination create, in the long run, dissent; too much dissent, even when successful, causes new concentrations of power fostering further dissent down the road. Political democracy institutionalizes dissent by offering elections for people to vent their anger, but democracy is never completely successful on the score; as a result, social movements often bordering on rebellion and even civil war emerge in even the most democratic society. The capacity of a society to absorb and accommodate rather than repress dissent is a key to its stability and viability. These are not abstract issues, for you confront them each time a crowd forms, a subgroup protests some condition, or a broad spectrum of people mobilize to address a grievance. I have lived through, and participated in, two such movements—the Civil Rights Movement and the antiwar movement against American involvement in Vietnam. You will, no doubt, be involved in other such movements, or at least watch one from the sidelines. At stake will be the capacity to maintain order, accommodate grievances, and limit abusive concentrations of power.

SUMMARY

1. Dissent is the process of mobilizing to protest against a perceived problem in a society.
2. Dissent is often generated by inequalities and people's sense of injustice or by other grievances that serve as a basic precondition to collective action. However, dissent can also be about a specific issue or problem that is not directly connected to inequalities.
3. A social movement is more likely to emerge in political democracies that reveal many voluntary organizations that can serve as templates or models and that reveal low levels of coercive repression.
4. Participation in a social movement increases with (a) intensification of dissent, (b) social networks for recruiting members, (c) beliefs and frames justifying

the goals of a movement, and (d) organizational resources in the form of a social movement organization.

5. Under these preconditions and their intensification, several of theories have been offered to explain collective outbursts and crowd behavior: (a) contagion theory stressing the face-to-face interaction of individuals; (b) convergence theory emphasizing self-selection of predisposed individuals into crowd situations; (c) emergent norm theory stressing that through interaction people develop norms in crowd situations that then guide their behavior; and (d) interaction ritual theory stressing that crowd behavior involves the same elements—co-presence, rhythmic interaction, common focus of attention, heightened emotional arousal, collective solidarity, and action—as normal routine interactions among small numbers of individuals in encounters.

6. Crowd behavior is then initiated with precipitating incidents that galvanize generalized beliefs expressing grievances. To become an effective social movement, those in crowds must have resources—organization, financial, symbolic, membership, networks—to sustain their protest activities.

7. The aftermath of successful social movements is often typified by repression of a counter-movement, with this repression often going against the original goals of the movement and, thereby, eventually causing yet another round of crowd behavior and social movement organization.

KEY TERMS

Collective Behavior: Field of study focusing on the sudden transformations of culture and social structures through such processes as dissent, riots, revolutions, fads, and social movements.

Contagion Theory: Early theory of collective behavior emphasizing the effects of interaction in intensifying people's emotions and, hence, potential for collective behavior.

Convergence Theory: Approach emphasizing that people self-select themselves into crowd situations rather than being swept away by a "mob mood."

Crowd Behavior: Gatherings of people acting together with reference to some stimulus, situation, or goal.

Interaction Ritual Theory: Theoretical approach emphasizing that all interactions reveal certain elements of rituals—co-presence, common focus of attention, rhythmic communication, emotional arousal, and solidarity—with crowd actions being only a special case of the more general process of interaction rituals.

Resource Mobilization Theory: Approach to the study of social movements emphasizing that crowd mobilization and persistence of a social movement are related to the resource base of those involved.

Revolution: Rapid and violent mobilization of people who seek to overthrow a political regime.

Social Movement Organization (SMO): Organizational structure, typically organized bureaucratically but also involving many volunteers, that seeks to direct a social movement by recruiting new members, securing financial contributions, lobbying, and relying on collective behavior.

Chapter 23

Revolution, War, and Terrorism

More than virtually any other animal, humans kill each other. Some have argued that humans are naturally violent, but there is little evidence that violence is part of our biology. Hunter-gatherers of the past may have become violent if they found themselves in competition for resources, but there was usually plenty of territory and food so that people did not have to fight. It was with horticulture, when humans began to settle down, that chronic warfare emerged; and here the cause seems more sociological than biological. People in one village were often in competition for resources with those in other villages; add to this source of conflict the fact that larger groups of kin were forced together, and it is perhaps not so surprising that internal feuds and external warfare were typical of horticulturalists. When humans must live under crowded conditions, when they must compete for scarce resources, and when there is inequality in the distribution of resources, they often turn violent. Dissent crosses a threshold, and people begin to engage in acts of violence. There may be something in humans that makes them violent when they feel crowded, fearful, and angry over injustice, but it is more likely that it is the way humans organize themselves and the kinds of cultural symbols they develop that make them perhaps the most violent species on earth.

Collective Violence in Societies

Violence is the use of physical force to inflict harm on others. Humans are so violent that we need to classify varying types of collective violence. One kind of violence is *person-to-person*. This kind of violence is almost always defined as deviant and as a "crime" in societies, with specified penalties for its commission. Robbery that involves physical force, murder, revenge, and other individual violence acts are very typical in human societies; and the rates of person-to-person violence increase as societies grow, urbanize, and reveal inequalities.

In this chapter, our concern is with *collective violence* that involves individuals who are, to varying degrees, organized to commit violent acts against others. Such collective violence usually brings about social change, even if it is unsuccessful. As violence is crushed, those who do the repressing will have changed society toward a more centralized political regime engaged in tight control and monitoring of people's activities. And, if the violence of one set of individuals is successful in bringing about certain goals, the new regime will change the society to realize its goals, while repressing those who fought against these goals.

A **revolution** is a mass uprising of people who use violence in an effort to overthrow the existing political elite and install a new government as well as new ways of organizing activity in society. A **civil war** is the military mobilization of at least two large segments of the population in a society and their use of violence against each other. The distinctions between a revolution and a civil war are often hard to draw because they reveal similarities. There are, however, critical differences. First, revolutions are always directed at the political elite, whereas civil wars are not always so—although in the end, the government must become an active participant as it attempts to restore order. Second, revolutions often spring spontaneously out of crowd behavior (e.g., a riot that draws organization from within itself), whereas civil wars usually involve considerable military planning, stocking of resources, mobilization of personnel, and other military strategies. Third, revolutions tend to be of short duration. If they persist, they evolve into civil wars in which both sides increasingly become organized militarily and use military tactics. Figure 23.1 delineates how revolutions can emerge from other forms of collective behavior and become transformed into civil war.

In contrast to a revolution or a civil war, a **war** is the political mobilization and organization of military personnel by at least two societies and the systematic use of violence by these military personnel against each other and, potentially, against nonmilitary members of each society. War is thus highly organized violence of identifiable societies against each other, whereas revolution and civil war involve violence among the members of the same society.

At times, though, revolutions and civil wars can become the vehicle by which outside societies indirectly wage war. If outside societies assist revolutionaries or take a side in a civil war, for example, they are in essence waging war against at least a portion (usually the established government) of that society.

Terrorism is deliberate violence against not just governmental targets of an enemy regime, but against broader segments of the population. Terrorism is designed to do exactly what its name implies: to instill fear and terror in the general population and, thereby, to erode the legiti-

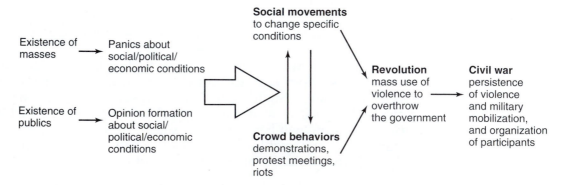

Figure 23.1   Collective Behavior, Revolutions, and Civil Wars

macy of the political regime that organizes a population. Terrorism is used when it is difficult to confront an enemy directly and openly because of the overwhelming military superiority of the enemy. Terrorism is greatly facilitated by active markets for materials that can be used to make weapons which can be carried and set off in public places. At times terrorism can be part of a revolutionary strategy to overthrow a particular political regime, as is perhaps the case in Indonesia today. At other times, terror is strategy to demoralize a regime and, thereby, to have them retreat from a territory, as has been the case with car bombings by radical factions of both Protestant and Catholic Irish. At still other times, terror is used to prevent compromise by warring regimes because the terrorists seek complete victory, as is the case with those who use violence to keep the Israeli-Palestinian conflict from being resolved. At other times, terrorism is used to strike back at an enemy whose actions, whether intentionally or not, interfered with the goals of terrorists, as was the case with the attack by the Al Queda on the World Trade Center on September 11, 2001.

These distinctions among revolution, civil war, war, and terrorism are not hard and fast; they often blend into each other, but they nonetheless give us a way to organize the discussion of violence within and between societies. Let us begin with revolutions and then move to civil wars, war, and terrorism.

Revolutions

Revolutions only occur when there is inequality in the distribution of valued resources and when political leadership has denied the general population procedures for redressing their grievances. Inequality and oppression alone do not cause revolutions, however. Several additional conditions must also exist. First, those who are deprived must be able to communicate their grievances to each other; physical contact and crowding in urban areas thus facilitate the development of a revolution. Second, the deprived must develop at least the beginning of an ideology, or set of beliefs, that articulates their grievances, feelings, and deprivations. Third, they must have begun to question the legitimacy of political leaders, believing them to be unfit to rule. Fourth, there must be at least a few individuals who are considered leaders and who, through their charisma, express the frustrations of the deprived. And fifth, there must be a sudden rise in people's *sense* of deprivation.

This last condition appears to be critical. It has long been noted that, ironically, revolutions tend to occur in societies in which the standard of living has been rising. The sense of deprivation is not absolute but relative to the rising expectations that come with an improved standard of living. It is not that life is good, for inequalities are the ultimate force behind revolutions. Rather, as the quality of life improves, people come to *expect* it to become even better in the future. Revolutions seem to occur when all of the other conditions listed above are present *and* when there is a sudden gap between what people expect and what they actually have.

The argument presented in Figure 23.2 can be summarized as follows (Davies 1969): First, revolutions occur in societies in which material

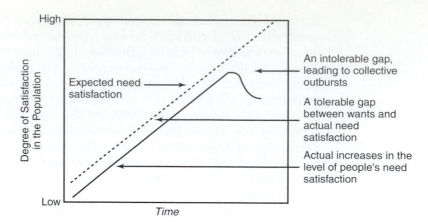

Figure 23.2   Revolutions, Expectations, and Sense of Deprivation
Source: Davies, 1969.

conditions have been improving and in which people begin to accept—indeed, to expect—continued betterment of their lives. Second, people will tolerate some discrepancy between what they want or expect and what they actually get. When this gap suddenly widens as a result of a downturn in people's material well-being, however, their sense of deprivation escalates, and they become capable of rioting and perhaps of joining a larger revolutionary movement.

Often, this sudden increase in the discrepancy between expectations and their fulfillment can be created in other ways. There can be a sudden leap in expectations and needs (as opposed to a downturn in actual material well-being). Such leaps in expectations are often generated by political leaders who simply promise too much. Or, opposition leaders can mobilize people's perceptions in a way that raises their expectations or lowers their sense of material well-being. In all these cases, the major stimulus to the revolution is a widening of the gap in people's expectations and what they perceive their actual situation to be. People's sense of deprivation is heightened and makes them easy targets for revolutionary mobilization, if the other preconditions are present.

The early stages of a revolution are often little more than a riot, as people express their anger and frustration. But if leaders and an ideology exist and if the deprivations are deeply felt, the protesters can frequently be mobilized into a revolutionary force. The Iranian revolution of 1979, for example, began as a series of street riots and then escalated to an attempt to oust the Shah. The American Revolution started as a quasi-riot, the Boston Tea Party, but unlike the revolution in Iran, it became a military confrontation between two armies, and so, it might be more correctly labeled the First American Civil War. The Russian and Chinese revolutions were also civil wars in that initial revolutionary activity gradually grew less spontaneous and increasingly revolved around military confrontations between organized armies.

There have been very few revolutions in which crowd behaviors led to the rapid overthrow of a political regime. Typically, the regime can fight back and hold off revolutionaries. Thus, the success of a revolution depends upon the strength of the state. Two conditions appear to weaken the state—one economic and the other symbolic or cultural. When the state experiences a fiscal crisis because of corruption, patronage to elites, military adventurism, and other practices, it is often vulnerable to a successful revolution. It simply does not have the money to pay police and soldiers to fight back, and the economic problems of the society as a whole are so pervasive that even some elites and members of the military join in the actions against the state. The other condition is symbolic, involving the delegitimatization of political elites and the state. Fiscal crisis is one source of delegitimatization; another is for the state to lose a war, thereby eroding away people's support for its activities. Thus, revolutions often come after a regime loses a war (Skocpol 1979) and/or experiences a severe fiscal crisis (Goldstone 1990). Only when states are weakened and revolutionaries are sufficiently organized can revolutions be successful. Much more typical is for initial revolutionary violence to be crushed, forcing revolutionaries to spend some time becoming better organized into an army that can more effectively engage the regime in a civil war.

Civil Wars

Civil wars do not always evolve from revolutions. Regional, ethnic, and subcultural variations in a society are often a source of tension and conflict. These tensions will be particularly intense when one region, ethnic group, or subculture dominates the government and imposes its will on other ethnics, subcultures, and regions. Under these conditions, riots and revolutions can evolve into civil wars after a prolonged period of tension in which the various parties arm themselves, develop leaders, and organize militarily. Sometimes a particularly harsh response to a demonstration can be the stimulus for more formal military organization. At other times, the mobilization takes place over a long period of time in anticipation of full-scale warfare.

Once initiated, civil wars tend to continue for a considerable period of time. Also, they are usually very violent and involve the loss of many lives. The reasons for their length and level of violence reside in the very conditions that caused them. First, because the parties in civil wars usually have strong ethnic, regional, and cultural differences, they define their adversary in very negative terms to justify abuse of the enemy. Second, because civil wars are usually fought along regional lines, each party invades the other's "homeland." As they do so, attacks on both military and nonmilitary targets are considered legitimate, especially as the enemy is seen as a threat to a "way of life." Third, because a civil war cannot occur without at least some balance in coercive power, the war can drag on. Indeed, a revolt that is immediately crushed is a rebellion or revolution that failed. The American Civil War (1860–1865) lasted so long and was so violent because both parties were equally matched, intensely patriotic about their regions and "way of life," and well-organized militarily.

A civil war against a government controlled by a foreign nation takes on new dimensions. If the occupying nation is a colonial power that actually rules the country and uses cadres of its own troops in conjunction with local recruits, revolutionary activities—crowds, riots, demonstrations—are typical. But if the colonial power persists, organized military efforts may follow. Depending upon the respective strengths of the colonial power and the rebels, the war may drag on, be crushed, or force the colonial power to withdraw.

When a foreign government leaves an indigenous "front" government in place and relies upon its threat of invasion to sustain order, full-scale wars often emerge from riots, revolutions, and civil wars. These third-party efforts at faltering governments generally transform what otherwise would have been a short revolution into a prolonged civil war. Supplying arms to assist a weak government sustains the conflict, and each side becomes increasingly organized to wage war. Only when the assisting party enjoys enormous military superiority and the ability to use it can a civil war be averted.

Still, as the United States learned in Vietnam and as the Soviet Union learned in Afghanistan, overwhelming military might is often not enough to suppress a civil war. When the rebellious faction against a regime is well-organized, has at least some military technology, and enjoys widespread support from the public, the ability of external intervention by a military power may be limited. Such is particularly likely to be the case when the regime being supported by an external political power is corrupt and not held in high esteem by its own supporters.

War

A Brief History of Warfare

War involves the mobilization of armies by one nation or population to invade the territories of another nation or population. The history of war began when humans settled into stable communities and claimed territories for themselves. Prior to this time, hunters and gatherers may have clashed, but generally there was nothing to fight over, and conflict was unnecessary. Horticulturalists were usually in a chronic state of war with neighboring tribes and villages; and so, war involving organized armies representing established populations comes with simple horticulture. As agricultural technologies improved and as more land-feeding larger populations came under cultivation, war became increasingly more violent. And as transportation technologies (ships, domesticated animals, carts, chariots, etc.) and weaponry (metal arms, high-powered bows, armor, massed armies, firearms) improved, the warfare became not only more violent but also more extensive. Warfare came to involve patterns of conquest, empire building, and collapse from internal revolution or from invasion by external forces.

A history of warfare thus reveals efforts by one population to conquer another, to take its resources, and if possible to conquer additional populations and take their resources. How far this process can go depends upon several factors (Collins 1975).

1. The superiority of one society's weapons over those of another determines how many other populations they can conquer.
2. The transportation technologies and the geography of a region set boundaries on how far conquest can extend.

3. Communication technologies also set limits because without adequate contact with political leaders, there are restrictions on what armies may do.

4. The mode of organization of the army determines how many soldiers can be mobilized, transported, and used in conquests.

5. The pattern of political control of conquered populations sets limits on the capacity to engage in further conquest (if resources and personnel must be used to subdue one population, they cannot be used to conquer another).

6. The productive surplus of the economy of the conquering and conquered populations determines how large an army can be supported, for how long, and how far from the homeland.

As each of these limiting factors has been overcome, the violence of warfare and the span of territories conquered has increased. The first "empires" were constructed around 3000 B.C. in Mesopotamia and the Nile Valley, as one city state could conquer a few of its neighbors. These empires were limited by the logistics of transportation, communication, weaponry, organization, political control, and economic production and distribution. And so, they periodically collapsed internally or were overrun by forces from the outside. Indeed, one of the ironic results of creating an empire through conquest is that the conquered learn the military technologies of their conquerors and, as a result, can better resist their subjugation. Moreover, outsiders learn and copy transportation and communication technologies, modes of army organization, and other techniques that made the conquering power initially successful. As a consequence, these outsiders can invade an empire and prevail, especially because the loyalty of the conquered cannot be relied upon. Of course the result of invasion is a new empire that, like the one it replaced, is vulnerable.

Since around 3000 B.C. to the present, this pattern of growth through conquest, internal collapse through revolution or external invasion, and reconquest of territories has recurred. In the past, the Mesopotamians, Egyptians, Assyrians, Persians, Greeks, Romans, Germans and Huns, Scandinavians, various Chinese dynasties, Aryans, Mongols, Moguls and other Islamic groups in the eastern hemisphere; and the Maya, Inca, and Aztecs in the New World all reveal this pattern of building up an empire, only to have it collapse from internal revolt or invasion by an external enemy. And more recently, the history of Europe over the last few hundred years has involved this pattern of conquest, collapse, and reconquest. In the last century, the two world wars as well as various limited ones have all involved efforts of one power to expand its empire, repel its enemies, or consolidate its hold on a territory or people.

In these processes, military superiority is obviously critical, with shifts in the balance of power coming with technological breakthroughs. Some of these are listed in Table 23.1. The development of weapons has now reached a new stage in human history; we now have the capacity to destroy not only an enemy but virtually all human beings and most other life forms. Moreover, the proliferation of nuclear weapons has created a situation in which to use them on an enemy would be to invite the retaliation that would, in essence, destroy most life on earth.

Table 23.1 Critical Developments Affecting the Course of Warfare

By the Time of	Developments in Warfare Technology
1500 B.C.	Development of the two-wheeled, horse-drawn chariot
1200 B.C.	Development of cheap iron and metal weapons that could supply mass armies
900 B.C.	Riding of horses and the use of a bow and arrows on horseback
600 B.C.	Use of heavy armor, the bureaucratic organization of mass infantry and naval fleets, armor plating for riders on horseback
A.D. 1500	Firearms and cannons, large warships with cannon weapons
A.D. 1900	Tanks, automatic weapons, airplanes, cars, trucks, mass infantry, metal ships powered by forces other than wind
A.D. 1920	Poison gas
A.D. 1930	Submarines
A.D. 1945	Nuclear weapons, guided missiles
A.D. 1950	Jet-propelled aircraft with nuclear weapons, missiles with nuclear warheads
A.D. 1955	Biological weapons
A.D. 1965	Multiple-head nuclear missiles

The advances in military technology, especially nuclear and biological weapons, take on new urgency in a world increasingly dominated by markets for weapons. Technologies and the weapons themselves can be smuggled out of a powerful nation and sold on a "black market" to less powerful nations or terrorists. The end result is for no nation to be safe from the horrors of modern warfare.

Modern Warfare

Although the threat of a nuclear and biological war between the two superpowers of the last century—the United States and Soviet Union—has diminished, the spread of nuclear and biological weapons of mass destruction to other, less stable nations increases the likelihood that these weapons will be used. Moreover, it is only a matter of time before a terrorist organization secures a nuclear weapon and, thereby, increases the chances of a nuclear detonation in an urban area. Moreover, terrorist groups can now secure or make biological weapons, although they lack an effective delivery system to make them weapons of mass destruction.

Today, war must be viewed in this context whereby weapons smuggling and black markets allow less powerful nations and terrorist groups to secure the weapons that were once exclusive to the great powers. Moreover, the more limited wars being fought are super-heated because ethnicity and religion are often involved. The Middle East, India and Pakistan, portions of Central Africa, Indonesia, and other "hot spots" in the world are not just about control of territory; they are intensified by religious and ethnic divisions that make the conflict "moral" and, hence, potentially more violent. And, if a superpower like the United States is pulled into these wars, it too becomes a target for terrorist cells aligned with one of the parties—as the United States learned on 9/11.

Moreover, some wars are now fought with terrorists at the vanguard. Often a government quietly supports terrorists, or at least feels that it cannot repress terrorists, who then engage in acts of violence against the population of an enemy state. Because terrorists are usually out of the direct control of any state or government, they are difficult to manage, with the result that negotiations between governments can be sabotaged by terrorist campaigns—as has been the case in the middle east. Thus, achieving and maintaining peace is now even more problematic.

The Consequences of Mass Violence

The Aftermath of Mass Violence

Revolutions are fought against what are perceived to be repressive and unresponsive governments. Often an ideology accompanies a revolution, convincing believers that "the people" will rule, that heavy-handed governmental control will wither away, or that government will "represent the average citizen."

The realities of revolutions are very different. If a revolution is unsuccessful, the repression and persecution of "enemies to the state" is extensive and brutal. If a revolution is successful, the problems of how to govern in the chaotic aftermath of violence are enormous. The result is usually a centralized government that regulates and controls people's activities. Figure 23.3 outlines some of these problems and how they force tight political control.

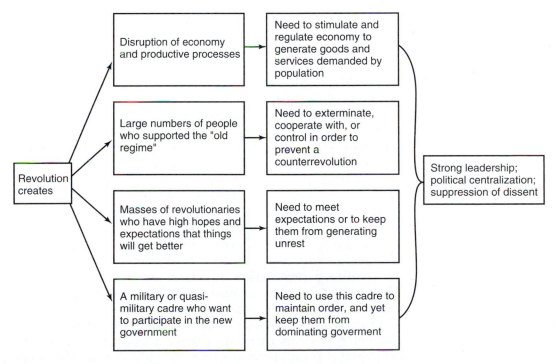

Figure 23.3   Revolutions and Their Aftermath

After a revolution, the economy is in chaos and productivity is essential to realize the promises of revolutionary leaders. A large number of people who supported the old regimes must be managed and controlled. There are the masses that supported the revolution and now expect things to be better. Meeting their demands—managing, controlling, and manipulating them so that they do not become restive—is vital. The "shock troops" of the revolution, who define solutions to problems in terms of violence and who possess the power to coerce, must be brought into government but kept from getting out of hand. The result of all these pressures is for a centralized, dictatorial, and repressive government to emerge in the name of the revolution. Although the government may indeed improve the situation of the average person, it rarely does so democratically and peacefully.

These problems are compounded after a civil war because the defeated enemy is organized militarily and must be prevented from reorganizing or becoming a guerrilla force. Moreover, because a civil war lasts longer than a revolution, the economy is more disrupted and less oriented to domestic production. Not only this, but the population has usually done without many goods and services and expects them to become available as soon as the war is over. Because a civil war has also killed more people, wasted more resources, and engendered the hurt and anger of more people on both sides who have lost loved ones and had their lives disrupted, there is always a problem of how to heal wounds and recover lost resources. The result is often a strong and dictatorial government, no matter which side has won the war. Yet, if a civil war is fought to vanquish an occupying army, then a less dictatorial form of government is possible—as was the case for the American Revolution.

The Effects of War and War Preparedness

When a war occurs, it dramatically alters the structure and culture of a society, and the longer a war continues, the greater is this alteration. Moreover, the threat of war and the resulting mobilization to be prepared when it comes has much the same effect as actual war on the structure and culture of a society.

Probably the most dramatic effect of war and preparation for war is the alteration of economic processes. Wars, or fears of wars, shift productive processes toward the manufacture of military hardware. In modern industrial economies, the result is the investment of technological capacities into "weapons systems" and the commitment of huge amounts of tax resources to military procurement. Such distortion of economic processes creates shortages of goods and services during war; in nonwar times, the domestic economy cannot compete, as it might otherwise, in world markets in which other competitors do not devote so much technology and capital to war preparedness.

Military production *decreases* economic growth, as is outlined in Figure 23.4. The main reason is that military technology is stockpiled and cannot easily be inserted into the domestic economy to create jobs or to expand production. Another reason is what can be called the multiplier effect. Investment in a piece of equipment in the domestic economy—say, a bulldozer—compared to one in the military—such as a tank—has very different effects on the economy. After the tank is built,

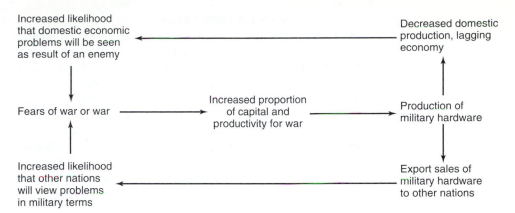

Figure 23.4   War and Productivity

its effects on the economy recede, whereas the bulldozer keeps working. For example, if the bulldozer clears land for the building of a house, it sets into motion jobs for carpenters and others who build the house, banks who finance the house, real estate brokers who sell the house, and service people who help maintain the house. And each time the bulldozer is used, it starts this chain reaction. In contrast, the tank sits on a military base; if used, it does little for a domestic economy.

Increases in military production not only place a drain on the domestic economy, they increase the sale of weapons to other nations. These sales make up for some of the lost profits in the nonmilitary economy, but they also lead to the proliferation of weapons around the world. This proliferation leads other nations to see problems in military rather than diplomatic terms, thus increasing the likelihood of war and, if terrorists can secure these weapons on the black market, acts of terrorism.

Wars or fears of war also increase the presence of military leaders as heads of governments or as prominent officials in civilian governments. The growth of the Pentagon in the United States, for example, is the result of not only several actual wars over the last 50 years (World War II, Korea, Vietnam, the Gulf War, and Iraq) but also of a prolonged "cold war" with the Soviet Union. The existence of a large military contingent in government increases the likelihood that "military options" will be given considerable weight in making political decisions, thereby increasing "fears of the enemy" and the inclination to take military action. These processes are diagrammed in Figure 23.5.

At the cultural level, wars or fears about them increase a population's sense of national identity and its patriotic fervor. Such cultural

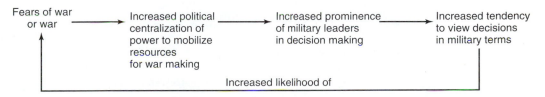

Figure 23.5   War and Government

unity is often necessary to inspire willingness to sacrifice for military mobilization and to accept increasing political control. As cultural beliefs
stress nationalism, patriotism, and unity, they operate to legitimate the
military bias in political decisions. In so doing, they increase the possibility of war. The Korean and Vietnam wars, for example, could not have
been legitimated without a sense of cultural unity over the "American
way of life" and fears about "the specter of communism." Of course, the
lack of consensus on the United States' involvement in Vietnam eventually forced revisions in policies. Without cultural consensus about the
"dangers" posed by the enemy, it becomes difficult to sustain a war. Yet,
the recent invasion of Iraq by the United States was supported by patriotic fervor that, in turn, allowed the department of justice to sustain policies that limit citizen's rights in the "Patriot Act."

Terrorism

Is Terrorism Increasing?

The term *terrorism* encompasses a variety of political activities, but at the
core is the intent to use violence to achieve political ends. Terrorists operate outside the existing political system and generally the goal is to
change this system through instilling fear in the general population that,
in turn, will reduce the legitimacy of a political regime. Terrorist organizations vary in how they are structured and how they operate (Tilly
2004). Some rely more heavily on coercion (i.e., attacks involving violence) whereas other terrorist organizations only periodically use violence; others are well-organized within a society and concentrate on the
use of terror within their own society for clear political objectives; and
still others are organized outside of their targeted society and enter the
society to commit acts of terrorism for political ends that may extend beyond the targeted society's borders (as was the case with the September
11 attack on the United States).

The dramatic events of September 11 may give the impression that
terrorism is increasing around the world. In fact, the overall trend in the
number of terrorist attacks has been declining. The U.S. State Department (2000, 2001, 2002) has collected data on the number of attacks
each year since 1980. In 1980, there were about 500 terrorist attacks;
this figure went up to nearly 700 in the late 1980s; however, with some
spikes here and there, the number has been declining ever since. There
were, for example, 346 attacks in 2001, a number that is far less than evident in the late 1980s. The level of casualties also declined with the number of attacks until 1999 where they increased and, then, in 2001, they
increased dramatically with the 3,000 deaths in the World Trade Center

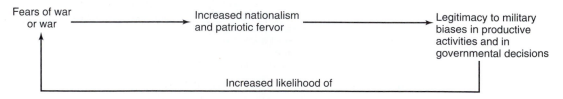

Figure 23.6   War and Cultural Beliefs

towers alone. Just whether the decline in the number of attacks will continue or the number of recent deaths are anomalies is difficult to gauge, but it is clear that acts of terrorism may not be as widespread as they appear, especially to Americans who were somewhat insulated to terrorist events that have been occurring all over the world for many decades. Indeed, terrorism has existed for a very long time; thus, it is not a new phenomenon. Its persistence suggests that it can be explained sociologically.

Explaining Terrorism

It is easy to assume that acts of terrorism are committed by madmen and zealots in the name of some political or religious dogma (Oberschall 2004). However, terrorism is a kind of collective action, granted one involving planned violence, that can be understood by the same forces that generate all collective behaviors (Oberschall 2004; see Chapter 22). First, there must be widespread dissatisfaction with present conditions. Second, there must emerge an ideology or set of beliefs that arouse emotions and articulate grievances. This ideology must focus people's attention on political leaders and, if an international organization, on leaders in particular nations that are assumed to be the cause of deprivations and grievances. Third, there must be some capacity to organize; and so, there must be financial resources, a cadre of activists willing to engage in action, a system for recruiting new members, a network of communication, and an organizational structure that can coordinate and control actions. Fourth, there needs to be political opportunities revolving around existing points of tension and collective action, abusive practices by a state that arouse anger among the masses, shifts in public opinion, and other factors that give terrorists an opening for action. Under these conditions, terrorism becomes likely and, indeed, inevitable.

Once conflict is joined between terrorists and their enemy, the solidarity of the two sides generally increases. This is often termed the **law of complementary opposition** because conflict will lead each party to centralize leadership, repress deviance or anyone who goes against the cause, legitimate actions with more intense ideologies, and organize people in more hierarchical forms to assure that coordination and control operate effectively. Once the respective parties are so organized, violence can escalate. For example, the attack on the World Trade Center led to the invasion of Afghanistan and Iraq by the United States under very high levels of American patriotism, centralized control, and suspension of some traditional civil rights of those accused of "war crimes." We can see complimentary opposition on the American side, but what about the other side? There can be little doubt that Al Queda is more centralized, more ideologically committed, and more likely to attack symbols of American dominance, even as agents of the United States seek to root out the members of Al Queda. Thus, once terrorists and their targets become locked into conflict, the respective structures of each part become more likely to engage in violence.

World System Dynamics and Terrorism

There have been acts of terrorism on American soil that have little to do with the rest of the world. The bombing of the federal building in Oklahoma is but one example, although a particularly deadly one. Here the terrorists had their own political agenda. The attack by Al Queda on September 11, 2001 and previous attacks by a variety of terrorist organizations on American targets abroad all point to a different kind of terrorism, one that perceives the dominant military and economic power in the world as an enemy. These perceptions are easily maintained because of the United States' heavy involvement over many decades in the middle east. Even efforts to broker peace between Israelis and Palestinians or to liberate Kuwait from Iraq can be used to mobilize anti-American sentiments. Similarly, the invasion of Iraq has drawn terrorists to Iraq to pursue their cause.

Communication and transportation technologies make the coordination of this kind of world action possible. People in remote parts of the globe can coordinate actions at any other part of the world. The United States is a particularly tempting target because it stands alone in its involvement in world affairs; although Americans may perceive themselves to be humanitarian (especially when ideologically mobilized), those who have resentments against various political regimes come to see the United States as the enemy. Indeed, corrupt political leaders will often encourage their disaffected masses to see the United States as the doer of wrong, thereby diverting attention from themselves. Or, those leaders who seek help from the United States in maintaining control of their populations not only intensify the resentment against them but against the United States as well.

Most acts of terrorism still occur for political reasons by actors within a given society for purposes unique to that society. But, the globalization and the rise of America as the dominant world power have made terrorism on a global scale not only easier to conduct but it has painted a bullseye on symbols of American domination.

SUMMARY

1. Humans are violent. Whether or not this propensity for violence is part of our biology is debatable, but it is clear that once humans settled into permanent communities, violence became habitual.

2. Person-to-person violence is usually seen as deviant and criminal, whereas collective violence involving the mobilization of many individuals takes on several different forms: crowd behavior that attacks a target, revolutionary action where crowds seek to overthrow a political regime, civil wars where armies are organized to overthrow a political regime, terrorism where sporadic violence against governmental and civilian targets are designed to demoralize a population and delegitimate its government, and war between societies in which full armies are mobilized to defend or conquer the entire society.

3. Revolutions usually fail because the state can fight back and crush revolutionary crowds. When the state is weak, however, revolutions can sometimes succeed in throwing out a political regime.

4. Failed revolutions often evolve into civil wars as the revolutionaries take their time and mobilize full armies that can march on a government. Civil wars are typically long and bloody, killing many soldiers and civilians.

5. Terrorism is very much like other forms of collective action because it involves the perception of grievances, ideological mobilization of emotions,

organization and recruitment of people committed to the cause, and opportunities to put into action violence against selected targets.

6. War almost always leads to centralization of power in government, ideological solidarity, repression of dissent, and distortion of economic production
away from domestic to military needs. Moreover, war biases governmental
decision making toward the military as opposed to diplomatic options.

7. Terrorism is promoted by globalization because terrorists use the communication and transportation infrastructures that make globalization of the
economy possible. As the lone superpower in the world, the United States is
a likely target for terrorists operating in the international arena.

KEY TERMS

Civil War: The clash of two armies within a society, with one seeking to defend
a political regime and the other attempting to overthrow the existing regime
and install another.

Complementary Opposition, Law of: The tendency for parties to any conflict to
become more organized along several fronts, including centralization of
power, creation of hierarchy, propagation of unifying ideologies, and repression of dissent.

Revolution: The rapid formation of angry crowds who then seek to overthrow a
political regime.

Terrorism: The use of violence against governmental and civilian targets by an
organized group seeking to demoralize a population, weaken and delegitimate
a government, and promote a political agenda.

Violence: The use of physical force designed to inflict harm.

War: The organized conflict between two or more nations, involving the mobilization or armies and invasion of the territories of another nation.

Chapter 24

Globalization

For better or worse, the people of the world are becoming increasingly connected to each other. Societies have always had relations with each other, but these relations tended to be confined to neighboring populations. Truly global sets of relations began slowly at first but are now in place. And today, virtually the entire world—except for a few remote outposts—is connected. How did this dramatic transformation come about?

Forces of Globalization

Technological Innovations

Globalization is not possible without innovations in communication and transportation technologies. The first people who built long-distance, ocean-going canoes and other sea craft were innovators because they made it possible to travel to distant places across the oceans; similarly, innovations in land transportation, from the wheel that could carry cargo over long distances to the use of pack animals for carrying people and goods, opened new possibilities for relations among people from different and distant societies. Infrastructures were also critical innovations because by building roads, ports, canals, and other facilities, it became possible to move people and products long distances. Thus, as technologies were used to build new modes of transportation, the populations of the world were on the way to globalization. Today, people and freight can move about the globe within a day through air travel and vast cargoes can be carried across the ocean in containers stacked and unloaded by computers on large ships with less than a dozen crew members.

Communication technologies advanced more slowly because without electricity, information could not travel very fast or very far. Communication had to be carried on the means of transportation, neither one of which was very fast until the late nineteenth century. At times, messages could be sent at a rapid pace through lights in towers that were lined up, but these messages could not go very far because building and maintaining towers was expensive. With electricity, however, communication increasingly became global. The telegraph was the first innovation; later came the telephone, and today messages can go at the speed of light through fiber optic cables and can be compressed, bounced off satellites, and decompressed in voice or tabular form.

As long as humans had to walk to travel, there were limitations on globalization. But with each new technological innovation in communication and transportation technologies, it became possible for people of the world to be connected.

Warfare and the State

Another great force behind globalization has been the desires of one government to control the population of another society. The reasons for conquest have varied, but the mobilization of armies to conquer another society always generates intersocietal relations. And, if an army can be successful, its government will often continue to conquer other populations and build up an empire. The largest empire ever built was by the Mongols who controlled China, the middle east, and portions of eastern Europe before the empire disintegrated. Empires have come and gone, but they have always created relations among societies that often endure after the empire has collapsed. Thus, although warfare spreads misery, it has historically been an important force in globalization.

Today, it is difficult to build an empire by conquest alone. The last big military empire—the Soviet Union—collapsed in the early 1990s. To initiate military aggression now generally brings in other military powers, thus raising the costs of military actions against other societies dramatically. In the place of military empire building, empires are now often based upon economic domination and control of markets.

Markets

We are so used to markets that we may not fully appreciate what a revolution they represented in human affairs. Markets provide both a place and mechanism for exchanging objects of value. The first markets were ad hoc, as people gathered to trade goods, tools, and other resources. Barter was the principal means of exchange, but once money and credit were introduced into markets, they could expand dramatically. With a medium like money, people can express their preferences in unlimited ways because they no longer need to have a good or commodity that someone else wants; they can use money to buy what they want. And, with credit it becomes possible to buy when you do not have the money on the promise to pay later. Once markets using money and credit emerged, they expanded in several senses. First, the sheer volume of goods and later services that could be exchanged increased. Second, the diversity and varieties of goods and services that could be bought and sold grew dramatically. And third, the scope of markets across territories expanded into systems of long-distance trade.

Once markets facilitated long-distance trade, they increased the probability of globalization. Goods from the far east, the Americas, and other parts of the world could come to Europe, and finished products using resources from the Americans could be sent back as finished goods. As transportation and communication technologies expanded, the rate, volume, and scope of trade could all increase. Any part of the world is now tied into a system of markets. You can use your credit card to buy products all over the world, and people elsewhere on the globe can do the same thing. More significantly, wholesalers and retailers can buy and sell with the click of a button on their computer, setting into motion the movement of goods and services.

Problems with Globalization

Outsourcing and the Loss of Jobs

We live in a society where the effects of globalization seem positive, but a moment's reflection reveals many profound problems. Close to home, your future job could be exported—or "outsourced" in current lingo—to someone in another country who will perform this job for much less money (see Table 17.4). This outsourcing of work has already occurred for many manual jobs in shoes, clothing apparel, toys, electronics, and a wide variety of goods that you buy without thinking about *who* is making these goods and *where* they are being made. Professional services are also moving overseas because they can be performed much more cheaply. Capitalists will always seek the cheapest labor costs, and many people all over the world are desperate for work, even highly educated professionals who look upon wages that you and I might view as too low in a much more positive light.

The very networks of communication and transportation that make the flow of goods and services around the world also make the loss of jobs in developed countries to less developed countries a trend of the future—a trend that will affect your prospects for prosperity. The wonders of a global world can become horrors to the professionals of the future.

Stalled Development

Many of the arguments for free and open trade among nations, including manufacturing jobs, go as follows. True, jobs are lost in the short run in more developed nations as manufacturing seeks lower priced labor, but as the underdeveloped world begins to perform jobs that were once performed in the developed world, people's incomes will slowly rise, with the result that in the long run, these workers will be able to purchase more expensive goods and services from the higher priced labor force of developed nations. Is this scenario accurate, or is it an ideology justifying inequality? No definitive answer is possible because the world is in the middle of the scenario, but Mexico can provide an instructive lesson. For a time, Mexico became a place where foreign manufacturers settled, especially along the northern border, to produce goods for a much less cost than was possible in the United States. The presumption was that wages would slowly rise in Mexico, allowing Mexican households to purchase goods manufactured in the United States. The North American Free Trade Agreement (NAFTA) was based upon these assumptions, and although it is still too early to tell, what has happened in Mexico is revealing: many of the manufacturing facilities along the border have shut down, as companies moved their production to cheaper priced labor in Asia. Wages rose for a while in Mexico, and in many sectors of the Mexican economy they still are on the rise, but at the same time, many workers are now out of a job, forcing them into lower wage occupations or, as is often the case, encouraging their illegal immigration into the United States.

Thus, globalization not only affects developed countries like the United States and Canada, it has enormous effects on developing nations where labor is just beginning to earn a living wage. Manufacturers will flee such higher priced labor if they perceive that they can reduce labor costs somewhere else. The result is for much of the rapidly developing world to be subject to the same problems as the even higher priced labor of postindustrial societies: the loss of manufacturing jobs. But, unlike the advanced postindustrial societies, there is not the same breadth of manufacturing that can absorb some of the laid-off workers, nor is there the high-technology sector or a large range of high-skill professions to sustain the purchasing power of people in developing countries. In contrast, jobs lost overseas in a wealthy country like the United States can, to a degree, be made up by new kinds of service jobs that are the backbone of a postindustrial society. So, even as computers are built in countries like Taiwan and Korea, the technology that allows them to be built is generated in America—thus creating jobs for Americans. Similarly, Nike shoes may be made in southern Asia, but they are designed and marketed by professionals in the United States. Developing countries like Mexico and most of Latin America do not have this large technology or professional sector to fall back upon. Moreover, they do not have the same broad mix of manufacturing jobs that can provide employment for some of those who have been laid off. These dynamics repeat themselves again and again all over the world as capital and manufacturing flee to the lowest priced labor.

Environmental Degradation

Manufacturers not only move to places where labor is less costly, they also move to places where environmental restrictions are lax. Controlling effluents into the environment is, like labor, a cost that cuts into profits. Thus, manufacturers will move to places where people are desperate for jobs and where governments are willing to cut some slack on environmental controls. Thus, just as the postindustrial societies of the world are making significant gains in controlling pollution, which is indeed a world problem, developing countries often encourage the movement of polluters to their shores—thereby increasing not only greenhouse gases but effluents of all kinds into the world's ecosystem (see Chapter 25 for more details).

World Inequality

Many of the aforementioned problems above revolve around a basic fact: inequality in the world system. People in poor countries are desperate for jobs and income at any cost. Their governments teeter on the brink of internal conflict if they cannot make daily life better for their citizens. And, even as capital and manufacturers move about in search of lower cost labor and favorable political environments, the fact is that world-level inequality is increasing. The rich in affluent countries are getting richer, while the poor in underdeveloped nations are becoming poorer, relative to others in the world. Globalization would seem to provide an answer to world inequality in its capacity to move capital and jobs around the globe, but thus far, the world economic system has yet to reach the poorest of nations. Many additional problems besides inequality itself—revolution, war, and terrorism, to name a few—are directly connected to patterns of inequality.

World-Level Misery

At the top of the stratification system are the early industrializing societies of Europe; the United States and Canada; and select Asian societies like Japan, Singapore, and Hong Kong, China. At the bottom are over a billion people who live on just one dollar per day. The United Nations provides several definitions of poverty to gauge the level of deprivation that people must endure. **Absolute poverty** is defined as a situation where people do not have enough money for survival, with two distinct subcategories: *world poverty* where people live on less than $365 per year and *extreme poverty* where individuals must live on less than $275 per year. There are over 600 million people living in such extreme poverty, and many hundreds of millions at or just above the world poverty level. For example, the World Bank (2000) estimates that 49% of those in sub-Saharan Africa and 44% of those in South Asia live below world poverty levels. The United Nations also formulates a human poverty index that measures several dimensions of life, such as how long one is likely to live, how well off people are economically, how much knowledge people have or can acquire, and how included they are in the social fabric. At one time this was termed the "misery" index because so many people in the world have little income, few opportunities for education, and short lifespans. Because standards of living are so different between postindustrial societies and poor nations, a sliding scale is necessary in this index for industrialized and developing countries, but the index of human misery is nonetheless revealing. In some countries such as Ethiopia, well over 50% fall into the most deprived categories, but even in some industrial societies, significant numbers exist in poverty. For example, in Russia almost 30% are in poverty and almost 14% fall below the standards of the world poverty index and cannot meet minimal standards of subsistence. There is also what is sometimes termed **double deprivation** in poverty rates because women and children are much more likely to be in poverty than adult males. For example, although the data are somewhat dated, the United Nations Commission on the Status of Women (1996) found that women constitute 60% of the world's population but receive just 10% of the income and hold only 1% of the world's wealth, while taking up two thirds of all working hours. These problems are compounded by the fact that, on the whole, the poorest populations are the fastest growing, assuring that most people and particularly women and children will remain at the bottom levels of the global stratification system.

Determining the Level of World Inequality

One rough measure of global inequality is *per capita GNP*. This figure is calculated by adding up the total number of goods and services, or gross national product (GNP), for a society. Then, this sum is divided by the total number of people in this society. The resulting number is **per capita inequality**. This figure tells us very little about inequalities within a society, because these are averaged out, but it can give us a sense for differences in income across societies. This measure is, however, only reliable for societies with a money economy; many poor populations trade in services and barter goods with the result that the per capita GNP for these societies in which many non-cash transactions occur is not very reliable. Table 24.1 reports the rank-order in the GNP per capita figures for 1999, as compiled by the World Bank (2000), for selected countries. As is evident, Luxembourg has the highest per capita GNP figure ($42,930 per year) whereas Mozambique has the lowest ($80 per year).

Trends in Inequality

Determining whether or not world inequality is increasing is difficult for a variety of methodological reasons (see Babones and Turner 2004, for a review). Part of the problem is that some very large nations, such as India and China, have increased per capita income; and so, when they are averaged into calculations, they skew the data because the populations of these societies represent 20% of the world's population. Moreover, just how one measures money also makes a difference. If purchasing power of

Table 24.1   Per-Capita Income of Top and Bottom 20 Nations

Top 20 Nations			Bottom 20 Nations		
Rank	Country	Per Capita Income (US$)	Rank	Country	Per Capita Income (US$)
1	Luxembourg	41,210	142	Yemen	260
2	Switzerland	40,630	143	Guinea-Bissau	250
3	Japan	39,640	144	Haiti	250
4	Norway	31,250	145	Mali	250
5	Denmark	29,890	146	Bangladesh	240
6	Germany	27,510	147	Uganda	240
7	United States	26,980	148	Vietnam	240
8	Austria	26,890	149	Burkina Faso	230
9	Singapore	26,730	150	Madagascar	230
10	France	24,990	151	Niger	220
11	Iceland	24,950	152	Nepal	200
12	Belgium	24,710	153	Chad	180
13	Netherlands	24,000	154	Rwanda	180
14	Sweden	23,750	155	Sierra Leone	180
15	Finland	20,580	156	Malawi	170
16	Canada	19,380	157	Burundi	160
17	Italy	19,020	158	Tanzania	120
18	Australia	18,720	159	Zaire	120
19	United Kingdom	18,700	160	Ethiopia	100
20	United Arab Emirates	17,400	161	Mozambique	80

Source: Population Concern (2003).

money is used, one conclusion can be drawn; however, when the exchange rate of the money on the world money market is employed, another conclusion emerges. We need not go into the details of measurement problems; rather, let us cut to the bottom line.

Despite the measurement problems, the general pattern of inequality is clear. The data clearly indicate that the spread between rich and poor nations is increasing. Whatever modest improvements in income there are in poor nations, they are still falling further behind the more dramatic increases in the income of rich nations. The developing nations in between the richest and poorest nations reveal a variety of patterns. Some like India and China are increasing per capita income, whereas other developing countries have suffered reversals or have not gained in per capita income. Thus, there is great flux in the middle portions of the world income distribution. But what is clear is that well over a billion people live in true misery, and their fate in life is not getting better (Babones and Turner 2004).

Problems Posed by World Inequality

Malthusian Problems.   At least 1.2 billion people live at or below the level of subsistence by any standards; and this situation represents a humanitarian problem of why so many people must live in such misery. More practically, populations that have exceeded their resource base always generate Malthusian pressures. Thomas Malthus proposed that populations grow geometrically (2, 4, 8, 16, 32, etc.) while resources grow arithmetically (1, 2, 3, 4, 5, etc.). The result, or **Malthusian Correction,** is that a rapidly growing population soon runs out of resources, setting into motion what he termed the "four horsemen" of war, disease, pestilence, and famine. Poor people in crowded nations will be visited by some or all of these horsemen, and in a global world, the horsemen can ride right into the backyards of affluent nations.

People are not only dying from poor nutrition in many parts of the world, but areas in their societies are becoming breeding grounds for new kinds of diseases, or variants of older ones, that, in a world where germs can move across the globe in a matter of hours, pose potential problems for everyone, even those in the developed world. If individuals could live substantially above subsistence, the threat of a pandemic would be greatly reduced.

Disease is not, of course, the only Malthusian pressure. War between populations and, more significantly, among subpopulations within societies, will increase when people lack resources. Traditional rivalries, past enemies, members of different ethnic groups, and other lines of division are often aggravated when access to resources—land, jobs, patronage, political power, health care, and the like—is seen in zero-sum terms. What one segment of a population receives is seen by another as depriving them of their due, leading the latter to violence that, in turn, breeds counter-violence in potentially escalating spirals. Indeed, the globe is covered with hot zones where inequalities within and between populations have caused warfare and other acts of violence. Like disease, these wars do not always stay local. Terrorists tend to see the developed and rich nations of the world as somehow implicated in the misery of people—often correctly—and they strike out at their overseas enemies.

Thus, when people are poor and angry, their anger often comes to the shores of developed nations.

Geopolitical Problems.   Inequalities among nations almost always generate political problems. Strong wealthy nations tend to exploit weak and poor nations, with the consequence that the latter come to resent the actions of the developed world. Whether through empire-building, colonization, or exploitive practices of multinational corporations, tensions exist between the developed and underdeveloped world. These tensions manifest themselves in many ways: border conflicts, internal revolts against political leaders who have supported colonial powers or exploitive multinational corporations, renewed rivalries among ethnic groups, and as is now evident, acts of terrorism against those who are seen to exploit the resources and sovereignty of a nation. These kinds of political problems are aggravated when wealthy nations export the resources of poor nations with the help of elites who skim profits for themselves, aggravating internal inequalities. The fact that many of the terrorists working against the United States come from Saudi Arabia is not surprising because inequality has been increasing over the last decades in Saudi Arabia during the period when the United States has supported corrupt leaders to assure a stable supply of oil. And, it is often the frustrated middle classes of these societies rather than the abject poor who become the ideological spokespersons and front-line combatants in conflict with rich powers. For these middle classes, internal inequalities have shut off sources of capital that could provide the career opportunities for which they have been trained and rightly feel entitled. Coupled with mobilization of the poor masses, this kind of threat to the developed world is considerable, especially as the elements of nuclear bombs and biological toxins circulate in underground world-level markets.

As a general rule, then, inequality always creates tensions, not only within a society but also between societies. As these tensions lead to mobilizations within societies, they often have consequences outside a society's borders, encouraging military adventurism from hostile neighbors or encouraging leaders to engage in external conflict to deflect attention from internal domestic problems. And, if any of these regional conflicts pulls in more advanced nations who have interests in, or alliances with, the conflicting parties, then the possibility of wider geopolitical tensions increases. Thus, as long as there is global inequality, geopolitical conflicts will have ample fuel.

Geoeconomic Problems.   Global inequality encourages developed nations to export labor and manufacturing costs to poorer nations with cheap pools of labor and unregulated manufacturing sectors. This kind of development causes problems at both ends of this exchange: wealthy nations continue to lose manufacturing jobs to poorer nations, thus increasing welfare burdens and other problems associated with loss of unskilled and semi-skilled jobs; and poorer nations develop dependencies on the technology and capital of wealthy nations that, at any time, can be moved to another poor nation. The end result is that wealthy nations are generating a divide between their high-technology and high-skill sectors, on the one side, and their marginally employed and unskilled poor sectors, on the other, whereas many poor nations are undergoing dependent development on conditions imposed by foreign capitalists.

Another geoeconomic pattern is for residents of poorer nations to migrate, often illegally, to wealthier nations in search of low-skill jobs. These kinds of migratory patterns create a large foreign-born work pool in host countries that typically arouses ethnic tensions and deprives low-skill native workers of potential jobs. At the same time, the country of origin for workers often becomes dependent upon the income (sent home) of their emigrants, with the result that the economy of the poorer country that is exporting workers does not develop the structural base to employ all of its citizens. Of course, this is often a blessing for an under-developed economy that exports its unemployment problems while receiving the currency of more developed nations, but although this pattern generates short-term benefits to poorer countries, it stagnates development in the long run because it does not encourage elites to deploy capital to develop the economic structures that can employ all of its citizens. Instead, development is uneven and does not address the problems that are causing workers to emigrate.

At times, migrants are the skilled workers or the entrepreneurs of a poorer nation who fill in holes and gaps in the labor markets of a host nation, but in emigrating, they deprive their country needed human capital. For example, the United States simply cannot produce enough skilled scientists to fill all positions, and thus, it must import them from poorer countries like India; although this exchange appears even—India cannot employ all of its skilled workers and the United States needs them—it works against both countries because U.S. educational policies are not adjusted to fill skilled positions, whereas India loses the vanguard of human capital for future development. In more recent years, however, countries like India have been able to retain many skilled workers as higher technology companies have emerged in India. This recent trend is part of the reason for India's economic growth and rising national income; and it confirms the need of societies to retain skilled workers and create economic structures that can employ them (rather than letting them emigrate to more developed nations). A further benefit of developing countries creating new, higher technology economic structures is that it levels exchange relations between developed and developing nations, and in so doing, reduces dependence of poorer nations for foreign capital and technology.

Yet, as long as there are large gaps in the incomes of people around the world, capitalists will have incentives to export labor costs, and in so doing, increase dependencies of poorer nations on richer ones. These dependencies may not be as disruptive as former patterns of colonization, but they can retard the development of poor nations because the capital and technology are not under their sovereign control. The result is that modest gains in income may ensue (until capitalists leave for greener pastures of even cheaper labor in another society), but at the price of longer term national development that can coordinate technology, capital, and labor on its own terms. These problems of underdevelopment will be compounded dramatically if advanced economies of industrial and postindustrial nations have extracted the natural resources of a poorer nation, thus leaving it without a resource base for future development. This problem is compounded when political elites have used their position to skim surplus wealth for privilege rather than reinvestment in expanding indigenous production (such will be the fate, for example, of Saudi Arabia, which at some point in the future will have squandered to elite privilege the vast resources that it obtained from oil production).

Explaining Global Inequality

There are no universally accepted explanations for world inequality. Indeed, the ebb and flow of historical empires, the early industrialization of the west, the unequal distribution of natural resources, and other unique historical events still help account for some patterns of inequality. Such historical explanations, however, do not capture all of the dynamics involved. The problem with all of these explanations is that they are loaded with ideological overtones; as a consequence it is difficult to have a rational debate about the explanatory power of each explanation. There are now three basic types of modes of explanations of world inequality: (a) modernization theories, (b) dependency theories, and (c) world systems theories.

Modernization Approaches.   **Modernization theories** argue that the values, beliefs, and motives of people must change before a society can develop economically, and so, it is not surprising that advocates of this approach emphasize the functions of the educational system in creating people with "modern" attributes. What are these modern attributes? The lists vary but include such changes as: the abandonment of traditional beliefs in favor of an active and manipulative stance toward the world, the internalization of achievement motives and values, the development of acquisitive orientations, and the desire to use and enter markets in preference to traditional patterns of ascription for assigning roles.

Critics of this approach have argued that it blames the victims for their lack of economic progress; although this interpretation is not without merit, it ignores the fact that before these changes in human capital can occur, there must be free and dynamic markets, universal education, rational organization systems, and capital available for economic development. If these more macrostructure conditions do not exist, it is difficult to transform people; but conversely, if individuals remain locked into traditional patterns of ascription, they will undermine efforts to alter macrostructural changes in a society.

Dependency Approaches.   The **Theory of Dependency** emphasizes that the lack of development of some countries is the result of policies of more developed nations. Nations have difficulty developing and moving out of poverty because of their dependency on more powerful countries that, in essence, exploit them. When a more powerful country takes control of a less powerful one to extract resources or when multinational corporations secure resources at the cheapest price, the dominant nations and their corporations gain control over significant segments of the economy and political system of poorer nations. Then, this control is used to extract a nation's resources without reinvesting capital in ways that would encourage broad-based development. As a consequence, a society becomes dependent upon more powerful nations or multinational corporations for capital, technology, and employment opportunities that are used not for the development of the dependent country as a whole but for the well-being of the more powerful nation or the profits of multinationals. This dependency is compounded by the dominant power's use of coercion to maintain control, or in more recent times by cooptation of corrupt political regimes who support the interests of outside nations or multinationals to maintain their privilege.

This approach has merit but it does not explain all global inequality. Many poor nations have never been dependent; they simply have been poor for many centuries. Other formerly dependent colonies, such as Singapore, Hong Kong, India, and even many Latin American countries, now enjoy considerable prosperity, perhaps as a result of investment by former colonial powers and multinationals. Dependency theory certainly has an element of truth, and it does correct for the lack of attention by modernization theories to the system of relationships in which a society has been historically implicated.

World Systems Approaches.   Dependency theories are a kind of world system approach, but adding certain conceptual elements has created a **Theory of World Systems.** The most critical element is the division of societies into core, peripheral, and semi-peripheral. *Core* societies are economically developed and politically dominant, using their power and economic resources to control world-level markets, extracting resources from poor *peripheral* countries, often through arrangements with *semi-peripheral* nations that stand between poor nations and the core. Core nations seek to extract resources and use cheap labor for their benefit, whereas semi-peripheral countries try to develop and enter the core so that they too can exploit weaker nations. Much of this analysis is historical and the three-part categorization of societies into core, semi-periphery, and periphery has many problems. As a consequence, this approach increasingly emphasizes the international division of labor in which various nations stand at somewhat different points in world markets. The core nations still use their political power, but more significantly their multinationals invest in poor countries to produce products less expensively. Semi-peripheral countries like Korea, Singapore, China, India, Mexico, and others at this level of development often use the capital and technology of the core, but seek to develop their own export-oriented industries, thereby gaining some control over their economic fate while increasing production and national income. The periphery either stands outside of this system, as is the case for countries like Ethiopia and much of sub-Sahara Africa, or becomes the place where both core and semi-periphery seek cheap raw materials, labor, and manufacturing venues. As the world system has evolved over the last 50 years, core nations increasingly export their labor and manufacturing costs to the periphery and semi-periphery. Indeed, in extreme cases such as shoe and clothing manufacturing, or low-end computer technologies, the core only designs and markets a product that often goes through various steps in the manufacturing that cut across the borders of several countries. Those semi-peripheral countries like Korea, China, India, Singapore, and Mexico, that can begin to gain some control over how multinationals invest and that can generate their own industrial base independently from the capital and technology of core nations, are likely to experience the greatest amount of economic development and rise in national income. Those that cannot do so, however, remain poor or stagnate; and of course, those countries that are so peripheral as to be virtually ignored by the core and semi-periphery are not likely to develop at all because they simply do not have access to capital, technology, or organizational systems that can move them out of poverty.

World systems theories, like dependency theories, have the virtue of emphasizing the connectedness of the nations through market and geopolitical dynamics. Increasingly, it is the fate of a nation in the world's markets that determines its capacity to develop. If it has few indigenous resources that are useful to industrial powers, if its labor pool is too unskilled or isolated, if it has no capacity to develop and use technologies, or if it has no capital to stimulate domestic investment in production, it will remain isolated from world markets. If a nation can provide cheap labor and low-cost manufacturing environments, it can experience some development but if a country is wholly dependent upon the capital and technology of multinationals of core and semi-peripheral nations, it will be difficult in the short run to develop economically. Over the long run, however, rising national income might spur less dependent domestic production, which can lead to development and some independence, but if multinationals come and then leave, they are likely to throw these developing nations into an economic tailspin. Semi-peripheral development is most likely when a society has a favored geopolitical position, as does China, and the capacity to develop export-oriented industries that are not wholly dependent upon foreign capital and technology. As production and national income rise, these translate into more internal market demand that stimulates further independent development. It is countries in this situation that have caused the dichotomization of world societies. They have become more affluent, moving in the same direction as the European-origin core and leaving behind those nations who remain outside the dynamic markets of the world system or who remain dependent on core and semi-peripheral nations.

Factors Favoring or Retarding Economic Growth

None of these approaches, even if we had outlined them in more detail, is adequate for the job of explaining global inequality. They do, however, emphasize important elements of a theory that has yet to be formulated. This theory will emphasize the elements that retard and accelerate the capacity of a society to generate capital for investment in organization systems that can employ the eligible population in the production of goods and services which can then be sold on both domestic and international markets. If societies can initiate development along these lines, its growth and rising national income will reduce global inequality. What conditions favor or retard such growth? The following conditions will encourage development:

1. A skilled population that can take advantage of capital investments and entrepreneurial activities creating employment opportunities.
2. Free markets, directly connected to foreign markets, that can attract capital and technology and that can be used to export domestically produced goods and services.

3. A favorable geopolitical position that can attract the interests of key core nations for political alliances which can then be traded for economic resources and foreign investments.

4. Governments committed to economic development, even if such commitments potentially pose long-term challenges to their rule.

5. Governments and/or economic actors that can avoid high levels of dependency on foreign nations for key technologies and capital, while being able to convert foreign investments into productive industries serving domestic markets.

This list is obviously very cursory, but it does reflect the elements that encourage development. This list, however, should be viewed in the context of the conditions that retard development:

1. Overpopulation that drains resources from government for welfare programs and that could otherwise be used for capital investments in production and education.

2. Lack of indigenous natural resources that isolate a poor population because foreign capital will not be attracted to invest in extraction industries and that force industries to purchase goods on international markets under unfavorable bargaining conditions.

3. Political-religious systems using traditional symbols to legitimate themselves which, in turn, will work against modernization of values, attitudes, beliefs, and motives of the population that would attract capital in search of cheap labor, that make use of imported capital and technology, and that would encourage free markets.

4. Geopolitical isolation of a nation from the interests of core or semi-peripheral countries that decreases their bargaining position with core and semi-peripheral nations over the exchange of political alliance for economic resources.

5. Corrupt political regimes that extract surplus capital for privilege, while spending capital to maintain coercive control of a population, thereby denying the economy needed capital, discouraging the liberating effects of free markets, and repressing innovative and entrepreneurial organizations.

Because so many countries can be characterized by this second list, world-level poverty will persist and, indeed, increase. The few core nations and ambitious semi-periphery countries that meet the conditions of the first list will grow wealthier. In the end, world inequality will increase and pose severe problems for globalization.

SUMMARY

1. For the first time in human history, relations among societies are global, with most societies connected to each other.

2. Globalization became possible with dramatic advances in communication and transportation technologies. War has been another force of globalization, particularly in the recent past as empires have formed and collapsed.

Today, markets are more critical to globalization, especially dynamic markets using high speed communications and advanced systems of transportation.

3. Globalization generates many problems, including (a) the outsourcing of jobs in nations with high-priced labor and governmental regulations to nations with lower priced labor and fewer governmental regulations, (b) stalled development as a result of multinational corporations pulling out of countries in which they had once invested capital for manufacturing, (c) environmental degradation, and (d) inequality.

4. Inequality is a particularly vexing problem because the gap between the rich and poor nations of the world appears to be widening. People in the poorest nations live miserable lives and out of such inequality emerge additional problems: (a) the likelihood of a Malthusian correction that will also invade the developed world; (b) geopolitical problems revolving around internal conflict and terrorism; and (c) geoeconomic problems such as uneven development, economic dependency, and mass migrations from poor to more affluent nations.

5. Efforts to explain world-level inequalities include (a) the modernization approach emphasizing the characteristics—skills, cultural orientations, and motivations—of human capital are critical to economic development that can reduce inequalities; (b) the dependency approach that emphasizes the effects of poor nations becoming dependent upon the government and/or multinational corporations of a rich nation; and (c) the world systems' approach stressing the place of a society in the system of core, peripheral, and semi-peripheral nations. None of these approaches adequately explains either world system dynamics as a whole or the problems of world-level inequality.

KEY TERMS

Absolute Poverty: United Nations' definition for people who do not have enough money for survival, with two subcategories: *world poverty* where people live on less than $365 per year and *extreme poverty* where people live on less than $275 per year.

Dependency, Theory of: Approach that seeks to explain the lack of economic development in a nation as an outcome of its dependency on more powerful nations or the multinational corporations of these powerful nations for technology, capital, and market access, with the result that the internal economy does not develop across all sectors.

Double Deprivation: United Nations' term for the poverty of women and children who are not only poor economically but suffer additional burdens because of their membership in devalued categoric units.

Globalization: Process whereby most nations of the world are connected via communication and transportation technologies and market relations.

Malthusian Correction: Outcome of a situation where a population has grown beyond its resource base, with the result that disease, war, famine, or pestilence (the "four horsemen") are likely to increase and kill off a substantial portion of the population. In a global world, a Malthusian correction in one nation often spills out onto the world stage.

Modernization, Theory of: Approach that seeks to explain the economic development, or the lack of development, in terms of the characteristics of human capital, particularly motives, value orientations, and skills.

Per Capita Inequality: Statistic reporting the average income for all members in a society, achieved by dividing the total gross domestic product by the number of people in a society.

World Systems, Theory of: Approach that seeks to explain the development of relations among nations in terms of their place at the core, periphery, and semi-periphery of a system of societies who are connected by economic and political relations.

Chapter 25

Population
and Ecology

Humans live on a kind of spaceship enclosed by the atmosphere. This ship is now crowded with too many fellow travelers who increasingly engage in forms of economic activity and community organization that are highly disruptive to the forces of nature that sustain the livability of earth's astronauts. There is, then, a fundamental relationship between the number of people on earth and the sustainability of the ecosystems on which all life forms depend for survival. This relationship is mediated by the ways in which this larger number of people becomes organized and by the cultural ideologies that they hold. If people are organized into dense urban communities, engage in industrial production, create market demands for an increasing number of consumer goods, and view nature as a garbage dump, the effects of too many people on the ecosystem are dramatically accelerated. Thus, population and ecological problems are inherently sociological because the number of people in a society, their distribution in space, their patterns of organization, their storehouses of cultural symbols, and their effects on the environment are all interrelated.

Two of the most important changes in the world today are the continued growth of the world's population, the organization of this growing population into industrial modes of production, and the ecological effect that industrialization and high consumption have on the world's ecosystem. These changes have already killed off many species that otherwise might have survived, and the ultimate question is whether or not humans may succeed in killing themselves off as environmental problems escalate.

The science that studies populations is called **demography** and the goal of demography is to understand population growth or decline, population characteristics, population movements, and population trends. The science of the environment is termed **ecology** and its goal is to understand the relationships not only among life forms but also between these forms and the inorganic environment. Sociology as the science of human organization stands between these two disciplines by studying how the organization of a population affects, and is affected by, other life forms and the inorganic environment. Let me begin our analysis with the science of demography.

Population and Demography

Population Size and Growth

The *size* of a population—that is, the absolute numbers of people in a society—is sociologically the most important demographic feature of a society because size affects the kinds of social structures that must be created to support and organize the population. The **rate of population growth,** or the speed with which new people are being added, is also important because this rate determines how much burden is being placed on existing social structures and how much change in these structures will be necessary to accommodate new people. The **growth rate** of a population is calculated by dividing the existing size of a population at the beginning of a given year into the net population increase or loss (i.e., new births minus deaths) at the end of the year. The resulting figure will give you a percentage per year increase or loss in a population. This percentage will usually sound very small—say a 2% or 3% increase—but this figure is only for one year; if a population reveals a 3% growth rate, the population would double in less than 25 years and it would increase many, many times over 100 years. It is for these reasons that demographers are interested in dimensions of *birth rates* and *death rates;* the relationship between these will determine the size of a population and its rate of growth.

The **crude birth rate** is the number of live births for 1,000 members of a population in a given year. In the United States, for example, this crude rate is a little less than 16 per 1,000 Americans, but it is over 50 in Kenya. Such rates give us a rough basis for comparison, but more refined calculations are usually needed. As a result, the **general fertility rate** is used as a way of factoring in age spans, usually the span of years during which women are fertile. This consideration produces a statistic that measures the total number of births per 1,000 women in the 15 to 44 age span, or child producing years. By knowing the rate of actual births among those who can give birth, we have a much more refined statistic. We can make this statistic even more refined if we want, producing an **age-specific fertility rate** that calculates live births per 1,000 in a year for particular age brackets, say 15-25 or 25-40. For example, we might want to compare the age-specific rate for young women in a society for different years, thereby allowing us to determine if those in their most reproductive years are indeed having more or fewer babies.

The **crude death rate** is calculated like the crude birth rate, except this time we calculate the number of deaths per 1,000 people in a population. In the United States, for instance, the crude death rate per 1,000 people is less than 9, whereas for much of central Africa it is approaching 50 per 1,000. One can also calculate an **age-specific death rate** to see the age brackets in which people are likely to die. If a society has a high figure for 50- to 60-year-olds, this tells us that many people are dying early. One of the most useful applications of an age-specific rate is the calculation of the **infant mortality rate,** which tells us the number of one-year-olds or less per 1,000 live births who die. Some African societies have rates over 200 per 1,000, whereas the rate in the United States is around nine, a figure that sounds much better but is still higher than most other industrial nations. This rate thus tells us that in the United States, a lot of babies are dying because they do not have adequate health care.

The Demographic Transition

As noted earlier, the relationship between birth and death rates influences the size of a population as well as its rate of growth. Other factors can come into play, such as migration into or out of a society, but the birth and death rates are crucial to understanding the growth of a population. For example, most of the growth in the population in the United States comes from immigration and the high birth rates of new immigrants.

For most of human history, birth and infant mortality rates were both high and the age-specific death rate would indicate that many people died early in their lives. There were perhaps as many as 3 million hunters and gatherers 40 thousand years ago; this figure might have gone as high as 5 million when horticulture was introduced. When agriculture emerged on a wide scale some 5,000 years ago (Wilford 1981), the population grew some more, although period waves of war, famine, disease, and pestilence—what Thomas Malthus called the "four horsemen"—would knock the population down, only to have it grow again. Thus, the rate of population growth for most of human history was not high, primarily because high birth rates were accompanied by high death rates. By the time of Christ, at 1 A.D., there were 200 million people on earth; by the early 1800s this figure had jumped to 1 billion; and today, the number of people on earth has passed 6 billion and is still growing, as is summarized in Figure 25.1. There has been, therefore, an accelerating rate of population growth since the spread of agriculture, as can be seen in Figure 25.2.

In his famous essay on population, Thomas Malthus (1798) argued that populations grow in a geometric or exponential pattern (2, 4, 8, 16,

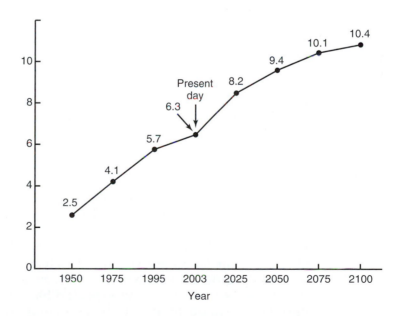

Figure 25.1   Recent Trends and Future Projections in Population Growth
Sources: United Nations, *World Population Prospects.* United Nations (1998, 2000); World Population Clock (2003).

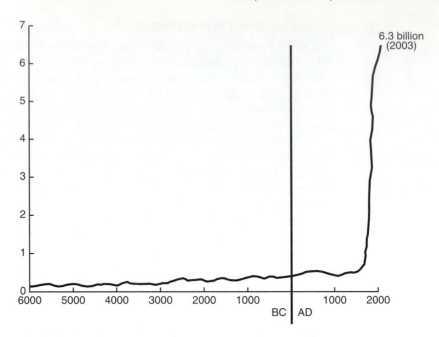

Figure 25.2   Long-Term Population Growth
Source: Population Reference Bureau, "How Many People Have
Ever Lived on Earth?" *The Population Bulletin,* 18 (February
1996 United Nations Yearbook (1978, 2000); World Population
Clock (2003).

32, 64, etc.), whereas resources remain stable or grow only at an arithmetic rate (1, 2, 3, 4, etc.). Populations will, therefore, grow until they
overwhelm the (economic) means of subsistence, *unless* this growth is
checked by famine, disease, pestilence and war—forces that had helped
stem the tide of population growth up to Malthus' time and thereafter.
But as has become evident, these forces have not been enough because
populations continue to grow. Industrialization and the concurrent rise
of medicine and science as institutions have drastically changed Malthus'
calculations, although the spread of AIDS throughout central Africa and
the scare of the SARS outbreak in 2003 signal that in the long run perhaps the world will experience a Malthusian correction to rapid growth.

For now, death and mortality can be reduced with the applications of
technologies—for example, pesticides that kill off those insects that cause
disease and ruin crops and medical advances that cure illness and disease
while reducing infant mortality. Disease and famine were thus reduced as a
check on population growth; we are seeing the result in explosive rates of
population growth in many parts of the world (Ehrlich and Ehrlich 1990).

However, something unexpected has also been occurring: birth rates
have also been declining. In the most modern societies, they are very low
and, at times, are below the replacement rates needed to keep a population at a given size. Malthus implied that birth rates would always remain high, but he was wrong. His miscalculation alerts us to what is
called the **demographic transition** (Almgren, 1992).

The basic idea behind the *demographic transition* is this (Davis 1945): As societies industrialize and become more modern, people begin to have fewer babies, and at the same time, new technologies decrease death rates. But there is a lag between when the death rate declines and when the birth rate begins to go down; it is during this lag period that a population explosion may occur. People are still having many babies because of cultural beliefs and lifestyles that presumed a large portion of babies would die, that valued having large families, and that needed larger families as labor and as a source of security in old age. When the infant mortality declines and older people live longer, people do not immediately lower their fertility; they keep on reproducing at the old rate, thereby increasing dramatically the size of the population. But eventually, birth rates decline as large families become a burden in non-agricultural work, as beliefs change to a more modern profile, as people are mobile in pursuit of education and careers, and as people seek to consume and enjoy the good life. The sequences in the demographic transition are delineated in Figure 25.3.

Europe went through this transition first, and 20 years ago there were great fears that the Third World would not do the same. In fact, it seemed like the death rate would decline *without* the lagged drop in the birth rate. The Third World would thus use modern technology to lower death rates, but not adopt the lifestyle of smaller families. But slowly, the birth rates of many Third World societies are beginning to decline, signaling that the world population explosion may not be as big and loud as once feared.

However, population will increase for quite some time, even if the birth rate dropped to replacement levels, because the large bulges of younger children produced before the birth rate declined must work their way through their child-bearing years. The world is not free from a

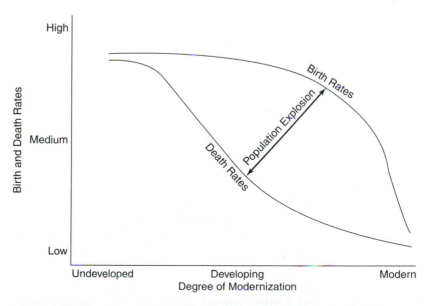

Figure 25.3   Dynamics of the Demographic Transition

Malthusian catastrophe yet, but it looks much better for the human species than it did two decades ago.

Characteristics of the Population

Demographers also analyze the characteristics of a population. One of the most important characteristics of a population is its **age composition**, or the percentage of the population at various ages—say, 0–4, 5–9, 10–14, 15–19, 20–24, and so on up to 80+. Examples of age composition are outlined in Figure 25.4. The age composition can tell us a great deal and inform public policy. For example, if a high percentage of a population is in the younger age cohorts, then a population will grow as these people enter their child-bearing years. Or to illustrate further, if younger cohorts constitute a smaller percentage of the 20- through 40-year-olds in a population, as is the case in the United States, then the population as a whole will become older, and the care of the elderly will soon be a major policy issue—as it is in the United States. You will, in all likelihood, increasingly resent your social security taxes that are used to pay for health care (Medicare) and other benefits for the elderly. And given the age composition of the population, you will have reason to be concerned because the "baby boomers" who are now close to retirement will have to be supported by a smaller and smaller group (you and those behind you).

Another characteristic of a population is its **sex ratio**, or proportion of men to women. This can become a significant concern if this ratio becomes unbalanced, as would be the case when war kills off a high proportion of the young men (as it has indeed done throughout the ages).

Another characteristic is the **ethnic composition** of a population, and the various rates (birth, death, and growth) for each ethnic subpopulation. If one ethnic subpopulation is growing, while others are stable, then this change is going to be reflected in ethnic tensions. White prejudice and discrimination against Latinos in America are, to some extent, fueled by fears about their growing numbers relative to whites.

Thus, by knowing some basic characteristics of a population, we can plan—given the political will—and develop policies that take into account demographic realities. Although the numbers and statistics of demographers may seem dry and dull, they have enormous implications for your well-being.

Population Movements

The size and characteristics of a population are affected by *migration*, or the movement of people into, out of, and within a society. When migration involves people coming into a society, **immigration** is occurring; when people move out of a society, **emigration** is evident; and when movement is within the regions of a society, **internal migration** is the appropriate term. The *net migration rate* is the increase or decrease of a population per 1,000 members that comes with migrations.

Migrations occur because of a combination of push factors, or those forces prompting people to leave one area, and pull factors, or those conditions that make a destination attractive (Long 1988). For example, most of you reading this book are the descendants of European, Asian, and Latin American immigrants who found economic, political, and social conditions in their society of origin unpleasant (the push factors)

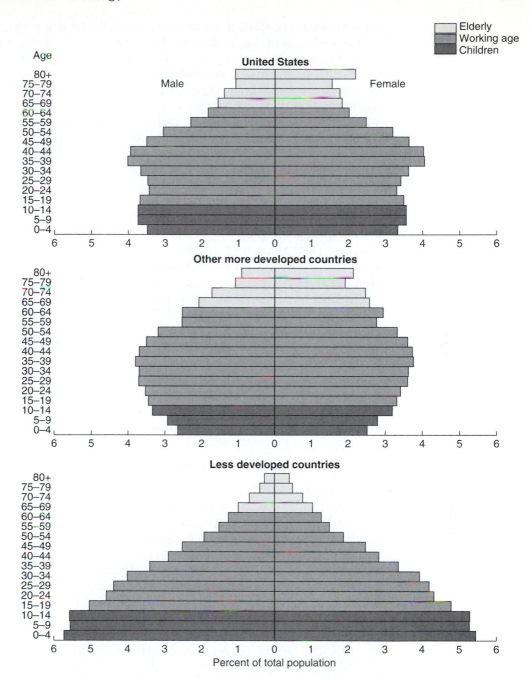

Figure 25.4   Age Distribution in Economically Developed and Less Developed Nations
Sources: U.S. Census Bureau, International Data Base; Census 2000 Summary File 1.

and who, at the same time, perceived the United States to be comparatively free, open, and filled with opportunities (the pull factors). The same is also true with internal migrations: first the movement westward, then the movement from colder to warmer climates where new businesses were created, then back for a while to the older regions, and now some movement again to the Sunbelt. All of these movements reflect push factors (loss of a job, cold weather) and pull factors (new job opportunities, warmth). Indeed, by some projections, the populations of the northeast will grow very little, and the midwest will decline as a result of internal migration patterns, whereas the south and west will continue to grow, and dramatically so, not only because of internal migrations but also because of immigration from other countries.

Today, as noted earlier, much of the growth in the American population is from immigration and, along with this, from the higher birth rates of many immigrants. Many of the ethnic tensions and political pressures at all levels of government in the United States today come from the turmoil created by migration of ethnic subpopulations into a region. It would, for example, be impossible to understand the social, economic, and political dynamics of the southwest without taking into consideration the immigration of Mexicans and Asians into the communities of this area. The same was true for the northeast and midwest with the immigration of Europeans between 1850 and 1920, and to a lesser extent today, with the immigration of Puerto Ricans and Asians. Thus, migration patterns are more than a bunch of dry statistics because these statistics give you some sense of the magnitude of the internal movements of Americans and the immigration of new ethnics. All of these movements will influence your job, schooling, political standing, and many other aspects of your lives. Add to the migration patterns the rate and character of population growth, and we can see how crucial the science of demography is for understanding a society.

Ecology and the Environment

It is, at times, hard to remember that humans are only one species among millions. Our complex patterns of organization sometimes appear to insulate us from immediate interaction with the natural environment, leading us to forget a very fundamental fact: like any animal, we are dependent upon complex chains, cycles, and flows among species as well as between species and the physical-chemical environment. As noted earlier, the science of *ecology* studies these interrelations among species and the physical-chemical conditions of all life. As the most disruptive species on earth, the analysis of **ecosystems** or the particular patterns of relations among species and their physical-chemical environments must include the study of human culture and social organization (J. Turner 1976, 1977, 1985c; Turner and Musick 1985).

Ecosystem Processes

For our purposes, we might visualize the ecosystem as a web of chains, flows, and cycles among those forces sustaining life. A *chain* is a form of interdependence among species. The most important example is a **food chain** in which one species becomes food for another. At one end of this chain are micro organisms that take energy directly from the sun, whereas at the other end are animals like you and I who eat a wide variety of other animals and plants. An **ecosystem cycle** is a form of interdependence that feeds back on itself, creating a loop; a good example is the photosynthesis of the sun's energy by plants that then become food for herbivores (plant eaters), some of whom become food for carnivores (meat eaters), and all of whom become food for micro organisms that decompose dead plants and animals into nutrients for plants engaged in photosynthesis of the sun's energy. An **ecosystem flow** is the broader movement of forces, energy, and various forms of organic and inorganic matter through an ecosystem. In the cycle above, the sun's energy flows through the ecosystem, with much of it lost as heat; or the forces of wind, rain, and tidal energy flow through ecosystems, taking with them other organic and inorganic materials.

Of particular importance are those chains, cycles, and flows that renew the soil, air, and water. For without these **renewable resources,** as they are often called, plant and animal life would not be possible—and this, of course, includes you and me. *Stock resources,* such as fossil fuels, metals, and chemicals, are stored in the ecosystem and are not renewable; indeed, they are taken out of the ecosystem and hence depleted, although many are recyclable as well. Although depletion of stock resources is a problem for humans today, it is not nearly so fundamental as the disruption of the chains, cycles, and flows renewing the water, soil, and air on which life on earth depends. Thus, patterns of human organization have depleted many of the earth's stock resources, but more significant, human culture and organization are disrupting the processes of regeneration of renewable resources.

Ecological Disruption

Industrial production and mechanized agriculture generate an enormous tonnage of waste residues—sewage, carbon dioxide, heat, chemicals, organic, pesticides, industrial slag, radioactivity, nitrogen oxides, carbon monoxide, ash, sulphur, heavy metals, and so the list goes on. As these are dumped into the ecosystem, they begin to disrupt those processes renewing the soil, water, and air as well as basic chemical balances such as the ozone layer; as a result, they begin to kill off species in those chains, cycles, and flows on which we as a species depend for life.

Air pollution is directly affected by chemicals spewed into the air, as are chemical balances in the upper atmosphere (e.g., the clear depletion of the ozone layer protecting us from the sun's ultraviolet rays). These pose health problems, but the more fundamental problem is the runoffs from toxic chemicals dumped into lakes, rivers, and streams that flow to the oceans and begin to kill off many micro organisms and, potentially, the ocean's phytoplankton producing 80% of the air in our atmosphere. Soil pollution comes from the dumping of wastes, particularly harmful residues of pesticides and chemical fertilizers, which accumulate and percolate through the soil, killing off the micro organisms that aerate and refertilize the soil. Moreover, these wastes disrupt the food chains of larger animals or directly kill insects and animals. The end result is that many of the organisms responsible for the renewal of the soil are being destroyed, reducing the capacity of the soil to produce crops for food. Water pollution is a particularly difficult problem because water flows to all parts of the ecosystem. And if waste residues enter at one point in the ecosystem, they are moved to other points, becoming more concentrated and killing both micro and more macro organisms.

Water and soil pollution are given much less attention than air pollution; yet they are far more serious for balances in the ecosystem. They are less visible and immediate, but they are more significant for the long-term survival of humans and other species. Air pollution may take a few years off your life; water and soil can potentially kill off the species.

Population, Pollution, and Sociocultural Organization

The basic problem in both local and world ecosystems is you and I, along with all of our fellow human beings. As populations have grown, as industrial production has expanded, as high-yield mechanized agriculture has become necessary to feed us all, and as consumption and needs for the "good life" have escalated, humans produce more, consume more, and dump more. The more we dump, the more disrupted are those processes renewing the air, soil, and water.

At the cultural level, values and beliefs emphasize achievement, consumption, and materialism that, in turn, create demand for production and consumption of goods. These cultural tenets encourage the development of mass produced goods requiring high levels of energy and widespread use of chemicals, many of which find their way into the ecosystem. And to consume large quantities of goods also means that many of them will be dumped when no longer needed, again finding their way into the ecosystem.

These cultural and economic patterns are reinforced by political systems where increased production and consumption are necessary for the legitimacy and careers of politicians. Stratification aggravates these political pressures because those who enjoy the good life usually want more, whereas those who have little want a piece of the affluence. The end result is more pressures for mass industrial and agricultural production, with its inevitable concomitant: pollution and disruption to the ecosystem. These dynamics of ecological disruption are outlined in Figure 25.5.

As the world seeks to industrialize, problems of pollution will escalate. Often societies undergoing industrialization do so under pressure from their large and restive populations; as a result, government does not impose environmental controls because they are costly. Thus, at the very time when the postindustrial nations are engaged in efforts at pollution control, the rest of the world is embarked on a rapid path of industrial development. Moreover, some of this development is by companies from postindustrial nations that set up dirty factories in foreign countries in an effort to avoid the strict standards of their home country. As the four billion people in industrializing countries begin to consume at a high level, not only will the industries that generate the products that are consumed pollute, but as these products are consumed, they will be dumped as garbage into the ecosystem. Even when industrialization is not occurring, population growth in the developing world pushes people to engage in more intensive agriculture, clearing forests and using wasteful planting systems. For example, much of the Amazon rainforest, which has important though not fully understood effects on the world's climate, is being decimated, as are the forests of south Asia and central Africa. Thus, even a low technology activity—forest clearing for agricultural lands with axes

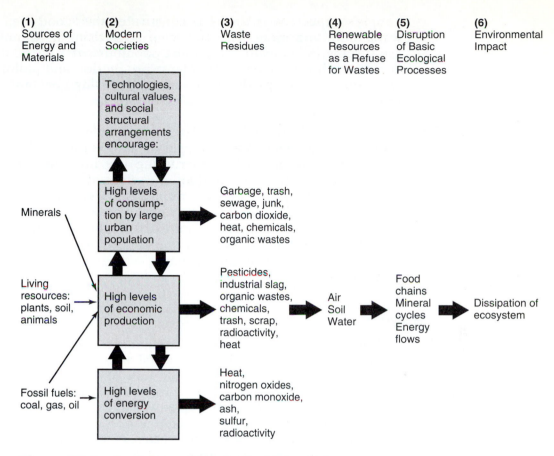

Figure 25.5   Society and Ecological Disruption
Source: Turner, 1976a.

(and at times, chain saws and bulldozers)—can have effects on not only the local ecosystem but also on the cycles, flows, and chains of the world ecosystem.

Still, we must remember that, even though the postindustrial nations of the world constitute a relatively small percentage of the world's population, they probably account for over half the harmful effluents and garbage dumped into the world's ecosystem. The reason for this high percentage is that these postindustrial nations produce and consume so much more than people in developing countries; even though postindustrial countries have initiated serious efforts at pollution control, they are still the major problem in sustaining ecological balances.

Globalization of the economy accelerates these trends of ecological disruption. As the large populations of Asia are viewed by capitalists as a source of cheap labor, factories are moved to these nations, especially if local governments do not impose too many environmental restrictions. And, as those who work in factories secure wage incomes, they become consumers seeking the goods that you and I take for granted, thereby ratcheting up industrial production and pollution even more. Media also contribute to this process because advertising on a global scale raises people's expectations for what constitutes the "good life," making them want more and more. The effects of advertising in stimulating demand are turning individuals in the most populous parts of the world into consumers—whose demands stimulates production and pollution. However, we should not forget that this same advertising constantly escalates the much higher levels of consumption among residents of postindustrial societies as well.

The psychologist Roger Brown once said that "the smart money is on the insects" who have managed to survive for hundreds of millions of years. Humans may be so disrupting the life support systems of the spaceship earth that we could kill ourselves off. There are too many people on the planet now, and the numbers are growing, thankfully at a decreasing rate. But even if the number of people on earth levels off, each person will consume more as industrialization continues in the less developed world, thereby aggravating the ecological crisis that is surely to come in the next few hundred years.

SUMMARY

1. The number of people, their distribution and patterns of organization, and their effects on the environment are all interrelated and important topics.
2. The science of demography is the study of population, its size and growth, its characteristics, and its movements. Of particular importance are growth patterns and the demographic transition.
3. Ecosystems are constructed from the relations among life forms and inorganic matter through a series of chains, cycles, and flows.
4. Patterns of human organization now disrupt these processes as they sustain the renewable resources on which all life on earth depends. Modernization of the less developed world and globalization of capitalism increase the likelihood that increased production and consumption will disrupt both local and world ecosystems.

KEY TERMS

Age Composition: Percentage/proportion of a population in various age brackets.

Age-specific Death Rate: Number of deaths per 1,000 people in particular age range or brackets, such as 65 to 75-year-olds or any bracket chosen for analysis.

Age-Specific Fertility Rate: Number of live births per 1,000 people in a particular age range or bracket, such as 15 to 25-year-olds, 26 to 40-year-olds, or any range chosen for analysis.

Crude Birth Rate: Number of live births per 1,000 people in a given year.

Crude Death Rate: Number of deaths per 1,000 people in a given year.

Demographic Transition: Pattern of population growth in the transition to modernity, during which death rates decline first in the face of continued high birth rates followed, eventually, by a decline in birth rates.

Demography: Science of population processes, especially the characteristics, distribution, movement, and growth/decline of populations.

Ecology/Ecosystem: The study of/and system of relations among life forms, as well as between life forms and the physical environment.

Ecosystem Cycle: Form of interdependence in which processes fold back on themselves, creating cycles of events and interdependencies.

Ecosystem Flow: Movement of energy, organic matter, and inorganic matter through an ecosystem.

Emigration: Movement of people *out of* a society.

Ethnic Composition: Proportions of various ethnic subpopulations in a society and the birth, death, and growth rate associated with each.

Food Chain: Linking of life forms as food for each other.

General Fertility Rate: Total number of live births in a given year for each 1,000 women in their child-bearing years (usually defined as 15 to 44 years of age).

Immigration: Migration of people *into* a society.

Infant Mortality Rate: Number of one-year-olds and below per 1,000 live births who die in a given year.

Internal Migration: Movement of people *within* a society.

Migration: Movement of people into, and out of, a society.

Population Size: Absolute number of people in a society.

Rate of Population Growth: Increase (decrease) in the size of a population in a given year calculated by dividing the size of a population at the beginning of a year into the net increase (or decrease) of people during the year.

Renewable Resources: Those resources that can be renewed by virtue of ecosystem chains, flows, and cycles. Air, water, and soil are the three most basic renewable resources.

Sex Ratio: Proportion of men to women in a population.

References

Aguirre, Jr., Adalberto. 2004. *American Ethnicity.* New York: McGraw-Hill.

Aitchison, Jean. 1978. *The Articulate Mammal.* New York: McGraw Hill.

Alexander, Jeffrey C., ed. 1985. *Neofunctionalism.* Beverly Hills, CA: Sage.

Alexander, Jeffrey C., et al. 1986. *The Micro-Macro Link.* Berkeley, CA: University of California Press.

Alford, Robert R., and Roger Friedland. 1985. *Powers of Theory: Capitalism, the State and Democracy.* Cambridge, UK: Cambridge University Press.

Allan, Kenneth and Jonathan H. Turner. 2000. "A Formalization of Postmodern Theory." *Sociological Perspectives.* 43:363–85.

Allport, Gordon. 1954. *The Nature of Prejudice.* Cambridge, MA: Addison-Wesley.

_____. 1979. *The Nature of Prejudice* (25th anniversary edition). Reading, MA: Addison-Wesley.

Almgren, Gunnar. 1992. "Demographic Transition." In *Enclycopedia of Sociology,* ed. E. Borgatta and M. Borgatta. New York: Macmillan.

Anderson, Craig A., and Brad J. Bushman. 2002. "The Effects of Media Violence on Society." *Science* 295:2377–79.

Apple, Michael W. 1982. *Education and Power.* Boston, MA: Routledge and Kegan Paul.

Apple, Michael W., and Lois Weis. 1983. *Ideology and Practice in Schooling.* Philadelphia: Temple University Press.

Asch, Solomon E. 1952. Social Psychology. New York: Prentice-Hall.

Avery, Christopher, Andrew Fairbanks, and Richard Zekhauser. 2003. *The Early Admissions Game: Joining the Elite.* Cambridge, MA: Harvard University Press.

Babbie, Earl. 1992. *The Practice of Sociological Research.* 3d ed. Belmont, CA: Wadsworth.

Babones, Salvatore J. and Jonathan H. Turner. 2004. "Global Inequality." In *Handbook of Social Problems: A Comparative International Perspective.* George Ritzer, ed. Newbury Park, CA: Sage.

Bagby, James W. 1957. "A Cross-Cultural Study of Perceptual Predominance in Binocular Rivalry." Journal of Abnormal and Social Psychology. 54:331–34.

Bales, Robert F. 1950. *Interaction Process Analysis.* Cambridge, MA: Addison-Wesley.

Bandura, Albert. 1977. "Self-efficacy: Toward a Unifying Theory of Behavioral Change." *Psychological Review* 84: 191–215.

Beeghley, Leonard. 1983. *Living Poorly in America.* New York: Praeger.

Bell, Daniel. 1973. *The Coming of Post-industrial Society*. New York: Basic Books.

Bell, Wendell. 1958. "Social Choice, Life Styles, and Suburban Residence." *The Suburban Community*. Edited by William M. Dobriner. New York: Putnam.

Bellah, Robert. 1964. "Religious Evolution." *American Sociological Review* 29: 358–74.

Bendix, Reinhard. 1968. *Max Weber: An Intellectual Portrait*. Garden City, NY: Doubleday.

Bennett, Neil G., A. K. Blanc, and D. E. Bloom. 1988. "Commitment and the Modern Union." *American Sociological Review* 53: 127–38.

Berger, Bennett M. 1960. *Working Class Suburb*. Berkeley, CA: University of California Press.

Berger, Joseph and Morris Zelditch, Jr. 1985. *Status, Rewards and Influence*. San Francisco: Jossey-Bass.

Berger, Joseph, David G. Wagner, and Morris Zelditch. 1989. "The Growth, Social Processes, and Meta Theory." In *Theory Building*, ed. J. H. Turner. Newbury Park, CA Sage.

Berger, Joseph, M. H. Fisek, R. Z. Norman, and M. Zelditch, Jr. 1977. *Status Characteristics and Social Interaction: An Expectation States Approach*. New York: Elsevier.

Berger, Joseph, S. J. Rosenholtz, and M. Zelditch, Jr. 1980. "Status Organizing Processes." *Annual Review of Sociology* 6: 479–508.

Berger, Joseph, T. L. Conner, and M. H. Fisek, eds. 1974. *Expectation States Theory: A Theoretical Research Program*. Cambridge, MA: Winthrop.

Biddle, Bruce J. 1992. "Role Theory." In *Encyclopedia of Sociology*, ed. E. F. Borgatta and M. L. Borgatta. New York: Macmillan.

Blake, Judith, and Kingsley Davis. 1964. "On Norms and Values." In *Handbook of Modern Sociology*, ed. R. L. Faris. Chicago: Rand McNally.

Blumberg, Rae Lesser. 1984. "A General Theory of Gender Stratification." *Sociological Theory*. 2:23–101.

Blumer, Herbert. 1969. *Symbolic Interaction: Perspective and Method*. Englewood Cliffs, NJ: Prentice Hall.

_____. 1978. "Collective Groupings." In *Collective Behavior and Social Movements*, ed. L. E. Genedie. Itasca, IL: Peacock.

Bonacich, Edna. 1976. "Advanced Capitalism and Black-White Relations in the United States." *American Sociological Review*. 38:583–94.

Bourdieu, Pierre. 1984. *Distinction: A Social Critique of the Judgement of Taste*. Cambridge, MA: Harvard University Press.

Bowles, Samuel, and H. Gintis. 1976. *Schooling in Capitalist America*. New York: Basic Books.

Brantlinger, Ellen A. 2003. *Dividing the Classes: How the Middle Class Negotiates and Rationalizes School Advantage*. London: Routledge.

Braudel, Fernand. 1982. *The Wheels of Commerce: Volume 2 of Civilization and Capitalism, 15th-18th Century*. New York: Harper and Row.

_____. 1977. *Afterthoughts on Material Civilization and Capitalism*. Baltimore, MD: John Hopkins University Press.

Brines, Julie and Kara Joyner. 1999. "The Ties That Bind: Principles of Cohesion in Cohabitation and Marriage." *American Sociological Review*. 64:333–55.

Brint, Steven and Jerome Karabel. 1989. *The Diverted Dream*. New York: Oxford University Press.

Brown, Roger W. 1972. "Feral and Isolated Man." In *Language*, ed. V. P. Clark, et al. New York: St. Martins Press.

Burke, Peter J. 1991. "Identity Processes and Social Stress." *American Sociological Review*. 56:836–49.

Burt, Ronald S. 1980. "Models of Network Structure." *Annual Review of Sociology* 6:79–141.

Camic, Charles. 1979. "The Utilitarians Revisited." *American Journal of Sociology* 85 (3):516–50.

Campbell, John L. 2004. *Institutional Change and Globalization*. Princeton, NJ: Princeton University Press.

Cantril, Hadley. 1941. *The Psychology of Social Movements*. New York: Wiley.

Carneiro, Robert. 1970. "A Theory of the Origin of the State." *Science* 169:733–38.

Carroll, John B., ed. 1956. *Language, Thought and Reality: Selected Writings of Benjamin Lee Whorf*. Cambridge, MA: MIT Press.

Castells, Manuel. 1998. *The Rise of the Network Society, Volume 1*. Oxford: Blackwell.

Centers for Disease Control. 2002. Atlanta, GA: CDC Printing.

Chafetz, Janet Saltzman. 1990. *Gender Equality: An Integrated Theory of Stability and Change*. Newbury Park, CA: Sage.

Chafetz, Janet. 1990. *Gender Equity: An Integrated Theory of Stability and Change*. Newbury Park, CA: Sage.

_____. 1984. *Sex and Advantage: A comparative Macro-Structural Theory of Sexual Stratification*. Totowa, NJ: Rowman and Allanheld.

Chambliss, William. 1978. "Toward a Political Economy of Crime." In *The Sociology of Law*, ed. C. Reasons and R. Rich. Toronto, Canada: Butterworths.

Chandler, Teritus. 1987. *Four Thousand Years of Urban Growth: An Historical Census*. New York: St. Davids University Press.

Charles, Maria, and David B. Grusky. 2004. *Occupational Ghettos: The Worldwide Segregation of Women and Men*. Stanford, CA: Stanford University Press.

Chase-Dunn and Thomas D. Hall. 1997. *Rise and Demise: Comparing World-Septems*. Boulder, CO: Westview.

Chronicle of Higher Education. 2003. *Almanac Issue, 2003–4*. August 29.

_____. 2004. *2004–5 Almanac Issue*. August 27.

Cicourel, A. V. 1964. *Method and Measurement in Sociology*. New York: Free Press.

Coleman, James S. 1990. *Foundations of Social Theory*. Cambridge, MA: Belknap.

Coleman, James S. 1991. *Foundations of Social Theory*. Cambridge, MA: Harvard University Press.

Collins, Randall. 1975. *Conflict Sociology*. New York: Academic Press.

_____. 1976. Review of "Schooling in Capitalist America." *Harvard Educational Review* 46:246–51.

_____. 1979. *The Credential Society*. New York: Academic Press.

_____. 1981. "On the Micro-Foundations of Macro-Sociology." *American Journal of Sociology* 86 (March):984–1014.

_____. 1984. "Statistics vs. Words." *Sociological Theory* 2:329–64.

_____. 1986. "Interaction Ritual Chains, Power and Property." Pp. 177–92 in *The Micro-Macro Link,* ed. J. Alexander, et al. Berkeley, CA: University of California Press.

_____. 2004. *Interactional Ritual.* Princeton, NJ: Princeton University Press.

Collins, Randall, and Scott Coltrane. 1991. *Family Sociology.* Chicago: Nelson-Hall.

Coltrane, Scott and Randall Collins. 2001. *Sociology of Marriage and Family.* Belmont, CA: Wadsworth.

Comte, Auguste. 1830–1842 [1896]. *Course of Positive Philosophy.* London: George Bell and Sons.

_____. 1851–1854. *Systeme De Politique: ou, Traite De Sociologies, Instituant La Religion De L'humanite.* Paris: L. Mathias.

Cooley, Charles Horton. 1902. *Human Nature and the Social Order.* New York: Scribners.

_____. 1909. *Social Organization.* New York: Scribners.

Coser, Lewis A. 1956. *The Functions of Social Conflict.* London: Free Press.

Cosmides, Leda. 1989. "The Logic of Social Exchange." *Cognition.* 31:187–276.

Dahl, Robert A. 1961. *Who Governs?* New Haven, CT: Yale University Press.

Dahrendorf, Ralf. 1958. "Out of Utopia: Toward a Reorientation of Sociological Analysis." *American Journal of Sociology* 74 (September):115–27.

_____. 1959. *Class and Class Conflict in Industrial Society.* Stanford, CA: Stanford University Press.

Damasio, Antonio. 1997. "Towards a Neuropathology of Emotion and Mood." *Nature.* 386:769–70.

_____. 1994. *Descartes' Error: Emotion, Reason and The Human Brain.* New York: Putnam.

Darwin, Charles. 1859. *On the Origin of Species.* London: J. Murphy.

Davies, James C. 1962. "Toward a Theory of Revolution." *American Sociological Review* 27:5–19.

_____. 1969. "The J-Curve of Rising and Declining Satisfactions as a Cause of Some Great Revolutions and Contained Rebellion." In *Violence in America,* ed. D. Graham and T. Gurr. New York: Bantam.

Davis, Kingsley. 1940. "Extreme Social Isolation of a Child." *American Journal of Sociology* 45:554–64.

_____. 1945. "The World Demographic Transition." *Annals of the American Academy of Political and Social Science* 237:1–11.

_____. 1947. "A Final Note on a Case of Extreme Isolation." *American Journal of Sociology* 52:432–37.

Davis, Kingsley, and Wilbert Moore. 1945. "Some Principles of Stratification." *American Sociological Review* 4:431–42.

Denzin, Norman K. 1970. *The Research Act: A Theoretical Introduction to Sociological Methods.* Chicago: Aldine.

Dogan, Mattei, and John D. Kasarda. 1988. *The Metropolitan Era.* 2 vols. Newbury Park, CA: Sage.

Domhoff, William G. 1967. *Who Rules America?* Englewood Cliffs, NJ: Prentice Hall.

_____. 1970. *The Higher Circles: The Governing Class in America*. New York: Random House.

_____. 1978. *Who Really Rules?* Santa Monica: Goodyear.

_____. 1983. *Who Rules America Now: A View for the '80s*. Englewood Cliffs, NJ: Prentice Hall.

_____. 1990. *The Power Elite and the State*. New York: Aldine de Gruyer.

_____. 2002. *Who Rules America?: Power and Politics*. Boston: McGraw-Hill.

Drucker, Peter. 1959. *Landmarks of Tomorrow*. New York: Harper and Row.

Durkheim, Émile. 1891 [1975]. *Montesquieu and Rousseau*. Ann Arbor: University of Michigan Press.

_____. 1893 [1947]. *The Division of Labor in Society*. New York: Free Press.

_____. 1895 [1938]. *The Rules of the Sociological Method*. New York: Free Press.

_____. 1897 [1951]. *Suicide*. New York: Free Press.

_____. 1912 [1965]. *The Elementary Forms of Religious Life*. New York: Free Press.

Earle, Timothy, ed. 1984. *On the Evolution of Complex Societies*. Malibu, CA: Undena.

Ehrlich, Paul, and Anne H. Ehrlich. 1990. *The Population Explosion*. New York: Simon and Schuster.

Eisenstadt, S. N., and A. Shachar. 1987. *Society, Culture and Urbanization*. Newbury Park, CA: Sage.

Ekman, Paul. 1982. *Emotions in the Human Face*. Cambridge, UK: Cambridge University Press.

_____. 1992a. "Are There Basic Emotions?" *Psychological Review*. 99:550–53.

_____. 1992b. "Facial Expressions of Emotion." *Psychological Science*. 3:34–38.

Ellis, Albert. 1945. "The Sexual Psychology of Human Hermaphrodites." *Psychosomatic Medicine* 18:108–25.

Epstein, S. 1980. "The Self-concept: A Review and the Proposal for an Integrated Theory of Personality." Pp. 27–39 in *Personality: Basic Issues and Current Research*. Englewood Cliffs, NJ: Prentice Hall.

Erikson, Erik H. 1950. *Childhood and Society*. New York: W. W. Norton.

Etzioni, Amitai. 1961. *A Comparative Analysis of Complex Organizations*. New York: Free Press.

_____. 1964. *Modern Organizations*. Englewood Cliffs, NJ: Prentice Hall.

Farkas, George, 2004. "The Black-White Test Score Gap." *Context* 3:12–19.

Farley, Reynolds. 1964. "Suburban Persistence." *American Sociological Review*. 45:38–47.

Feagin, Joe R. 1991. *Racial and Ethnic Relations*, 3d ed. Englewood Cliffs, NJ: Prentice Hall.

Federal Reserve System. 1992. "Preliminary Report of a Survey of Wealth." Washington, DC: U.S. Government Printing Office.

Federal Reserve System. 2003. "Survey of Consumer Finances." Washington, D.C.: U.S. Government Printing Office.

Fischer, Claude S. 1976. *The Urban Experience*. New York: Hancourt.

_____. 1982. *To Dwell Among Friends*. Chicago, IL: University of Chicago Press.

Forstmann, Theodore. 1999. "A Competitive Vision for American Education." *Imprints* 28 (September 8):1–4.

Freud, Sigmond. 1938. *The Basic Writings of Sigmund Freud.* New York: Random House.

Fried, Morton H. 1967. *The Evolution of Political Society.* New York: Random House.

Frisbie, Parker W., and John D. Kasarda. 1988. "Spatial Processes." Pp. 629–66 in *Handbook of Sociology,* ed. N. J. Smelser. Newbury Park, CA: Sage.

Gans, Herbert J. 1962a. *The Urban Villagers.* New York: Free Press.

_____. 1962b. "Urbanism and Suburbanism as Ways of Life" in *Human Behavior and Social Processes.* Edited by Arnold M. Rose. Boston, MA: Houghton Mifflin.

_____. 1967. The Levitt Owners: *Ways of Life and Politics in a New York Suburb.* New York: Basic Books.

Garfinkel, Harold. 1967. *Ethnomethodology.* Englewood Cliffs, NJ: Prentice Hall.

Gecas, Viktor. 1982. "The Self-concept." *Annual Review of Sociology* 8:1–33.

_____. 1985. "Self Concept." Pp. 739–41 in *The Social Science Encyclopedia.* London: Routledge and Kegan Paul.

_____. 1986. "The Motivational Significance of Self-Concept for Socialization Theory." *Advances in Group Processes* 3:131–56.

_____. 1989. "The Social Psychology of Self-efficacy." *Annual Review of Sociology* 15:291–316.

_____. 1991. "The Self-Concept as a Basis for a Theory of Motivation." Pp. 171–87 in *The Self-Society Dynamic: Cognition, Emotion and Action.* Cambridge, UK: Cambridge University Press.

Gecas, Viktor, and Michael L. Schwalbe. 1983. "Beyond the Looking Glass Self: Social Structure and Efficacy-Based Self-Esteem." *Social Psychology Quarterly* 46:77–88.

Geschwind, Norman. 1965a. "Disconnection Syndrome in Animals and Man, Part I." *Brain.* 88:237–94.

_____. 1965b. "Disconnection Syndrome in Animals and Man, Part II." 88:585–644.

Geschwind, Norman and Antonio Damasio. 1984. "The Neural Basis of Language." *Annual Review of Neuroscience.* 7:127–47.

Giddens, Anthony. 1971. *Capitalism and Modern Theory: An Analysis of the Writings of Marx, Durkheim, and Max Weber.* Cambridge, UK: Cambridge University Press.

_____. 1976. *New Rules of Sociological Method.* London: Hutchinson Ross.

_____. 1984. *The Constitution of Society.* Berkeley, CA: University of California Press.

_____. 1993. *New Rules of Sociological Method: A Positive Critique of Interpretative Sociologies.* Stanford, CA: Stanford University Press.

Gilmore, Samuel. 1992. "Culture." In *Encyclopedia of Sociology,* ed. E. F. Borgatta and M. L. Borgatta. New York: Macmillan.

Goffman, Erving. 1959. *The Presentation of Self in Everyday Life.* Garden City, NY: Anchor Books.

_____. 1961. *Encounters.* Indianapolis, IN: Bobbs-Merrill.

_____. 1967. *Interaction Ritual: Essays on Face-to-Face Behavior.* Garden City, NY: Anchor Books.

_____. 1974. *Frame Analysis: An Essay on the Organization of Experience.* Boston: Harper and Row.

Goffman, Erving. 1963. *Behavior in Public Places: Notes on the Social Organization of Gatherings.* New York: Free-Press.

_____. 1971. *Relations in Public: Micro Studies of the Public Order.* New York: Basic Books.

Goffman, Erving. 1961. *Encounters.* Indianapolis, IN: Bobbs-Merril.

_____. 1963. *Behavior in Public Places.* New York: Free Press.

Goldstone, Jack. 1990. *Revolution and Rebellion in the Early Modern World, 1640–1848.* Berkeley, CA: University of California Press.

Goode, William J. 1960. "A Theory of Role Strain." *American Sociological Review* 25:483–96.

Greer, Scott. 1956. "Urbanism Reconsidered: A Comparative Study of Local Areas in Metropolis." *American Sociological Review.* 21:19–25.

Gup, Ted. 1992. "What Makes This School Work?" *Time* 140. (December 21): 63–65.

Habermas, Jurgen. 1968. *Knowledge and Human Interest.* London: Heineman.

Habermas, Jurgen. 1970. *Knowledge and Human Interest.* London: Heineman.

Halfpenny, Peter. 1982. *Positivism and Sociology: Explaining Social Life.* London: Allen and Unwin.

Hall, Edward T. 1959. *The Silent Language.* New York: Doubleday.

Handel, Warren. 1982. *Ethnomethodology: How People Make Sense.* Englewood Cliffs, NJ: Prentice Hall.

Hannan, Michael T., and John Freeman. 1977. "The Population Ecology of Organizations." *American Journal of Sociology* 82 (March):929–64.

_____. 1984. "Structural Inertia and Organizational Change." *American Sociological Review* 49:149–64.

_____. 1986. Where Do Organizational Forms Come From?" *Sociological Forum* 1:50–72.

_____. 1987. "The Ecology of Organizational Founding: American Labor Unions, 1836–1985." *American Journal of Sociology* 92: 910–43.

_____. 1988. "The Ecology of Organizational Mortality: American Labor Unions, 1836–1985." *American Journal of Sociology* 94:25–52.

_____. 1989. *Organizational Ecology.* Cambridge, MA: Harvard University Press.

Hare, A. Paul. 1992. "Group Size Effects." In *Encyclopedia of Sociology,* ed. E. Borgatta and M. Borgatta. New York: Macmillan.

Harris, Chauncey, and Edward Ullman. 1945. "The Nature of Cities." *The Annals of the American Academy of Political and Social Sciences* 242:7–17.

Harvey, David. 1989. *The Conditions of Postmodernism.* Oxford: Blackwell.

Hawley, Amos H. 1950. *Human Ecology.* New York: Ronald Press.

_____. 1981. *Urban Society: An Ecological Approach.* New York: Ronald Press.

_____. 1986. *Human Ecology: A Theoretical Essay.* Chicago: University of Chicago Press.

Hechter, Michael. 1987. *Principles of Group Solidarity.* Berkeley, CA: University of California Press.

Herberg, Will. 1955. *Protestant-Catholic-Jew.* New York: Doubleday.

Hirschi, Travis. 1969. *Causes of Delinquency.* Berkeley, CA: University of California Press.

Hobbes, Thomas. 1651 [1947]. *Leviathan.* New York: Macmillan.

Hochschild, Arlie R. 1979. "Emotion Work, Feeling Rules, and Social Structure." *American Journal of Sociology.* 85:551–75

Hochschild, Arlie, with Anne Machung. 1989. *The Second Shift: Working Parents and the Revolution at Home.* New York: Viking.

Hoyt, Homer. 1939. *The Structure and Growth of Residential Neighborhoods in American Cities.* Washington, DC: U.S. Government Printing Office.

Hunt, Morton. 1985. *Profiles of Social Research. The Scientific Study of Human Interaction.* New York: Russell Sage Foundation.

Hunth, Floyd. 1953. *Community Power Structure.* Chapel Hill: University of North Carolina Press.

Hurd, Richard M. 1903. *Principles of City Growth.* New York: The Record and Guide.

James, William. 1890 [1980]. *Principles of Psychology.* New York: Dover.

Jameson, Frederic. 1984. *The Postmodern Condition.* Minneapolis, MN: University of Minnesota Press.

Janis, Irving L. 1972. *Victims of Group-Think.* Boston: Houghton-Mifflin.

_____. 1982. *Groupthink: Psychological Studies of Policy Decisions and Fiascos.* Boston: Houghton-Mifflin.

Jencks, Christopher, and Meredith Phillips, eds. 1998. *The Black-White Test Score Gap.* Washington, DC: Brookings Institution Press.

Johnson, Allen W., and Timothy Earle. 1987. *The Evolution of Human Societies: From Foraging Group to Agrarian State.* Stanford, CA: Stanford University Press.

Kahlenberg, Richard D. 1996. *The Remedy: Class, Race and Affirmative Action.* New York: Basic Books.

Kellerman, Henry. 1981. *Group Cohesion.* New York: Grune and Stratton.

Kelley, Harold H. 1958. "Two Functions of Reference Groups." In *Readings in Social Psychology,* ed. G. E. Swanson. New York: Holt.

Kemper, Theodore D. 1987. "How Many Emotions Are There? Wedding the Social and the Autonomic Components." *American Journal of Sociology* 93:379–99.

Kluckhohn, Clyde. 1951. "Values and Value Orientations in the Theory of Action." In *Toward a General Theory of Action,* ed. T. Parsons and E. Shils. New York: Harper and Row.

Kluegel, James, and Eliot Smith. 1986. *Beliefs about Inequality: Americans' Views of What Is and What Ought to Be.* Hawthorne, NY: Aldine de Gruyter.

Kogan, Neil, and M. A. Wallach. 1964. *Risk Taking.* New York: Holt, Rinehart and Winston.

Kornhauser, Ruth. 1978. *Social Sources of Delinquency: An Appraisal of Analytic Models.* Chicago: University of Chicago Press.

Kornhauser, William. 1961. "Power Elite or Veto Group?" *Culture and Social Character.* Edited by Seymour Lipset and Les Lowenthal. Glenroe, IL: Free Press.

Kroeber, A. L., and Clyde Kluckhohn. 1973. *Culture: A Critical Review of Concepts and Definitions.* New York: Vintage Press.

Kroeber, Alfred, and Talcott Parsons. 1958. "The Concept of Culture and Social System." *American Sociological Review* 23:582–83.

La Piere, Richard T. 1934. "Attitudes vs. Actions." *Social Forces* 13:230–37.

Lash, Scott and John Urry. 1994. *Economics of Signs and Space.* Newbury Park, CA: Sage.

Lemert, Edwin M. 1951. *Social Pathology.* New York: McGraw-Hill.

_____. 1967. *Human Deviance, Social Problems and Social Control.* Englewood Cliffs, NJ: Prentice Hall.

Lenski, Gerhard. 1963. *The Religious Factor.* Garden City, NY: Anchor.

Lenski, Gerhard. 1966. *Power and Privilege.* New York: McGraw-Hill, reprinted by the University of North Carolina Press.

Lenski, Gerhard, Jean Lenski, and Patrick Nolan. 1991. *Human Societies: An Introduction to Macrosociology.* New York: McGraw-Hill.

Lewis, Oscar. 1965. *LaVida.* New York: Random House.

Lieberson, Stanley. 1985. *Making It Count: The Improvement of Social Research and Theory.* Berkeley, CA: University of California Press.

_____. 1992. "Small N's and Big Conclusions." *Social Forces* 70 (2):307–20.

Lifton, Robert Jay. 1961. *Thought Reform and the Psychology of Totalism.* New York: W.W. Norton.

Linton, Ralph. 1936. *The Study of Man.* New York: Appleton-Century Crofts.

Liska, Allen E. 1981. *Perspectives on Deviance.* Englewood Cliffs, NJ: Prentice Hall.

Long, Larry. 1988. *Migration and Residential Mobility in the United States.* New York: Russell Sage.

Lopreato, Joseph. 1989. "The Maximization Principle: a cause in search of conditions." *Sociobiology and The Social Sciences.* Edited by K. Bell and N. Bell. Lubock, TX: Texas Tech University Press.

Luhmann, Niklas. 1982. *The Differentiation of Society,* trans. S. Holmes and C. Larmore. New York: Columbia University Press.

Luker, Kristen. 1984. *Abortion and the Politics of Motherhood.* Berkeley, CA: University of California Press.

Machalek, Richard and Michael N. Martin. 2004. "Sociology and the Second Darwinian Revolution." *Sociological Theory.* 22:455–76.

Madoo-Lengerman, Patricia and Jill Niebrugge-Brantly. 1998. *The Women Founders,* 1830–1930.

Malthus, Thomas R. 1798 [1926]. *First Essay on Population.* New York: Kelley.

Marsden, Peter, and Nan Lin, eds. 1980. *Social Structure and Network Analysis.* Newbury Park, CA: Sage.

Martineau, Harriet. 1838a. *Illustrations of Political Economy.* London: Fox.

_____. 1838b. *How to Observe Morals.* London: C. Knight.

Marx, Karl. 1867 [1967]. *Capital: A Critical Analysis of Capitalist Production.* New York: International Publishers.

Marx, Karl, and Friedrich Engels. 1846 [1947]. *The German Ideology.* New York: International Publishers.

_____. 1848 [1978]. *The Communist Manifesto.* Pp. 469–500 in *The Marx-Engels Reader,* ed. Robert Tucker. New York: Norton.

Maryanski, Alexandra, and Jonathan H. Turner. 1991. "Network Analysis." In J. H. Turner, *The Structure of Sociological Theory.* Belmont, CA: Wadsworth.

Maryanski, Alexandra. 1997. "African Ape Social Networks: A Blueprint for Reconstructing Early Hominid Social Structure." Pp. 28–42 in *The Archaeology of Human Ancestry,* ed. J. Steele and S. Shennan. London: Routledge.

Maryanski, Alexandra R. and Jonathan H. Turner. 1992. *The Social Cage: Human Nature and The Evolution of Society, Stanford,* CA: Stanford University Press.

_____. 1992. *The Social Cage: Human Nature and the Evolution of Society.* Stanford, CA: Stanford University Press.

Massey, Douglass S., Camille Z. Charles, Garvey F. Lundy, and Mary J. Fischer. 2003. *The Source of The River: The Social Origins of Freshmen at America's Selective Colleges and Universities.* Princeton, NJ: Princeton University Press.

Mauss, Marcel. 1925. *The Gift* trans. I. Gunnison. New York: Free Press.

McAdam, Doug. 1987. *Political Processes and the Development of Black Insurgency, 1930–1970.* Chicago: University of Chicago Press.

McAdam, Douglas, John D. McCardy, and Meger, Zald. 1988. "Social Movements." *Handbook of Sociology,* Neil J. Smelsh, ed. Newbury Park, CA: Sage.

McCall, George P. and J.L. Simmons. 1978. *Identities and Interactions,* New York: Basic Books.

McCarthy, John D., and Mayer Zald. 1977. "Resource Mobilization and Social Movements." *American Journal of Sociology* 82 (6): 1212–41.

_____. 1988. "Social Movements." In *Handbook of Sociology,* ed. N. J. Smelser. Newbury Park, CA: Sage.

McDonough, Patricia M. 1997. *Choosing Colleges: How Social Class and Schools Structure Opportunity.* Albany State University of New York Press.

McKenzie, Roderick. 1933. *The Metropolitan Community.* New York: McGraw-Hill.

McPherson, J. Miller. 1981. "A Dynamic Model of Voluntary Affiliation." *Social Forces* 59:705–28.

_____. 1983. "An Ecology of Affiliation." *American Sociological Review* 48:519–32.

_____. 1988. "A Theory of Voluntary Organization." Pp. 42–76 in *Community Organizations,* ed. C. Milofsky. New York: Oxford.

_____. 1990. "Evolution in Communities of Voluntary Organizations." Pp. 224–45 in *Organizational Evolution,* ed. Ji Hendra Singh. Newbury Park, CA: Sage.

Mead, George Herbert. 1934. *Mind, Self, and Society.* Chicago: University of Chicago Press.

Mehan, Hugh, and Houston Wood. 1975. *The Reality of Ethnomethodology.* New York: Wiley and Sons.

Merton, Robert K. 1949. "Discrimination and the American Creed." In *Discrimination and National Welfare*, ed. R. H. MacIver. New York: Harper and Row.

_____. 1957. "Role-Set: Problems in Sociological Theory." *British Journal of Sociology* 8 (1957):106–20.

_____. 1968. *Social Theory and Social Structure.* New York: Free Press.

Merton, Robert K., and Alice S. Rossi. 1957. "Contributions to the Theory of Reference Group Behavior." In *Social Theory and Social Structure*, ed. R. K. Merton. New York: Free Press.

_____. 1968. "Continuities in the Theory of Reference Groups and Social Structure." In *Social Theory and Social Structure*, ed. R. K. Merton. New York: Free Press.

Meyer, John W. 1977. "The Effects of Education as an Institution." *American Journal of Sociology* 83 (1):55–77.

Miller, Walter B. 1958. "Lower Class Culture as a Generating Milieu Gang Delinquency." *Journal of Social Issues.* 10:5–19.

Mills, C. Wright. 1956. *The Power Elite.* New York: Oxford University Press.

Miyamoto, Frank S. 1970. "Self, Motivation, and Symbolic Interaction Theory." Pp. 271–85 in *Human Nature and Collective Behavior*, ed. T. Shibutani. Englewood Cliffs, NJ: Prentice Hall.

Money, John, and Anke Ehrhardt. 1972. *Man and Woman, Boy and Girl.* Baltimore, MD: Johns Hopkins University Press.

Morris, Aldon D. 1984. *The Origins of the Civil Rights Movement: Black Communities for Change.* New York: Free Press.

Murdock, George P. 1949. *Social Structure.* New York: Macmillan.

_____. 1965. *Culture and Society.* Pittsburgh, PA: University of Pittsburgh Press.

Nadel, S. F. 1957. *The Study of Social Structure.* London: Cohen and West.

National Council of Churches. 2004. *Yearbook.* New York: Abingdon Press.

Nolan, Patrick and Gerhard Lenski. 2004. *Human Societies: An Introduction to Macrosociology.* Boulder, CO: Paradigm Press.

Nolan, Patrick and Gerhond Lenski. 2004. *Human Societies.* Boulder, CO: Paradigm Publishers.

NORC. 1982. *Prestige Rankings.* Chicago: National Opinion Research Center.

Oberschall, Anthony. 2004. "Explaining Terrorism: The Contributions of Collective Action Theory." *Sociological Theory.* 22:26–37.

OCED. 2000. *Comparative Tax Rates.* Paris: OCED.

Park, Robert E. 1916. "The City: Suggestions for the Investigation of Human Behavior in an Urban Environment." *American Journal of Sociology* 20:577–612.

_____. 1936. "Human Ecology." *American Journal of Sociology* 42:1–15.

Park, Robert E., and Ernest W. Burgess. 1925. *The City.* Chicago: University of Chicago Press.

Parkinson, C. Northcote. 1957. *Parkinson's Law.* Boston: Houghton-Mifflin.

Parsons, Talcott. 1951. *The Social System.* New York: Free Press.

_____. 1953. "A Revised Analytical Approach to the Theory of Stratification." In *Class, Status, and Power*, ed. R. Bendix and S. M. Lipset. New York: Free Press.

_____. 1966. *Societies: Evolutionary and Comparative Perspectives.* Englewood Cliffs, NJ: Prentice Hall.

_____. 1971. *The System of Modern Societies.* Englewood Cliffs, NJ: Prentice Hall.

Perrow, Charles. 1967. "A Framework for the Comparative Analysis of Organizations." *American Sociological Review* 32:194–208.

_____. 1986. *Complex Organizations.* New York: Random House.

Peter, Laurence F., and Raymond Hull. 1969. *The Peter Principle.* New York: Morrow.

Phillips, Bernard S. 2001. *Beyond Sociology's Tower of Babel: Reconstructing the Scientific Method.* New York: Aldine de Gruyter.

Piaget, Jean. 1948. *The Moral Judgement of the Child.* Glencoe, IL: Free Press.

_____. 1952. *The Origins of Intelligence in Children.* New York: International Universities Press.

Pierce, T.M. 1964. *Federal, State, and Local Government in Education.* Washington, D.C.: Center for Applied Research in Education.

Plutchik, Robert. 1962. *The Emotions: Facts, Theories and a New Model.* New York: Random House.

Plutchik, Robert, and Henry Kellerman, eds. 1980. *Emotion: Theory and Research Experience.* New York: Academic Press.

Pondy, Louis. 1983. *Organizational Symbolism.* Greenwich, CT: JAI Press.

Popper, Karl R. 1959. *The Logic of Scientific Discovery.* London: Hutchinson.

_____. 1969. *Conjectures and Refutations.* London: Routledge and Kegan Paul.

Quinney, Richard. 1970. *The Social Reality of Crime.* Boston: Little-Brown.

_____. 1979. *Criminology.* 2d ed. Boston: Little-Brown.

_____. 1980. *Class, State, and Crime.* 2d ed. New York: Longman.

Reynolds, Vernon. 1976. *The Biology of Human Action.* San Francisco: W. H. Freeman.

Ritzer, George. 1975. *Sociology: A Multiple Paradigm Science.* Boston: Allyn and Bacon.

Ritzer, George. 2004. *The Globalization of Nothing.* Thousand Oaks, CA: Pine Forge Press.

Roethlisberger, Fritz, and W. J. Dickson. 1939. *Management and the Worker.* Cambridge, MA: Harvard University Press.

Rokeach, Milton. 1973. *The Nature of Human Values.* New York: Free Press.

_____, ed. 1979. *Understanding Human Values: Individual and Societal.* New York: Free Press.

Ropers, Richard H. 1991. *Persistent Poverty: The American Dream Turned Nightmare.* New York: Plenum Press.

Rose, Arnold M. 1967. *The Power Structure: Political Process in America.* New York: Oxford University Press.

Rosenberg, Morris. 1979. *Conceiving Self.* New York: Basic Books.

Rosenthal, Robert and Lenore Jacobson, 1968. *Pygmalion in the Classroom.* New York: Holt, Rinehart and Winston.

Rossi, Peter, James Wright, and Andy Anderson, eds. 1985. *Handbook of Survey Research.* Orlando, FL: Academic Press.

Sachs, Peth. 2003. "Class Rules: The Fiction of Egalitarian Higher Education." *The Chronicle of Higher Education,* Section 2, July 25:7–10.

Sahlins, Marshall. 1972. *Stone Age Economics.* New York: Aldine.

Sanchez, Rene. 1998. "Urban Students Not Making the Mark." *Washington Post.* (January 8): A18.

Savage-Rumbaugh, E.S.D., D. Rumbaugh, an K. McDonald. 1985. "Language Learning in Two Species of Apes." *Neuroscience and Biobehavioral Reviews.* 9:653–65.

Scheff, Thomas J. 1966. *Being Mentally Ill: A Sociological Theory.* Chicago: Aldine.

Schiller, Bradley R. 2004. *The Economics of Poverty and Discrimination.* Upper Saddle River, NJ: Prentice Hall.

Schutz, Alfred. 1932 [1967]. *The Phenomenology of the Social World.* Evanston, IL: Northwestern University Press.

Seboek, T. A., ed. 1968. *Animal Communication.* Bloomington: Indiana University Press.

Seidman, Steven, and David G. Wagner, eds. 1992. *Postmodernism and Social Theory.* Oxford, UK: Blackwell.

Sherraden, Michael. 1991. *Assets and the Poor: A New American Welfare Policy.* Armonk, NY: M. E. Sharpe.

Shibutani, Tamotsu. 1955. "Reference Groups as Perspectives. *American Journal of Sociology* 60 (May):562–69.

Shotola, Robert W. 1992. "Small Groups." In *Encyclopedia of Sociology,* ed. E. Borgatta and M. Borgatta. New York: Macmillan.

Simmel, Georg. 1956. *Conflict and the Web of Group Affiliations,* trans. K. Wolf. New York: Free Press.

Silberman, Charles E. 1971. *Crisis in the Classroom: The Remaking of American Education.* New York: Vintage.

Singer, Milton. 1968. "Culture: The Concept of Culture." In *International Encyclopedia of the Social Sciences.* New York: Macmillan.

Singleton, Royce, and Jonathan H. Turner. 1975. "Racism: White Oppression of Blacks in America." Pp. 130–60 in *Understanding Social Problems,* ed. D. Zimmerman and L. Weider. New York: Praeger.

Sjoberg, Gideon. 1960. *The Preindustrial City.* New York: Free Press.

Skocpol, Theda. 1979. *States and Social Revolutions.* New York: Cambridge University Press.

Smelser, Neil J. 1963. *Theory of Collective Behavior.* New York: Free Press.

Smircich, Linda. 1983. "Concepts of Culture and Organizational Analysis." *Administrative Science Quarterly* 28:339–58.

Smith, Adam. 1776 [1937]. *An Inquiry into the Nature and Causes of the Wealth of Nations.* New York: The Modern Library.

Smith, Kevin B. 1985. "I Made It Because of Me: Beliefs About the Causes of Wealth and Poverty." *Sociological Spectrum* 5:17–29.

Snow, David A., and Robert D. Benford. 1988. "Ideology, Frame Resonance, and Participant Mobilization." *International Social Movement Research* I:197–217.

Snow, David A., Louis A. Zurcher, and Sheldon Ekland-Olson. 1980. "Social Networks and Social Movements: A Microstructural Approach to Differential Recruitment." *American Sociological Review* 45:787–801.

Sorokin, Pitirim. 1937. *Social and Culteral Dynamics, 4 volumes.* New York: American Book.

Spectorsky, A.C. *The Exurbanites.* Philadelphia, PA: Lippincott.

Spencer, Baldwin, and F. J. Gillian. 1899. *The Native Tribes of Central Australia.* 2d ed. London: Macmillan.

Spencer, Herbert. 1850 [1872]. *Social Statics.* New York: D. Appleton.

_____. 1862. *First Principles.* New York: D. Appleton.

_____. 1894–1896. The Principles of Sociology, 3 volumes. New York: Appleton-Century.

_____. 1864–1867 [1887]. *The Principles of Biology,* 2 vols. New York: D. Appleton.

_____. 1873. *The Study of Sociology.* London: Kegan Paul.

_____. 1873–1934. *Descriptive Sociology:* Groups of Sociological Facts. 16 columes published by various publishers.

_____. 1874–1896 [1898]. *The Principles of Sociology,* 3 vols. New York: D. Appleton.

Stapnski, Helene. 1998. "Let's Talk Dirty." *Amerrican Demographics.* 20:50–56.

Stark, Rodney, and W. S. Bainbridge. 1980. "Secularizations, Revival and Cult Formation." *Annual Review of Social Sciences of Religion* 4:85–119.

Stark, Rodney. 1981. "Must All Religions Be Supernatural?" In *The Social Impact of New Religious Movements,* ed. by B. Wilson. New York: Rose of Sharon Press.

_____. 1992. *Sociology,* 4th ed. Belmont, CA: Wadsworth.

Statistical Abstracts of The United States, 2003. Washington, D.C.: U.S. Government Printing Office.

Steinberg, Jacques. 2002. *The Gatekeepers: Inside The Admissions Process of a Premier College.* New York: Viking Press.

Stephan, H. 1983. "Evolutionary Trends in Limbic Structures." *Neuroscience and Biobehavioral Reviews.* 7:367–74.

Stephan, H. and O.J. Andy. 1969. "Quantitative Comparative Neuroanatomy of Primates." Annals of New York Academy of Science. 167:370–87.

Stryker, Sheldon. 1980. *Symbolic Interaction: A Social Structural View.* Menlo Park, CA: Benjamin-Cummings.

Sullivan, Harry Stack. 1953. *The Interpersonal Theory of Psychiatry.* New York: W. W. Norton.

Sumner, William Graham and Albert Galloway Keller. 1927. *The Science of Society, 4 volumes.* New Haven, CT: Yale University Press.

Sutherland, Edwin H. 1924. *Criminology.* Philadelphia: J. B. Lippincott.

_____. 1939. *Principles of Criminology.* Philadelphia: J. B. Lippincott.

Sutherland, Edwin D., and Donald R. Cressey. 1986. *Principles of Criminology.* Philadelphia: J. B. Lippincott.

Swanson, Guy. 1960. *The Birth of the Gods.* Ann Arbor: University of Michigan Press.

Tilly, Charles. 1978. *From Mobilization to Revolution.* Reading, MA: Addison-Wesley.

_____. 2004. "Terror, Terrorism, and Terrorists." *Sociological Theory.* 22:5–13.

Time Almanac. 2002. Boston: Information Please.

Tooby, John and Leda Cosmides. 1989. "Evolutionary Psychology and the Generation of Culture." *Ethology and Sociobiology.* 10:29–49.

Tumin, Melvin M. 1953. "Some Principles of Stratification: A Critical Analysis." *American Sociological Review* 18:387–93.

_____. 1967. *Social Stratification: The Forms and Functions of Inequality.* Englewood Cliffs, NJ: Prentice Hall.

Turk, Austin T. 1969. *Criminality and Legal Order.* Chicago: Rand McNally.

Turner, Jonathan H. 1972. *Patterns of Social Organization: A Survey of Social Institutions.* New York: McGraw-Hill.

_____. 1976. *American Society: Problems of Structure.* New York: Harper and Row.

_____. 1977. *Social Problems in America: The Structural and Cultural Basis.* New York: Harper and Row.

_____. 1981. "Emile Durkheim's Theory of Integration in Differentiated Social Systems." *Pacific Sociological Review* 24 (4):187–208.

_____. 1983. "Theoretical Strategies for Linking Micro and Macro Processes: An Evaluation of Seven Approaches." *Western Sociological Review* 14 (1):4–15.

_____. 1984a. *Societal Stratification: A Theoretical Analysis.* New York: Columbia University Press.

_____. 1984b. "Durkheim's and Spencer's Principles of Social Organization." *Sociological Perspectives* 27:21–32.

_____. 1985a. "In Defense of Positivism." *Sociological Theory* 3 (Fall):24–30.

_____. 1985b. *Herbert Spencer: A Renewed Appreciation.* Newbury Park, CA: Sage.

_____. 1985c. *Sociology: The Science of Human Organization.* Chicago: Nelson-Hall.

_____. 1986a. "The Mechanics of Social Interaction." *Sociological Theory* 4:95–105.

_____. 1986b. "Toward a Unified Theory of Ethnic Antagonism: Preliminary Synthesis of Three Macro Models." *Sociological Forum* 1 (Summer):403–27.

_____. 1988. *A Theory of Social Interaction.* Stanford, CA: Stanford University Press.

_____. 1990. "Durkheim's Theory of Social Organization." *Social Forces* 68:1–15.

_____. 1991. *The Structure of Sociological Theory.* 5th ed. Belmont, CA: Wadsworth.

_____. 1993a. "Inequality and Poverty." In *Social Problems,* ed. George Ritzer and Craig Calhoun. New York: McGraw-Hill.

_____. 1993b. *Classical Sociology Theory: A Positivistic Interpretation.* Chicago: Nelson-Hall.

_____. 1995. *Macrodynamics: Toward a Theory on the Organization of Human Populations.* New Brunswick, NJ: Rutgers University Press.

_____. 1997. *The Institutional Order.* New York and London: Longman.

_____. 1999. "Toward a General Sociological Theory of Emotions". *Journal for the Theory of Social Behaviour.* 29:109–62.

_____. 2000. *On the Origins of Human Emotions.* Stanford, CA: Stanford University Press.

_____. 2001. "Social Engineering: Is This Really as Bad as It Sounds?" *Sociological Practice* 6: 1–10.

_____. 2002. *Face-to-Face: Toward a Sociological Theory of Interpersonal Behavior.* Stanford, CA: Stanford University Press.

_____. 2003. *Human Institutions: A Theory of Societal Evolution.* Boulder, CO: Rowman and Littlefied.

_____. 2003. *Human Institutions: A Theory of Societal Evolution.* Boulder, CO: Rowman and Littlefied.

_____. 2003. *The Structure of Sociological Theory, 7/e.* Belmont, CA: Wadsworth.

Turner, Jonathan H. and Pedro Payne. 2002. "Power, Politics and African Americans." *Sociological Views on Political Participation in the 21st Century.* Edited by Betty A. Dobratz, Timothy Buzzell, and Lisa Waldner. New York: JAI Press.

Turner, Jonathan H. and Royce R. Singleton. 1978. "A Theory of Ethnic Oppression." *Social Forces.* 56:1001–08.

Turner, Jonathan H., and Alexandra Maryanski. 1979. *Functionalism.* Menlo Park, CA: Benjamin-Cummings.

Turner, Jonathan H., and Charles E. Starnes. 1976. *Inequality: Privilege and Poverty in America.* Santa Monica, CA: Goodyear.

Turner, Jonathan H., and David Musick. 1985. *American Dilemmas.* New York: Columbia University Press.

Turner, Jonathan H., and Edna Bonacich. 1980. "Toward a Composite Theory of Middleman Minorities." *Ethnicity* 7:144–58.

Turner, Jonathan H., and Peter Molnar. 1993. "Selection Processes and the Evolution of Emotions in Humans." *Biology and Culture* (in preparation).

Turner, Jonathan H., Leonard Beeghley., and Charles Powers. 1989. *The Emergence of Sociological Theory.* Belmont, CA: Wadsworth.

Turner, Jonathan J., Leonard Beeghley, and Charles Powers. 2002. *The Emergence of Sociological Theory.* Belmont, CA: Wadsworth.

Turner, Jonathan H., Royce Singleton, and David Musick. 1984. *Oppression: A Socio-history of Black-White Relations in America.* Chicago: Nelson-Hall.

Turner, Ralph H. 1962. "Role-Taking versus Conformity." In *Human Behavior and Social Processes,* ed. A. Rose. Boston: Houghton Mifflin.

_____. 1968. "Social Roles: Sociological Aspects." *International Encyclopedia of the Social Sciences.* New York: Macmillan.

_____. 1978. "The Role and the Person." *American Journal of Sociology* 84:1–23.

_____. 1980. "Strategy for Developing an Integrated Role Theory. *Humboldt Journal of Social Relations* 7:123–39.

Turner, Ralph H. and Lewis Killian. 1978. Collective Behavior. Englewood Cliffs, NJ: Prentice-Hall.

Turner, Ralph H., and Lewis M. Killian. 1987. *Collective Behavior.* 3d ed. Englewood Cliffs, NJ: Prentice Hall.

Turner, Stephen Park, and Jonathan H. Turner. 1990. *The Impossible Science: An Institutional History of American Sociology.* Newbury Park, CA: Sage.

U.S. Bureau of the Census. 1983, 1991. *Current Population Reports.* Washington, DC: U. S. Government Printing Office.

U.S. Bureau of the Census. 2002. *The Asian Population 2000.* Washington, D.C.: U.S. Bureau of Census.

U.S. Bureau of the Census. 2003. "Current Population Reports." Washington D.C.: U.S. Government Printing Office.

U.S. Bureau of the Census. 2003. *Populational Characteristics*. Washington D.C.: U.S. Government Printing.

U.S. Bureau of the Census. 2005. *World Population Clock*. www.census.gov/main/www/popclock.html.

U.S. Department of Labor. 2003. *Women in the Labor Force*. Washington D.C.: U.S. Government Printing Office.

U.S. Department. 2002. Office of the Coordinator of Counterterrorism. "Patterns of Global Terrorism."

U.S. State Department. 2000. Office of the Coordinator of Counterterrorism. "Patterns of Global Terrorism."

U.S. State Department. 2001. Office of the Coordinator of Counterterrorism. "Patterns of Global Terrorism."

U.S. Women's Bureau and National Committee on Pay Equality. 2003. Washington, D.C.: U.S. Government Printing Office.

United Nations, 1991. *World Trends in Population*. New York: United Nations Publishing.

United Nations. 1996. *The World's Women 1995: Trends and Statistics*. New York: U. N. Publications.

United Nations. 2000. *Human Development Report 2000*. New York: Oxford University Press.

United Nations. 2002. *Human Development Report 2002*. New York: Oxford University Press.

United Nations Yearbook. 1978. *World Population Trends*. New York: United Nations.

United Nations Yearbook. 2000. *World Population Yearbook*. New York: United Nations.

Van Ausdale, Debra and Joe R. Feagin. 2001. *The First R: How Children Learn Race and Racism*. Boulder, CO: Rowman and Littlefield.

Van den Berghe. 1981. *The Ethnic Phenomenon*. New York: Elserier.

_____. 1991. "Once More with Feeling: Genes, Mind and Culture." *Behavioral and Brain Sciences*. 14:317–318.

Wallace, Anthony F. C. 1966. *Religion: An Anthropological View*. New York: Random House.

Wallerstein, Immanuel M. 1974. *The Modern World System: Capitalist Agriculture and the Origins of the European World Economy in the Sixteenth Century*. New York: Academic Press.

Ward, Lester. 1883. *Dynamic Sociology*. New York: D. Appleton.

Weber, Max. 1904 [1949]. *The Methodology of the Social Sciences*. New York: Free Press.

_____. 1904–5 [1958]. *The Protestant Ethic and the Spirit of Capitalism*. New York: Scribners.

_____. 1905. *The Protestant Ethic and the Spirit of Capitalism*. New York: Free Press.

_____. 1922/1978. *Economy and Society: An Outline of Interpretive Sociology*, ed. G. Roth and C. Wittich. Berkeley: University of California Press.

Webster, Murray Jr., and Martha Foschi. 1988. *Status Generalization: New Theory and Research*. Stanford, CA: Stanford University Press.

Westerly, William A. 1956. "Secrecy and The Police." Social Forces. 37:254–57

White, Lynn K., and Alan Booth. 1985. "The Quality and Stability of Re-marriages." *American Sociological Review* 50:689–98.

White, Lynn K., and John N. Edwards. 1990. "Emptying the Nest and Parental Well-Being." *American Sociological Review* 55:235–42.

Whyte, William Foote. 1989. "Advancing Scientific Knowledge through Participatory Action Research." *Sociological Forum* 4:367–86.

Whyte, William Foote, and Kathleen King Whyte. 1984. *Learning from the Field: A Guide from Experience.* Beverly Hills, CA: Sage.

Whyte, William H. 1957. *The Organization Man.* Gonden City: New York.

Wilford, John Noble. 1981. "Nine Percent of Everyone Who Ever Lived is Alone Now." *New York Times,* October 6:13.

Williams, Jr., Robin M. 1970. *American Society: A Sociological Interpretation.* New York: Knopf.

Wilson, William J. 1987. *The Truly Disadvantaged.* Chicago: University of Chicago Press.

Wirth, Louis. 1938. "Urbanism as a Way of Life." *American Journal of Sociology.* 44:8–20.

Wolff, Edward N. 1987. "Estimates of Household Inequality in the United States." *Review of Income and Wealth* 33:231–42.

World Bank. 2000. *Global Poverty Report (July).* New York: World Bank Publication.

Zald, Meyer N., and John D. McCarthy, eds. 1979. *The Dynamics of Social Movements.* Cambridge, MA: Winthrop.

Zimbardo, Philip. 1972. "Pathology of Imprisionment." *Society,* 9:4–8.

Index